D0629738

HM
131
•A39

Organizations and Environments

HOWARD E. ALDRICH

Cornell University

WITHDRAWN

.Tennessee Tech. Library
Cookeville, Tenn.

Prentice-Hall, Inc., Englewood Cliffs, New Jersey 07632

284646

Library of Congress Cataloging in Publication Data

ALDRICH, HOWARD.
    Organizations and environments.

    Bibliography: p. 351
    Includes index.
    1. Organizational change.   2. Organizational research.
3. Social sciences.   I. Title.
HM131.A39   301.18'32   78–21592
ISBN 0–13–641431–1

for Penny

© 1979 by Prentice-Hall, Inc., Englewood Cliffs, N.J. 07632

All rights reserved. No part of this book may be reproduced in any form or by any means without permission in writing from the publisher.

Printed in the United States of America

10   9   8   7   6   5   4   3   2   1

Prentice-Hall International, Inc., *London*
Prentice-Hall of Australia Pty. Limited, *Sydney*
Prentice-Hall of Canada, Ltd., *Toronto*
Prentice-Hall of India Private Limited, *New Delhi*
Prentice-Hall of Japan, Inc., *Tokyo*
Prentice-Hall of Southeast Asia Pte. Ltd., *Singapore*
Whitehall Books Limited, *Wellington, New Zealand*

CONTENTS

PREFACE

I could never understand why sociologists studying organizations were apparently content in focusing on single organizations and ignoring the societal context of what they observed. Perhaps things began to go awry when organizational sociology slipped out of mainstream sociology in the 1960s and drifted aimlessly during a period of great ferment in other sociological specialties. Failing to ground their studies in a political and historical context, organizational sociologists lost touch with developments in other disciplines as well. While grand theory was superceded by historically-informed and period-specific explanations in many social scientific investigations, quite a few organizational sociologists were drawn into "systems theory" and "contingency theories" of dubious historical relevance. While European theorists were delivering body-blows to American theories of stratification, social mobility, and the role of the state in advanced industrial societies, much of organizational sociology remained curiously parochial. The promise of organizational sociology, as revealed in the work of Philip Selznick, James Thompson, and others was not entirely lost, however, and during the 1970s a renewed sense of excitement crept into the field.

In trying to write a book on organizational sociology for both students and colleagues, I decided there was no point in either reviewing all of the "perspectives'' advanced by theorists in the past two decades, or in re-creating the seemingly endless debates over measurement and method that have plagued the field. Rather, I have attempted to present a perspective that integrates concepts and research findings from all social science disciplines studying organizations while retaining the gains made by historically and politically sensitive investigators in the United States and abroad. With a slight shift of emphasis from an original investigator's intentions, I found that a great deal of the literature in economic history, industrial economics, the social-psychology of organizations, organizational sociology, and political sociology could be integrated into an encompassing framework. Of course, achieving such integration has its costs (as I'm sure critics of the book will point out).

From beginning to end, this book is focused on a central unifying theme: organizational change. Each chapter deals with a different aspect of the question, "Under what conditions do organizations change?" Theoretical integration across the chapters is achieved through the population ecology model of organizational change. It captures the essential features of sociology's emerging concern for relations between organizations and their environments, and stresses the inseparability of mainstream sociology and organizational sociology.

The population ecology model explains organizational change by focusing on the nature and distribution of resources in organizations' environments, rather than on internal leadership or participation in decision making. The model provides a comprehensive framework within which organizational change and persistence can be studied, calling our attention to a level of analysis often overlooked in traditional approaches. Organizations are examined as representatives of types found in populations consisting of hundreds and often thousands of similar organizations, thus using an aggregate as opposed to an individual level of analysis. Investigators using the population ecology model cannot avoid dealing with the societal context within which organizations are created, survive or fail, and rise to prominence or sink into obscurity.

Studying variations over time in organizational forms requires not only longitudinal research designs but also knowledge of historical trends and changes in political systems, modes of economic production, law, patterns of international trade, and other topics often neglected in case studies or surveys of isolated organizations. Whenever possible, I have put illustrative case material into its proper historical context. For example, I examine the historical conditions under which new forms of organizations emerged during the rise of capitalism in the West and during industrialization in the United States.

Politically sensitive issues, often ignored in previous research, are highlighted throughout the book. The "environment" in population ecology studies, properly conceived, does not refer simply to elements "out there" beyond a set of focal organizations but rather to concentrations of resources, power, political domination and, most concretely, other organizations. There is no danger of a conservative "new orthodoxy" developing in organizational sociology, as long as investigators remain sensitive to the issues raised in this book. One chapter, for example, deals with corporate ownership and control and the exercise of economic power, and another treats organizations as prized objects of intraorganizational struggles.

I prefer textbook authors taking a critical stand toward the literature they review, and thus I have critically reviewed others' research rather than merely summarizing it. I have sought to give students an appreciation of the conceptual and methodological issues facing organizational sociology, at the same time revealing to my colleagues where I stand. Taking my cue from other books I admire, I've included a great deal of descriptive material that illustrates theoretical principles (or occasionally just adds a bit of light to an otherwise tedious point).

Simple ideas are often stumbled upon quite slowly. In retrospect, the roots of the ideas in this book were laid down about a decade ago, when I sat through courses in organizational sociology and human ecology in successive terms at the University of Michigan. Reading James Thompson and Amos Hawley back-to-back (and then going on to political sociology) was a mind-expanding experience, and the possibilities of a synthesis have intrigued me ever since. I began teaching courses on organizations and environments in the early 1970s, and finally realized—as I suppose all authors must—that only by suppressing my monumental degree of ignorance in a host of areas would I gain the courage to undertake a book of this nature. Happily, I had long since discovered that ignorance is no bar to obtaining a hearing in the sciences (as a philosopher of science explained to me, we achieve progress only by rejecting false ideas), and so I plunged ahead.

Along the way, many friends and acquaintances were implicated in my effort, and to prevent them from denying any connection with this work, I've decided to give them due credit. Many people read a first draft of the book—some were paid to, some did it out of friendship, and others shared office space with me! In addition to reading the manuscript, Charles Perrow and Mayer Zald have been conducting unofficial tutorials for me for almost a decade, and they set high standards for an aspiring author. They disagree in significant measure with parts of my argument, and I've benefitted immeasurably from their criticisms. Bob Stern, Paul Hirsch, and David Knoke made extensive comments, suggested additional references, and contributed new substantive examples.

Joyce Rothschild-Whitt and Jane Weiss heightened my political sensibilities and pointed out passages where I strayed from the objective of stressing conflict and change. John Child and I have enjoyed an extensive correspondence over the years, and his criticisms sharpened my presentation of "strategic choice" and its limitations. William Clute, Jerry Hage, Dick Hall, Marshall Meyer, Mike Moch, Bonnie Payne, and Hans Pennings also took the time to make written comments and I am grateful to all of them.

Many of the book's ideas were initially developed in collaborative writing with others. Diane Herker co-authored a paper on boundary spanning roles with me, and Lena Kolarska and I have written several papers critical of Albert Hirschman's work. Sergio Mindlin's re-analysis of the Aston group's data formed the basis for several joint papers on interorganizational dependence, and Jeff Pfeffer and I wrote a paper explaining how and why we viewed organizational change differently (in the guise of a comprehensive review article on organizations and environments). Albert J. Reiss, Jr., originally sparked my interest in the external conditions constraining organizational autonomy, while also teaching me a great deal about social science research. David Whetten and I worked together on a multi-community study on interorganizational relations, with special attention paid to the problems of aggregation and measurement.

Several people read sections of the book and discussed their reactions with me: Ken Benson and Andrew Pettigrew, who reminded me that I was only partially successful in building "process" into my argument; John Kimberly, who apart from useful suggestions, also offered me the hospitality of his lovely apartment in Paris several times; and Jean Millar and Anthony Manero, who cast doubts on the wisdom of the entire enterprise.

A year spent in England and Germany provided an opportunity for leisurely reading and reflection on the state of organizational sociology, and I am indebted to Mike Aiken for suggesting it. The International Institute of Management in Berlin, the Centre for Environmental Studies in London, and Nuffield College, Oxford, generously provided support that made the year possible.

My colleagues at the New York State School of Industrial and Labor Relations, Cornell University, supported my work in countless ways. Sam Bacharach stood firm as a friend as well as colleague when it counted, continually reminding me of the complex and contradictory nature of social life. Tove Hammer, Karl Weick, William Foote Whyte, and Larry Williams read drafts of papers, furnished obscure references, and contributed to the quality of my working life. At Prentice-Hall, Ed Stanford convinced me that this book could be written, and then Irene Fraga, Kitty Woringer, and Alison Gnerre helped make it a reality.

Penny, Steven, and Daniel helped me keep the whole effort in perspective. Perhaps the book would've been finished more quickly without them, but then I would never have seen the marine Venus, climbed Cinder Cone, walked across the Charles Bridge, or spent a week in Pen-y-Gwyd.

1 Introduction

The major focus of this book is on organizational change—the conditions under which organizations are created, grow, establish relations with important actors in their environments, adopt tactics for survival, and, quite often, fail. Organizational sociology normally focuses on the internal workings of organizations, following a tradition begun with Frederick W. Taylor's "scientific management" earlier in this century, and continued by Elton Mayo, Chester Barnard, Melville Dalton, and others. I will argue that this perspective is not wrong, but rather that it is incomplete. Many questions of interest to organizational sociologists today require a perspective on organizations that takes account not only of the internal structure of organizations but also the forces in their environments that set limits to organizational discretion. Many social scientists have begun to incorporate environmental concepts into their work in the past decade, with James Thompson's book (1967) perhaps being the major turning point.

The large volume of research and writing on organizations and their environments is a relatively recent development, but an interest in organizational environments is not: Max Weber's historical and comparative studies in the late nineteenth and early twentieth centuries examined the effect of social structure on bureaucracy; Selznick's studies of the Tennessee Valley Authority (1949) and the

Communist Party (1960) explicitly included the environment as a major external constraint; and Bendix (1956) analyzed the relationship between managerial ideologies and social structure in an historical study of England, Russia, the United States, and East Germany. Economists, especially those working in industrial economics, have examined the conditions under which firms acquire power to modify situations of economic competition to their advantage (Scherer, 1970), thus acquiring power over their markets. Anthropologists and sociologists theorizing about societal evolution have, of necessity, treated "environment" as a central topic (White, 1949; Parsons, 1966).

My objective in this book is not to develop another theory of organizations, but rather to show that the literature on organizations can be recast into an organization-environment framework that brings together research on internal organizational structure *and* organizational environments. This is accomplished by elaborating upon a three-stage population ecology model that makes explicit the conditions under which organizations (or any social systems) change their structure and processes. Conversely, I will also use the model to account for stability and lack of change.

THE REALITY OF ORGANIZATIONS

Organizations are all around us and thus we tend to take their existence for granted. They are simply a non-problematic element in our everyday lives and, as such, we shut them out of our consciousness. They hover around the edges of our life-space as rather vague entities, for most of us experience life in terms of person-to-person and not person-to-organization relations. When do we notice the reality of organizations? Organizations typically become evident to us when a problem or crisis occurs. For example, the introduction of a computer course scheduling system throws registration for college classes into disarray, and students want to know "who's responsible?"; our new car is recalled by the manufacturer to correct a defective engine mount, and we are made dimly aware of the existence of a federal agency monitoring auto safety standards. In a particularly severe winter there is suddenly not enough natural gas to satisfy customer demand, causing shops and factories to shut down and forcing millions out of work. We learn that there probably is enough natural gas to satisfy short-term needs, but because of a complex regulatory system producers find it cheaper to sell in intrastate rather than in interstate markets. Fuel exists, but organizations cannot or will not deliver it to us.

In each instance, the reality of organizations as possessing an existence independent of their members and with power over peoples' lives exerts itself. The objective reality of organizations is felt, subjectively, pressing itself upon us. At times it can be an overwhelming presence, as the first day on a college campus or at a new job confirms. Initial anxiety quickly passes, however, and it is a rare individual who has sleepless nights worrying about the organizations in his or her life.

Instead, we recognize a simple fact of life—organizations are necessary and important because they enable people to accomplish *collectively* what cannot be accomplished by individuals acting on their own. The maintenance of complex industrial societies is inconceivable without the existence of large-scale organizations, together with a great number of very small organizations.

In an organizationally complex society, we can write an individual's biography as a series of encounters with organizations (Tausky, 1970). Consider your own "career" as a participant in, and supplicant to, the organizations you'll meet from birth to death:

You're born in hospital

Your birth is registered by a city or country bureau of records

You're educated in a school system, assigned to a variety of teachers in your thirteen years in the system

When old enough, you're licensed to drive by a state agency

You're loaned money for your first car or house by a financial institution

If you travel abroad, you'll be required to carry a passport issued by an agency of the national government

Your marriage is registered by the bureau of records

Home furnishings and food are purchased from businesses whose owners you do not know

By the time you're thirty years old, you'll have moved at least twice, relying upon a moving company to transport your belongings from dwelling to dwelling

Quite likely, you, or someone you know, will be granted a divorce by state courts, with the aid of a law firm

At your death, you'll be ministered to by representatives of at least three organizations—a law firm, the church, and the undertaker!

There are two ways to read this record of person-to-organization encounters. First, we could consider organizations the servants of individuals, making possible an infinitely more varied and full life than would otherwise be possible. Optimistically, the record is one of organizations serving *our* needs. Second, we could read this biography as one of people enslaved and dominated by organizations, subject to arbitrary and impersonal dictates, and powerless to fight back. No entertainer has caught this image of man-against-the-organization better than Charlie Chaplin in his film, *Modern Times*. In his first day on the job, we see him as a dazed worker being pushed, punched, cajoled, and ultimately sucked up into the machinery, spinning about in the wheels and cogs of the production process. Pessimistically, the record is one of men and women performing for the benefit of organizational needs.

There is no way to choose a value-free position on this issue. These contradictory images motivate much of the literature on organizations, in both the scholarly and popular press. Writers assert that the tension between individuals and organizations can be a creative, liberating, alienating, or destructive force. As there is no necessarily correct position, it is my intention simply to keep the issue alive throughout the book, leaving the choice, quite properly, to those who have to make the decision in their own "organizational careers."

DEFINITION OF AN ORGANIZATION

People writing about organizations usually take for granted our ability to identify organizations, and indeed, theorists and investigators appear untroubled by accepting a commonsensical conception of "organization." Nevertheless, defining a concept in *analytic* terms is generally a useful endeavor, if for no other reason than that it reveals hidden assumptions about what is studied.

A definition should highlight the *social* nature of organizations—they are products of, and constraints upon, social relations. Thus, I propose the following definition: *organizations are goal-directed, boundary-maintaining, activity systems*. This definition has the advantage of logically implying other concepts that are significant for the study of organizational change, and it directs our attention to organizing as a continuous process (Weick, 1969).

Goal-directed

Organizations are purposive systems (Parsons, 1956). To an observer, members of organizations behave *as if* the organization has a goal. This is not the same as asserting that organizations *do* have goals, but only that much of the activity we observe appears directed toward some common purpose. This means that at least some of the time we will observe task-oriented behavior, as opposed to purely sociable interaction (Aldrich, 1971b). Some organizations may have multiple or contradictory goals, but a unity of purpose is still evident among various groups within the organization. Inferring organizational goals from participants' behaviors allows us to identify "operative goals" (Perrow, 1961) and avoids the knotty problem of reconciling "official goals," espoused by leaders, with what's actually going on in an organization.

Boundary-maintaining

The establishment of an "organization" implies that a distinction has been made between members and non-members—some persons are admitted to participate in the organization, whereas others are excluded (Weber, 1947, pp. 139-46). Modern organizations typically define members contractually, but in an earlier age membership was often ascriptively based. Persons were organizational members not on the basis of an employment contract or voluntary affiliation, but on the basis of ethnicity, kinship, or wealth (Coleman, 1970).

Maintaining a distinction between members and non-members involves establishing an authority, either exercised collectively or delegated to a specific role, empowered to admit some and exclude others. Under this definition, friendship circles or casual associations would not be considered organizations, whereas most social clubs and fraternal associations would be. Our ability to uniquely define a particular organization ultimately rests on developing a reliable scheme for identifying members and, by implication, the complementary set of non-members. From an organization's perspective, the ability to *control* boundaries is critical for the maintenance of organizational autonomy. When the boundaries of an organization become blurred for an observer, it is probably a sign of a change in the relative power of the organization vis-à-vis its population. The boundary-maintaining process becomes visible on those occasions when it is severely tested, such as when blacks or Jews sought admission to exclusive fraternities, country clubs, or elite law firms.

Activity Systems

Organizations possess a *technology* for accomplishing work, whether it's a technique for processing raw materials or people. "Activities" emphasizes that technology affects social relations in organizations by structuring transactions between the roles that are the building blocks of an organization. An activity system thus consists of a bounded set of interdependent behaviors, with the nature of the interdependencies contingent upon technology's form. Consider, for example, the interdependent activities involved in a dress-making firm: pattern making, marking of the cloth, cutting the cloth, allocation of various pieces to different groups of seamstresses, sewing, putting the pieces together in a finished garment, and, of course, supplying the materials and maintaining the tools and machines required. In large firms, each activity may constitute a different role, filled by a different person.

The division of labor between activities in an organization leads to role differentiation and specialization of function. In smaller organizations, role differentiation—people fulfilling different roles in the organization—may involve simply a difference between a leader or manager and other members. Larger organizations are more highly differentiated, and a great deal of research in organizational sociology concerns the relationship between organizational size and role differentiation (Blau, 1972; Child, 1973).

Theorizing about organizations as activity systems biases our thinking toward a concern for processes. By definition, many of these processes are goal-directed and boundary-maintaining, and these characteristics, in turn, are central to the open- or natural-system model of organizations that Thompson (1967) identified as the emerging focus of organizational sociology. Focusing on processes also makes salient the dialectical tension between members' behaviors, which threaten to push an organization into ultimately contradictory activities, and leaders' efforts at pulling members' contributions together into a coordinated whole. Organization theorists were traditionally more concerned with harnessing members' behaviors in the interests of fulfilling organizational goals than in considering the costs to individuals of organizations' structural constraints.

ORGANIZATIONAL STRUCTURE: CENTRAL VARIABLES

Defining organizations as goal-directed, boundary-maintaining, activity systems conveys an image of organizational processes, but we can still raise the question of what holds an organization together. I have said nothing about members' motives or a sense of common purpose—neither is a necessary element of a definition. If we do not assume that all members enter organizations with similar motives, or pursue a common personal goal, then what binds the members together into a collective enterprise?

Coordination and Authority

Coordinated activity gives organizations the appearance of being goal-directed, and such activity usually occurs at the command of dominant members. Beginning with Max Weber's studies in the last decade of the nineteenth century, sociologists have sought the grounds upon which dominance of some members over others is legitimated. Specifically, *why* do people follow the authoritative commands of organizational leaders and administrators? The exploration of this question carried Weber into a more general examination of the structural arrangements in large-scale organizations that make coordinated action possible.

Weber approached the study of organizations through his study of power and authority relations in political structures and public bureaucracies. *Power* is defined as the possibility of imposing one's will upon the behavior of others: "The chance of a man or of a number of men to realize their own will in a communal action even against the resistance of others who are participating in the action" (Gerth and Mills, 1958, p. 180). In the short run, coordinated action based solely upon power relations between ruler and ruled may suffice, but unmediated dominance is an unstable base upon which to erect a long-lived organization.

If political structures, public bureaucracies, and large-scale organizations are to survive, a means must be found to legitimize the exercise of power in the eyes of those who are being ruled. Weber identified *authority* as the means by which dominance was cloaked with legitimacy and the dominated accepted their fate. An *authority relationship* is a power relationship which rulers—those imposing their will on others—believe they have a right to exercise power and, most important, the ruled consider it their duty to obey. An authority relationship contains the element of reciprocity that is lacking in uncontrolled power relationships.

Clearly, organizations founded solely on the ability of rulers to dominate the ruled, without a reciprocal belief by the dominated that the relationship is legitimate, face a constant problem of the erosion of their power. Organizations without legitimacy must devote considerable resources to social control. Authority relations, by contrast, make possible the exercise of domination over large numbers of people, as belief in the legitimacy of authority leads to an acceptance of control procedures.

As organizations grow and exceed the scope of one person's ability to supervise, domination can no longer be exercised on a one-to-one basis. Large-scale organization requires an administrative apparatus to execute the commands and bridge the gap between leaders and the led. Indeed, the level at which a belief in the legitimacy of the leaderships' authority is crucial is *not* the lowest level of an organization, but rather among the members of the administrative apparatus. Political structures, public bureaucracies, and most other organizations can survive a high level of disaffection and alienation among the dominated, as long as the administrative personnel remain convinced of their own legitimacy.

Given the fundamental importance of authoritative relationships, the question Weber posed was what *kinds* of beliefs legitimize the exercise of power in the eyes of rulers and the ruled? On the basis of his historical investigations, he identified three principles of legitimation of authority: charismatic, traditional, and legal. Each principle implies a different type of administrative structure, with differing limits on the exercise of power by rulers or leaders.

Charismatic authority.   Charisma means literally a "gift of grace," "*extraordinary* quality of a person, regardless of whether this quality is actual, alleged, or presumed" (Gerth and Mills, 1958, p. 295). Charismatic authority is legitimated by the belief the governed have in the exceptional qualities of their leader, and charismatic leaders justify their authority by their exceptional deeds. Prophets, warrior chieftains, heads of political factions and social movements, and religious leaders exemplify this type of authority.

Because it is based upon a belief in seemingly magical powers and exceptional virtues, such authority is limitless. The only constraint on the orders of charismatic leaders is the personal capabilities of their followers. Followers or disciples accept arbitrary dictates because they have "faith" in their leaders. The administrative structure under charismatic leaders is loose and unstable, dependent upon the whims and desires of the leader. If the leader dies or is otherwise removed, the organization faces a crisis of succession to the leadership post. If the organization is to survive, stability must be introduced into the structure, in a process labelled the "routinization of charisma." When the Reverend Martin Luther

King, Jr., was assassinated in 1968, the loss of his charismatic leadership threw the Southern Christian Leadership Conference into a turmoil, with opposing factions supporting Ralph Abernathy and Jesse Jackson. The organization split, with Jackson breaking away to find Operation Breadbasket in Chicago.

Charismatic leaders are important figures in the study of organizational change because of their role in creating new organizations and disrupting established ones. "Charismatic domination means a rejection of all ties to any external order in favor of the exclusive glorification of the genuine mentality of the prophet and hero. Hence, its attitude is revolutionary and transvalues everything; it makes a sovereign break with all traditional or rational norms: It is written, but I say unto you" (Gerth and Mills, 1958, p. 250).

Traditional authority.   Legitimation of traditional authority stems from a belief in the inviolable nature of everyday routine and the unchanging past. People obey out of respect for the ruler's traditional status and the belief that tradition is the best guide to behavior. Obviously, leaders have a strong vested interest in promoting such beliefs, and infractions of the leader's commands are said to result in magical or religious evils.

The feudal lord or small town community leader, who command by virtue of their inherited statuses, exercise traditional authority. Orders and decisions of the traditional leader are personal, rather than based on formal rules or law, but are not as arbitrary as those of the charismatic leader, as they must fall within the limits fixed by custom. The administrative structure under traditional authority consists of patriarchal household or patrimonial bureaucracy, made up of officials who depend solely upon the leaders and whose interests are linked to them. Continuity in administration is not as problematic as under charismatic authority, as officials have tradition and custom to guide them in daily decisions.

Legal authority.   The legitimation of legal authority is a belief in the law, not in a charismatically gifted person nor upon sacred tradition or obligations toward a traditional leader. People obey laws under legal authority not because they are issued by a charismatic or traditional leader, but because they believe that the laws were enacted through proper procedure. "Submission under legal authority is based upon an *impersonal* bond to the generally defined and functional 'duty of office'" (Gerth and Mills, 1958, p. 299). One's duty of office is fixed by rationally established norms, and is arrived at through commonly agreed upon principles of rationality, rather than through the visions of a charismatic leader or repetition of traditional practices.

Rulers or leaders have authority to issue orders because they were elevated to their positions by legal procedures. Authority is strictly limited to areas of competence defined by law, and if the rules are followed, the administrative structure is highly stable.

The administrative structure under legal authority is called a *bureaucracy*; it is a structure characterized by a belief in rules and legal order in the carrying out of organizational tasks. Weber argued that legal-bureaucratic authority had become the dominant organizing principle in modern society, displacing the ad hoc, patriarchal, and patrimonial forms of organization. "The decisive reason for the advance of bureaucratic organization has always been its purely technical superiority over any other form of organization. The fully developed bureaucratic mechanism compares with other organizations exactly as does the machine with the non-mechanical modes of production" (Gerth and Mills, 1958, p. 214). In writing of the bureaucratization of modern society, he noted that the bureaucratic form of administration had penetrated all institutions: the church, army, universities, and, above all, the state. The spread of bureaucratization was spurred by the general trend of the rationalization of social life.

Weber was particularly interested in the political effects of the bureaucratization of administration. On the one hand, he noted bureaucrary's impact in the leveling of social differences, while on the other hand he wrote of its tendency toward concentration of the means of administration in the hands of a few. His discussion of power in bureaucracies and of the power of bureaucracies in society is still relevant today. The following warning will be as relevant in the 1980s as it was in the earliest decade of this century:

> Once it is fully established, bureaucracy is among those social structures which are the hardest to destroy. Bureaucracy is *the* means of carrying "community action" over into rationally ordered "societal action." Therefore, as an instrument for "societalizing" relations of power, bureaucracy has been and is a power instrument of the first order—for the one who controls the bureaucratic apparatus (Gerth and Mills, 1958, p. 228).

Bureaucratic Structure

Weber not only analyzed the tendency of bureaucracies to accompany the increasing rationalization of social life, but also identified the reasons for the technical superiority of bureaucracy over previous forms of organization. Since most modern organizations resemble the bureaucratic type portrayed by Weber, it is imperative that we understand its features if we wish to understand the conditions under which organizational structures change. Weber presented the characteristics of bureaucracy as an *ideal type*—an analytically-constructed model, extracted from systematic observations of many bureaucracies. He recognized that the characteristics might be present in particular bureaucratic structures in varying degrees, as is evidenced by his use of qualifying phrases such as "more or less," "normally," and "usually."

Social scientists studying organizations disaggregated Weber's portrait of an ideal-typical bureaucracy into its component parts and used them as *variables* in analyzing organizational structures (Hall, 1963). As they were adapted to the demands of research, the variables became detached from their original context. It is clear, for example, that Weber had in mind fairly large administrative structures: the church, the army, political parties in the United States, the state apparatus of the Roman and Egyptian empires, or the social Democratic party in Germany. Nevertheless, the dimensions have been found useful when applied to smaller-scale organizations, and while some investigators may have neglected the association between these characteristics and organizational efficiency (Weber's concern), occasionally critics speak out to remind us of Weber's intent (Perrow, 1972).

Seven characteristics enjoy a special place in the list of variables used in modern organizational research, as will be evident from the studies reviewed in this book. I will give the characteristics labels that match them with current conceptions of organizational structure, and will discuss the advantages accruing to organizations falling toward the "bureaucratic" end of a dimension. Treated as variables, rather than components or properties of an ideal type, the structural characteristics Weber identified are perfectly general dimensions that may be applied to any organizational structure. Recent research demonstrates that the dimensions may vary independently of one another—they are not perfectly correlated in any population of organizations—and thus most social scientists prefer to theorize about specific variables, rather than "bureaucracy" as a form. Our image of bureaucracy is so strong, however, that even social scientists often slip into writing about "bureaucratic organizations," and I will periodically do the same.

Specialization.   The duties of each role are clearly specified in bureaucratic organizations, with each member operating in a fixed and official jurisdictional area. A highly rationalized division of labor limits each member to only a subset of the organization's tasks, thus increasing organizational efficiency as members gain experience and learn to do their job well. Specialization also increases efficiency by reducing the chaos and uncertainty that would result if members were free to take on any task in the organization, regardless of their training or experience.

Formalization and standardization.   As an organization becomes more bureaucratized, the extent to which the duties of each role are formalized through rules and regulations expands. Weber observed that the management of modern organizations is based on written documents and files, which is the highest degree of formalization. Formalization of duties reduces uncertainty that would otherwise confront members faced with variability in customers, raw material, relations with other members, or simply the problem of how to allocate their time. Most organizations dealing with large constituencies develop standardized procedures that members follow when dealing with clients, such as presenting them with standard forms to be completed or recording a credit card transaction in exactly the same manner for every sale.

Rules are the basis of self-protection for organizational members, as they reduce internal conflict (Perrow, 1972). Departments and their members occupy a specific role in the organizational division of labor, and formalization of duties limits the demands others can make on persons in a particular role. A response to a difficult or unusual request is typically "that's not my job."

Decentralization. In a bureaucratic organization, the responsibility for making routine operating decisions is delegated to the various units and departments, rather than remaining in the hands of the chief administrator. Although it is paradoxical, given the common stereotype of bureaucracies as highly centralized and monocratic, delegation of authority is actually a requisite for efficient operations in a bureaucracy. Centralization of authority is limited to important policy decisions and planning, and top administrators deal only with exceptional and unusual cases that subordinates cannot handle. This type of structure frees the top administrator or leader for making long-range decisions, and can be contrasted with decision making under charismatic or traditional authority, wherein leaders are involved in almost all decisions.

Efficient bureaucracies centralize the authority to make *non-routine* decisions, while routine decisions are made by lower-level staff. The hallmark of a highly bureaucratized organization lies in the ability of clerks, foremen, lower-level supervisors, and ordinary members to handle most of the everyday tasks of the organization without involving their immediate supervisors. Successful decentralization allows the organization to reap the maximum benefits from specialization and formalization, as it minimizes communication costs and the drain on scarce managerial or leadership time.

Hierarchy. A highly bureaucratic organization is characterized by an official hierarchy of authority that establishes "a firmly ordered system of super- and subordination in which there is a supervision of the lower offices by the higher ones" (Gerth and Mills, 1958, p. 197). The hierarchy is both a structure of domination and a channel through which decisions can be appealed from lower ranks to higher ranks. An organization and its clients benefit from an officially recognized hierarchy of authority, as it makes decision makers visible and thus accountable for their actions.

Each role is subject to discipline from a role above it in the hierarchy, but such authority extends only to the formal duties of the role. The private life of an employee is free from the organization's authority. Again, contrast this situation with the fate of a member under charismatic or traditional authority, where the organization potentially has access to a member's entire life-space.

Limited rewards to officeholders.   The "means of administration"—the resources of the organization—are attached to the office, not the officeholder. Weber noted that office holding is a "vocation," not to be exploited for side benefits such as extorting money from clients or appropriating organizational resources. A member implicitly accepts an obligation to faithfully perform the duties of office, but gains no personal rights to the office. Weber noted that in the Middle Ages the practice of "office farming" was quite common: Persons were induced to occupy positions in the state bureaucracy with the promise of being able to arrange their own methods of tax collection and the opportunity to put state-owned land to personal use. In modern organizations, while it is no longer legitimate, white-collar employees stock up on envelopes, pencils, use the telephone for personal calls, and pad their expense accounts. Opportunities for blue-collar workers are more limited, but employees of firms with equipment repair shops may find ways to reduce the cost of auto maintenance or appliance upkeep. Bureaucratic structure is designed to reduce such exploitation of the organization.

Universalistic performance standards.   Hiring and promotion in a highly bureaucratic organization are ideally based on competence and universalistic standards. Competence may be measured by one's educational qualifications, previous training, standardized tests, or performance in office, but whatever the criterion, it is applied on a non-personalistic basis. Efficiency is achieved because employees are chosen for their ability and technical knowledge, rather than on technically irrelevant criteria such as race, sex, or kinship ties. As battles over equal opportunity hiring and promotion of blacks and women in the United States attest, particularistic standards are still a characteristic of many otherwise bureaucratically structured organizations.

Career advancement opportunities.   Bureaucratically structured organizations ideally provide their members with the prospect of career advancement, and increasing authority and income within the organization. Mobility through the ranks is based on universalistic criteria and is a way of motivating persons to perform well continually. Efficiency is increased because members are offered a strong inducement to do their jobs well and they adopt a long-term perspective on membership in the organization. Not all modern organizations or occupations offer the possibility of a career, and some economists argue that the business sector is split into two parts—one with an internal labor market and the other without (Doeringer and Piore, 1971). An organization with an internal labor market offers employees the opportunity to gain organization-specific skills, which give them access to jobs with higher pay or more responsibility. Organizations without internal labor markets, such as small, family-owned retail and service establishments, represent a career dead-end for their employees.

Summary of bureaucratic structural characteristics.   If we ignore the variable nature of the seven characteristics and concentrate only on the "bureaucratic" extreme of each dimension, we can grasp the fundamental feature of bureaucratic efficiency: bureaucracy tries to eliminate or control all extra-organizational influences on the behavior of its members. Bureaucratic characteristics are designed to close off the organization from unwanted influences, insofar as this is possible. These structural features are chosen on the basis of rational criteria, and another way to remember the central feature of the bureaucratizing process is to think of it as the exercise of control on the basis of the rational use of information.

OPENING UP THE BUREAUCRATIC MODEL
OF ORGANIZATIONS

As a model for managing organizations, bureaucracy is unassailable. Given the proper set of conditions, leaders and administrators could do no better than to follow the recommendations implicit in Weber's description of bureaucracy; it is a technically superior instrument for accomplishing complex tasks. As Perrow (1972) and others have noted, many criticisms of bureaucracy are misplaced, as Weber did not argue that bureaucratic structure constituted a universal organizing principle. His chief concern was with the administration of nation-states and other large-scale undertakings, such as armies and political parties. Weber could not have foreseen the uses to which his model would be put by sociologists and others studying industrial organizations, voluntary associations, and other forms of organization.

Weber's work was not widely available in the English language and in the United States until the late 1940s, but social scientists interested in the management of organizations (in the decades following World War I) were developing a conception of internal organizational structure very similar to his. Borrowing many of their concepts from military terminology, management scientists wrote of the necessity for unity in the chain of command, achieving an optimum ratio of subordinates per supervisor, and improving lines of communication. The central question for these theorists was how to design an efficient organizational structure—a question that was also at the center of Weber's work.

For purposes of analysis and prescription, the environments of organizations were taken as given, or else outside forces acting on organizations were assumed to be predictable. Theorists assumed that goals were known, technology was well-understood, and resources were available to support the organization. These assumptions are very much the same as those Weber made in developing his ideal-typical model of bureaucracy. The underlying premise of these models was that organizational structure is designed through deliberate choice, and that choices reflect a non-ambiguous goal (Thompson, 1967). For management scientists, industrial economists, and others, this was both a model of organization and a sought-after goal.

A concern for maximizing efficiency (given the assumption of stable goals, technology, and funding) leads to the creation of organizational models very much like Weber's conception of bureaucracy. Thus the various management-oriented models began to blend together with Weber's model in the literature on organizations in the 1950s. As Thompson (1967) notes, such models are oriented chiefly to managing organizations, rather than understanding them. People often fail to consider under what conditions the bureaucratic model could most appropriately be applied and what conditions limit its usefulness when they follow such models. For example, the destructive effects of rationalization's consequences for wage-workers were overlooked, and some theorists have argued that the "degradation of labor" is a direct result of applying rational-scientific methods of analysis to the jobs people have in *all* organizations (Braverman, 1974).

The factors taken as given by these rather closed models of organizations are most easily discerned when they are related to the definition of an organization presented earlier: a goal-directed, boundary-maintaining, activity system. The bureaucratic model, strictly applied, takes goals, boundaries, and activity systems as non-problematic for an organization's structure. Under these conditions, there are no barriers to adopting the seven characteristic features of bureaucracy, and administrators and leaders can direct their attention to maximizing efficiency.

The pure bureaucratic model never totally dominated the sociological literature; Selznick (1949), Bendix (1956), Thompson (1960), and others maintained a concern for organizational environments in their writings. I believe that the non-cumulative nature of much of this work, as contrasted with research focused more narrowly on intraorganizational structure, was due to the lack of an all-encompassing theoretical perspective. The bureaucratic model was well-developed, parsimonious, and easy to apply in case studies of single organizations. Nevertheless, what Thompson (1967) calls an open- or natural-system model was kept alive, and it ultimately attracted enough attention to become a specialty area within organizational sociology. A few case examples, based upon the goals-boundaries-activity system definition of an organization, will indicate the flavor of the more open orientation.

Organizations in Relation to Environments

Goals may be imposed on an organization by the environment.   The bureaucratic model presumes that organizational goals are known and are an unambiguous guide to action. An example taken from a study by Maniha and Perrow (1965), however, highlights a situation in which organizational objectives follow from pressures imposed on an organization by outside elements. In the early 1960s, a Youth Commission was created in Ann Arbor, Michigan, with the official goal of "appraising conditions and influences affecting youth, evaluating existing services, and recommending measures to promote the best interests of children and youth in the city." The technology of the new organization was only vaguely spelled out, and an opening was left for the possibility of an action role for the group.

During its first year, the Commission played a wait-and-see role, listening to suggestions from various community groups but resisting pressures for a more active role. A benign report was issued that assured other agencies and groups that the Youth Commission was not going to be a threat to their roles and interests in Ann Arbor. At the beginning of its second year the Commission elected a new chairperson who had no organizational role directly involving youth, and thus could act as a free agent. This is not to say that he planned an aggressive role for the Commission, but only that he had no vested interest in it playing a passive role.

A major change occurred in the Commission's environment during its second year—other organizations began to view the Youth Commission as a vehicle for the realization of their own ends. First, the Ann Arbor city council considered enacting an anti-brawling ordinance, but before taking action, the council asked the Youth Commission to study the situation and make recommendations. Given the nature of the request, this was tantamount to asking the Commission to become a part of the legislative process, a step on the road to assuming a more active role. Second, the United Fund asked the Commission to co-sponsor a seminar, which was very well received by the local media, generating a great deal of favorable publicity for the Commission.

Third, the Probate Court asked the Youth Commission to "look into" a project offering protective services for juveniles, such as protection from parental abuse. A judge from the Probate Court arranged a meeting between the Commission and a representative of a state-wide project, and told the assembled group that he felt the Commission ought to sponsor a program to aid troubled youth. Subsequently, a meeting was held with the heads of agencies dealing with youth, and an unquestioned assumption of the meeting was that the Commission would sponsor a study and take the lead in disseminating its results.

By the beginning of its third year, the "no-action" policy was thoroughly compromised, even though Youth Commission members didn't openly acknowledge it. The Commission was taking the lead in youth protective services and was considering adding a staff person to coordinate the work of all the involved groups. Although this shift in goals was made possible by the election of a more receptive Commission chairperson, the actual push toward an action role came from outside the organization's boundaries.

Organizations' goals can be generated by external forces, such as other groups seeking to use the organization to further their own ends, as occurred in the case of the Youth Commisssion. Other examples include the use of the Democratic Party by the AFL-CIO to press for minimum wage legislation, and the use of the American Medical Association and its journal by the ethical drugs industry to advertise its products (Hirsch, 1975b). The bureaucratic model must be modified to recognize organizational goal-setting as a result of interaction between organizations and their environments (Thompson and McEwen, 1958).

Organizational boundaries are not fixed. Organizational boundaries— defined in terms of membership—may vary, depending upon internal needs and the degree of threat posed by an organization's environment. Organizational strategy in times of interorganizational conflict may be thought of as a choice between two options: constricting or expanding organizational boundaries. Member participation, under normal circumstances, is important because organizational maintenance depends upon members sustaining the activity system. Members constitute critical resources in a conflict, as the more active the participation, the greater the chances of success in the conflict. Strategy may take the form of constricting the boundaries of the organization by strengthening the requirements of participation, with each member asked to do more in conforming to organizational rules and ideology. Raising performance standards means, in many cases, expelling weaker members from the organization.

The Black Panther Party, a militant black organization that began in Oakland, California, in the early 1960s exemplifies the boundary constriction strategy. At times, thousands claimed to be members of the organization, but when the group became subject to severe police and FBI harassment in the late 1960s, the leadership claimed less than a thousand members. Ideological standards were raised, and they became the source of violent conflict within the Black Panthers. The organization split into warring factions, with the opponents trading charges of ideological impurity and opportunism. A similar conflict befell the Students for a Democratic Society (SDS), a predominantly male, leftist-oriented group that became increasingly politicized through the 1960s. The conflict culminated in a split in the late 1960s that sent the most militant faction underground—the "Weather Underground." Surviving factions accepted only the ideologically committed, and the danger of police discovery kept most working subgroups of the organization quite small.

Strategy may also take the form of expanding organizational boundaries to include as members persons from competing organizations or from the potentially troublesome environment. This strategy poses problems for an organization because taking on new, unsocialized members means more work for current members. Expansion is easiest in organizations without a highly specific belief system or stringent participation requirements, and in organizations with slack resources to distribute to new members.

The most well-known example of boundary expansion in the organizational sociology literature is Selznick's (1949) study of co-optation of business and agricultural interests in the Tennessee Valley Authority (TVA) case. Faced with potentially crippling hostility from powerful elements in its environment, the TVA expanded its boundaries to take them in. The Democratic Party in the United States is remarkable in its ability to absorb divergent interests and dissident groups under the same organizational umbrella. When potential opposition groups arose, such as the coalition that supported Eugene McCarthy's unsuccessful attempt at the Democratic presidential nomination in 1968, the party simply expanded to take in all but the most committed opponents.

Organizational boundaries are not firmly fixed and may vary, depending on the situation an organization faces. Expansion and contraction are two extremes of a range of boundary-maintaining strategies open to leaders and administrators. Moreover, often organizations have no discretion in the matter—either boundaries change or survival becomes problematic. A revised model of organizational structure must take this into account.

Activity systems are not equally adapted to all environments.   Managerial theories of organization structure usually make the choice of an activity system non-problematic, assuming that administrators will choose the activity system and technology that is most suited to the organization's environment. In this example, the focus will be on the technological aspect of activity systems. Whether technology is based on people- or material-processing, little attention is paid to the prospect of changing conditions that could make it non-effective, or, worse still, fatally unfit for the environment an organization operates in. Emery and Trist (1965) provided an example of a food canning company in England after World War II that failed to modify its technology to keep pace with the times and consequently suffered a severe financial decline.

The ACME Vegetable Company produced a canned vegetable that accounted for about 65 percent of the vegetables sold in its market, with this proportion quite stable before and during the war. Top administrators, believing their environment was stable, convinced the parent company to invest millions of dollars in building a new automated factory. Since the new technology only attained highest efficiency when run at a high volume, it constituted a built-in rigidity in the operations of ACME.

ACME's environment, however, was not stable. Four developments occurred while the new factory was being built. First, after World War II, the removal of controls on sales of metal products made cheap metal cans easy to obtain, and the resumption of international trade sparked a large market in imported fruits. The fruit trade was seasonal and to take up their slack capacity, the small companies sought an off-season activity. They discovered the availability of large quantities of vegetables from the United States due to a side effect of the development of quick-frozen foods. Vegetable crops that were unsuitable for freezing but that were suitable for canning became available at cheap prices. These developments had the effect of substantially increasing competition in ACME's market.

Second, the increasing affluence of post-war English society meant that a large number of people could afford quick-frozen, as opposed to canned, vegetables. Frozen-food companies began to erode ACME's once-dominant position in the market. Third, increasing affluence meant that people had access to a wider variety of vegetables than just the line produced by ACME. Fourth, as in the United States, major changes were taking place in the English food-retailing industry. Food retailing became increasingly concentrated in the hands of supermarkets and large grocery chains. One of the marketing strategies of these organizations was lower prices; they wanted to sell cheaper "house" brands, rather than relying upon well-known, independent producers' brands. Supermarkets and chains placed bulk orders with the smaller canning firms and, within a few years, retailers' own brands captured almost 50 percent of the market.

ACME's automated factory couldn't be adapted to the new situation until new products could be developed with a sales volume large enough to justify high volume production. Developing new products required research and development and large scale market research, but ACME had structured itself on the assumption that these strategies would not be needed. The company could not afford to make the necessary adjustments to the changed environments and consequently had to be reorganized, after massive internal disruptions and conflict.

A particular technology is effective only insofar as it is appropriate to the environment an organization faces, as this example demonstrates. No matter how *internally* efficient the technology-activity system, the loss of external relevance dooms an organization to inferior status unless it has other sources of power over its environment. The American steel industry has lagged behind its foreign competitors under a shield of oligopolistic pricing and common values regarding a reluctance to diversify or innovate. Rapid growth in the availability of cheaper steel from Western Europe and Japan in the 1970s has caused massive employment loss and corporate reorganizations in many steel companies. Most organizations have only a limited degree of freedom from environmental forces, and a model of organizational change must treat technology, as well as goals and boundaries, as subject to environmental constraints.

SOURCES OF CHANGE

In choosing to study organizational change, we face the question of how to organize our inquiry. How are we to decide where to look for the sources of change in organizational forms and functions? Which academic disciplines can we draw upon? A reasonable answer would be that we make use of whatever concepts and perspectives are relevant to the specific instance of change we examine. However, as the examples in the preceding section show, it is useful to have an idea of the range of possible answers to the question of "how do we account for change?"

Leadership

Social-psychology and administrative science emphasize the role of key individuals as leaders and innovators in organizational change. Entrepreneurial theory in economics attributes the creation of firms to farsighted action by individuals willing to take risks in uncertain economic environments. As Perrow (1970, p. 2) noted, administrators and others assert that, after all, "organizations are people" and therefore the study of organizations is really the study of persons who happen to occupy organizational roles. No one can deny that organizations are sustained by social relations and that interpersonal interaction is the lifeblood of organizational routine; but such a view is incomplete.

Viewing organizational change solely as the product of key decisions by leaders or members fails to take into account the significant constraints that confront "people" as they go about their everyday duties. Even entrepreneurs whose names we associate with spectacular successes in American corporate history appear slightly less heroic when we examine the inconsistent records they compiled. Henry Ford founded his enormously profitable automobile company in 1903 (as a minority shareholder) only after being associated with two previous corporate failures. William Durant, founder of General Motors in 1908, did so poorly that by 1911 he was replaced as head of the company by outside financial interests. He then created another auto company—Chevrolet—and through its success returned to head General Motors again in 1916. Such examples are even more common in the small business community, as the very high failure rate of small firms reflects the constant shuffling of workers into and out of self-employment.

After reviewing the debate between theorists over whether leaders can make a large difference in organizations, Hall (1977) suggested two ways of resolving the issue. First, "leadership" depends on the degree of congruence between a situation and the characteristics of the leader. This position leaves room for individual initiative, but also directs our attention to the *context* within which "leadership" is exercised. Second, the higher a leader's position and the more centralized the decision-making structure, the larger the impact he or she can make. This proposition is eminently plausible, but it must be qualified by the first proposition—high rank opens up the possibility of making an impact, but the contingency of matching "leadership" to the context still holds. Lieberson and O'Connor's (1972) study of 167 large corporations found only limited effects of leadership changes on company performance, net of industry and company effects. Generalizing from their findings is risky, however, given definitional dependence between their three performance variables and the lack of organization-specific control variables.

Assessing the contribution that leaders make to organizational change is quite difficult in societies that place great value on "leadership," and attribute success or failure to individual rather than social structural characteristics. Organizational failures are generally followed by a search for the individual responsible, and the annual turnover of managers in professional sports reflects, in part, this ritual scapegoating (Gamson and Scotch, 1964). The basis of structure selection, experienced as "success" by a given organization, may be imperfectly understood by organizational members. Without knowledge about the experience of other organizations, especially those experiencing "failure," it is difficult for the members of a single organization to accurately account for the source of their success. It is equally difficult, of course, for members to understand the causes of failure. Under conditions of uncertain and ambiguous information, members fall back on cultural and organizational stereotypes for an explanation of success and failure, and "leadership" is a popular choice.

Other Organizations

Economics and human ecology emphasize the role of other organizations in supplying (or withholding) resources in the interorganizational division of labor. As will be noted throughout this book, organizations in industrial societies control and allocate the bulk of societal resources through the production of goods and services and the payment of wages and salaries. Differentiation and specialization within the organizational population lessen the possibility of any single organization achieving self-sufficiency, thus requiring most organizations to enter into transactions with others to obtain resources that cannot be generated internally (Levine and White, 1961). Organizational differentiation and specialization of function are likely to lead to interorganizational dependencies whenever some organizations manage to acquire monopoly control over important resources and are able to defend their position. By manipulating interorganizational dependencies, dominant organizations have a major impact on the behavior of other organizations in the population.

The organizational population is highly stratified, and so the potential impact of dominant organizations is widespread. For example, in 1972, approximately 2 percent of all business organizations in the United States accounted for over 76 percent of all business receipts. Among active corporations in 1972, 0.10 percent controlled 61 percent of all corporate assets. Whether intended or not, any action by the very largest organizations reverberates throughout the entire population—setting wage scales, product quality standards, supplying top-level officials for Presidential cabinets, or intervening in the internal affairs of foreign countries.

Any particular organization may be enmeshed in a web of dominant and subordinate relations with dozens of other organizations, but the full effects of dependencies will be felt only when dominant organizations make demands on subordinate organizations. The manipulation of authority is a common strategy to ensure organizational dominance, as is vertical integration, interlocking directorates, discriminatory pricing, exclusive dealing arrangements, and the formation of cartels. These strategies are most readily used by the largest and most stable organizations. Their resources provide a base that cushions them against occasional strategic failures, as well as making possible expensive maneuvers that smaller organizations would never dare attempt.

Political science and public administration furnish insights into political and legislative demands for and constraints on organizational change. The past several decades are replete with examples of organizational change mandated by legislative or regulatory action: pollution and gasoline mileage standards for new automobiles that led to changes in automotive design; occupational safety and health standards that mandated changes on the shop floor to eliminate risks to workers; capital exporting restrictions in the early 1970s that affected corporate foreign investment; and federal subsidies for graduate education that first boosted and then deflated enrollment in graduate social science programs, thus affecting the size and operating procedures of social science departments. Legislative and regulatory action has also had the opposite effect—that of inhibiting or prohibiting organization change. The conservative procedures for allocating new trucking and airline routes, initiated by the Interstate Commerce Commission and the Civil Aeronautics Board, have been a major barrier to the entry of new firms into these industries.

Social and Cultural Forces

An examination of the historical record by sociologists, historians, anthropologists, and others points up the community and societal context within which organizational change occurs. Social movements, changes in societal values, cross-societal diffusion of innovations, and the incorporation of peripheral areas into the world capitalist system (Wallerstein, 1974), have had major impacts on the production of new types of organizations and the transformation of old ones.

In all industrializing societies, entrepreneurs have had to fight to win acceptance for the new pattern of economic activity made necessary by industrialization (Bendix, 1956). The creation of new organizational forms has been limited until industrialists could win over or neutralize a politically dominant aristocracy and the newly recruited work force. The position of the state has been crucial in these confrontations. From the very beginning, industrialization in Russia was both stimulated and controlled by the state. In contrast, the rising entrepreneurial class of England had a great deal of autonomy from the state, relative to Russian industrialists, and they were left free to develop new enterprises. Chinese society presents an interesting third case, as their industrialization never really got underway until the late 1940s when the Chinese communists took control. Even though Chinese authorities prior to the 1940s had recognized the importance of industrialization, they were in no position to promote it. Industrialization, when it did occur, took place in the port cities, where foreign intervention and influence were strongest.

There are many examples of organizational innovations that have transferred readily from one society to another: workers' councils, job design by industrial engineers, and the use of electronic computers in payroll and accounting departments. We must also recognize, however, that innovations have failed when introduced into societies with non-supportive cultural and institutional traditions. The McDonald's fast food corporation, after extensive preparation, introduced several outlets in England and achieved instant success. Establishing outlets in Japan in 1971 was more difficult, as Japanese consumers were not easily persuaded to switch from their traditional diet of fish to a meal of beef and bread. In spite of this, McDonald's ranked seventh in sales among food service enterprises in Japan by 1977, with 105 walk-in outlets opened in six years, and with the prospect of becoming number two by 1978. In contrast to McDonald's fairly rapid growth in Japan, its attempt to penetrate the French market was impeded by traditional French eating habits, and by 1977 only two successful outlets were open in Paris.

Of the three possible sources of change (leadership, other organizations, and social and cultural forces), two direct our attention to forces outside an organization. Both the second and third possibilities give less weight to leadership and more to external constraint. This book will focus on demonstrating the value of an organization-environment perspective.

SUMMARY

A truly open model of organizational change does *not* take the environment as given, and does *not* assume a completely known or controllable internal structure (Thompson, 1967). A strict application of the bureaucratic model leads to a focus on efficiency, while the theoretical focus of a more open model is on effectiveness, survival, and adaptation to changing environments. This model shifts our attention to variables not directly controlled by members of organizations, as discussed in the three examples presented above.

The concept of efficiency has mainly an internal relevance (to maximize internal control and communication), whereas the concept of effectiveness refers to an organization's ability to exploit its environment in the acquisition of scarce resources (Yuchtman and Seashore, 1967). How do members and leaders cope with the uncertainty produced by environmental elements and forces beyond their control? Instead of treating the various characteristics of organizational structure (hierarchy, specialization, and so forth) as resulting from deliberate and informed choice by members, a more open model treats structure as partially a response to organizations' adaptations to their environments. Organizations are shaped, pushed, and pulled in directions unintended and unforeseen by members. The model presented in the next chapter does not deny the importance of leaders' and members' choices in shaping organizational structures and processes. It points, instead, to a more balanced viewpoint: how, under what conditions, in which specific ways, are environments, as opposed to individuals, the driving force underlying organizational change?

Central Themes of the Book

After presenting the population ecology model of organizational change in Chapters 2 through 5, the remaining chapters deal with various issues of organizational change and stability. The following four are among the more important issues covered.

Differential survival and success (Chapters 5, 6). Why do organizations with similar objectives or products and comparable services differ rather drastically in terms of their survival and success? When organizations start out with similar chances for success, which aspects of their environments and managements account for such differences in outcome? About half of all small businesses fail within two years of their creation, and probably less than one in five ever achieve anything resembling "success" (Mayer and Goldstein, 1961). At the other extreme, the very largest corporations rarely, if ever, "fail" (in the sense of going out of business). Instead, if they disappear it is by takeover by or merger with another firm. Of the 100 largest publicly held manufacturing corporations in the United Kingdom in 1948, 36 had disappeared by 1968, but 27 of these "deaths" were due to mergers and the other 9 to government takeover (Whittington, 1972).

The divergent paths followed by Sears, Roebuck and Company and by Montgomery Wards during the 1940s resulted in substantial success for Sears and troubles for Wards (Chandler, 1962). Whereas Sears changed its internal structure to match what was happening in its environment—by establishing direct-selling stores in the suburbs, regionalizing its administrative structure, and creating a hierarchy of store sizes to match market conditions—Wards continued with its ill-fated strategy of catalog stores in the central business district urban areas and little differentiation in store size by market area.

The creation of organizations (Chapters 7, 12, 13). Under what conditions do organizations come into being? Examination of the historical record reveals a rather curious phenomenon: while certain types of organizations have a relatively constant birth rate over a fairly long time span, e.g. grocery stores, others have been created in great spurts of activity, followed by or interspersed with, almost no new starts at all. Most men's social fraternities in the United States were founded in three waves: 1840–1850, 1865–1870, and 1900–1920 (Stinchcombe, 1965). During the first period most were founded at northern colleges, during the second period in the South (later spreading to northern colleges), and in the third period they were founded at a variety of locations by groups excluded from the original social fraternities, e.g. Jews, Catholics, and blacks.

Many of the largest and most important United States government agencies were created in a burst of activity during the 1930s, evidently as a response to the crisis of the Great Depression (Grafton, 1975). The Securities and Exchange Commission, the Federal Communications Commission, and the Federal Housing Authority were created in 1934, and the National Labor Relations Board, the Social Security Administration, and the Rural Electrification Administration were created in 1935.

Goal succession and organizational transformation (Chapters 8, 9).   Why do organizations sometimes radically change their structure and processes and become something that was completely unforeseen at the time of their creation? This question differs from that of creation in that it refers to an organization undergoing a transformation from one organizational form to another, e.g. from a social movement to a sociable organization (Aldrich, 1971a). The Women's Christian Temperance Union (WCTU) began with the objective of wiping out alcohol as a social problem among the working class. Middle- and upper-middle class women were recruited to improve the general welfare of the working class, and the movement reached its zenith with the enactment of Prohibition. The repeal of Prohibition and other changes in the social environment led to the organization's transformation into a social club for the lower-middle class, limited to occasionally expressing its "moral indignation" against the drinking habits of the middle class (Gusfield, 1955).

Similarly, the Young Men's Christian Association was transformed from a religiously-oriented social movement to a youth service organization after being transplanted from London to the United States (Zald, 1970). In the past decade, a number of American oil companies have made the transition from being "in the oil business" to "being in the energy business" through their acquisition of coal mining firms and their expansion into atomic and other energy souces. For example, through 1975 Exxon had spent about $100 million on nuclear research.

Managing the environment (Chapters 9 through 13).   What tactics and strategies do organizations choose, or have forced upon them, to cope with potentially problematic aspects of their environments? How are disruptive or unwanted influences dealt with? One problem many organizations face is how to socialize members into the organizational culture, particularly when new members bring with them values and behavior that conflict with standard operating procedures. Rookie police officers enter their departments highly-motivated, idealistic, and committed to the organization. Idealism is quickly lost, and recruits learn that zealousness in the performance of their duties only causes trouble. Motivation decreases as a recruit learns the ropes, and "the model adjustment of the novice patrolmen of the occupational culture is best epitomized by the 'lay low, hang loose and don't expect too much' advice frequently heard" (Maanen, 1975, p. 225).

Businesses and local governments responded to the increased strength of labor unions with the creation of special industrial or employee relations units, just as they responded to the consumer movement of the 1970s with the creation of consumer relations units. Mergers, joint ventures, and the creation of special boundary-spanning roles are examples of the types of adaptations to problematic environments that are reviewed later.

A common theme running through the four issues just outlined is that organizational change is a consequence of organizations interacting with their environments. Sometimes organizations merely react to environmental conditions, whereas in other instances members are active in challenging the environment and perhaps even reshaping it. Regardless of whether the initiative lies within an organization or outside of it, the major contribution of organizational sociology in the 1970s was to explicitly add the environment concept to studies of organizational stability and change.

2 The Population Ecology Model

Opening up our model of organizations has not meant replacing the Weberian model of internal structure with something else, but rather placing it in its proper context. The bureaucratic model remains paramount as an account of how behavior in organizations is coordinated, but theorists now recognize other bases of coordination, such as relying upon self-regulation by members selected through tough entrance requirements or commitment to a participatory ideology (Rothschild-Whitt, 1976). Similarly, examples presented in the previous chapter show how the elements in the definition of an organization (goals, boundaries, and technologies) may vary with changing environmental conditions. The change in emphasis from a more closed or rational system model to an open or natural system model brought confusion into theorizing about organizational change, as sociological developments in the study of social change failed to diffuse into the study of organizational change. Evolutionary theories of social change depend heavily upon the natural selection model borrowed from biological and human ecologists, although the model has not yet achieved complete acceptance (Nisbet, 1969; Lenski, 1976). We cannot review the history of sociology's somewhat fickle romance with evolutionary theory—alternating enthusiasm and disillusionment—but it is useful to review a few issues that hampered acceptance of the theory, after presenting an overview of the theory itself.

The population ecology model represents an attempt to explain the *process* underlying change. It differs from "evolutionary approaches" that simply classify societies or organizations on the basis of unilinear schemes, such as from least to most developed. The model rejects the teleological implications inherent in theories of societal or organizational development, just as reform Darwinists rejected the notion of a final, perfect society. A focus on process and a willingness to leave open the ultimate course of organizational change makes the natural selection model perfectly compatible with the open or natural systems view of organizational structure described in the last chapter. In calling it a natural selection or ecological model, I wish to emphasize that the process of organizational change, while controlled by the environment, does not necessarily mean progress to higher forms of social organization or to better organizations. The process of natural selection means organizations are moving toward a better fit with the environment, nothing more. It also refers to the process of environments changing and thereby inducing change in their organizational populations, such as occurred in the United States during the period of rapid industrialization from 1860–1910. Managerial staffs proliferated, hierarchies of authority lengthened, cost accounting became common, and labor became a "problem." Whether these changes represented better or worse forms of organization is a moot point from the perspective of the population ecology model, for the relevant question is whether we can explain *why* such changes spread through almost all of the organizations in that evolving environment.

In its original form, the model is applicable to the population level of organizations, rather than at the level of individual units. However, following Hannan and Freeman (1977), I will argue that the model can be successfully applied to studies of single organizations, with little loss of generality. The model is not intended to account for short-run changes, which are temporary responses to local conditions, but rather for long-run transformations in the form of social organization. The ability to make short-term changes in response to local conditions is, of course, itself a result of long-term changes brought about through natural selection. Organizational forms are typically identified through empirically derived taxonomies, such as mechanistic-organic or bureaucratic-professional groups, but such typologies are not usually developed rigorously enough to permit a very comprehensive ecological analysis (McKelvey, 1975). Earlier attempts at constructing typologies focused on goals (Etzioni, 1961; Blau and Scott, 1962), but recent efforts have focused on activity systems, especially on technology and types of control and communication systems (Perrow, 1967; Woodward, 1965; Pugh, Hickson, Hinings, and Turner, 1968).

AN OVERVIEW OF THE POPULATION ECOLOGY MODEL

The population ecology model, based on the natural selection model of biological ecology, explains organizational change by examining the nature and distribution of resources in organizations' environments. Environmental pressures make competition for resources the central force in organizational activities, and the resource dependence perspective focuses on tactics and strategies used by authorities in seeking to manage their environments as well as their organizations. The three stages of variation, selection, and retention constitute a general model of organizational change, which explains how organizational forms are created, survive or fail, and are diffused throughout a population. Although the general perspective is labelled the "population ecology model," the term "natural selection" is used occasionally to emphasize the perspective's intellectual heritage.

Organizational *forms*—specific configurations of goals, boundaries, and activities— are the elements selected by environmental criteria, and change may occur either through new forms eliminating old ones or through the modification of existing forms. Environmental *niches* are distinct combinations of resources and other constraints that are sufficient to support an organization form. Organizational forms, then, are organized activity systems oriented toward exploiting the resources within a niche.

Selection pressures may favor or eliminate entire groups of organizations, such as industries, and the changing population distribution of organizations in a society reflects the operation of such selection pressures. Organizations are loosely coupled systems, and so it is possible for them to change at the level of specific activities or components. These specific activities or components include the number of departments, various decision-making styles, or types of control structures. The three elements of the definition of *organization* given in the first chapter are clues to how organizational forms may differ from one another. Examples presented throughout this book will indicate just how difficult it is to unambiguously identify a unique "organizational form."

Variation

Variation within and between organizations is the first requirement for organizational change, and there must also be variation across environments if externally directed change is to occur. Some variations arise through members' active attempts to generate alternatives and seek solutions to problems, and the rational selection model of traditional organizational theory focuses on such planned variations. The population ecology model, however, is indifferent to the ultimate source of variation, as planned and unplanned variation both provide raw material from which selection can be made. I review arguments for the strategic choice position and note that, while there are some occasions on which "strategic choice" may be exercised, there are usually severe limits to decision-maker autonomy. Many opportunities are closed to organizations because of economic and legal barriers to their entry, most organizations are not powerful enough to influence their environments, and perceptual distortions and illusions bias most decisions. Error, chance, luck, and conflict are more likely sources of variation, although they are devilishly difficult to theorize about.

Two types of variation create the possibility of external selection pressures affecting the direction of organizational change. First, there are variations between organizations in their overall form—between industries, within industries, across the public and private sectors, and across local communities. Such variation is likely to be introduced into the organizational population whenever new organizations are created. Increasing exposure to ideas from other societies or regions, the spread of a secular world view and faith in science, improved communication and transportation technology, and immigrant status in a foreign land are conditions promoting the creation of new organizations. Changing selection criteria and the breakdown of existing retention mechanisms may make the formation of new organizations easier, and certain periods in history are associated with revolutions in organizational forms. The late nineteenth century witnessed the emergence of giant corporations resulting from horizontal mergers, and conglomerates appeared *en masse* after World War II.

Second, variation within organizations opens them to the potential for change or transformation. Growth is a common source of within-organization variation, as increasing complexity and control problems lead to fundamental changes in organizational practices. As growth is inevitably tied to increasing environmental munificence, changes in environmental richness or in technologies permitting greater exploitation of environments are typically associated with organizational change. Turnover in members and leaders, seasonal variations in procedures, and random deviations from standard practices—whether intentional or accidental—give environments an opportunity to produce internal organizational change and transformation.

Selection

According to the population ecology model, selection of new or changed organizational forms occurs as a result of environmental constraints. Organizations fitting environmental criteria are positively selected and survive, while others either fail or change to match environmental requirements. If selection criteria favor administrative rationality and formalized control structures, for example, bureaucratically structured organizations will be chosen at the expense of non-bureaucratic organizations.

Environments are described in terms of either the resources or the information they make available to organizations. The information approach relies heavily on theories of perception, cognition, and decision making, with organizational members acting on the information they glean from typically incomplete searches of their environments. A major factor explaining organizational change is thus variation in information, as filtered through members' perceptions of their environments. Changes in communication technology, improvements in methods of recording and storing information, the breakdown of barriers to information flow, and innovations that enhance people's understanding of their environments are aspects of social change that increase the likelihood of changes in organizational forms.

The resource approach treats environments as consisting of resources for which organizations compete, highlighting the amount of resources and the terms on which they are made available. Selection occurs through relative rather than absolute superiority in acquiring resources, and an effective organization is one that has achieved a relatively better position in an environment it shares with others, rather than the hypothetical "best" position. Resources can be ranked in terms of why they are sought: liquidity, stability, universality, and lack of alternatives. Each distinct combination of resources and other constraints that support an organization form constitutes a niche, defined in ecological terms as "any viable mode of living."

Six dimensions are used to characterize the way in which enviroments make resources available to organizations, and may eventually allow us to deductively identify niches, even when they are not occupied. These dimensions are: environmental capacity, homogeneity-heterogeneity, stability-instability, concentration-dispersion, domain consensus-dissensus, and degree of turbulence. They affect the distribution of resources in environments, and together could be used as an accounting scheme for describing social change in terms of its relevance to organizational change. Just as organizational complexity is sustained in part by consistent environmental pressures, so population complexity is maintained by similar wide-ranging external pressures. Changes that add or remove constraints and resources from environments will affect organizational population diversity, directing our attention to such societal changes as the increasing importance of national markets and the growing role of national governments in the affairs of local communities.

Retention

Retention of organizational forms in a population or of specific structures and activities within an organization is affected by environmental and organizational characteristics. Knowledge of previously successful forms is institutionalized in the socialization apparatus of societies—schools, families, churches, public agencies—and in cultural beliefs and values defended by dominant organizations and institutions. With industrialization there has been a trend toward the externalization and rationalization of culture, and oral traditions are now less important than the material artifacts of a society: written records, machinery, the physical and material components of communities, and general capital improvements. Technological change, especially in the form of electronic information transmittal and retrieval systems, has vastly simplified the task of preserving valuable information.

Social stability and its effects are seen most clearly in the major role the state plays in the creation and maintenance of organizations. As the major constraint on organizational formation and persistence, the state's role appears in many guises: Political stability and ideological legitimation, educational systems, improvements in transportation and communication networks, national economic planning, and other state investments affect the terms on which resources are made available to organizational entrepreneurs. Institutions such as calculable law and an independent judiciary, and state-supported banks and corporations, affect the probability that organizational forms will persist if successful and that unimaginative entrepreneurs will be able to copy them.

Stability in the structure and activities of individual organizations is a central focus of traditional organizational analyses, and most of the characteristics of the ideal-typical bureaucracy contribute to the retention of a specific organizational form. Documents and files are the material embodiment of past practices and are handy references for persons seeking appropriate procedures to follow. Specialization and standardization of roles limit members' discretion and protect organizations against unauthorized variation from official policies, although loose coupling within organizations creates opportunities for deviance that are hard to root out. Centralization of authority and formalization of duties also limit role discretion, channeling members' activities in ways that make them accountable to higher authorities. Bureaucratic structures and procedures thus help preserve existing organizational forms, provided environmental selection criteria are met.

Variation, selection, and retention thus constitute the three stages of the organizational change process. Variation generates the raw materials from which selection, by environmental or internal criteria, is made; retention mechanisms preserve the selected form. The model can be applied to the selective retention or elimination of entire organizations or their components.

EVOLUTIONARY THEORY:
PRELIMINARY CONSIDERATIONS

The evolutionary model has been objected to on political and methodological grounds. Politically, evolutionary theory is often condemned as legitimation for conservative political ideology regarding the worst injustices of industrial society. Methodologically, evolutionary theory is often rejected as unscientific because, while it can explain change *ex post facto,* it cannot predict change *ex ante.* The political objection will be discussed below, with the methodological issue taken up after the population ecology model is presented.

Some people react negatively to the idea of applying evolutionary theory to the study of social organization because of a misunderstanding of modern evolutionary concepts (Hofstadter, 1945). Charles Darwin's writings on the origin of biological species spawned an interest in evolutionary social theory in the late nineteenth centruy, but there are two rather different interpretations of its application to societal evolution. The two interpretations have been labelled "Conservative" versus "Reform" Darwinism (Zachariah, 1971).

Conservative Darwinism

The original "social Darwinists"—E. A. Ross and Herbert Spencer—helped generate a world-view that laid the groundwork for a science of society. They also espoused a socio-political ideology that offends the moral sensibilities of twentieth-century social theorists. The major contribution of conservative Darwinists was their insistence that the human is a part of the natural world, and as such can be studied like any other part of nature. Nothing is sacreligious about studying norms, customs, or societal institutions if social organization is examined with the same methods of investigation that are applied to other biological communities. Conservative Darwinists went a step further than this, however, and derived a political message from their efforts: They argued that social change should occur *naturally,* rather than being forced by the interventions of social "do-gooders."

The key concept of conservative social Darwinism was the "struggle for existence." Following their image of nature as being in a perpetual state of fierce and relentless competition, they argued that only the strongest survive. By definition the survival of the fittest was nature's way of culling the weak from the strong, with those who survive being the fittest. Survivors from this social struggle, which was taking place in all societies, exemplified the wisdom of nature's selection process, and collectively they contributed to the development of civilization.

Pursued to a logical conclusion, the political implication of this position was that it is improper to use social agencies to intervene in the social struggle. The division "between employers and their men was held to illustrate the survival of the fittest and most virtuous, since the one possessed the power to originate and conduct great enterprises and the other 'obviously' did not" (Bendix, 1956, p. 259). Intervention was unnecessary, as "hardships can't be eradicated by trying to make things easier for anyone."

Another key concept of conservative social Darwinism was "progress." Evolution was not a haphazard process; conservative Darwinists believed in progress because they believed in *purpose*. They departed from a strict Darwinian view, which avoids an assessment of the ultimate state toward which a species is evolving. Purposive, rather than natural, selection guided the course of social evolution. Theirs was an Aristotelian world-view: They believed that all reality moves toward an immanent perfect state, and this conflicts sharply with the neutrality of a pure Darwinian view.

Reform Darwinism

Reform Darwinists broke with the conservatives by distinguishing between pre-human and human phases of evolution, and they argued for a discontinuity in the evolutionary process between human society and previous levels of organic evolution. They noted that humans would use thier superior mental capabilities to oppose and reverse some "natural" changes, such as intervening to affect the causes of human mortality and fertility. Natural selection included constructing social institutions to change people's life chances, and selection need not be only accidental. This is purposive selection, but it deals with the level of specific behaviors and institutions, and it is carried out by men, not some higher purpose.

Reform Darwinists criticized the uncritical use of the concept of a "struggle for existence," pointing out that nature is not always in a state of fierce and unrelenting competition. Examination of food chains and the "web of life" by biological ecologists reveals many instances of symbiotic relationships between species, with hierarchies of dominance limiting all-out war between the species (Hawley, 1950). "Fitness" need not mean simply being the strongest and most brutal, but rather a species (or, in human society, humans) who were best adapted to existing conditions. Defining fitness in relative terms undercuts the moral fervor of the conservative Darwinist notion of fitness.

Zachariah (1971) concluded that reform Darwinists brought the concept of "progress" under the control of people, giving it a relative rather than absolute frame of reference. A social definition of progress may depend, for example, on reducing or eliminating competition, as in the control of warfare. Not only individuals, but aggregates of individuals could engage in purposeful activity to advance their own interests. Consider, for example, unions championing the interests of workers against management, a development that was anathema to conservative social Darwinists. This view legitimated the evolution of the state into the role of an intervening agent.

Modern evolutionary theory is distinctly "reform-oriented," and is indifferent to whether selection is controlled by market forces or by the state. As will be noted shortly, this is not the same as asserting that humans control their destiny, for the natural selection model emphasizes sources of change that are rather intractable to human manipulation. Nevertheless, current evolutionary theory is a vastly different enterprise than the one which enrolled Herbert Spencer, William Graham Sumner, A. G. Keller, and others in a celebration of the "survival of the fittest" at the turn of the century.

THE THREE STAGE PROCESS: VARIATION, SELECTION, RETENTION

The natural selection model identifies three states in the process of change in living systems. Campbell (1969) outlined the three stage process and insightfully pointed out the relevance of the natural selection model for the study of social organization. The following discussion depends heavily on his analysis, as well as that of Buckley (1967) and Hawley (1950). I will present organizational examples in the next section, after the process itself is explained.

The Occurrence of Variations

The first stage in the natural selection process is the occurrence of variations, for whatever reason: planned, unplanned, haphazard, systematic, random, predictable, or heterogeneous variations in some activity, behavior, or structure. Variations are the raw material from which the selection process culls those structures or behaviors that are most suitable, given the selection criterion. In organic evolution, variations occur through the random process of genetic mutations, while in the learning processes of individual organisms, variation occurs in exploratory responses made to stimuli. A baby babbling in its crib is an example of haphazardly generated variation.

Consistent Selection Criteria

The second stage is the operation of consistent selection criteria that differentially select or selectively eliminate certain types of variations. In organic evolution, the differential survival of certain mutant forms that are better able to exploit the food supply in their environment reflects the operation of resource-based selection criteria. In the learning process, there is differential reinforcement of particular exploratory responses by animals. Differential reinforcement of certain utterances gradually channels the production of a baby's sounds toward those common in the baby's culture.

A Retention Mechanism

The third stage of the natural selection process involves the operation of a retention mechanism for the selective retention of the positively selected variations. Retention occurs when selected variations are preserved, duplicated, or otherwise reproduced so that the selected behavior is repeated on future occasions or the selected structure appears again in future generations. In organic evolution, the retention mechanism is the chromosome-gene system, which ensures rigid duplication of selected structures in the succeeding generations of plants and animals. Positively selected variations survive and reproduce others of their own kind. In the learning process, the memory system ensures that positively selected responses can be recalled for future use. A baby's speech patterns become and remain comprehensible to others in the same culture because they are retained in the baby's memory.

The natural selection model is perfectly general and may be applied to any situation where the three stages are present. The three stage model completely describes trial and error learning, organic evolution, and, as I shall argue in the remainder of this chapter, socio-cultural and organizational evolution. When the three conditions of the model are met, "an evolution in the direction of better fit to the selective system becomes inevitable" (Campbell, 1969, p. 73). A "better fit" doesn't mean that there is only one fit—selection is a matter of *relative* superiority over other forms.

THE THREE STAGE MODEL APPLIED TO ORGANIZATIONS

The population ecology model is very well developed in biographical ecology, and the question facing sociologists is whether we can identify similar processes at the level of social organization. If the processes are isomorphic—similar in form—then we can use many of the insights of evolutionary theory to understand organizational change. The variation-selection-retention model gives us a very powerful framework for explaining how organizations change in ways that make them more fit for the environment they face. In the following sections, I will sketch the relevance of the natural selection model to organizational theory in general terms, and in subsequent chapters I will return to the first two stages, using the principles given here to review recent research in organizational sociology. As before, I rely heavily on Campbell's (1969) insightful presentation.

Variation in Organizational Populations

The natural selection model is indifferent to the ultimate source of variation, as both planned and random variation serve equally well in providing the raw material from which selection is made. The general principle is that the greater the heterogeneity and number of variations, the more the opportunities for a close fit to environmental selection criteria. Three examples of variation within organizational populations indicate the applicability of the variation stage to understanding organizational change: (1) variation between organizations in their overall form; (2) variation within internally differentiated organizations; and, (3) variation over time in the performance of important organizational activities.

First, there are variations between organizations in their overall form, such as between bureaucratic versus non-bureaucratic, or capital intensive versus labor intensive, organizations. Variation between organizations is inherent in the interorganizational division of labor across industries, and since the distribution of organizations by industry is changing over time, clearly selection at this level is occurring. There are also variations among organizations in individual industries and at the level of production for specific markets (Hirsch, 1975a). Until the 1850s, almost no American manufacturing firms employed full-time professional managers, as the owner or his relatives performed whatever managerial duties were required. In the 1850s, as the scope of markets increased and large-scale production became technologically feasible (due to improvements in transportation, communication, and machine technology), firms switching to full-time professional managers gained a competitive advantage over others (Chandler, 1977). Variation between firms with professional managers and those without provided the opportunity for external selection criteria to operate.

Variation between organizations.   Variation may be introduced into the organizational population by the creation of new organizations or the transfer of existing organizations to new owners or sponsors. Economic organizations, for example, are created by entrepreneurs who are seeking profit and who are also confronted with the risks of undertaking a new venture. The rate of creation of new business organizations is quite high in the United States, as is the failure rate, as shown in Table 2.1. In 1957, 398,000 new businesses were begun; 376,000 transferred to a new owner; and 335,000 failed outright. Between 1944 and 1954, over 5.4 million new businesses were established in the United States, most quite small, and another 4.5 million were transferred to new owners. The rate of new business creation has varied over time, and also varies by industry, as shown in Table 2.1. Unfortunately, the time series reported in Table 2.1 ends in 1962 and has not been updated. Recent information on business undertakings and failures is available only for corporations, which make up about one-seventh of the business population.

There are a large number of voluntary associations and social movements that come and go quite regularly (Hausknecht, 1962; Zald and Ash, 1966), introducing a great deal of "between-organization" variation into the organizational population. In one of the few attempts ever made to systematically list a portion of the non-business organizational population, the Department of Commerce in 1949 estimated that there were 4,000 Chambers of Commerce; 70,000 labor unions; 10,000 women's organizations; and 15,000 civic service groups, luncheon clubs, and similar organizations of business and professional people. The validity of these figures cannot be judged, as the Department did not reveal how they were compiled (Smith and Freedman, 1972).

More comprehensive information on variation at the level of organizational types is available from studies of single communities, or subpopulations of specific organization types. These studies suggest that sociological theories of organizations have severely underestimated the total number and variety of organizations. An extremely detailed case study of voluntary associations in Birmingham, England, (Newton, 1975) uncovered 4,264 organizations, grouped into thirteen rather heterogeneous categories for purposes of analysis (see Table 2.2). Birmingham is England's second largest city, with slightly more than one million inhabitants, and thus there are roughly 4 voluntary associations for every 1,000 people. If Birmingham is representative, this implies the existence of several hundred thousand voluntary associations in the whole of England.

W. Lloyd Warner's studies of American communities provide additional information on voluntary associations' diversity. In the 1930s, a New England

TABLE 2.1 Number of new, discontinued, and transferred businesses, by major industry group: 1940 to 1962. (In thousands)

Year	All Industries	Contract Construction	Mfg.	Wholesale Trade	Retail Trade	Service	All Other
New Businesses							
1962	430	60	25	25	168	91	61
1960	438	66	27	24	170	89	62
1957	398	57	25	23	166	71	56
1954	366	62	25	21	147	61	50
1951	327	54	28	21	123	53	48
1948	393	65	35	24	151	73	45
1946	617	95	63	45	234	117	64
1943	146	9	25	8	50	28	26
1940	275	22	29	20	118	49	36
Discontinued Businesses							
1962	387	63	29	20	158	67	50
1960	384	64	29	19	157	65	49
1957	335	57	29	17	137	53	43
1954	319	48	30	18	134	48	40
1951	276	44	23	13	113	47	37
1948	282	36	27	19	98	62	38
1946	209	26	24	11	66	44	38
1943	337	26	22	20	160	71	38
1940	318	30	22	14	138	74	41
Transferred Businesses							
1957	376	13	15	12	252	56	28
1954	371	13	15	12	250	53	27
1953	378	14	17	13	253	55	26
1951	358	11	16	11	241	53	25
1948	501	71	29	17	327	79	33
1946	627	18	37	26	399	107	39
1943	250	4	17	7	122	70	39
1940	241	7	18	6	60	105	44

New businesses include only firms newly established. *Discontinued businesses* include closures of all kinds without reference to the reason for going out of business. A firm which is maintained as a business entity but undergoes a change of ownership is counted as a *transferred business,* not as a discontinuance.

Source: U.S. Bureau of the Census, *Historical Statistics of the U.S., Colonial Times to 1970, Bicentennial Edition, Part 2,* 1975, p. 913.

Original Source: U.S. Bureau of Economic Analysis, Survey of Current Business. Originally from data supplied by Bureau of Old-Age and Survivors Insurance and the IRS.

town of 17,000 inhabitants had approximately eight hundred adult voluntary associations (Warner, 1953, p. 192). In the 1940s, an Illinois town of about 6,000 inhabitants contained 133 voluntary associations (Warner *et al.,* 1949). These figures show that there were between 25 and 50 voluntary associations per 1,000 people in these smaller communities, again implying that there is a great deal of diversity within the population of American voluntary associations.

TABLE 2.2   Voluntary associations in Birmingham, England: Population statistics.

Type of Organization	Number in City	% of Total
Sports and hobbies	2,144	50
Social welfare	666	16
Cultural	388	9
Trade associations	176	4
Professional	165	4
Social	142	3
Churches and religious	138	3
Armed forces and veterans	122	3
Youth	76	2
Technical and scientific	76	2
Educational	66	2
Trade unions	55	1
Health	50	1
Total	4,264	101

Kenneth Newton, "Voluntary Organizations in a British City: The Political and Organizational Characteristics of 4,264 Voluntary Associations in Birmingham,"*Jour. Vol. Action Res.*, 4 (Jan-April 1975); 43-62.

Variation within organizations.   A second type of variation affecting organizational change is variation *within* differentiated organizations, such as in individual abilities to fill particular roles. Following suggestions made by Buckley (1967) and Hannan and Freeman (1977), I will apply the natural selection model not just to the survival or failure of entire organizations, but also to the partial modification of structure and activities falling short of the elimination of the total organization. This modification of the biological model takes into account the capacity of social organizations to change through structural alteration, a process qualitatively different from limited short-run homeostatic changes made by individual biological organisms. Organic evolution proceeds by a process of differential survival of entire units, whereas the changing of social organization can also occur through adaptations in one area of structure or activities while the rest of the organization remains intact.

Modifying the natural selection model in this fashion complicates an ecological analysis, since the criterion for successful adaptation to the environment is changed from the easier-to-observe survival or failure to structural stability or change. Characteristics of a population of organizations may change, not only because of differential mortality, but also because surviving organizations have undergone significant internal transformations. The more internal variation within organizations, the greater the likelihood that adaptive variations will be produced.

Turnover in members and especially leadership roles is an example of internal variation that may lead to survival with structural modifications. Voluntary associations typically select new slates of officers once a year, and the more open the process, the greater the likelihood that the organization will present a set of activities to the environment slightly different from the preceding year. New officers have different priorities, possess different skills, and make new kinds of mistakes. Some large business enterprises, in recognition of the potential adaptive advantages in personnel movement through various roles, make a policy of shifting as much as one-quarter of their managerial level staff to new responsibilities each year.

Variation over time.   A third source of variation in organizational populations arises from variations over time in carrying out important activities. In all but the most tightly controlled organizations, we can expect that no task is ever performed exactly the same way twice. Consider the many ways of interviewing a client, preparing a meal, or making a sale. In some instances, especially in organizations with unstandardized procedures and low formalization of rules and regulations, differences over time may be very large indeed. The cumulation of random errors in the performance of duties allows organizations to drift into unchartered regions and, possibly, into deterioration *or* advantageous innovation (Hirschman, 1970).

Innovating organizations may introduce variation into a population by deliberately varying from customary forms of behavior. Innovation, however, need not be a consciously planned strategy and may be a result of imperfect attempts to imitate other organizations perceived as successful (Alchian, 1950). Prevailing beliefs in most Western societies discourage people from interpreting the advantages that come their way as products of "luck" or "chance," and attempts to do so are often taken as a subtle form of boasting. Social scientists are not immune from the pervasive need to find structure in the world, as shown by the hostility that greeted the attempt by Jencks and his colleagues (1972) to explain a great deal of socioeconomic achievement as the result of idiosyncratic ("chance") events.

A key difference between the natural selection model and traditional theories of organizational change lies in the assignment of the *source* of variation. Planned variation—strategy and choice—is one source of variation, but any variation will do. Hence, the natural selection model emphasizes chance events, error, and luck. Given the rational model bias of traditional organizational and economic research, there have been few attempts to test the hypothesis that unplanned variations play an important part in change.

The Selection Process Applied to Social Organization

A critical difference between the natural selection model and other models of organizational change lies in the relative importance of environmental selection as opposed to intraorganizational factors. If environmental selection criteria are to have an effect, two conditions must be present (Campbell, 1969): (1) there must be a high rate of variation; and, (2) there must be a fairly high mortality rate for the activities, structures, or organizations involved. Variation provides the raw material for the selection process, and a high mortality rate for individual organizations increases the possibility of environmentally-relevant selective survival. Three examples of selection, matching the previous examples of sources of variation, will be presented: (1) selective survival or elimination of whole organizations; (2) selective diffusion or imitation of successful innovations of partial organization structures or activities; and, (3) selective retention of successful activities resulting from variations in behavior over time.

Selective survival.   The first and purest form of environmental selection is the *selective survival or elimination of entire organizations*—organizations either are fit for their environment, or they fail. If selection criteria favor administrative rationality in organizational control structures, then we might observe that non-bureaucratically structured organizations fail, leaving only bureaucracies. Organizational forms survive or fail depending upon their fitness for a particular environmental niche. A niche is created by the intersection of resource constraints—an abstract resource space consisting of a unique combination of resources (information, access to materials, customers, and so on) that could permit a form to survive there. Forms thus take advantage of a niche's resource-space. A small neighborhood grocery store occupies a niche defined in economic, geographic, and cultural space: a specific location provides access to a population of potential customers with need for food products, perhaps with cultural tastes for a particular line of products, and a value orientation toward supporting local merchants. Variations in the organizational forms exploiting this niche include whether a grocery store employs only family labor (thus lowering costs), is autonomous or part of a chain (thus gaining the benefits of subsidized advertising), and makes only cash sales or offers credit (thus creating the possibility of losses due to bad debts).

Most organizations are small and are in that segment of the population potentially subject to selective elimination. The only systematic information available on organizational failures covers just the business sector, and as the figures in Table 2.1 show, the business failure rate in the United States is quite high. Most businesses are operated on a small scale, making them highly vulnerable to failure.

Two-thirds of all businesses take in less than $25,000 in receipts per year, and nearly three-fifths of all corporations have less than $100,000 in assets. In the retail trade and service sectors, a substantial proportion of all businesses have *no* paid employees, as shown in Table 2.3. Except for manufacturing establishments, most employees work at sites employing less than one hundred people, In the five industry sectors portrayed in Table 2.3—manufacturing, construction, retail trade, merchant wholesalers, and service businesses—90 percent of all establishments employ less than 100 people, and the majority of all establishments employ less than 10 people. (Note that since some organizations operate at more

TABLE 2.3   Size of establishment by industry: 1972 (Includes only establishments operated throughout the entire year)

			Industry		
Size class	*Mfg.*	*Construction*	*Retail*	*Merchant Wholesaler*	*Services*
% establishments with *no* paid employees	(NA)	(NA)	32.2	(NA)	56.0
		Cumulative Percent of Establishments			
0 to 9 employees	50.8	80.3	77.9	70.4	84.6
0 to 49 employees	77.6	97.1	97.7	97.1	97.7
0 to 99 employees	89.0	98.9	99.3	99.2	99.1
% employees working in establishment with 100 or more employees	75.2	(NA)	17.5	13.8	28.3

Key: (NA) indicates the information is not available.

Sources:

U. S. Bureau of the Census, Census of Manufactures, 1972. *Subject Series: General Summary, MC72(1)-1,* Table I-98.

U.S. Bureau of the Census, Census of Wholesale Trade, 1972. *Subject Series: Establishment Size and Firm Size, WC72-S-1,* Table ID.

U. S. Bureau of the Census, Census of Construction Industries, 1972. *Area Series, United States Summary, CC72-A-10,* Table 3A.

U. S. Bureau of the Census, Census of Retail Trade, 1972. *Subject Series: Establishment and Firm Size, RC72-S-1,* Table 1B.

U. S. Bureau of the Census, Census of Selected Service Industries, 1972. *Vol. I. Summary and Subject Statistics,* Table 1B.

than one site, the information in Table 2.3 understates somewhat the size of employing organizations.)

Two characteristics of industrial societies limit the applicability of this purest form of selection to a large subset of the total organizational population. First, the population of business organizations is divided into a small segment of very large organizations with a high rate of failure. Second, the growth of the public sector of industrial societies has caused governments at all levels (community, regional, and national) to appropriate and reallocate between two-fifths and three-fifths of national income, with a high proportion of these funds used to support public sector organizations. Each characteristic deserves further examination.

Within the business sector, the bifurcation of the population into segments differentially vulnerable to failure has been accelerated by two trends. First, businesses have increasingly adopted a corporate form of legal organization,

41

gaining status as an entity with limited liability under the law. Corporations are still outnumbered by sole proprietorships (operated by an individual as more or less an extension of his or her personal economic affairs) and partnerships (like proprietorships, but with more than one owner), constituting about one-seventh of the business population. However, corporations account for the bulk of business receipts in the United States, as shown in Table 2.4, taking about 85 percent of all receipts in 1972. Proprietorships are the dominant legal form, but most are quite small: about 77 percent of them took in less than $25,000 in receipts in 1972, and 95 percent of all proprietorships took in less than $100,000.

Another trend evident among both incorporated and non-incorporated businesses is the increasing concentration of wealth in the hands of the very largest organizations, which are a tiny minority of the population. As shown in Table 2.4, in 1972 only 1.7 percent of all businesses took in more than $1,000,000 in receipts, but they accounted for 76.3 percent of all receipts. Dominance by the very largest organizations is especially evident within the corporate sector, as shown in Table 2.5, which gives information on the asset size of all corporations in 1955, 1965, and 1972.

Most corporations have less than $100,000 in assets, but they account for less than 2 percent of all corporate assets. At the other extreme, 6.6 percent have $1,000,000 or more in assets, and at the very top of the corporate pinnacle, 0.1 percent have $25,000,000 or more in assets. This one-tenth of one percent of all corporations with a quarter-billion dollars or more in assets accounted in 1972 for 60.8 percent of *all* corporate assets. Seventeen years before, in 1955, the top 0.1

TABLE 2.4   Proprietorships, partnerships, and corporations: Number and business receipts, 1972.

Size Class of Receipts	Total Number (thousands)	Total Receipts (in billions)	Number (thousands) Prop.	Part.	Corp.	Receipts (in billions) Prop.	Part.	Corp.
Total	12,978	2,494.7	10,173	992	1,813	276.0	104.3	2,114.1

	Percent Distribution							
Under $25,000*	67.7	2.2	76.7	53.5	25.3	17.0	3.5	0.2
$25-49,999	10.8	2.0	10.7	13.2	10.0	14.0	4.3	0.3
$50-99,999	8.3	3.1	7.1	12.5	13.2	18.2	8.3	0.8
$100-199,999 } $200-499,999 }	9.8	10.8	3.6 1.6	10.3 7.3 } 31.9		18.1 17.1	13.6 20.5 } 6.5	
$500-999,999	1.6	5.7	0.3	1.9	8.6	7.0	12.4	5.1
$1,000,000 or more	1.7	76.3	0.1	1.3	11.0	8.6	37.4	87.1

*Includes firms with no receipts.

Source: U.S. Bureau of the Census, *Statistical Abstract of the U.S.: 1975,* Table 803, p. 491.

TABLE 2.5 Active corporations, by asset size. (Figures are estimates, based on samples of active corporations filing income tax returns.)

Asset Size of Class	Number of Active Corp. (thousands)			Total Assets (in billions)		
	1955	1965	1972	1955	1965	1972
Total number	807.3	1,424.0	1,812.8	899	1,724	3,257
	Percent Distribution					
Under $100,000	60.9	59.4	57.8	1.8	1.6	1.0
$100-999,999	32.2	34.5	35.6	8.5	8.3	6.0
$1,000,000-10,000,000	5.9	5.2	5.4	15.3	12.0	8.2
$10,000,000-25,000,000	0.6	0.5	0.6	8.1	6.7	5.3
$25,000,000-50,000,000	0.1	0.2	0.3	6.2	5.7	5.0
$50,000,000-100,000,000	0.1	0.1	0.1	6.5	6.1	5.3
$100,000,000-250,000,000	0.1	0.1	0.1	10.3	9.6	8.4
$250,000,000 and over	0.1	0.1	0.1	43.4	50.0	60.8
Total	100.0	100.0	100.0	100.0	100.0	100.0

Source: U.S. Bureau of the Census, *Statistical Abstracts of the U.S, 1975,* Table 816, p. 497.

Original Source: U.S. IRS, *Statistics of Income, Corporate Income Tax Returns.*

percent accounted for 43.4 percent of all assets. Clearly, businesses with millions of dollars in assets are substantially protected from the threat of direct elimination by failure. Large businesses rarely disappear, and when they do it is almost always because of mergers or acquisitions, as will be examined in a subsequent chapter.

The second characteristic of industrial societies that limits the applicability of the pure form of the natural selection model is related to the expanding role of government. Organizations that come under the protection of various national, regional, or local governments have very low failure rates, such as public hospitals, social service agencies, schools, and various nationalized industries.

A large proportion of governmental income is allocated to the support of public sector organizations, which are consequently protected against the possibility of failure. National foundations and nonprofit trusts support other organizations, which are therefore also insulated from the prospect of rapid demise. Public sector agencies and other protected organizations may still undergo structural modification, but they will not, mostly likely, face total elimination. National governments have come to the aid of privately-owned businesses (especially large firms such as Lockheed Aircraft Corporation in the United States, or the Chrysler Corporation in England), further reducing mortality rates in that sector. In some instances government aid has led to the nationalization of industries, such as the railroads in the United States and Western Europe, and airlines in Western Europe and most other industrialized nations. Thus a successful form of adaptation might consist of an organization managing to have itself (or the class of organizations it represents) classified among those receiving government subsidies. Similarly, a small firm acquired in a take-over action by a large corporation finds its survival assured and perhaps its owners handsomely compensated. Of course, the take-over may also mean the loss of the firm's identity and the indiscriminate dismissal of employees.

The importance of national governmental intervention in the economy should not be minimized, even in such avowedly private enterprise systems as we find in the United States. In 1973, 13,742,000 persons were employed by governments in the United States, 2,663,000 by the federal government and 11,079,000 by state and local governments. Public sector employment was about one-fifth the size of employment in the private sector. Moreover, in recent years government has taken the lead in the creation of new jobs. Between 1973 and 1976, about 700,000 new jobs were created in the private sector and 1,300,000 in the public sector. The phenomenon of bursts of activity in the creation of organizations, to be considered in a subsequent chapter, is especially noticeable in the public sector. In 1950 there were 641 public institutions of higher education in the United States, and still only 701 in 1960. Over 300 new institutions were created in the decade of the 1960s, and by 1974 there were 1,200 publicly supported institutions of higher education in the United States, an increase of 69 percent in fourteen years, compared to a less than 10 percent increase in the decade preceding 1960.

Environmental selection of entire organizations, then, occurs most often with small businesses (which are far more numerous than large businesses, although not nearly as significant economically), organizations not subsidized by governments, and voluntary associations. Less complete forms of selection, however, exist for all organizations; particular structures or activities may be eliminated, added, or modified without the destruction of the existing form. As is the case in organic evolution, selection among organizations is on the basis of relative rather than absolute advantage, except for absolutely nonviable forms.

Selective diffusion.   A second type of environmental selection is *selective diffusion or imitation of successful innovations in structure or activities* across organizations in a population. In the traditional model of organizational change, diffusion and borrowing are a result of strategic choices made by leaders or managers. To apply the natural selection model, however, we can disregard the motives for choice and assume only that organizations adopting the innovations of relatively successful organizations will have at least a short-run advantage over others. Detroit auto manufacturers (and their employees) resisted the adoption of an assembly-line production system until Henry Ford installed one and began to produce cars at such volume and low cost that their markets were threatened

(Braverman, 1974). At that point they were forced into adopting a similar production process.

If information flows freely throughout a population, the selective diffusion of innovations can be an important selection mechanism for changes that do not require the elimination of entire organizations. Organizational intelligence units play an important role in keeping authorities informed of new developments *before* they become a threat to an organization's existence (Wilensky, 1967).

Diffusion and borrowing are matters of external selection because of the need for a certain degree of compatibility between the structures and activities of innovating and imitating organizations. Compatibility between two organizations is thus part of the selective criteria. Selective diffusion and borrowing will occur most readily when organizations are relatively similar and there are few constraints on communication, thus allowing the free flow of information (Stinchcombe, 1965). "Choice" can be incorporated into the natural selection model by noting that opportunities for borrowing are open to many potential organizations meeting the compatibility requirement, but that the act of borrowing involves a strategic choice by the borrower.

Selective retention of successful activities.   A third type of selection is that of *advantageous activities that are happened upon in the normal course of variation in their performance over time.* Variations in task performance that prove successful will be selected if they occur frequently enough and there exists a mechanism for retaining the process. Such selection will be facilitated if there are persons in the organization with the capability of remembering the successful activity, or if the organization's files permit easy review of past actions. The process of selection of variations across occasions may occur indirectly through the selective promotion to leadership roles of persons whose past behavior has been most adaptive and successful in a given environment (Campbell, 1969). Selection would have its greatest impact if the promotion system itself were modified when a consistent pattern in the advancement of persons varying activities proved to be adaptive.

Having reviewed some examples of the natural selection process, we can return to the question of whether there are any general principles to help us identify when selection is occurring. Campbell (1969, p. 75) noted a major difference between research into organic versus social evolution. Biologists and zoologists have given us a good understanding of the selection system operating on plant and animal species, and "we know the physics of air, water, and light to which flying, swimming, and seeing creatures must conform." We need much better knowledge of organizational types and appropriate environments before we can do as well in understanding organizational change.

We have two guidelines, mentioned earlier, for identifying where selective criteria could have made an impact on the evolution of an organizational form:

relatively high variation and mortality rates. Thus, we would expect to find external selection criteria having an impact on organizational survival in the segment of the population previously identified as small and subject to high turnover, but not in the segment identified as economically dominant or protected by government legislation. However, particular activities or partial structures of economic dominants may be subject to selective criteria, as, for example in the means used to acquire new funds for capital expenditures or in methods of expansion. Alexander (1971) demonstrated that after traditional forms of mergers were challenged by antitrust authorities in the 1950s, large firms switched to rarely-challenged conglomerate mergers.

Internal selection criteria.   The focus has been on *external* selection criteria to this point; that is, pressures external to organizations. We must be aware that an organization's internal diffusion, imitation, and promotion systems may be selective in ways that are irrelevant to environmental fitness. This is especially likely in organizations that have achieved some degree of insulation from environmental pressures. Campbell (1969) has described two types of internal selectors that are especially interesting.

First, there are pressures in organizations that encourage internal stability and compatibility. Frequent interaction between members leads to positive reinforcement of interpersonal behavior, which is rewarding for the people involved, and to the elimination of incompatible behavior. Interdepartmental and other intraorganizational activities are influenced similarly towards maintaining consistency and a reasonable degree of harmony. "Thus any social organization tends to move in the direction of internal compatibility, independently of increased external adaptiveness" (Campbell, 1969, p. 76). Organizations that are protected from their environments may even move *away* from external relevance, as in so-called "ossified" organizations. Public bureaucracies are often accused of being non-responsive to their clients because members are too caught up in rules and regulations designed to smooth internal functioning.

Second, there are internal selection criteria that continue as vicarious representatives of past external criteria. Procedures that were once selected because they fit the context an organization found itself in may be irrelevant or even maladaptive to the current situation. The example of ACME vegetable canning company, given in the last chapter, is a case in which decisions were made on the unstated assumption that the environment would remain the same. Thus, the decision-making structure led to the commitment of funds to an inappropriate use. Similarly, the American armed forces continued for some time to use a promotion system for officers that rewarded battle experience, rather than rewarding those with the technical sophistication required by a modern weapons system and long-range strategic planning of modern warfare (Janowitz, 1959).

Retention Systems in Organizations

The retention stage can be interpreted as the stability in organizational forms or in specific structures and activities of individual organizations. Retention in social organization analysis is different from that of organic evolution in that social scientists have not identified a social analogue to the rigid duplication process of the gene-chromosome system. Nevertheless, there are some general characteristics of social retention mechanisms that have been identified, and these can be extended to an examination of organizational forms and activities.

Retention of successful adaptations in social systems depends upon the retention and transmission of knowledge from one generation to the next. Using traditional sociological concepts, we say that *culture* is transmitted via the *institutionalization* of beliefs and values, thus ensuring retention. In preliterate societies with few written records, knowledge is passed through the generations by an oral tradition—passed from the elders to the young by word of mouth —and there are strong sanctions against innovation or variation in information passed along (Campbell, 1969). Pressures against varying from successful traditions result from the extreme vulnerability of societies with few surplus resources to short-run misfortunes. A series of unsuccessful variations may mean not the selective elimination of specific practices but instead failure for the entire society. The natural selection model explains sanctions against variation not in terms of deliberate design, but by the fact that societies *without* such sanctions will be less likely to survive. As surplus resources accumulate, variation and innovation are less threatening and innovators may find a niche in the societal division of labor that is explicitly recognized (Lenski, 1966).

As societal forms have matured, there has been a trend toward the externalization and rationalization of culture. Material culture rather than the oral tradition now carries societal traditions and history, and there is less danger of adaptations being lost due to random variations. Written records, machinery, the physical and material components of cities, and the general capital improvements in a society represent the externalization of past successful adaptations to its environment. Lenski documented the long-term trend in the advance of technology, and the increase in the scale and complexity of social structures (Lenski, 1975). No presumption is made that such trends will continue forever, and it is possible that the depletion of vital resources required by industrial societies will produce a different future. It is clear that social retention systems are much more complex in industrial as compared to pre-industrial societies.

Retention systems may reside both in a social system and its environment, and I will point out some intraorganizational mechanisms in the next section. A strong argument can be made that very complex structures can only be maintained by consistent environmental pressures (Campbell, 1969). Without consistent environmental pressure, two factors combine to disrupt the complexity of a structure. First, the continuous occurrence of random or haphazard variation, if unchecked by selective elimination and retention, gradually begins a system to a simpler and less organized state. Second, strong internal selection pressures exist that are biased toward simplicity and standardization in the interests of stabilizing organizational activities. Deviance is rooted out and there are strong pressures toward a uniformity of outlook among members. These two pressures, if not countered by strong environmental pressures that reward complexity, will eventually remove a structure's complexity. In organic systems the simplification process would take many generations, but in social systems we can envision the process occurring over the life of a single organization. This principle helps us understand why some overly-complex structures "degenerate" into simplicity or disorder, and also emphasizes that not all organizational change is toward a better fit vis-à-vis the environment.

Complex interorganizational arrangements, such as oligopolies, cartels, and coalitions, are highly vulnerable to short-term deviations from agreed-upon policies by members. Members of such arrangements are under heavy pressures to make their own unique adaptations to local environmental pressures, and there are few external pressures to preserve the complex command and control system necessary to coordinate members' actions. Systems insulated from the first type of problem still face the second, which is a drift toward internal simplicity at the expense, perhaps, of external relevance. In general, if we observe a complex and long-lived structure, we should look to the environment for the source of pressures that have maintained it.

Retention: Some organizational examples.   Much of the past research on organizational structure and process is actually concerned with internal and external retention mechanisms, although investigators have not usually put their work into a natural selection framework. The analysis of retention supplied by traditional organizational sociology is so thorough that, apart from this chapter, it is not necessary to spend much time on the issue itself. The concept of retention is used in later chapters dealing with specific issues, such as the association between the time of founding and organizational structures and the role of dominant organizations in interorganizational networks.

External pressures for retaining a given form or partial structure include all the environmental forces that originally selected the form, partial structure, or activity. Competitive pressures on business firms, member pressures on voluntary associations, and political pressures on public agencies help explain the retention of past structures in these organizations. Some organizations, especially publicly supported ones, generate external pressures intentionally to help maintain their current forms and practice. The United States Department of Defense usually manages to "leak" proposed defense budgets to friendly members of Congress and defense contractors as a way of marshalling support to resist budget cuts.

Shared interorganizational beliefs and other forces that induce common perceptions among persons and information processing and transmitting organizations may assist in the retention of a limited range of forms. Business schools, training and educational institutes, consulting firms, and trade or professional associations promote specific procedures and organizational forms that become part of the culture of an organizational population. Some procedures catch the popular fancy and spread to most organizations, where they become entrenched and encrusted with organizational mythology. An example of this is the spread of divisional as opposed to functional forms of departmentalization that occurred after World War II in the United States.

Folk wisdom and rules of thumb (Scherer, 1970) are also part of interorganizational culture. They play a role in the retention of specific forms because they become part of the habitual behavior of members and are resistant to change. Since selective elimination or retention depends on variation in the forms of a population, widespread habit can effectively insulate a population against a changing environment if no competing forms arise in other industries or subpopulations and new entrants adopt the traditional behavior or structure. Recall that selection is on the basis of relative superiority rather than absolute advantage, and any force preventing one organization from gaining an advantage over the others will inhibit the process of organizational change at the level of new organizational forms.

The characteristics of bureaucracy, described in the previous chapter, can be thought of as contributing to the retention of a specific organizational form. Documents and files are the archetypal characteristic of bureaucracy; as the material embodiment of past practices, they are ready references for appropriate procedures, to be followed by normal contingencies. Specialization and standardization of roles limit member discretion and thus protect organizations against random variation from official policy and prescribed activities. Given that leaders and managers have a clear image of their organization's character (Selznick, 1957), centralization of authority allows them to preserve it. Making membership in a bureaucracy a career and basing mobility through the ranks on universalistic performance criteria rewards persons for conforming to their specialized and standardized duties. Formalization and an official hierarchy of authority circumscribe the exercise of role discretion, limiting opportunities for variation. Bureaucratic administrative structure and procedures thus help preserve the integrity of organizational forms, increasing the probability of their retention, if environmental selection criteria are met.

Recruitment and socialization of new members enhance continuity of structure by facilitating the transmission of organizational culture. At a minimum, new members learn attitudes and actions appropriate to their positions, such as through apprenticeship programs in the skilled trades which enable young people to learn on the job and gradually acquire the skills of workers they observe. Many organizations hold periodic training sessions for their members as a way of reminding them of organizational expectations, especially for members who have extensive contact with outsiders. Salespeople, for example, need occasional refresher courses on the virtues of their products and on how to make a sale, because they spend a great amount of time working inside other organizations.

Continuity in leadership may be another retention mechanism preserving patterns of structure and activities. Similarity in succeeding groups of leaders is enhanced by a stable selection and promotion system that rewards and filters people according to their similarity in outlook and background to current leaders. Screening and filtering are conducted by those already in leadership positions, and because people are attracted by others like themselves, a strong bias is exerted toward perpetuating established leadership patterns. Further, since the promotion of leaders is based on their experience and expertise in dealing with critical environmental contingencies (to the extent that the definition of significant uncertainties remains the same), similarity in leadership characteristics is assured (Pfeffer, 1977). Organizations that are marketing-oriented, for example, tend to promote people with sales or marketing experience. Such persons, because of similar backgrounds and socialization, will have fairly similar ideas about organization policy.

Organizational retention: A laboratory experiment.   Zucker (1977), using an ethnomethodological approach, conducted research on the persistence of organizational practices and standards over time. She noted that two previous explanations of cultural persistence—defined as stability in beliefs and practices over successive generations of organization members—have a number of flaws. "Functional necessity" arguments lapse into tautology, equating persistence with necessity, and vice versa. "Social control" is not a universal explanation, as some actions persist despite the absence of direct sanctions. "Internalization" of practices through the recruitment and socialization of new members is a stronger argument, and Zucker investigated to determine under what conditions the internalization process has the strongest impact.

The ethnomethodological approach, following Berger and Luckmann (1967), focuses on Durkheim's concepts of *exteriority* and *objectivity*. When acts are perceived as objective and exterior, they are most likely to be taken for granted and are thus more easily institutionalized. Institutionalization defines what is expected and what others will perceive as "rational" acts. *Objectivity* is achieved when members can repeat an act without changing the common understanding of it, and *exteriority* is achieved when meanings are widely shared among members.

What types of settings are most conducive to generating institutionalization? Personal influence is a weak condition, for we have only another person's word for what is "objective." However, within an organization there are high expectations that people know what they are doing, especially since their perceptions of reality appear to be shared. This expectation is heightened for new members when definitions of reality are provided by persons occupying offices and authoritative positions. Zucker didn't mention a condition that is clearly critical to this process: namely, that a person coming into an organization must be predisposed to accept the presence of authority. This predisposition will have been instilled from birth by the socializing institutions of society—family, schools, churches, and the mass media.

Zucker tested the hypothesized relation between institutionalization and cultural persistence in three laboratory experiments. The autokinetic situation was used, which is built on the fact that when a stationary point of light is presented in a totally darkened room, it appears to move. Subjects' perceptions of *how much* it moves can be manipulated by having confederates of the experimenter make false reports of their own perceptions to the naive subjects (new organization members). Through controlled manipulations, Zucker created three conditions of increasing degrees of institutionalization: a purely personal influence condition, a condition emphasizing the organizational context, and a condition utilizing a confederate person in a "formal office" (based on the organizational context condition). The question then was under which conditions the arbitrarily created standard (how much the light moved) would be passed on between generations in the laboratory room as new subjects replaced the experienced ones.

Zucker's predictions were confirmed: "As predicted, it was found that the greater the degree of institutionalization, the greater the generational uniformity of cultural understandings, the greater the maintenance without direct social control, and the greater the resistance to change through personal influence [when a confederate came in and give arbitrarily "low" responses]" (Zucker, 1977, p. 742). This experiment provides an explanation for *why* the characteristics of bureaucracy are so effective in contributing to the retention of specific organizational form. Documents and files, formalization and standardization of practices, and the exercise of control by legitimate authority heighten new members' expectations that the established reality is unshakable and firmly grounded in its own reality. The more successful the institutionalization process, the less likely members are to question the established order, and the more likely they are to acquiesce in those bizzare rituals that pass for "standard operating procedures" in most organizations. The process is not deterministic, however, and the possibility is always open that some members fail to comprehend or actively resist the official version of organizational reality. This creates the variation that is the first stage of the change process.

A METHODOLOGICAL ISSUE

One of the major problems in using the natural selection model of organizational change is the difficulty of avoiding circular or tautological arguments (Campbell, 1969). Critics question whether it is valid to build explanations by retrospectively constructing rationales for changes that have already occurred. Evolutionary theory focuses on differential survival rates only known in retrospect—after the fact—and dangers of tautological explanation appear great. We may find ourselves saying that bureaucratic organizations were produced by selection criteria favoring bureaucratic organizations, which hardly constitutes a proper explanation!

In spite of the difficulties involved in applying the natural selection model, we can, following Scriven (1959, p. 477), note that "one cannot regard explanations as unsatisfactory when they do not contain laws, or when they are not such as to enable the event in question to have been predicted." Evolutionary explanations are scientifically legitimate, even if they can't be used to predict the exact nature of changes.

A major question is the similarity in logical status between prediction and explanation. At the most abstract level, the two appear similar: To predict requires that we posit a correlation between present and future events; to explain, we posit a correlation between past and present events. In each case, we derive an event from the general laws connecting it to antecedent conditions, and if we can plausibly do so, we say we have "explained" the consequent event from the antecedent. However, in a world of events connected in a probabilistic rather than deterministic manner the similarity is more apparent than real. If there are a multitude of antecedent events that are likely to occur, but not with absolute certainty, then prediction becomes problematic. The costs of acquiring relevant information may well be prohibitive, and the feasibility of assembling and interpreting it in time to make a prediction may be remote.

Explanation and prediction differ in the demands placed on an analyst. "What we are trying to provide when making a prediction is simply a claim that, *at a certain time,* an *event* or state of affairs will occur. In explanation we are looking for a *cause,* an event that not only occurred earlier but stands *in a special relation* to the other event. Roughly speaking, the prediction requires only a correlation, the explanation more" (Scriven, 1959, p. 480). We can make predictions about events from indicators that are not causes of the events; predicting changes in the weather by observing changes in barometric pressure would be an example of this. Similarly, meteorologists are quite good at explaining weather patterns spawning violent storms, even if they are nearly incapable of predicting when such storms will occur. Explanation is possible, in this case, because meteorologists understand the causal principles underlying weather changes, which contain a large element of uncertainty.

Hypothetical Probability "Predictions"

If we understand the nature of the environment in which a particular form is most fit, then we might argue that we can predict whether the form will survive if the environment should change to another, specified, state. It is obvious that few, if any, characteristics contribute to fitness in all environments, and biological ecologists can do quite well in identifying specific characteristics of species relevant to fitness in specific environments. Organizational sociologists have paid little attention to the issue of organizational environments, and so we have little knowledge of the contribution to fitness of specific organizational characteristics in given environments. In either situation, however, we will not be able to predict a species's or organization's fate unless we can predict *how* the environment is changing.

Scriven (1959, p. 478) noted that difficulties in predicting environmental changes do not invalidate the natural selection model:

> However, these difficulties of prediction do not mean that the idea of fitness as a factor in survival loses all its *explanatory* power. It is not only true but obvious that animals which happen to be able to swim are better fitted for surviving a sudden and unprecedented inundation of their arid habitat, and in some such cases it is just this factor which explains their survival. Naturally we could have said in advance that *if* a flood occurred, they would be *likely* to survive; let us call this a hypothetical probability prediction. But hypothetical probability predictions do not have any value for actual prediction except in so far as the conditions mentioned in the hypothesis are predictable or experimentally producible; hence there will be cases where we can *explain why* certain animals and plants survived even when we could not have *predicted* that they would.

If we understand the general nature of selection principles, then inability to predict changes in the principles does not mean we cannot retrospectively reconstruct the impact of past selection principles on the course of change.

Retrospective Causal Analyses

We can avoid the problem of constructing tautological explanations if we are strict in our adherence to a set of three principles. In drawing up an explanation of an observed change in terms of hypothesized causes, we have to show that: (1) the cause was, in fact, present; (2) *independent* evidence supports our claim that it can produce this effect—in practice, this obligates us to find comparison cases and argues against attempting to explain truly unique events; and, (3) no other possible causes could have produced this effect. The last condition also argues for a comparative approach, so that other possible explanations can be identified and tested for in our analysis.

If our knowledge of the principles of selection are well-grounded empirically and theoretically, enabling us to reliably recognize the operation of selection effects when they occur, then we can "identify the causes of events *after* they happen, without committing the fallacy of *post hoc ergo propter hoc. . .*" (Scriven, 1959, p. 481). In a rather morbid example, Scriven (1959, p. 479) noted that, "We are not hard put to explain that a man's death was due to his being struck by an automobile, even when we could not have predicted the event." We need not ask for a complete account of all the factors contributing to a particular outcome, settling instead for a useful and enlightening partial account. Thus we can understand and accept an explanation for how business firms adapted to the energy crises of the 1970s—such as by converting from natural gas to coal power—without being concerned as to whether we could have predicted if and when a crisis would occur.

The Natural Selection Model Cannot Explain Everything

We must avoid a simple-minded application of the "survival of the fittest" principle, or we shall fall into the same trap as the conservative Darwinists. It is not always the case that the "fittest" survive, given the elements of chance and luck that have been emphasized as part of the natural selection process. Some perfectly fit persons and organizations fail because they happen to be in the wrong place at the wrong time, and it is not universally true that fitness determines survival. The natural selection model refers to a *tendency* for those species and organizations most fit vis-à-vis their environments to survive. Equating "fitness" with "survival" would rob the model of any claim to scientific status and reduce it to a tautology.

Just as the "fittest" sometimes fail, because of random variations in the selection process, so patently maladaptive organizations sometimes survive. Neo-Darwinism contains the concept of "random preadaption," referring to the phenomenon of apparently unfit adaptations prospering. Some non-adaptive partial structures or activities survive because they are tightly linked to an adaptive characteristic, because they are insulated from direct environmental pressures, or simply by chance alone. Whatever the reason, we must be alert to the logical fallacy of concluding, as the earliest social Darwinists concluded, that "what exists is the fittest." This same difficulty, of course, plagues attempts to develop a truly rigorous "functional theory" of social stratification (Tumin, 1953).

However, in terms of likelihoods and probabilities, the presumption remains that a thriving organization is adaptive to its environment. The burden of proving that an apparently successful organization is a maladaptive one falls to those who assert it isn't. They might do this by pointing out environmental trends that will soon eliminate an organization's market, such as a farsighted observer might have done for buggy-whip manufacturers in the 1890s, or for manufacturers of mechanical calculators in the 1970s who failed to convert quickly to electronic components.

SUMMARY

The population ecology model of organizational change is taken from a model well-developed in biological ecology and is one that is enjoying increasing use in the social sciences (Lenski, 1976). Given the existence of the three components—variation, selection criteria, and a retention mechansim—change in the direction of greater fit of a social system to its environment is inevitable. The model has to be modified in its application to organizations to take into account the possibility of altering structures and activities on a partial basis. This modification also allows us to study the evolution of individual organizations adapting to their environments. In subsequent chapters I will elaborate on issues raised when considering the variation and selection stages of the model, with a key issue being the extent to which reform Darwinists are correct in believing that people, at last, have achieved some control over their environments.

The description given in this chapter indicates that the population ecology model differs from traditional explanations of organizational change in several ways. First, it focuses on the nature and distribution of resources in organizations' environments as the central force in change, rather than on internal leadership or participation in decision making. Second, it examines organizations as representatives of types found in populations consisting of hundreds and often thousands of other organizations, thus using an aggregate as opposed to an individual level of analysis. Third, it takes into account the historical context within which organizations emerge, paying particular attention to political and economic conditions. Finally, the population ecology model re-establishes the link between organizational sociology and the general analysis of social organization that was weakened in the decades following World War II.

3 ENVIRONMENTS: SOME GENERAL CONSIDERATIONS

The population ecology model turns our attention toward the environment as a major force shaping organizational change. Selection occurs as a consequence of environmental pressures—if an organization, structure, or activity fits environmental requirements, it is selected. Making use of the model, however, requires a clear conception of what "the environment" is and how it affects organizational structure and activities. In this chapter the methodological implications of using the population ecology model to study change are discussed, and six dimensions of environments that exert selective pressure on organizations are presented. All are defined in terms of their effect on resources sought by organizations.

ENVIRONMENTAL VARIATION

Variation within and between organizations is the first requirement for organizational change; there must also be variation across environments if externally-directed change is to occur. Traditional studies of organizations typically focus on internal variation, whereas the natural selection model emphasizes the sources of variation in environments that select out certain types of behaviors or structures. An environment without variation—a prospect difficult to conceptualize, even abstractly—would be irrelevant to organizational change, for its eternal constancy would present the same set of selection rules to all organizations for all time. Once fitness were achieved by the population, reproduction of the same forms could continue forever. Only when variation in the environment exists, in time and space, are external conditions relevant to organizational change. As I shall argue in following chapters, organizational sociologists are quite fortunate in having environments of almost endless variation and complexity to study. The problem is not one of finding variation, but of conceptualizing it.

The concept of variation, because it refers to variation in both organizations *and* environments, requires an examination of both sides of the organization-environment relationships in order to understand change. We cannot make predictions about the effect of environmental characteristics without knowing more about the organizational population in question, and we cannot predict the adaptiveness of organizational structure without knowledge of environmental contexts. One problem with traditional approaches to the study of organizations is that organizational properties have been investigated without regard to their contributions to fitness in varying or diverse environments. Investigators haven't learned what particular combinations of internal organizational characteristics are most effective in permitting organizational survival or growth.

The growing popularity of "contingency theories" of organizations, in the past decade, reflects an attempt by investigators to take account of contextual differences. Contingency theories posit that whether a particular organizational form is effective depends on the nature of the environmental context, or, in population-ecology terms, in the fit between the form and its niche. Most research on contingency models is oriented more to designing than to understanding organizations and rests on incomplete conceptions of the environment. Little cumulation of the results of "contingency" research is possible, because no commonly agreed upon theoretical scheme has been adopted. Environments are defined in terms of members' perceptions, resources, uncertainty, and other disparate schemes. Perhaps most important is contingency researchers' focus on cross-sectional studies of fairly large, stable organizations, rather than on longitudinal studies of representative populations (Kimberly, 1976a) in varying environments.

The concept of variation is directly related to a point that is very easy to overlook: The organizations we usually study are a highly select (and biased) group, compared to the total population of new starts, successes, and failures. The study of successful organizations—those still available for investigation—may be quite misleading insofar as it blinds us to essential differences between these successful organizations and those that are no longer in existence. This omission hampers the development of an empirically-based sociology of organizational change. As noted in the last chapter, rates of business starts, transfers, and failures are quite high in Western industrial societies. Hundreds of thousands of businesses in the United States are begun, change hands, or go out of business each year.

The population ecology model directs our attention to *turnover* in the populations of organizations studied, and stresses the high failure rate and transiency of most organizations. Surviving organizations are also relevant to this point, for many go through substantial transformations after their creation.

METHODOLOGICAL IMPLICATIONS

The methodological implication of examining turnover in a population of organizations is straightforward in principle, but extremely complicated in practice: It makes more sense to deal with issues mirroring what is actually happening in a population, rather than theorizing about organizations as if most were stable and lasted forever. We can best study the effects of environmental selection by observing the fate of large numbers of organizations over time. How badly are we misled by studying organization-environment interaction cross-sectionally—at one point in time—rather than taking a comparative, longitudinal view? A hypothetical population of organizations, shown in Figure 3.1 will be used to illustrate the dilemmas and dangers of cross-sectional research.

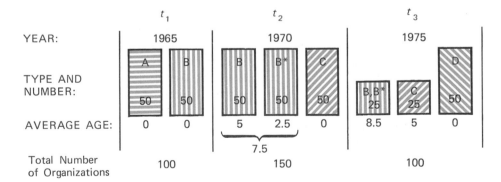

Figure 3.1. Longitudinal study of the evolution of organizational forms.

Notes: As and Bs were created prior to 1965.
          B*s were created between 1965 and 1970.
          Cs were created in 1970
          Ds were created in 1975.
          Form A is totally labor intensive, B is highly labor intensive, C is partially labor intensive and partially capital intensive, and D is highly capital intensive.

Assume that we are interested in the evolution of organizational forms, and we want to know which types of organizations are most fit for the environment from which we've drawn our sample. Assume further that we are collaborating with a naive investigator who is unaware of the importance of following a cohort of organizations over time. We begin our study in 1975, and since the population of organizations is fairly small in the industry and environment we've chosen, we include all of them in the sample. As shown in Figure 3.1, in 1975 we find 100 organizations of three forms: 50 Ds, 25 Cs, and 25 Bs. The Ds are all new, having been founded in the past year, the Cs are 5 years old, and the Bs average 8.5 years, with the oldest being 10 years old.

What can the naive observer conclude on the basis of this first cross section we have drawn? First he observes that the Ds are obviously inferior forms, for all of them were founded in the past year and evidently previous attempts at founding Ds were unsuccessful. The key difference between D and the other forms is that D is highly capital intensive, relying on a computer-controlled technology, whereas the other forms have more labor intensive technologies. Thus, the naive observer concludes that environmental selection criteria are operating against capital intensive forms.

Second, the naive observer concludes that form B is obviously more fit than Form C, because, while each constitutes 25 percent of the population, the Bs have had longer lives than the Cs. Form B is more labor intensive than form C, and so the observer takes this as confirming evidence for his initial hypothesis concerning environmental selection favoring labor intensive forms.

Armed with the natural selection perspective, we continue our investigation until we discover an archive containing complete information on all organizations in this industry and environment in 1970. We note that the population was larger then, consisting of 150 organizations, and then call the naive observer's attention to his mistaken interpretations. First, we now see that form D was a young form in 1975 not because it had been negatively selected against, but because it was a *new* form. Form D did not exist in 1970, and thus could not have been selectively eliminated. Second, contrary to the naive observer's interpretation, form B appears *less* fit than form C, as three-fourths of the Bs operating in 1970 failed by 1975, compared to only half of the Cs. We advance the tentative hypothesis that, between 1970 and 1975, environmental selection criteria favored capital intensive over labor intensive forms.

The naive observer is not deterred, however, and proceeds to an interpretation of the 1970 cross section. He concludes that, because no aged Cs were found, they were unfit for the environment at that time. The case of the new Ds in 1975 gives him pause, however. He also argues that surely form B was more fit than form C, since the Bs constituted two-thirds of the population and new ones were still being formed, as indicated by our finding some very young Bs as well as fifty that were five years old. (The 50 B*s were founded between 1965 and 1970.)

We then discover yet another cache of records, this one giving us complete information about the entire population in 1965, which is when the industry began. The naive observer is chagrined to find he is again in error, for both of his interpretations are proved false by the new information. First, form C was a new form in 1970, rather than a form negatively selected against in preceding years. Second, the major finding is that a form, A, existed in 1965 and did not survive to be included in the 1970 sample. It is now evident that the 50 Bs created since 1965 (B* in Figure 3.1) were taking the place of As that were failing. (Alternatively, perhaps organizations with form A were modifying their structures to become Bs.) Moreover, we learn that form A was even more labor intensive than form B, thus encouraging us to promote our earlier tentative hypothesis to the status of an empirical generalization: Environmental selection criteria favored capital intensive forms, in this industry, throughout the period of our study.

What may we conclude from this exercise? First, a cross-sectional study design that collected information from this population in only 1970 or 1975 would be seriously misleading, for it would lead to incorrect interpretations almost impossible to refute. A study design is required that covers a broad enough life span of an industry (or type of organization) to highlight the impact of a changing environment. Ideally, of course, an investigator should try to determine what happened *between* the three periods, t_1 to t_3, to make sense of the organizational change observed.

Second, the longitudinal design provides information supporting several generalizations about the direction of organizational and environmental change. A comparison of the relative frequency of forms at each point shows that the environment is evolving in a manner that differentially selects capital intensive over labor intensive forms, perhaps because labor costs are rising so rapidly that substituting machinery for labor is an increasingly sound investment. New forms of organization are being created in response to the changing environment, and forms are consistently selected for survival in a manner that favors capital intensive organizations. The environment changed in another way, too, as indicated by changes in the size of the population. Perhaps because 1970 was a peak year in the business cycle, the total population of organizations reached a high of 150, only to fall to 100 again in 1975 when the economy was in a downturn. This downturn accelerated the decline of form B, as 75 percent of them failed to survive.

The naive observer, suitably chastened, returns to us with a final question: Can we now simply extrapolate from the trend revealed in Figure 3.1 and predict what the population will be in 1980? From the population ecology perspective, our answer must be "no," for there is danger in extrapolating trends without comprehensive knowledge of how and why the environment is changing. The environment might be changing, for example, in ways that will once again favor form B or even A. This might be the case if resources required to sustain forms C and D become increasingly difficult to obtain at prices the organizations can afford. An investigator must know *why* particular forms are surviving and prospering, not just *which* survive. Knowledge of how and why the environment is changing would reveal, for example, if the trends observed are linear or cyclical.

Organizational and environmental variation occupy positions of equal importance in the natural selection model. Environmentally influenced change implies that environments, as well as organizations, are evolving. This has methodological as well as theoretical implications, as the example in Figure 3.1 has demonstrated. This example of hypothetical change should make us aware of the limits to our current knowledge of how and why organizations are changing, for sophisticated studies that follow a large population of organizations over time are extremely rare. Because there are few detailed historical studies of populations of organizations, most of the examples presented in this book are case studies or studies of extremely limited populations. Insightful case studies can tell us a great deal, however, especially those tracing the history of a particular organizational form. Also, studies of organizational failure are clearly as important as those of survival. For an insightful discussion of longitudinal research on organizations, see Kimberly (1976a).

THE ENVIRONMENT AS RESOURCE CONTROLLER

Environments affect organizations through the process of making available or withholding resources, and organization forms can be ranked in terms of their efficacy in obtaining resources. I will review theories that treat environments as information sources, but even these models must view information in view of its relevance for resource acquisition. If organization structure is defined as an information-processing system, then the ultimate test of efficiency is still the channeling of information to the proper roles so that appropriate decisions about resource acquisition and disposal can be made.

Yuchtman and Seashore proposed that organizational resources be defined as "generalized means, or facilities, that are potentially controllable by social organizations and that are potentially usable—however indirectly—in relationships between the organization and its environment" (1967, p. 900). This definition is useful in the population ecology framework because it emphasizes that organizations are in competition for resources—this is what makes resources valuable—and it takes into account the relative nature of concepts such as organizational effectiveness. As noted in the last chapter, environmental selection occurs through relative rather than absolute superiority, and an effective organization is one that has achieved a relatively better position in the environment it shares with others, rather than the best position. Provided we can define resources in general terms, we can compare organizations across environments.

The most general resource, and one sought by all organizations, is human activity. "The effectiveness of many organizations cannot be realistically assessed without some accounting for the organization's bargaining position with respect to the engagement of people in the service of the organization. One thinks, of course, of competition in the industrial or managerial labor market, but the idea is equally applicable to the competition, say, between the local church and local political party, for the evening time of persons who are potentially active in both organizations" (Yuchtman and Seashore, 1967, p. 900). Other general resources are power, influence, reputation, money, and knowledge.

Resources can be ranked on a series of dimensions that capture *why* a resource is sought, even though it is difficult to create a comprehensive list of resources themselves. First, the more liquid a resource, the more attractive it is to an organization. Liquid resources are easily converted into other resources, with money and credit being two prime examples. Liquid resources give an organization flexibility, whereas nonliquid resources tie an organization tightly to past practices. Second, resources that are stable and can be accumulated provide organizations with a cushion against environmental fluctuations, whereas unstable resources do not. Money and raw materials are examples of stable resources, while the technical competence of a research staff depreciates continuously without periodic re-education.

Third, some resources are sought by a large percentage of the organizations in an environment, and this universality makes them highly valued. Trained personnel, strategic geographical locations, favorable government regulations, and, of course, money are universal resources because of their relevance to nearly all forms of organization. Fourth, some resources are critical because there are no substitutes for them, and organizational technology is dependent upon them. Resources lacking substitutes are quite valuable, but organizations dependent upon such resources may attempt to develop alternatives to guard against the possibility of a restricted supply. Artificial fabrics took the place of cotton and wool, and synthetic rubber undermined the value of natural rubber partly because of availability and partly because the substitutes were adapted to a wider range of uses.

My objective in listing these characteristics of resources is more modest than that of Yuchtman and Seashore, as I make no assumption that resources can be defined in such general terms as to apply to all forms of organizations. Clark (1968, pp. 57-67), studying community decision making, compiled an abstract list of thirteen resources of social exchange and attempted to estimate the prestige and power value of each resource, its institutional importance, and how easily each resource could be converted into any other resource. The failure of Clark's efforts to generate much empirical research suggests that organization theorists should pay careful attention to specifying the precise context within which a resource is defined. Abstract lists are useful chiefly as a beginning point for more detailed investigation. Such dimensions are a guide for identifying forces in environments that make it difficult for organizations to obtain their requirements. Treating organizational activities as oriented toward resource procurement rather than more abstract goals focuses attention on specific elements in environments and should ultimately enable us to identify distinct niches. Niches will be defined in terms of the specific resources they make available rather than simply "viable modes of living."

DIMENSIONS OF ENVIRONMENTS

A search of the literature on organizations and their environments reveals six dimensions that various investigators have identified as important. The dimensions are relevant to environmental selection because they refer to the nature and the distribution of resources in environments, with different values on the dimensions implying differences in appropriate structures and activities. Each dimension should be viewed as a continuum rather than a dichotomy, as should be clear from the examples given. Variation exists within as well as between organizations, and thus while one dimension may be of special significance for one subset of organizational members or activities, it may have little relevance for another. I will present examples of the application of each dimension, pointing out its selective significance for organizational change.

Environment capacity (rich/lean): the relative level of resources available to an organization within its environment. This dimension also can be conceptualized as the extent to which an organization has to expand its area of operation to obtain the resources it requires, either to achieve stability or growth. Thompson (1967) suggested using the term "domain" to refer to an organization's area of operation—the range of products or services offered and the population served.

Organizations have access to more resources in rich environments, but such environments also attract other organizations. Stockpiling and hoarding of resources is probably not as prevalent in rich as in lean environments. Lean environments also promote cutthroat competitive practices, and apart from rewarding organizations capable of stockpiling and hoarding, lean environments reward efficiency in the use of resources. Two alternatives are open to organizations in lean environments: move to a richer environment, or develop a more efficient structure. The latter alternative can be accomplished by improving operating practices, merging with other organizations, becoming more aggressive vis-à-vis other organizations, or moving to a protected subenvironment through specialization.

Rich environments also have been seen as a barrier to the formation of interorganizational relations, at least of the more formalized kind. Aiken and Hage (1968) argued that the need for resources is an important determinant of forming interorganizational relations, and this need is missing for organizations in rich environments. However, rich environments have been viewed as preconditions to the formation of interorganizational linkages, as in the theory of oligopoly, since questions of domain protection and survival are not as urgent in rich as compared to lean environments.

Environmental capacity, or what ecologists call carrying capacity, sets limits on the size of a population of organizations. Assume that organizations are of uniform size and environmental resources are fixed, and assume further that new organizations can be started fairly easily, such as through imitation. Locally-owned restaurants and limited-price variety stores fit this description. In this case, we can use a logistic equation for growth of the population of organizations:

$$\frac{dx}{dt} = ax - bx^2$$

where x = the number of organizations in the population at a given time; a = the intrinsic rate of increase in the population, in the absence of resource constraints; b = the inhibiting effect of intrapopulation competition, which is the negative impact that organizations have on one another because they compete for a fixed supply of resources; a/b = the carrying capacity of the environment, given fixed organizational size; and dx/dt = the number of new organizations added per unit of time.

Given this set of assumptions, growth of the population would be quite rapid at first, but then would taper off as the carrying capacity was reached and the population entered a steady state, as shown in Figure 3.2. When the population (x) is small, the bx^2 term is insignificant and the equation reduces to $dx/dt = ax$; growth is then exponential. As time (t) increases and more generations are added to the population, x approaches a steady value and a point is reached at which no new organizations can be added unless others fail. Table 3.1 presents an example where the intrinsic rate of increase, a, is 0.5; the inhibiting effect of intrapopulation competition, b, is 0.01; and thus the carrying capacity is 50 (0.5/0.01). Note that growth is fairly rapid with each unit of time in the beginning, but as population size approaches 50, smaller and smaller numbers of organizations are added. When the carrying capacity is reached, no further population growth takes place.

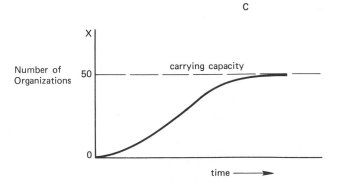

Figure 3.2.   Growth pattern of a population of organizations, assuming fixed organizational size and limited resources.

Table 3.1. Growth pattern of a population of organizations, given $a = 0.5$, $b = 0.01$, and $a/b = 50$.

If X then	ΔX	$=$	aX	$-$	bx^2
1	0.49	=	0.5	−	0.01
10	4.0	=	5.0	−	1.0
20	6.0	=	10.0	−	4.0
30	6.0	=	15.0	−	9.0
35	5.25	=	17.5	−	12.25
40	4.0	=	20.0	−	16.0
45	2.25	=	22.5	−	20.25
50	0.0	=	25.0	−	25.0

Note: For the definitions of a, b, and a/b, see the text.

When a steady state is reached, change can occur in four ways. First, the carrying capacity of the environment might be increased through the discovery of new resources or the recycling of old ones. Second, carrying capacity might decrease because irreplaceable resources are depleted and no substitutes are available, thus lowering population size. Third, the average size of organizations in the population might increase, as some gain an advantage over others and drive them out of existence or acquire them. Fourth, the average size of organizations might drop, as a previously indivisible factor of production becomes divisible. This might happen if technological innovations made available new production techniques that allowed efficient organizations to be half the size formerly required.

What if another type of organization, y, exists, which uses the same resources as type x? This might occur if fast-food restaurants specializing in roast beef are introduced to challenge fast-food restaurants specializing in hamburgers. There are two possibilities. First, the two forms, x and y, might coexist under very special conditions; namely, that growth in x has a greater inhibiting effect on itself than on y, and vice-versa. For example, the two forms could exactly divide the resources, so that there are twenty-five of each, and each is intrinsically inhibited from expanding beyond twenty-five members. This would hold true if the inhibiting effect of intrapopulation competition, b, were 0.02 for form x instead of 0.01 in Table 3.1, and if form y were similarly limited.

Coexistence could be achieved in another, perhaps more difficult, manner if leaders within each segment of the population came to an agreement on sharing the environment, rather than competing. Fast-food restaurants might agree to limit their expenditures on advertising or to refrain from price-cutting. Oligopolistic coalitions and cartels consist of organizations within the same niche that cooperate in the interests of joint survival, but they depend on collective agreements that are very difficult to maintain.

A second possibility is that the two forms use the same resources and there are no intrinsic limits that prevent their expansion to the point where interform competition occurs. If every new *y* takes resources from a potential *x*, then they are in the same niche and this situation cannot last. The form with any adaptive advantage over the other in obtaining resources will eventually eliminate the other if it persists in using its original form. Gause's principle of competitive exclusion was derived to cover this condition: "the greater the similarity of two resource-limited competitors, the less feasible it is that a single environment can support both of them in equilibrium" (Hannan and Freeman, 1977, p. 943). Competition will either eliminate one form, drive it into another environment, lead to its modification to resemble the more fit competitor, or end in some sort of agreement to share the environment. Consider the high degree of similarity among fast-food restaurants, regardless of whether they specialize in hamburgers, fish, roast beef, or tacos: large parking lots, self-servicing, precooked food, young staffs employed at the minimum wage, small tables for only two or four people, and a minimum of amenities so that customers are encouraged to eat quickly and leave. Restaurants not adopting this form find themselves at a severe competitive disadvantage.

Environmental homogeneity-heterogeneity: the degree of similarity or differentiation between the elements of the population dealt with, including organizations, individuals, and any social forces affecting resources. A homogeneous environment rewards the development of standardized ways of relating to the domain population, and may lead to the development of an undifferentiated set of products or services (Thompson, 1967). Homogeneity simplifies organizational activities because a small set of operating routines may suffice for a large population. Heterogeneity can often be troublesome, leading to intraorganizational conflict, if a people-processing organization seeks to transform a population of heterogeneous clients into highly specialized outputs (Hasenfeld, 1972).

Public service organizations are assigned quite heterogeneous client populations by law and thus would be expected to adopt strategies for obtaining a more homogeneous population, if smoother operating procedures are desired. With the proliferation of governmental social service legislation during the past two decades, there has been an expansion in programs offered that has had the effect of expanding the range of clients served while at the same time narrowing the range of any one program. Even within this differentiated population of social service organizations, there are still attempts to limit the types of clients served. This process is called "creaming" when used to select the most qualified clients.

The dimension of homogeneity-heterogeneity, when combined with the principle of competitive exclusion, can be used to generate a general principle of expected diversity in an organizational population. The principle of competitive exclusion can be formulated in a positive sense, which is that two organizational forms can only coexist in equilibrium in the same environment if they depend on *different* resources, or there are other constraints that limit competition between them. Laws and governmental rules and regulations are, of course, major constraints on competition and on the creation of new organizations in the same niche. Taking into account all the possible constraints on population growth, including the number of different resources plus other constraints such as laws, the general principle is that a population can only be as diverse as the environment sustaining it. A population of m forms can only be sustained in an environment with at least m different constraints on growth (Hannan and Freeman, 1977).

Note the similarity between this general principle of population diversity and the argument in the last chapter concerning the maintenance of complex structures. Complexity in the structure and activities of single organizations is maintained by consistent environmental pressures, and similarly, population complexity, is maintained by environmental complexity. This principle is useful mainly for its qualitative implications, for it is extremely difficult in practice to identify the unique environmental constraints sustaining unique organizational forms. However, it does alert us to search for environmental changes that add or remove resources and other constraints from environments, since population diversity will be affected by such additions and deletions.

The increasing importance of national markets and federal rules and regulations in the United States may have had the consequence of reducing or eliminating some local environmental heterogeneity. If local and regional constraints are replaced with more uniform national ones, then local homogeneity results and diversity in the organizational population should decrease. However, some national forces do not eliminate local constraints but rather add others, thus increasing environmental heterogeneity. Consequently, population diversity could increase.

Environmental stability-instability: the degree of turnover in the elements of the environment. A stable environment implies that organizations will be able to develop fixed sets of routines for dealing with environmental elements and consequently fairly formalized structures should be selected. Organizations will be positively selected by age when environments are stable, as the longer an organization is in the environment, the more its members learn, thus acquiring an advantage over new organizations. Conversely, when environments change from stable to unstable, established organizations may have more difficulty coping with the change than newly established organizations. Problems of adaptation are most severe when internal retention mechanisms are strong and there are few established procedures for responding to change. This dilemma is illustrated by the problems of traditional government social service agencies in the 1960s, which were staffed by career civil servants and had evolved into structures highly resistant to change. The new social service agencies created during the 1960s, such as Community Action Agencies, complained that the older agenices didn't respond quickly enough to their requests and newly militant (and sometimes organized) clients complained of the unsympathetic manner in which they were treated.

Small businesses in the inner-city neighborhoods of northern cities have been drastically affected by instability of residential populations since World War II.

Turnover in residents from white to black, because of white migration to the suburbs and black migration from the South, led to a decrease in relative economic status, which lowered the business carrying capacity of the neighborhoods. Failure rates are as high as one in ten per year, with not enough turnover from white to black ownership to make up for the large number of vacant shops. Negative selection affects mainly retail and service businesses, as nonlocally oriented businesses such as manufacturers are insulated from local environmental changes (Aldrich and Reiss, 1976).

Environmental concentration-dispersion: the degree to which resources, including the population served and other elements, are evenly distributed over the range of the environment or concentrated in particular locations. If resources are randomly distributed, little organizational learning is possible. If, however, resources are concentrated in identifiable units, then strategies for exploiting the organization's position can be worked out. Thus, position in the environment becomes important in the selection process when elements are concentrated rather than dispersed.

Social service organizations adapt to concentrations of their client populations, such as in a low-income "ghetto," by changing their recruiting and intake procedures. Outreach centers and neighborhood offices are commonplace in the structure of large urban social service agencies today. When client concentration is due to the presence of another organization, as with youth in schools, social service agencies respond by assigning permanent staff to the organizations as outreach workers.

Retail businesspeople in metropolitan areas must make decisions regarding location in order to maximize their access to a fairly dispersed population (Berry and Kasarda, 1977, pp. 248-67). Changes in the geographic distribution of socioeconomic groups between cities and suburbs drain central cities of upper-income customers and reconcentrate them in the suburbs. Some businesses have adapted by following population concentrations to the more affluent suburbs, while others have located in centrally placed shopping centers. Shopping centers concentrate the domain population by maximizing access to it, and from the clients' perspective, what is concentrated is a group of essential retail and service businesses at an easily accessible location.

Domain consensus-dissensus: the degree to which an organization's claim to a specific domain is disputed or recognized by other organizations, including governmental agencies (Levine and White, 1961). This concept is relevant chiefly to nonprofit organizations and the social services sector, as most profit-oriented businesses are, by definition, in competition with others for a larger piece of their shared domain. In the social services sector, domain conflict arises over alleged duplication of services and efforts by new agencies to encroach on the domains of established organizations.

The concept of domain consensus can be used to derive several hypotheses about organizational growth and development. Organizations attempt to capture a domain by differentiating themselves from other organizations with highly similar goals. Efficacy in acquiring resources is not only a matter of finding a niche where the organization successfully competes against other forms, but also it involves gaining legitimacy from key social control institutions, such as government and coalitions of dominant organizations (Warren, Rose, and Bergunder, 1974). The achievement of domain consensus thus involves negotiation, mediation, and compromise, as well as conflict.

Businesses are involved in disputes regarding domain defense at many levels of government. At the community level there are battles over zoning laws in developing suburbs, where perceived incompatible land users struggle with one another over the right to locate at choice sites. Communities, in turn, use exemptions from zoning laws, pollution ordinances, and other regulations as weapons in the intercommunity struggle to attract businesses. At the national level, regulated industries must win the approval of regulatory agencies to exploit resource opportunities, as with the awarding of routes in the airline and interstate trucking industries.

Social service agencies are particularly sensitive to encroachment on their domains, as they rely on protected markets for their clientele and don't use the marketing methods of the private sector, such as price competition and aggressive advertising programs. A great deal of interorganizational interaction thus involves negotiations over claimed areas of competence, and new organizational forms have emerged that fulfill the role of mediating domain conflicts. Community Chest, United Fund, Councils of Social Agencies, and other new forms arose in the period following World War I in the United States as a partial response to a welter of conflicting domain claims by private as well as public social service agencies. Block grants to communities under the federal sharing act in the 1970s embroiled city councils in conflicts between local groups, each after a share of the funds allocated for the "good and welfare" of the community.

Environmental turbulence: the extent to which environments are being disturbed by increasing environmental interconnection, and an increasing *rate* of interconnection (Emery and Trist, 1965; Terreberry, 1968). Increasing interconnection leads to externally induced changes in the nature of environmental selection criteria, produced by forces that are obscure to administrators and therefore difficult to predict or plan for. Implied in these changes is a decrease in local organizational autonomy and an inability to plan for the future. Turbulence refers not to chaos in the environment, but to an increasing causal interconnection that renders environments obscure to local observers. The causal laws connecting external events become incomprehensible to persons having no firsthand knowledge of the distant forces at work.

Turbulence can be conceptualized as an increase in *potential* as well as *actual* linkages. First, as environmental capacity increases there is an increasing number of organizations and new forms in the population, as reflected in increased diversity in the interorganizational division of labor. Increasing size and diversity in the population leads to an increase, by definition, in the possible number of links between organizations. In a population of n organizations, there are $n(n - 1)$ possible two-way links. To avoid counting links twice, we divide by 2 and the resulting formula for total ties is $n(n - 1)/2$. Linear increases in the number of organizations in the population produce large increases in the number of possible links, as each new organization could form a tie to all previous organizations. Each new organization adds $(n - 1)$ links to the pool of existing links, as shown when the above formula is applied to a population increasing from two to ten organizations: the number of links, beginning at two organizations, is three, six, ten, fifteen, twenty-one, twenty-eight, thirty-six, and forty-five. In a population of only ten organizations there are forty-five possible two-way interorganizational links; the possible number of links between voluntary associations in Birmingham, England (see Table 2.2) is over nine million!

Second, improved communication facilities, comprehensive transportation routes, increased specialization of organizational forms, and other forces have led to an increase in the number of links actually used. As communication and transportation networks in industrial societies have been extended on a nationwide basis, local organizations have found themselves caught up in a whirl of remote national events over which they have no control. Local labor and product markets are no longer as insulated as they once were, and fads and fashions—disseminated through national cultural media—sweep aside local differences. The increased role of national corporations in local economic life is represented by the impact of franchise operations on local retail and service businesses. Fast-food chains are backed by national advertising campaigns, sophisticated sales and employee training programs, and ready-made accounting systems that simply aren't available to local merchants. The increasing presence of the federal government in all aspects of the society adds or removes constraints in local environments in a way that local organizations find difficult to monitor or interpret. In these examples turbulence is defined from the perspective of *local* organizations—large national organizations with specialized planning departments might find these events well within their realm of understanding.

USING MULTIPLE DIMENSIONS IN UNDERSTANDING SELECTION

The six environmental dimensions were presented as independent units, but they will naturally be used in combination in analyzing organizational change. Emery and Trist (1965), in one of the best-known articles on environments, used three dimensions—stability, concentration, and turbulence—to illustrate how the distribution of resources in an environment might selectively reward the development of particular structures and activities. Four types of environment, which they labelled "causal textures," form a hierarchy of increasing complexity in

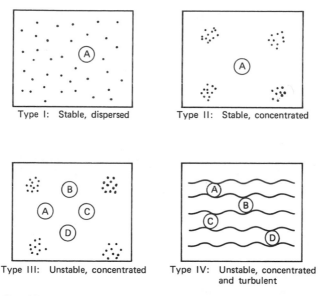

Type I: Stable, dispersed

Type II: Stable, concentrated

Type III: Unstable, concentrated

Type IV: Unstable, concentrated and turbulent

Note: A, B, C, and D represent organizations.
Dots represent resources.

Figure 3.3   Resource distribution in four types of environments.

their example. I have relabelled their dimensions to conform to those discussed above. The four environments are illustrated in Figure 3.3.

Four Types of Environment

Stable, dispersed environments.   In Emery and Trist's Type I environment, resources are dispersed to the point of being randomly distributed, and therefore no causal laws connect elements of the environment. The environment is stable and unchanging, but stability is of little help to organizations because a random environment contains no information. The only activities positively selected would be fairly simple *tactics*, which are short-run maneuvers in the vicinity of resources being approached. If environmental capacity is also low, then we might expect organizations of a larger size to be positively selected, as larger organizations could more easily tolerate the random shocks organizations face between opportunities for resource acquisition.

A Type I environment, curiously enough, allows the largest role for idiosyncratic and utterly subjective definitions of the situation facing organizations. It really doesn't matter how the environment is perceived, for just about anything will work (or not work) in a totally random environment. Of course, such an

71

environment is pure fantasy, because it is highly unlikely that structures as complex as organizations would arise in random environments. Nevertheless, we can conceive of situations where external events are equally meaningless to all participants and where chance perceptions therefore play an important role. The difference between this situation and a Type I environment is that in Type I environments there is no long-run pressure toward more adaptive perceptions.

Stable, concentrated environments. Type II environments contain information for the organizational population, as resources are no longer randomly distributed. The addition of concentrated resources has selective significance because some positions in the environment are now richer than others. If we think about Type II environments in terms of their general evolutionary significance, we can see that any living system that developed the capacity of *memory* would have a selective advantage over its rivals for the same resources. It could return to the optimal locations without wasting energy in the process, and could behave as if it had a plan.

Emery and Trist argued that Type II environments would reward the development of *strategic activities*, even if the activity was no more elaborate than the facility for locomoting in a straight line. The development of strategies illustrates the principle of *isomorphism*: organizational characteristics are modified in the direction of increasing compatibility with environmental characteristics. If environments move toward increasing structural complexity, then organizations will do the same. Strategies represent greater behavioral complexity than tactics because they involve a capacity for planning and the rudiments of a distinctive competence.

Unstable, concentrated environments. The addition of other organizations competing for the same resources changes a Type II into a Type III environment, as represented by the letters A through D in Figure 3.3. The existence of other organizations with similar needs now becomes the dominant characteristic of the environment, and ability relative to competitors becomes of selective significance. Instability arises from the addition of competing organizations because they disrupt the link between strategies and effectiveness established in stable, concentrated environments.

Type III environments would selectively reward the development of a capacity for *operations*, which consist of campaigns involving a planned series of tactical initiatives, reactions by others, and counteractions. Variations that have the potential for increasing the power of an organization will be positively selected, such as innovations increasing flexibility and the capacity to move at will. Larger size might give organizations such power, and over time the larger organizations might drive out the smaller ones. If no variations arise that permit dominant organizations to exist, then a purely competitive situation exists and we would expect all organizations over time to move toward very similar structures and activities. Such structural symmetry is another example of the principle of isomorphism.

Unstable, concentrated, and turbulent environments.   A Type IV environment in Emery and Trist's schema is characterized by a change in the nature of relations between environmental elements, which is a possible outcome of a Type III environment. This might occur as all organizations become able to use operations and grow skilled at concealing future moves and counter-moves. In Figure 3.3 a Type IV environment is portrayed as a series of wavy lines to convey the image that the "ground" is in motion—all organizations face an increase in uncertainty because the rules governing environmental changes are themselves changing.

Common values, if developed, could lead to domain consensus and the prospect of change back to a more certain situation. Terreberry (1968) argued that a Type IV environment would selectively reward organizations that developed efficient environmental monitoring, screening, and information-processing systems. As I noted in discussing turbulence, it is not the absence of causal laws but their obscurity that makes turbulence problematic for organizations. Any activity endowing an organizational form with even a slight competitive edge in forecasting and planning increases its relative survival prospects. In contrast to Type I environments, which allow for maximum idiosyncracy, Type IV environments demand efficacy in perception.

Short-run and long-run applications.   Emery and Trist's examples emphasize the isomorphism between the principles of short-run adaptation and long-run population changes. In the short-run, if we assume organizations are capable of piecemeal modification of structures and activities, we can predict the adaptations individual organizations are likely to make in their lifetime in Type I through Type IV environments. Our analysis would then be of organizations adapting to their environments. If we take a long-run view, we might assume organizational structures and activities are relatively fixed. Under this assumption, forms would be modified mainly through the replacement of old organizations by new ones. Movement of organizations toward a better fit with environmental characteristics, by developing tactical, strategic, or operation capabilities, would occur through the selection of entire organizations. Needless to say, we will rarely encounter such clear-cut cases.

SUMMARY

Variation within environments is as important as variation between organizations in permitting an understanding of organizational change. I have presented an example of the necessity for studying organization-environment interaction over

Table 3.2 Dimensions of organizational environments

Environmental Capacity: The relative level of resources available to an organization within its environment, varying from lean or low capacity to rich or high capacity environments.

Environmental Homogeneity-Heterogeneity: The degree of similarity between the elements of the domain population, including individuals and organizations. Varies from undifferentiated or homogeneous to highly differentiated or heterogeneous environments.

Environmental Stability-Instability: The degree of turnover in environmental elements. (Note that high turnover may still be patterned and is thus predictable.)

Environmental Concentration-Dispersion: The degree to which resources, including the domain population and other elements, are evenly distributed over the range of the environment. Varies from random dispersion to high concentration in specific locations.

Domain Consensus-Dissensus: The degree to which an organization's claim to a specific domain is disputed or recognized by other organizations.

Turbulence: The extent to which environments are characterized by an increasing interconnection between elements and trends, and by an increasing *rate* of inter-connection.

a fairly long time span, showing the errors of interpretation that arise in cross-sectional studies. Environmental variation in the availability of resources is the driving force in the population ecology model, but we have only a tentative understanding of the relative importance of particular resources and how to categorize them. Liquidity, stability, universality, and substitutability are four characteristics of specific resources that make them sought after, and may serve as a guide to identifying environmental niches. Six dimensions of environments that affect the distribution of and accessibility to resources are listed in Table 3.2, and examples of their application to understanding both short- and long-run change are presented. Subsequent chapters will draw on these dimensions in an examination of issues such as the conditions under which new organizational forms are created and interorganizational linkages are established.

4 Variation: Interdependence and Autonomy within Organizations

Traditional organization theory overemphasizes the functional interdependence and operating harmony of organizations. On theoretical grounds, this conception of organizations makes it very difficult to account for change, as variation is considered to be something organizations avoid. Theorists search for structure and stability rather than the sources of variability and disharmony. On empirical grounds, we know that this is an inaccurate interpretation of what actually happens inside organizations, as examples in the last three chapters should make clear. In this chapter I examine issues raised in applying the first stage of the natural selection model—the occurrence of variation—to the study of organizational change. Organizations will be portrayed as loosely-coupled systems that are subject to change because of error, creativity, luck, and conflict, as well as through planned innovation.

LIMITS TO COMPLEXITY

Challenges to Traditional Assumptions

The "everything's related" syndrome.   Many theorists in the social sciences and humanities argue that trying to understand and explain social life scientifically is too difficult because "everything is related to everything else." They argue that there are too many factors to cope with systematically. Analytic description is impossible because the richness of social life defies such description. As Nietzsche wrote, "Theory is gray, but green is the tree of life."

Consider for a moment, however, the type of system construction implied by these comments. *If* everything is related to everything else, then change anywhere would immediately reverberate throughout the system. Imagine that the floor of your room is covered with mouse traps, each set and waiting to be triggered, and that a ping-pong ball is perched on each, ready to be hurled into the air when the trap is set off. If a trap in any part of the room is triggered, the flying ping-pong balls will quickly set off every other trap in the room and in seconds the air will be filled with flying ping-pong balls and mouse traps. Clearly a highly interdependent system is also a highly unstable system, in the sense of being immediately sensitive to outside influences. This is a rather unsuitable arrangement for a society or an organization.

Is it then plausible to assert that "everything is related to everything else?" If someone in New York sneezes, does someone in Peoria catch cold? Does the failure of the ABC Laundry in Boston affect the unemployment rate in Hartford? If the sociology department at Ivy University declines in prestige, does the chemistry department cease to attract qualified post-doctoral students? Does a temporary increase in absenteeism in the shipping department of Allied Metal Products disrupt operations in the accounting department? There are countless examples, but the central point should be clear: Many situations in everyday life are only loosely related to one another, if at all, even within the same organization or group.

Things are not as complex as they seem.   Or, things are usually more simple than they first appear. This is the central premise of the evolutionary view of organizational change, for without the assumption of a loosely coupled world, a theorist's task is hopeless. As I will explain in the following sections, living systems (including organizations) achieve stability and continuity of existence precisely because they contain "holes." Not all possible links between people, departments, or organizations are realized, and many links develop in ways that promote stability. This is not to deny that turbulence, as defined in the last chapter, is an increasingly important characteristic of organizational environments, but increasing causal interconnection falls far short of joining all possible links.

LOOSE COUPLING AND HIERARCHY

A central characteristic of organizations and other living systems is "their relative independence of momentary environmental change" (Glassman, 1973, p. 84). Loose coupling exists when structures and activities in various parts of an organization are only weakly connected to each other and therefore are free to vary independently. Independence of organizations from momentary external changes is achieved through loose coupling within organizations, between organizations and their environments, and through the differentiation of organizations into hierarchically arranged subcomponents. After defining and illustrating loose coupling and hierarchy, I will point out their evolutionary importance.

Loose Coupling

The degree of coupling between persons, roles or units within organizations depends upon the activity of their common variables. If two elements have few variables in common, or if variables common to both are weak compared to other variables influencing the elements, then they are relatively independent of each other and thus loosely coupled. Weick (1976, p. 3) noted that loosely coupled events are "responsive *but* each also preserves its own identity and some evidence of its physical or logical separateness. . . each retains some identity and separateness and their attachment may be circumscribed, infrequent, weak in its mutual effects, unimportant, and/or slow to respond."

The *time* it takes one variable to affect another is an important linkage factor. How long does it take for an affect to appear, assuming that it does? The longer the time span, the looser the coupling. Using the familiar form of if-then statements from the philosopher's truth tables, we might characterize loose coupling as "if A, then B, eventually."

Also, linkages may be *deterministic or probabilistic*. If a linkage between two events or elements is not a one-to-one, cause-effect relationship, then we may question the strength of the coupling. The higher the probability of B adapting a particular condition because of the state of A, the tighter the coupling. Referring again to if-then statements, we might identify this property of loose coupling as "if A, then B, maybe."

The evolutionary importance of loose coupling will be discussed subsequently, but the relationship between loose coupling and current system stability should be clear: "Because component parts are semiautonomous, a massive action of the entire system is less probable in any given interval than an action of a component subsystem or linkage" (Glassman, 1973, pp. 85-86). In loosely coupled systems it is more difficult for changes in individual elements or units to affect the entire system than in tightly coupled systems. External events therefore do not ramify throughout an entire system, and subcomponents can achieve their own adaptation with local subenvironments. Consider again the example of a floor covered with mousetraps, but imagine now that tables and chairs have been placed in the room also. Adding furniture has substantially lessened the interdependence of the mousetraps and ping-pong balls, for the tables and chairs will shield some mousetraps and thus prevent them from being set off.

Loose coupling at the level of societal institutions is exemplified by the method of elections in some democratic countries, such as the United States. The long time span between elections prevents rapid changes of government in response to specific policies or short-run societal fluctuations. Thus the political system is loosely coupled to current social conditions, in contrast to political systems that permit a government to fall whenever it cannot command a majority vote in the legislature. A second example is group norms promoting stability by decoupling potentially extreme member behavior from a group's fate through prohibiting or severely circumscribing displays of interpersonal hostility. Norms regarding "good manners" prevent the introduction of potentially disruptive topics, and people quickly intervene to quiet angry members (Aldrich, 1971b). Values and norms venerating traditional customs and behaviors have the effect of maintaining loose coupling between new developments in the environment and organizational structure and activities.

Often loose coupling between events is due to the slippage between intention and action, as people find it difficult, impractical, or impossible to carry through on their intentions (Weick, 1976). Ambiguous goals, unclear technologies, inadequate resources, and conflicting motives lead people in directions that may be unintended by organizational authorities. Nonetheless, authority relations and task requirements generally combine with environmental pressures to hold organizations together, albeit not in the tightly coupled form described in management textbooks.

Hierarchy

A hierarchial system is composed of subsystems interrelated in such a way that subsystems at the bottom of the hierarchy are related to those at the top only through intermediate subsystems. Within each subsystem there may also be hierarchical relations, as exemplified in a typical organizational authority chart, shown in Figure 4.1. Organization charts are drawn up by administrators as a device for managing organizations, but we can also derive hierarchies by observing who interacts with whom, or in general, by observing patterns of influence in a system. Two features of hierarchies are of special importance: the span of a system—the number of subsystems into which a system is partitioned; and the number of levels in a system—the qualitative breaks in the structure between subsystems with large differences in influence. The span of the organization in Figure 4.1 is four and the number of levels is four or five, depending upon the division. When the number of levels is small, we speak of "flat" structures, and when the number of levels is large, we call the structure "tall" (Hall, 1977).

The concepts of loose coupling and hierarchy can be combined to generate a model of what Simon (1962) called a nearly decomposable system, as shown in Figure 4.2. This organization has four major departmental units, labelled A, B, C, and D; and each department consists of three members, labelled 1, 2, and 3. Some members know each other very well and communicate frequently, whereas others never speak to one another. Numbers in the cells of Figure 4.2 represent

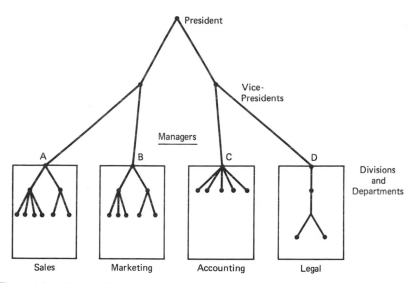

Figure 4.1. A typical hierarchy: An organization chart of official authority relations.

the probability of one speaking to another. For example, within department A, there is a 90 percent chance that member A_1 will communicate with A_3, and a 100 percent chance that A_1 will communicate with A_2. The chances are much less that members in department A will communicate with those in B or C, and almost nil that they will communicate with members in department D.

Imagine now that a rumor is introduced into department A; how will it spread throughout the organization? Hierarchy is built into the organization because the pattern of communication flow is from A to B to C, and finally to D, although this flow is not absolute. Loose coupling is present, as the major impact of a department is on the department adjacent to it in the hierarchy. Members have less chance of passing on rumors to other members who are more than one department away.

In the short-run, communication between departments is extremely limited, especially to those more than one step away. Tight coupling exists within departments, but loose coupling exists between them. In the long-run, the rumor will spread throughout the entire organization, with the aggregate outcome determined more by departments at the top than at the bottom of the hierarchy. Simon (1962) suggested as an example of this the problem of heat transfer between rooms in a building, where A, B, C, and D are the four major rooms and the subcomponents are cubicles within the rooms. Temperatures within rooms would very quickly equalize, given the pattern of tight coupling between cubicles, but it would take longer for temperatures in the entire building to equalize because of loose coupling between rooms.

79

Subsystem		A			B						D	
		1	2	3	1	2	3	1	2	3	1	2	3
A	1	—	100	90	70	60	70	30	10	40	10	0	0
	2	90	—	100	60	80	50	20	20	30	0	0	10
	3	90	90	—	60	60	60	20	30	20	10	0	0
B	1	10	20	0	—	90	100	80	60	80	10	20	30
	2	10	0			—	100	70	70	70	20	10	10
	3	0	20	10	100	90	—	80	70	70	30	10	20
C	1	10	20	20	0	30	30	—	90	100	70	60	70
	2	20	10	20	30	20	40	100	—	90	80	80	60
	3	10	20	30	30	0	40	90	100	—	70	70	80
D	1	0	0	0	20	0	0	20	30	10	—	90	90
	2	0	10	0	10	10	0	10	20	0	90	—	100
	3	10	0	0	0	20	10	20	10	10	100	100	—

Key: A, B, C, and D are departments.
A₁, A₂, A₃, B₁, etc. are department members.
Numbers in the cells represent the probability that member i will communicate with member j in a typical week.

Figure 4.2.   A loosely coupled, hierarchical system.

THE EVOLUTIONARY IMPORTANCE OF HIERARCHY AND LOOSE COUPLING

Hierarchy and loose coupling, as properties of organizational structure and activities, are important to the natural selection model because they help us understand the emergence and persistence of complex forms. Complex systems, whether organizational or organic, are able to evolve from simple systems much more rapidly when there are stable intermediate forms between the simple and the complex. Stable intermediate forms are able to survive long enough to move toward complexity if they are at least partially independent of their environments, and if various subparts of the evolving system can adapt autonomously to the local environments they face. If we understand the principles underlying the evolutionary importance of hierarchy and loose coupling, we can also understand their importance for strategic adaptations made by individual organizations.

The Importance of Hierarchy

Simon (1962) illustrated the evolutionary significance of hierarchy through the parable of Hora and Tempus, two watchmakers. Both produce watches that are identical, once assembled, but they use very different technologies in the assembly process. Hora's watch consists of 100 independent subassemblies of ten elements each, while Tempus has to put all 1,000 pieces of the watch together at the same time. If put down, Tempus's entire watch falls to pieces and he has to start over again.

Hora and Tempus run very small shops and, in addition to making watches, they also have to answer their phones. People phone in orders for watches, and each watchmaker has to put down whatever he is working on to answer the phone. Assuming that these calls come at fairly frequent and unpredictable intervals, who is most affected? Obviously Hora has an enormous advantage over Tempus, for the odds are much greater that Hora will complete a stable subassembly between incoming calls than that Tempus will put an entire watch together. For example, if calls come on the average of every eleven seconds, and it takes one second to joint two pieces together, then Hora will generally finish a subassembly between calls, while Tempus will never finish a watch! Apart from the implication that Tempus should enter another line of trade, what do we learn about the evolutionary importance of hierarchy from this example?

The evolution of a complex form from a simple one depends upon the number and span of the subassemblies that exist between them. It also depends upon the frequency of disruptive events in the environment. In sociocultural evolution, unlike the creeping gradualism of organic evolution, it is also possible that intermediate stages can be skipped entirely by social systems wishing to adopt new forms that have emerged elsewhere. This possibility has animated discussions about the best path for developing nations to follow in pursuing Western-style economic growth: Can Western industrial technology be imported without a nation passing through the intermediate stages that the developed nations experienced (Kuznets, 1959)?

For the mathematically inclined, the principle of intermediate stable forms is captured nicely in the following equation: The time required for the completion of a subassembly is proportional to $1/(1 - P)^s$, where s = the span of the assembly (the number of elements in the assembly), and P = the probability that a part will be dispersed by environmental disruption before another is added. Note that as P becomes smaller, $(1 - P)^s$ becomes larger, and the entire fraction becomes smaller, which means a faster completion time. For example, if $P = 0$ (there are no disruptions), then $(1 - P)^s$ reduces to $(1)^s$ or simply 1, and completion requires one unit of time. If, however, $P = 0.9$, meaning the probability of disruption is quite high, then $(1 - P) = 0.10$ and $(0.10)^s$ could be a very small number, depending upon the span. If the span = 4, then $(0.10)^4 = 0.0001$, and $1/0.0001 = 10,000$, which means a longer completion time.

The importance of the number of levels in the complex form also can be captured mathematically: The time required for the assembly of a complex system containing N elements is proportional to $\log_s N$, which is the number of levels in the system, assuming that the span is the same at each level of the hierarchy. (Remember that the logarithm is the power by which you would have to raise "S" to obtain "N") The number of levels, L, is computed from the formula $S^L = N$. In the example of Hora and Tempus, the number of levels in Hora's form is 3, as $\log_{10} 1000 = 3$. If the span of Hora's subassemblies were two instead of ten, the number of levels would be approximately nine, and it would take quite a bit longer to assemble a completed watch.

Complex forms, then, will evolve more rapidly and easily in uncertain environments when they are built upon stable intermediate forms. The number of component elements, the span of the intermediate forms, the number of levels, and the frequency of disruptions determine the likelihood that a complex form will evolve. Simon points out that the principle of hierarchy has an analogue at the level of organizational decision-making. Problem solving typically involves selective trial and error, and cues that indicate a partial solution has been reached play the role of stable intermediate forms. Decision makers retain these partial solutions and aggregate them to achieve an overall solution. Without intermediate partial solutions, progress toward a complete solution may well be impossible.

The Importance of Loose Coupling

Using the concept of hierarchy, we see that because complex systems are composed of many subsystems at lower levels of complexity, adaptation to a changing enviroment can only proceed at the pace of a system's component parts. New adaptations to the environment need not involve the complete remodeling of the entire organization, because loose coupling makes units temporarily or partially independent. Successful adaptations in one part of an organization can be safely insulated, and thus not changed further, while other parts of the organization are still adapting. The research and development department of a technologically complex organization may be oriented toward a scientific community whose time perspective is fairly long-run, whereas the marketing department may be oriented toward a consumer community whose time perspective is quite short. These two departments can coexist in the same organization precisely because they are only loosely coupled, and thus each does not have to respond to every adaptation the other makes.

The concept of loose coupling highlights an essential difference between the retention systems of organic as opposed to social systems, with organic systems much more insulated against short-term effects of the environment than social systems. At the organic system level, evolution occurs through natural selection rather than by the inheritance of acquired characteristics, and thus the environment is only loosely coupled to the fundamental form (morphology plus instinctive behaviors) of a species through the experience and acts of any single organism. It takes a long time, involving many generations of a species, for the environment to affect a species's form (Glassman, 1973), as the inability to inherit short-term acquired characteristics partially insulates a succeeding generation from the environment of its predecessor. At the level of social organization, there is something akin to the inheritance of acquired characteristics, as diffusion, borrowing, and socialization spread short-term learned adaptations throughout an organizational population. Thus, insulation of forms from current environmental fluctuations is not complete, and substantial change can occur within the span of a few years.

Weick (1976), building on the work of Buckley (1967), Glassman (1973), and Landau (1969), listed seven advantages of loose coupling for organizations, together with corresponding disadvantages, and several of his points concern loose coupling's evolutionary importance. First, as noted above, loose coupling allows portions of the organization to persist and evolve independently of other parts. This is advantageous for organizational change, as was pointed out in the parable of Hora and Tempus, because if all the components of an organization must come together in a new adaptive state at the same time, the probability of failure in an uncertain environment is quite high. Loose coupling, however, is nonselective regarding what is perpetuated, and may thus permit the retention of archaic traditions as well as adaptive changes. Second, loose coupling provides an organization with a selective sensing mechanism, in the same way that sand is a better medium to display wind currents than rocks. This heightened sensitivity, combined with high variability due to loose coupling (Buckley, 1967), may have the disadvantage of exposing an organization to the influence of transitory fads and fashions in its environment.

Third, as Glassman (1973) argued, loose coupling may be an excellent system for allowing local adaptation of organizational subunits facing environments that in the aggregate pose conflicting demands. Components can adapt without affecting or disrupting the overall adaptation of the whole, but this same characteristic may prevent the diffusion of desired system-wide changes.

Fourth, loosely coupled systems permit the retention of a greater number of mutations and novel solutions than do tightly coupled systems, as they survive in out-of-the-way units or rarely invoked practices. Weick called these protected and little used practices an organization's "cultural insurance" against cyclically changing or repetitive environments because ostensibly useless practices are allowed to persist until they are recalled or reused later. However, loose coupling may inhibit the diffusion of these adaptive practices to other parts of the organization.

Fifth, loose coupling permits the confinement of a breakdown in one part so that it doesn't affect the rest of the organization. A loosely coupled system with some degree of duplication and overlap is relatively immune to the failure of one component (Landau, 1969). A disadvantage of such insulation is that it may be difficult for the other parts of the organization, loosely coupled to the failing component, to assist in its repair or learn of its difficulties in time to take corrective action. Given the tendency of subunit heads to present themselves in the most favorable light, this disadvantage is a potentially serious one.

Sixth, loose coupling may permit greater self-determination by persons in organizational subunits, thus raising levels of involvement and generating a greater sense of efficacy among them. In environments changing in unpredictable ways, the only route to survival may be through granting a great deal of self-determination to members in positions having an immediate grasp of external events. The disadvantage of loose coupling in this case is that members are more or less on their own in contending with possibly hostile environments.

Seventh, a loosely coupled organization could be relatively inexpensive to run, as administrators could save the time and funds that would otherwise be devoted to ensuring tight coupling. However, loose coupling may lead to subunits using organizational resources for activities not desired by central administrators, thus actually increasing an organization's total costs. In the life cycle of most private firms, the founding entrepreneur typically exercises tight control over all aspects of organizational activities in the early stages of growth, moving to loose coupling only after the organization has grown too large for one-person supervision.

The adaptive advantages of loosely coupled systems in changing environments lead to the expectation that most organizational forms are loosely coupled. Loose coupling, combined with hierarchical form, enables simple forms to evolve into complex ones, and Simon (1962) asserted that loosely coupled hierarchies predominate among the complex systems in nature. As the examples should make clear, it would take a long time for a tightly coupled system to develop through natural selection, and given the disadvantages of tight coupling, it should take considerable skill and effort for humans to design tightly coupled organizations. "Loose" and "tight" couplings are, of course, matters of observer judgment, and presently the idea of loose coupling is useful in organizational analysis chiefly as a sensitizing device. Nevertheless, it is a needed corrective to the overly rationalized and harmonious image of organizations that is fostered by many organization theorists and administrators.

Forms of loose coupling.   Loose coupling is present in both an active and a reactive sense in formal organizations. *Active* loose coupling occurs when a subsystem of an organization is more tightly coupled to an environmental sector than other subsystems, and a feedback loop connects environmental conditions with organizational responses. A feedback loop is present when an organizational mechanism for monitoring the environment exists, and when the state of the environment (or intended target of the organization's action) is compared to some desired state by members of the organization. The feedback loop is closed when members of the organization take action to move the organization to the desired position vis-à-vis the environment, and the results of their actions are monitored and compared to the original condition. The cycle repeats until the desired state is achieved, whether it be one of selling a million toothbrushes or converting a million souls.

March and Simon's (1958) concept of the factoring of organizations into subprograms is an example of active loose coupling. Organizations are differentiated into departments and divisions, each oriented to a different part of the environment. There are prepared programs within each unit that are put into operation when a particular stimulus is presented to the division, department, or role by the environment. As programs accumulate, organizations develop a repertoire of activities that follow automatically when evoked by the appropriate cue, as in the appearance of a customer at a sales desk, the delivery of a shipment of raw materials, or the receipt of partially completed work from another department. The existence of performance programs allows organizations to avoid the dilemma of solving thousands of simultaneous equations that would result if each environmental demand required members to build a response from scratch.

In *reactive* loose coupling, an organization does not actively defend itself against the environment, as in the case of the feedback loop in active loose coupling (Glassman, 1973). Instead, certain properties of an organization's structure or activities insulate it from the direct impact of the environment, allowing the environment only limited access to the organization. The example of the method of elections in some nations, presented earlier, is a case of reactive loose coupling, as the impact of short-run economic or political conditions on the government is weakened by the long delay between elections. Reactive loose coupling is adaptive only when environmental pressures can be safely ignored, and active loose coupling is probably a more adaptive long-run structure.

Observing and understanding loose coupling and complexity. How will we really know relatively loose coupling when we see it? Could our attribution of loose coupling to a system simply be a matter of faulty methods, due to our inability to comprehend greater complexity (Weick, 1976)? Simon (1962, p. 977) adopted the position that our world is comprehensible to us because it is composed predominantly of loosely coupled, hierarchical systems: "The fact that many complex systems have a nearly decomposable, hierarchic structure is a major facilitating factor enabling us to understand, to describe, and even to 'see' such systems and their parts." This proposition could, of course, be reversed: If there are complex systems that are tightly coupled and nonhierarchical, then they are unknowable to us, for their complexity lies outside our range of observation and understanding. Powerful electronic computers and modern methods of analysis have given us the ability to simulate and create complex systems undreamed of in the last century, and perhaps someday Simon's proposition will be put to the test.

In searching for loose coupling, several problems confront an observer (Weick, 1976). Our attention tends to be drawn to things that vary the most, and things that vary little thus have low visibility. The most obvious and visible coupling within organizations may not necessarily be the most critical to an understanding of organizational change, especially if the really important events occur infrequently. The remedy for this problem is a thorough immersion into the affairs of the organization, coupled with knowledge of the way things work in other organizations. A second problem arises because people tend to overrationalize their behavior and attribute greater coherence and integrity to remotely connected organizational events than they, in fact, deserve. A great deal of communication within organizations consists of attempts to retrospectively reconstruct rationalizations of recent activities, giving them "meaning" in terms of avowed organizational goals (Silverman, 1970). Observers must be careful not to fall into the trap of taking participants' justifications for their behavior at face value. Detailed knowledge of the context of behavior, and comparative studies that reveal alternative activities that might have been observed, but were not, help an observer to guard against misinterpreting the nature of the couplings examined.

ERROR, CHANCE, AND CREATIVITY

Much of what happens in organizations is neither intended nor foreseen. Error, chance, and creativity play an important role in generating internal variability and hence affect the likelihood that organizational change will occur. Klingsporn (1973) contrasted the rather negative attitude of psychologists toward behavioral variability with the more positive attitude of biologists toward genetic variability. In trial and error learning experiments, psychologists treat the behavioral variability remaining at the end of the trials as an indication that the learning process has not been completed, and thus attitude toward variability as "error" carries over into the other social sciences. In the natural selection model, variability in a species's gene pool, an organism's behavior, or an organization's activities is considered to be a source of potentially adaptive characteristics. We might, indeed, argue that some unpredictable deviations are a good thing in all populations, for the unpredictable variability they make available occasionally permits totally new adaptations to the environment.

"An organism learning is the analogue of a population adapting, but the population is required to maintain a high degree of variability no matter to what ecological niche it has adapted, whereas the organism, when learning, is expected to lose all response variety and become completely uniform" (Klingsporn, 1973, p. 443). Klingsporn argued that an organism that did learn this way would be pathological and unfit, for in totally adapting to current demands, it would become vulnerable to short-range misfortunes produced by a sudden shift in demands. Thus he expects to find variability in the learning process because it is part of the organism's fitness. Because random variability is so important in the adaptability of learning organisms, Klingsporn asserted that this characteristic would itself be positively selected through natural selection. The propensity to vary behavior randomly gives an organism a "pure" source of variability—variability made available regardless of whether it is utilized. "No other arrangement would guarantee a greater potential for adaptability" (Klingsporn, 1973, p. 445).

Do organizations contain any sources of inherent variability? Certainly. They are filled with people, each with an irrepressible tendency toward varied behavior. Whether out of caprice, boredom, imaginativeness, forgetfulness, or just plain malice, people in organizations vary in the way they carry out their tasks over time and occasions. Formalization and standardization of procedures are designed to suppress the more flagrant departures from prescribed practices, and specialization of function plus circumscribed authority limits the impact any one member's deviations can have on an organization. Nonetheless, variability is a prominent feature of modern organization, as witnessed by the high level of employee and customer accidents, injuries, failures, and disasters, as well as malicious types of variability such as sabotage, malingering, and pilferage. Countering these rather negative examples are instances of variability that include humor and joking behavior, individual expressions of creativity and curiosity, humanitarian concern for clients, and heroic risk-taking because of a commitment to altruistic values.

Cataloging all the structural and social-psychological sources of variability would be a major undertaking, and this chapter has a more modest goal of simply reviewing key manifestations of organizational variability: loose coupling; error, chance, and creativity; conflict; and innovation, planned and unplanned. The *source* of random variability is not as important as the simple fact that variability occurs at all, for its presence opens the organization to influence from the environment and increases the likelihood of environmentally induced change.

A focus on error, chance, and acts of God as sources of variability does *not* absolve organization members of the responsibility for the consequences of their actions. Administrators often persist in some dangerous behavior while knowing full well its potentially disasterous consequences: The likelihood that thalidomide caused birth defects was recognized long before the drug was withdrawn from the market, and coal miner's black lung disease was known and recognized for thirty years in the United Kingdom's coal industry but was denied by United States mine operators. External constraints do not rob self-conscious persons of all their freedom, and those who claim so are guilty of "bad faith" (Berger, 1963) in denying responsibility for their actions (*see also* Hughes, 1964).

Chance-Prone Structures: Examples of Anarchy and Creativity

Some organizational forms have a high propensity for variability built into their structures, and accordingly are labelled "organized anarchies" (Cohen, March, and Olsen, 1972). In terms of the definition of an organization given in Chapter 1, organized anarchies can be characterized as having problematic goals or preferences, fluid boundaries, and an unclear technology. The university is the primary example of an organized anarchy cited by Cohen *et al.,* but many voluntary associations, research and development laboratories, and professional service firms (e.g., advertising, law) display similar characteristics. Goals are problematic because the organization operates on the basis of inconsistent and ill-defined preferences, perhaps because sizeable groups of members have very different reference groups and standards as to what the organizations should be doing. Preferences may be discovered after the fact, as members examine yesterday's actions and try to make sense of them.

Boundaries are fluid because participants vary in the amount of time and effort they invest in different activities, being highly involved in some decisions and not at all in others. Technology is unclear because the organization's own processes may not be understood by all members. Cause and effect relations between efforts and outputs may be ambiguous, and so members use simple trial-and-error procedures, applying relevant aspects of past experiences, or anything else that appears to work.

How are decisions made in this form of organization, if there are not consistent, shared goals and substantial participant involvement? The study made by Cohen and his associates suggests that decisions *will* be made, but in such a way as to introduce a very high degree of variability into organizational activities. Decisions are a result of the coming together of four relatively independent occurrences within an organization: the flow of problems, which may arise inside or outside the organization; the flow of solutions, which are lying in wait in the organization, ready to be activated if they are attached to a problem; the flow of participants, who come and go frequently, with variation in participation depending on other demands on participants' time; and the occurrence of choice opportunities, which arise from the demands made on the organization by outsiders or other units in the organization, such as signing contracts, hiring or firing people, allocating funds, or drawing up next year's budget.

These four flows or occurrences are brought together through the conjunction of two organizational structures—the decision structure and the problem-access structure. The term "decision structure" refers to the fact that organizations vary in the extent to which they allow various individuals and levels to make decisions about the organization's problems. At the two extremes, either everyone could be involved in deciding everything, or each person could specialize in only a limited range of decisions. Or, decisions could be ranked by importance, with more important decisions made by the people in higher levels of the organization. Whether the decision structure actually guides the way decisions are made depends, in turn, on the problem-access structure. Problems, which signal the occurrence of a choice opportunity, constantly flow through the organization, gaining access to various positions. Again, at the two extremes, everyone may have access to all problems, or problems may be directed to only specialized positions. Or, problems may be sorted out by level of importance, and then directed to the appropriate level for a decision.

Variability is an inherent property of organized anarchies because of shifting relationships between participants, problems, and solutions. Any given choice opportunity may bring together a completely different mix of decision maker, problem, and solution, depending upon other demands on participants' time, the order in which problems are processed on that occasion, and the availability of a solution. If participants' time is limited so that they can only attend to a few problems at a time, then the continuity normally introduced by having the same person deal with similar problems over time is lost. One of the striking things about universities is the way in which very similar issues are raised year after year, as new cohorts of staff and students enter, but different (temporary) solutions are found. Voluntary associations produce drastically different decisions from meeting to meeting, depending on who attends and which issues manage to find their way onto the agenda. Organized anarchies are not truly anarchies, of course, for there is stability in the decision and problem-access structures. Variability occurs because of the way people, problems, and solutions flow through these structures, and we would expect that monumental decisions would call forth a more stable set of decision rules.

Organizational Disasters

Sometimes the cumulation of random variability, errors, and bad luck leads not simply to organizational change, but to disaster. Turner's (1976) study of three major organizational disasters in Great Britain identified false assumptions, poor communications, cultural lag, misplaced optimism, and a large number of human errors as the factors contributing to disaster. An analysis of accidents in gold mines showed an average of 1.96 human errors per accident, whereas Turner's study found 36, 61, and 50 errors, respectively, in the three disasters. The disasters resulted from a complex tangle of events, aided by the unwitting assistance provided by misused organizational resources. As Turner (1976, p. 395) noted, "small-scale failures can be produced very rapidly, but large-scale failures can only be produced if time and resources are devoted to them."

The first disaster, in Aberfan, occurred when a portion of a coal mine refuse dump slid down into the village in 1966, killing 144 people, including 109 children in a school. The Hixon disaster involved an oversized truck (148 feet long) carrying a large transformer that was slow in clearing a railroad crossing and was hit by a train; eleven people were killed. The third disaster took place in Summerland. A holiday leisure complex of a new design—an open structure of steel frames covered with acrylic sheeting—caught fire with 3,000 people inside. In the ensuing panic, fifty people died. Turner reviewed each case and identified seven common features that precipitated the disasters.

First, rigidities in perception and overconfidence in existing organizational arrangements led people to disregard cues to the impending disaster. In the Aberfan case, industrial practices in the coal industry gave little consideration to refuse dumps, and mine inspectors were quite naturally more concerned with mine safety than with refuse dumps. Second, attention to easily identified minor problems—what Turner called "decoys"—distracted attention away from the really dangerous conditions. In the Hixon case, persons involved were concerned with the problem of taking an extraordinarily long load across a railroad crossing, but their attention focused on the hazard of getting tangled in the overhead electrical wires.

Third, organizational exclusivity and protection of boundaries led organizations involved to disregard complaints from non-members prior to the disasters, when there was still time for remedial action. Members of the focal organizations assumed that outsiders were poorly informed and had nothing to contribute. At Aberfan, the local borough council protested to the British National Coal Board about the danger posed by the refuse dump, but to no avail. Fourth, typical organizational problems of communication and information dissemination were magnified by the ill-structured nature of the problem. At Summerland, two of the most important building materials represented an innovation in construction techniques, and their possible reaction when exposed to fire was not well-understood. Somehow, waivers for their use were issued by the local planning authority.

Fifth, the involvement of strangers at an early stage in the budding disaster exacerbated an already dangerous situation. "Strangers are always located at the moment of danger at a site where they have a number of opportunities to manipulate the situation in ways not foreseen by those designing the abstract safety system" (Turner, 1976, p. 390). At Summerland, fire exits were clogged by parents who were trying to reach children trapped on another floor, in a children's film theater. Sixth, failure to comply with existing safety regulations, either because they were seen as irrelevant or as merely a nuisance to be avoided, made matters much worse than they otherwise would have been. In the Hixon case, the police had received all the information necessary to avert the disaster, yet they failed to act upon it. At Summerland, existing safety regulations governing theaters were simply inadequate to cover the new type of structure being built, and yet no action was taken to devise new regulations. Seventh, in each disaster persons involved minimized the imminent danger, underestimating the potential magnitude of a disaster and underplaying danger signs. At Summerland, the fire was discovered when it was still quite small, but the elaborate fire alarm system was not used.

Most errors in organizational activities do not lead to disasters, but given the resources involved, the potential for a large-scale disaster is ever-present. The disasters reviewed by Turner led to a number of changes in the organizations involved, as commissions of inquiry redefined problems and recommended appropriate precautions against future disasters. The major effect was an elaboration and extension of local and national government regulations to fill the gaps in organizational communication and decision-making revealed by the disasters.

Hermann's (1963) review pointed to similar communication failures occurring *during* crises. Disasters of precisely these sorts are unlikely to happen again; however, by definition, disasters are unusual events, produced by a chain of circumstances unforeseen by participants. The everyday occurrence of errors in organizational performance coupled with chance events will continue to produce occasional organizational disasters (as well as triumphs).

INTRAORGANIZATIONAL CONFLICT

Conflict within organizations is an important source of organizational variation, as disintegrative and independence-generating forces cause schisms between members, departments, programs, and other subunits. Because organizations are the fundamental social units of industrial societies controlling scarce resources and thus the nature of industrialization, conflicts within them are of much greater importance than interpersonal conflicts. Conflict within organizations is over the internal allocation of resources: who shall make the rules governing resource flows, what shall be the content of the rules, and who shall enforce them. Organizations create and hold wealth; allocate income, status, and prestige to their members; and thus affect members' life chances and power in the larger society (Pfeffer, 1977). Unless someone is independently wealthy, his or her ultimate source of wealth consists of payments received from an organization, making organizational affiliation a highly important investment.

Organizations' control over resources, and the consequences of control, makes organizational participation a game of high stakes. Members seek their proper share of whatever resources an organization has to confer, and some theorists have made the contest for control over organizational surplus the corner-stone of their perspective on organizations (White, 1974; Benson, 1977). Two general sources of conflict can be identified: divergent interests of members, and ambiguities in the definition of organizational reality.

The divergent motives of participants, and members' orientations to differing incentives, are major sources of conflict. There are often conflicts over priorities in maximizing values, such as between the values of economic efficiency and social efficacy. Conflicts arise because of the fundamental schism built into the authority structure of business firms: administrators' desires for control versus employees' desires for participation (Dahrendorf, 1959). As long as authorities insist on hierarchical control and limited access to decision-making, employees are likely to resort to strikes, mutinies, and other forms of conflict in pursuit of their goals (Lammers, 1969).

In pursuing their own interests or those of their subunit, participants come into conflict with others who wish to put resources to a different use. University department heads all pursue the goal of university effectiveness, but each thinks that this goal would be best served by the allocation of additional funds to his or her department to hire new faculty, support graduate students, or embark on new research projects (Pfeffer and Salancik, 1974). Construction workers may feel that one of the attractive side benefits of their job is the availability of tools to make repairs to their automobiles, but contractors may feel otherwise. The classic industrial conflict is, of course, that between unions seeking higher wages and employers seeking lower costs and greater productivity (Kornhauser, Dubin, and Ross, 1954; Shorter and Tilly, 1974).

Social movements within organizations, such as *coup d'etat*, insurgency, and mass movements, are important not only for their impact on organizational change but also because of their relationship to the larger trends and politics of societies. As Zald and Berger (1978, p. 825) noted, "struggles for executive office, clandestine product development, student revolts, the seizure of plants, the admirals' revolt or the fight for the control of unions, can be viewed as autonomous events, but such an analysis misses an important point: social movements in organizations are often the situs for the working out of political issues and trends of social change." Ultimately the study of organizational conflict must take account of cleavages and conflicts in organizations' societal contexts.

A second source of intraorganizational conflict is the ambiguity inherent in all complex activities, as persons work on an intersubjectively shared definition of their situation. Order is achieved through a process of negotiation and compromise, with agreed upon meanings of actions and intentions gradually arising over a series of encounters. Within organizations, a negotiated order arises against a context of organizationally defined goals and roles, and participant autonomy is thus fairly heavily circumscribed. There is room for ambiguity, however, because few structures are so well-defined as to meet all possible contingencies. Occupational groups may interpret the same regulations and objectives differently, and interpersonal differences based on ethnicity, sex, age, and socioeconomic origins impede attempts to settle on a single definition of the situation. As Dalton (1959, p. 215) remarked, "however well defined official tasks may be, and however neatly we think we have fitted our personnel to these roles, the inescapably fluid daily situation distorts expected working conditions. Circumstances require various out-of-role and unplanned actions."

Benson and Day (1976) pointed out that there are limits to the application of a negotiated order perspective on organizations, as participants typically are enclosed within constraints limiting the range of activities open to negotiation. Analysts using the negotiated order perspective happen to have chosen organizations for study that exemplify a rather atypical openness to negotiation, such as clinics and hospitals. Other organizations with unclear technologies and fluid participation (those we labelled organized anarchies in an earlier section) also provide wide latitude for participants to redefine major aspects of their work roles. These examples, however, should not blind us to the incontrovertible fact that much of what is "negotiated" in most organizations does not substantially alter their structure or goals.

Factors Producing Interunit Conflict

Organizational structure is both a source of control and communication *and* a mechanism generating variation and conflict. Some properties of organizations that give them their strength also contribute to weakening them. Walton and Dutton, (1969 p. 73) presented an analysis of a number of sources of interdepartmental conflict relevant to the analysis of any two units "that engage in any type of transaction, including joint decision making, exchanging information, providing expertise or advice, and auditing or inspecting." Examination of their scheme permits consideration of the work of several other investigators who have studied intraorganizational conflict.

Mutual task dependence.   Two units dependent upon one another for assistance in the performance of their tasks have a strong incentive to collaborate as well as to engage in conflict when things don't go according to plan. Loosely coupled units in an organization interact rarely, have little effect on one another, and thus have few opportunities for confrontation. Tightly coupled units, by contrast, are greatly aware of one anothers' existence and they realize the significance of each unit's failure to do its job properly. Thompson (1967, pp. 54-56) discussed two types of mutual task interdependence, although he didn't relate them explicitly to the issue of tight or loose coupling. Pooled interdependence is a condition in which each subunit contributes something to organizational performance and is supported in a general way by the entire organization. Coordination occurs through the standardization of procedures and outputs, and the organization is relatively loosely coupled in that each subunit carries on its tasks independently so long as the overall organization remains viable.

Reciprocal interdependence exists when the outputs of each subunit are inputs for others and subunits are symmetrically dependent on one another. This condition approximates tight coupling, and coordination is achieved through a continual process of mutual adjustment. Under conditions of mutual dependence, task overload may exacerbate the problem of scarce resources, leading to bargaining, increased conflict, and a decrease in the time available for cooperative interaction. It is not certain that high mutual dependence will cause high levels of conflict, however, as it may simply lead to increased emphasis on mutual trust and cooperation, depending upon the history of interdepartmental relations.

Task-related asymmetries.   If one unit is unilaterally dependent upon another, or the flow of influence is decidedly one way, prospects for conflict are much greater than in a condition of mutual dependence. Thompson (1967, p. 54) described this as a condition of sequential interdependence, in which one unit must take some action before another can accomplish its tasks. The second is thus dependent upon the first, in a serial fashion, and coordination occurs through planning. Conflict between staff and line employees is often due to the dependent position of staff vis-à-vis the line, as staff members are called upon for advice and assistance and must make an effort to blend their activities into line needs, whereas line employees are not similarly obligated toward staff members (Dalton, 1959). Assembly line operations sometimes lead to this kind of conflict, as one department's shoddy or incompleted work is left for the next department to complete, with the dependent unit in no position to retaliate. In an asymmetrical situation, the dominant unit has little incentive to cooperate with the subordinate unit.

A unit may increase its power over others because it controls critical uncertainties; this proposition forms the core of the "strategic contingencies" theory of intraorganizational power (Hickson *et al.*, 1971). Crozier's (1964) study of the position of maintenance engineers in a French factory found that they had a great deal more influence than would be expected from the official organizational hierarchy. He discovered that the engineers' power was based on their control over the one remaining source of uncertainty in an otherwise very well-understood technological process—the breakdown of machines. Several studies document that subunits acquire power by being the only unit able to cope with an uncertainty posing critical problems for an organization. Pfeffer (1977, p. 257) reviewed these studies and offered some rather cynical advice to subunits seeking to increase or retain their power: "This may be done by destroying sources of information relevant to how the job is done (e.g., the destruction of maintenance manuals as described by Crozier), developing specialized language and terminology which inhibits the understanding of the job by outsiders, and by restricting the distribution of knowledge concerning how the task is accomplished." Presumably a subunit's attempt to increase its power will be resisted by others, thus leading to further conflict.

Performance criteria and rewards.   Since it is difficult for administrators to evaluate the joint performance of two or more departments, performance criteria and rewards usually measure only the unique contribution of a single department. In the abstract this would seem the most equitable method, as it avoids penalizing a unit for the failures of others, but it can lead to conflict if maximizing performance on one criterion impedes the attainment of others. A sales department may wish to emphasize delivery speed and production of products with unique specifications as a means of retaining good customers, whereas the production department achieves maximum economies through long runs of producing identical products (Dutton and Walton, 1966). Dalton (1959) found that staff units were devoted to preserving the controls and regulations they had helped devise, while line units treated controls as bothersome constraints on their ability to respond flexibly to production problems. Organizational administrators have the ability, then, to create reward structures that either magnify or minimize interdepartmental differences.

The attempt to create harmonious structures by combining personnel from several units has spawned a new subfield of organizational development consultants who stress "matrix organizations." A matrix structure involves the assignment of persons to temporary project teams, as well as functionally specialized departments, with teams created on the basis of technical expertise and the need for rapid communication between specialists (Galbraith, 1973). Such structural innovations mitigate the conflict-producing potential of varying departmental reward criteria, but pose another problem of integrating the free-floating specialists back into a departmental home.

Role dissatisfaction.   Members bring a variety of hopes and aspirations to an organization, stemming from occupational socialization, previous organizational experience, and the internalization of cultural values. They sometimes find that the duties and rewards of their roles don't meet their expectations, and while alienation and withdrawal are a possible response, many persons begin searching for opportunities to embellish their roles. As Strauss (1962) pointed out in his study of purchasing agents, some persons in boundary-spanning roles—roles linking an organization to external units—are not satisfied with their subordinate position on the vertical axis of the organization, given their self-evident horizontal location of equality with other roles and departments. Thus, dissatisfied boundary-spanners take the initiative to increase their standing: personnel officers suggest changes in job descriptions before agreeing to post them; admissions or intake staff develop their own criteria of "worthy" applicants (Blau, 1951); and purchasing agents make informal compacts with salespeople from outside firms to push products their firm "really" needs (Strauss, 1962). If members perceive other units or roles as being more highly rewarded than theirs, one response is, of course, to leave the organization; another is to remain and seek allies in fighting to improve matters. Hirschman (1970) called these responses "exit" and "voice," respectively, and I will discuss them in a subsequent chapter on the maintenance of organizational boundaries.

Other sources of interunit conflict.   In addition to mutual task dependence, dependence on common resources can also provoke conflict if the resource is in short supply, as manpower, capital funds, and equipment are likely to be. Some large firms explicitly rationalize this conflict by creating semiautonomous "profit centers" within the firm, which then must negotiate for supplies with other departments, just as an outside company would. Communication obstacles arise through faulty communication channels, lack of a shared vocabulary, and the deliberate withholding of information as a power-gaining tactic. "Information is essential in order to affect any organizational decision. Consequently, secrecy, or the limitation of access to information is used strategically by power holders to enhance and maintain their capability for action in the organization" (Pfeffer, 1977, p. 246). Pettigrew (1972) presented an example of how a manager was able to influence a large-scale capital investment decision by his firm through the control and manipulation of information flowing between departments. By preventing the managers of the systems and programming departments from communicating directly with the firm's board of directors, the head of management services biased the board's decision in favor of the choice he preferred. Conflict magnifies pre-existing communication problems and may lead to an overall reduction in intraorganizational communications (Hermann, 1963).

Some theorists have suggested that internal organizational structure is disrupted by managerial or leadership succession (Gouldner, 1954). Subordinates and other members may react in a way that increases tension and conflict in the organization, for a number of reasons: differing values between the old and new managers, unfulfilled expectations generated by the previous manager's behavior, the decline of informal interaction between subordinates and the new manager, the lack of allies for the new manager to rely upon, and the tendency of subordinates to "test" the new manager. Variability is most likely to be introduced when succession is from the *outside* rather than promotion from within. To the extent these phenomena occur, variation is introduced into the organization and there is the possibility of change (Grusky, 1961, 1969; Guest, 1962; Helmich and Brown, 1972). However, most succession—except to top executives' posts—is quite routine; it is planned to occur at regular intervals and is taken for granted by members.

Summary

Intraorganizational conflict is a primary source of variation within organizations, and many other examples will be presented in subsequent chapters (see Table

Table 4.1   Sources of organizational conflict

General Sources:
1. Divergent motives of participants and members' orientations to differing incentives.

   Examples: Conflicts over setting priorities for goals and values, and over the extent of participation in decisions allowed to lower-level members.

2. Ambiguity in the definition of organizational reality and difficulties in the negotiation of organizational order.

   Examples: Racial and ethnic differences in perceptions of blocked career mobility chances, and occupational differences in perceptions of appropriate standards of quality.

Factors Heightening Intraorganizational Conflict:
1. Mutual task dependence: The tighter the bond between subunits, the greater the opportunity for conflict.

2. Task-related symmetries: The greater the degree to which a subunit depends on another subunit, the greater the tendency for the dominant unit to make demands leading to conflict.

3. Performance criteria with a differential impact on subunits: Criteria that are biased toward rewarding some departments at the expense of others provoke struggles to change the criteria or distort unit performance to meet the criteria.

4. Dissatisfaction with role allocations: If the duties and rewards of organizational roles don't match members' expectations, they may respond by withdrawing, leaving the organization, or organizing to change the established order.

4.1). Organizations are not neutral objects, passively responding to constituents' and members' needs, but rather are powerful centers of resources that are bound to conflict. Some conflicts have a purely personal referent, as individuals seek to improve their relative standing by gaining access to a larger share of organizational resources. Other conflicts, however, involve entire subunits and departments, partly because organizational differentiation incorporates such conflict into the organization and partly because coalitions of vested interests have very different ideas about the uses to which organizational resources should be put. Should more resources be assigned to operating funds in order to pay bonuses to company officers and make lucrative stock options available, or should more be spent on capital investment, raising the value of stockholders' equity? Should the American Civil Liberties Union put more resources into the defense of people accused of "political" offenses, such as flag burning or unlawful assembly, or should it devote its limited resources to collaboration with other organizations in cases involving the defense of the civil rights of blacks? Such conflicts have no obvious resolution, and it is from such tensions that organizational variability springs.

INNOVATION AND VARIABILITY

Innovating organizations may introduce variation into an organizational population by deliberately varying from customary modes of behavior. Innovation, however, need not be a conscious strategy and may be a result of imperfect attempts to imitate other organizations perceived to be successful, as noted by Alchian (1950, pp. 218–19): "While there certainly are those who consciously innovate, there are those who, in their imperfect attempts to imitate others, unconsciously innovate by unwittingly acquiring some unexpected or unsought unique attributes which under the prevailing circumstances prove partly responsible for the success." A continuing cycle of imitation-innovation occurs if other organizations attempt to imitate the unwitting innovator.

Alchian's comment raises a general issue that plagues attempts both to distinguish specific kinds of organizational change from others and to label them "innovations." How does an investigator decide *which* variations are new or different enough from past practices to be called "innovations," and if variation is a central property of all organizations, why bother? Adaptive variations leading to new organizational forms are not based on imitating previous forms, but on the ability to abandon old forms at the "right" time. Participants and organizational theorists sometimes fail to recognize the hit-or-miss nature of the innovation process: "Those who are different and successful 'become' innovators, while those who fail 'become' reckless violators of tried-and-true rules" (Alchian, 1950, p. 218). Fortunately, students of organizational innovation need not rely on the arbitrary and evaluative judgments of participants, for comparative research generally allows us to pick out, *ex post facto*, those variations significant enough to be studied as innovations.

Innovations are products or practices that are new to the organization adopting them, and really significant innovations are those which are new to all organizations of a similar form. There is debate in the field over this definition, as some theorists would reserve the term "innovation" for only the first appearance of a new practice or product, calling subsequent organizations that use the innovation "adopters" rather than "innovators." The spread of an innovation throughout a population represents the *diffusion* of an innovation, and *adoption* is the act of a single organization adapting the innovation to its own use. As with other types of variation, I am less concerned with the ultimate source of an innovation than with its diffusion and adoption throughout a population. In keeping with the ecological model's stress on material conditions, innovations are conceptualized in absolute terms—from the perspective of a knowledgeable observer—rather than in terms of participants' perceptions. No attention will be paid here to the invention process that leads to an innovation's first appearance, a topic covered quite well in Scherer (1970, pp. 346-62).

This brief review focuses on two types of innovations: technological, which are changes in products and production processes; and managerial, which are changes in the activities involved in organizational decision-making (Kimberly, 1978). Most innovations occur within established organizations and require only slight changes in organizational form for their survival. More radical innovations may require either drastic modification of an established form, such as the change from water-to steam-powered factories in the nineteenth century textile industry, or the creation of entirely new forms wholly designed around the innovation, such as the creation of retail photocopying shops in the 1970s. This perspective on organizational change is in its infancy and thus we have no firm guides for drawing the line between innovations-within-forms and innovations-of-forms, except after the fact. This issue is considered again in Chapter 5.

The Diffusion of Innovations

Kimberley's (1978) summary of the literature on managerial innovation identified two categories of factors affecting the rate, pattern, and completeness of the diffusion of innovations: (1) communication processes and the spread of information; and (2) characteristics of the innovation itself, such as cost or risk. Diffusion of innovations between organizations accounts for a large share of all innovations adopted, even by fairly large organizations. Business firms tend to innovate in areas where the potential for short-term profits are clearly visible, and thus the really major innovations—representing a technological breakthrough or with the potential for changing the character of an entire industry—tend "to come from sources other than firms within that particular industry" (Utterback, 1971, p. 80). Between 1920 and 1950, twelve of the eighteen major product innovations adopted by DuPont were created by firms or individuals outside of DuPont (Mueller, 1962). Jewkes *et al.* (1958) and Hamberg (1963) found that a majority of the most significant innovations since 1900 came from outside the large established firms (Utterback, 1971). Karpik (1972) argued that a defining characteristic of advanced capitalism is small innovating firms depending on larger, more heavily capitalized firms to develop and market their innovations. Utterback (1971, p. 84), in summarizing his study of thirty-two innovations developed by firms in the instrument industry, noted that his findings support those of Allen (1967), who found that information about advanced technology is primarily communicated through external discussion courses and technical literature. This communication tends to be through a few individuals who are identified as "technical gatekeepers" within the firm.

Organizations that are part of large, loosely coupled information networks are more likely to have members exposed to news concerning innovations than those in small, tightly coupled networks. Granovetter (1973) pointed out the importance of weak ties between social positions as facilitators of information diffusion. Organizations with strong ties to a small set of organizations may have members who are involved in frequent interaction, but very little new information is generated, as the same opinions are recirculated through the network. Organizations with weak ties to a large set of organizations, by contrast, may have members who see persons in any particular organization only rarely, but there is a greater potential for new information being passed on. New information is more likely to be generated because interaction in loosely coupled networks is, by definition, between organizations that have quite a few nonoverlapping ties to others and thus have access to different information sources. Czepiel's (1977) studies of the steel and electrical utility industries found large communication networks linking technical decision makers who used network contacts for information acquisition, validation, and verification.

Social movements often generate a large, loosely coupled information network within which information spreads rapidly. Political activism in the 1960s spawned the "alternative institutions" movement of the 1970s: small, democratically run retail and craft shops, "free" schools, health clinics, and other organizations with a strong ideological commitment to an alternative future for American society were formed. By making use of interpersonal ties from previous political movements (mainly the antiwar movement), over 15,000 alternative institutions were founded in less than a decade. Diffusion of innovations can thus be linked to the third stage of the population ecology model, retention, as the more widely diffused an innovation, the greater its likelihood of finding a niche and being retained in the population.

Opinion leadership is as important in the diffusion of organizational innovation as in any other social diffusion process (Becker, 1970). The two-step flow theory of the diffusion of political information can be modified to encompass the adoption of an innovation by an influential organization, which in turn is copied by members in other organizations who look to it for leadership. Czepiel's (1974) study of the adoption of the continuous casting process by thirty-two firms in the steel industry illustrates the importance of early adopting firms in the diffusion process. "Early adopting firms were each contacted by an average of 19.5 firms about the innovation, 15.0 of which had not yet adopted the innovation. Later adopters reported that an average of 10.7 firms had contacted them concerning the innovation; however, most of these contacts were from earlier adopters, an average of only 3.2 coming from firms which were to adopt later" (Czepiel, 1974, p. 177). Myers and Marquis (1969) examined over 500 innovations identified by over 100 firms as being their "most important" new products or processes, and found almost one in four were adopted from other firms.

An example of diffusion: Technological change in the machine tool industry.   An important aspect of industrialization is the changing historical role of the capital goods industries, especially that portion of the industry devoted to the production of durable goods. This sector is important because new product innovations and improvements depend upon the ability of the capital goods producers to make a machine that can turn out the new product. Rosenberg (1963), in an analysis of the evolution of the machine tool industry from 1840 to 1910, noted that prior to 1840, machines were made by the firms that used them to produce their final product and there was no separate machine tool industry in the United States. "The growth of independent machinery-producing firms occurred in a continuing sequence of stages roughly between the years 1840–1880. These stages reflect both the growth in the size of the market for such machines and the accretion of technical skills and knowledge (and growth in the number of individuals possessing them) which eventually created a pattern of product specialization by machine-producing firms which was closely geared to accommodating the requirements of machine users" (Rosenberg, 1963, p. 418). An important characteristic of these stages was the continual diffusion of innovations in one sector of the machine tool industry to other firms and industries.

The machine tool industry originated as a response to the requirements of a succession of industries. Machine tool firms were good at making products for their own industry, and their skills were readily transferrable to making machines to solve production problems of other industries. The results of these early attempts at making machine tools for other industries were quite visible, and they led to demands from many growing American industries for assistance. Growing demand allowed shops to specialize in only machine tools and at the same time to focus on a narrow range of products. Machine tool shops no longer had to produce their own finished goods as well as machine tools, and some even moved to concentrating on the production of a single type of machine tool.

Firms in industries producing quite different products nevertheless used highly similar production processes, and this similarity was an important asset to the infant machine tool industry. Even though firms were producing for highly differentiated markets and industries began to vertically disintegrate as markets expanded (firms could specialize in the components of a product, rather than making the entire product themselves), there was still a *convergence* toward the use of similar technology. For example, many industries (firearm, sewing machine, and bicycle producers) had to make use of metal-cutting and -shaping machinery. Two factors were particularly significant in the growth of the machine tool industry during this period. First the *development* of new techniques was assisted by the size of the market for machine tools, which was large because of the similar machine tool requirements of industries producing quite different finished products. Second, the *diffusion* of new production techniques to other industries occurred through a common technological core—the machine tool industry. Diffusion was aided by the concentration of the machine tool industry in the northeastern and north-central sections of United States, with the highest concentration in six industrial states: Ohio, Massachusetts, Connecticut, Pennsylvania, New York, and Illinois.

Diffusion arose from a common technological core because similar problems were encountered by machinery producers for all industries, and once these problems were solved in one industry, the stage was set for the diffusion of the technique to other industries. The machine tool industry became a center for the acquisition and diffusion of new skills and played a critical role in the industrial learning process. The skills and technical knowledge used in the machine tool industry were relevant throughout all machine using sectors, and thus it played an accidental but vital role in the transmission of technological innovations from one industry to another. The development and diffusion of the sewing machine's use is a case in point. "Out of the innumerable modifications of the sewing machine grew the vast boot-and-shoe and men's and women's ready-to-wear clothing industries; and the machine, by 1890, was used extensively in the production of such items as awning, tents and sails, pocketbooks, rubber and elastic goods, saddlery and harnesses, etc., and in bookbinding" (Rosenberg, 1963, p. 430). The sewing machine achieved widespread adoption after 1860 because it was a highly effective machine for performing operations common to many industries, and Rosenberg cites it as a major example of technological convergence.

The universal milling machine is another example of an innovation developed for one industry that diffused quickly through other industrial sectors. It was introduced in 1862 by the Brown and Sharpe Company of Providence, Rhode Island—a company that pioneered other innovations—and was first used to make gun parts. "It was an amazingly useful machine, which would not only cut the grooves of spiral drills but could be employed in all kinds of spiral milling operations and in gear cutting, as well as in the cutting of all sorts of irregular shapes in metal" (Rosenberg, 1963, p. 437). Within ten years, the universal milling machine was sold to manufacturers of hardware, tools cuttery, locks, arms, sewing machines, textile machinery, and locomotives. Some industries were especially fertile in the generation of innovations that would subsequently spread via the machine tool industry. The bicycle industry was the source of a number of technological spinoffs in the last quarter of the nineteenth century, including the improvement of ball bearings; the development of the flat link chain, which could be used for power transmission; and the development of tubular steel, orginially used in bicycle frames. The bicycle industry also furnished the nascent automobile industry with business and technical leadership, workshops and other facilities, and skilled labor, and the decline in the bicycle industry in the early 1900s coincided with the rise of automobile manufacturing.

The Adoption of Innovations

In his review of the literature on managerial innovation, Kimberly (1978) identified three questions regarding the adoption of innovations: (1) Why do some organizations adopt an innovation that others ignore?; (2) Why do some organizations adopt an innovation more rapidly than others?; and (3) Why are organizations selective in adopting some but not all innovations possible in their industry or niche? Asserting that innovations are adopted when participants perceive a *need* for the innovation avoids the questions posed, for members of some organizations perceive a need to adopt an innovation rapidly, while members of other organizations in the same industry (presumably facing the same environment) perceive no urgency in the matter and delay adoption as long as possible. Perception of a need is only one among many factors affecting whether an organization will adopt an innovation, and I argue in Chapter 6 that perceptions may, indeed, be a poor guide to adaptive organizational action.

Three categories of factors affecting the adoption of innovations were summarized by Kimberly (1978), with most of the propositions focusing on individual organizations rather than on populations: the personal characteristics of administrators, managers, and other members; structural characteristics of organizations, such as size or degree of centralization of authority; and relations between an organization and others in its environment. Underlying all the factors affecting adoption is the question of compatibility between organizational structure and activities and the nature of the innovation. In the absence of detailed information on a specific innovation's characteristics, only very general propositions can be formulated about the correlates of adoption.

First, some theories of adoption treat characteristics of administrators and other members as predictors of whether an organization will be receptive to innovations. Professional training, an open leadership style, and a cosmopolitan orientation create favorable conditions for the generation and acceptance of new ideas (Kaplan, 1967; Mytinger, 1968; Becker, 1970). Rational selection models of organizational change emphasize active innovation and search procedures as sources of variation and accordingly give great weight to management education as preparation for innovating administrators. The rational selection model is examined more fully in the next chapter and so a comprehensive discussion of this issue is deferred until then.

Second, some structural characteristics of an organization, such as the degree of centralization or formalization, affect the likelihood that members or subunits will have the autonomy and flexibility required to carry through on the adoption process. Other structural characteristics, such as size and level of organizational slack, affect the probability that an organization will be able to afford an innovation. In a study of 450 hospitals in the United States, Moch and Morse (1977) found that the adoption of innovations compatible with the interests of lower-level decision makers occurred most frequently in large, specialized, functionally differentiated, and decentralized hospitals. Presumably, under these conditions lower-level members had the degree of autonomy necessary to pursue goals compatible with their own interests.

Kimberly (1978, p. 17) argued that the impact of centralization and formalization depends on conditions in the environment: "When environments are stable and predictable, formalization and centralization may be positively related to adoption, while in cases of instability and turbulence, decentralization and non-formalization increase the probability of adoption." Instability and turbulence place heavy demands on an organization's control and communication activities, and greater delegation of authority and loosening of rules is required to allow members to respond to rapidly changing conditions. Stability and predictability allow administrators to follow through on their own plans for innovation, and a high degree of formalization and centralization hastens the implementation of such plans.

The relationship between size (measured by assets or revenues) and innovation is ambiguous, and empirical research does not support our intuitive expectations that larger organizations should be more innovative. Larger firms have *not* been found to spend proportionately more than smaller firms on innovative activity, and in some industries—particularly steel and pharmaceuticals—smaller firms spend proportionately more (Sharp, 1973). Larger firms fare no better than smaller ones in the results of their expenditures, as "the various studies of the determinants of inventive activity have found generally that at best large firms come up with proportionately the same number of inventions, and in a number of industries actually do relatively less, than the medium size firm. This [occurs] despite the fact that the larger sales and cash flow of the biggest firms should make inventive activity more profitable for them" (Mueller, 1972, p. 204). There is also little support for Schumpeter's (1934) thesis of a positive relationship between innovation and monopoly power, as firms in highly concentrated industries don't do consistently better than those in more competitive industries (Sharp, 1973, p. 140). The population ecology model would predict such findings, as firms in monopolistic and hence relatively secure markets are under little external pressure to change and there is a very low turnover rate.

These findings must be qualified in two ways. As a first qualification, we must distinguish between the creation of an innovation, and the production and marketing of the innovation. Karpik (1972) argued that under advanced technological capitalism, characterized by rapid technological change in production processes, smaller firms must turn to larger ones for production and marketing services. When larger firms are unable to acquire an innovation through licensing arrangements or imitation, they are often able to buy out the smaller firm. This sort of "adoption" represents a very different process than the diffusion of an innovation in an environment where all organizations are of roughly equal size.

A second qualification is that the concept of organizational slack may be more useful than size, as it refers to the resources available to be used on new projects without affecting an organization's financial stability. Organizational slack may vary independently of size, and there is no reason to expect that correlations between innovation and size are the same as those between innovation and level of slack resources. Adoption represents a decision about how organizational resources are to be allocated. If organizational slack is present, we can expect a contest for control over its allocation, and thus there may be an association between organizational conflict and innovation. The more visible the consequences of a proposed innovation, the greater the chances that a large number of subunits will be involved in the conflict.

A third set of factors affecting the adoption of innovations is the nature of an organization's relations with other organizations in its environment. In environments where the market for an organization's product is expanding, and where the number of competing organizations is low enough so that the absolute size of market shares is also growing, the frequency of innovation increases (Schmookler, 1966; Enos, 1962). As pointed out in the discussion of diffusion, organizations with links to others that serve as opinion leaders may adopt an innovation in imitation of the opinion leader. Joint ventures and programs are innovations undertaken by mutually dependent organizations when pooling resources for tasks neither could accomplish alone.

Summary of Innovation and Variability

Innovation, whether planned or unplanned, introduces variation into an organizational population. Whether a particular change in structure or activities will be called an "innovation" depends not only on the extent of its departure from previous forms but also on prevailing norms and standards defining "innovation." Thus a major error or disaster may lead to a drastic change in organizational procedures, as happened to the National Coal Board after the Aberfan mining disaster, but few observers are likely to call the disaster's consequences an "innovation." The study of innovation is linked to the more general study of differing organizational forms, especially since the processes involved in the diffusion of innovations can easily be generalized to the diffusion of new organizational forms. The case study of the machine tool industry in the nineteenth century reveals the overlap between these two processes, and an observer would be hard pressed to decide if "innovations" or "organizational forms" were the relevant units of analysis.

Table 4.2   Sources of variability within and between organizations

Loose Coupling: A low degree of constraint between roles, units, or activities within an organization. Active loose coupling is present when a feedback loop connects environmental or intraorganizational conditions with role or subunit responses. Reactive loose coupling is present in the form of buffering and insulating mechanisms that limit the impact of environmental or intraorganizational change.

Error, Chance, and Creativity: Unplanned deviations from prescribed practices that characterize all social systems. Organized anarchies are organizational forms with a low degree of constraint between participants, problems, and solutions. Organizational disasters result from the cumulation of unplanned deviations.

Intraorganizational Conflict: Conflict occurs in the struggle to control the allocation of organizational resources. Divergent motives of participants, conflicting demands on roles and subunits, and the ambiguity inherent in all social behavior produce potential conflict situations.

Sources of Interunit Conflict: (1) mutual task dependence; (2) task-related asymmetries; (3) conflicting performance criteria; and (4) role dissatisfaction.

Innovation: Variation may be a consequence of deliberate attempts to vary from customary modes of action, but some "innovations" are accidental. Innovations have a maximum impact when they diffuse throughout a population and are adopted by many organizations.

SUMMARY

In this chapter, the portrait of organizations drawn by traditional theories of organization has been questioned on theoretical and empirical grounds. Functional interdependence and operating harmony represent one side of organizational life, but in contrast there is also autonomy, variability, and conflict. The tension between these opposing forces may be thought of as dialectical, in the sense that conflict resolution is a temporary condition and the underlying pressures generating variability are unabated, regardless of the motives and interests of participants (Benson, 1977). However, there is no need to appeal to a mysterious dialectic astir in organizations, when we live in a world so filled with error, creativity, luck, and conflict. These forces suffice to explain the irrepressible tendency toward variability characteristic of all organizational structures and activities.

5 Environmental Selection: The Role of Resources and Information

The issue of organizational selection mechanisms, in its simplest form, is sometimes presented as the role of the environment *versus* the role of the humans. It is analogous to the nature-nurture debate over formative influences on child development, and just as fruitless. The more sociologically interesting issue is to determine under what conditions each is most influential, and what questions and explanations are made salient by our awareness of the issue. After presenting the underlying assumptions of proponents of each extreme, I will argue that part of the divergence of views stems from a failure to distinguish a resource from an information view of the nature of environments. This distinction, in turn, is used to classify various perspectives on selection, ranging from pure environmental selection to the exercise of choice by administrators and organizational elites, based on their perceptions of situations.

RATIONAL SELECTION VERSUS ENVIRONMENTAL SELECTION

One way to understand the key issues involved in the study of organizational change is to consider two ideal-typical models of structure selection—a rational selection (learning) model and an environmental selection model. They are isomorphic in terms of their underlying processes, as each is a specific instance of the variation-selection-retention scheme. Differences between them are a matter of emphasis and application regarding level of analysis, sources of variation, the selecting agent, and time frame.

As Perrow (1972) has pointed out, management scientists and traditional organization theorists place great faith in people's ability to learn the proper way to modify organizational structure for maximum efficiency. The level of analysis of traditional organization theory and research is individual units, and these units can be individual members, departments, or organizations. In contrast, the population ecology model is typically applied to populations of organizations, although the model can also be applied to the evolution of single organizations over time.

The rational selection model places heavy reliance on *active* alternative generation and search procedures as sources of variation. Planned variations, such as tactics and strategies in competitive situations, are emphasized, as is the socially constructed nature of organizations. Variations are selected in terms of their fit with a specific criterion, and it is assumed that structural and behavior patterns are selected, discarded, or modified on the basis of their contribution to the organization's goals (Benson, 1971). *Choice* characterizes rational behavior in organizations, and even though there are severe limits to cognitive rationality (March and Simon, 1958), the burden of choice is still on people as decision makers and generators of alternatives. The time frame for such theories and investigations is necessarily short-run, because individuals or single organizations are followed, not successive generations or populations of organizations.

In the population ecology model the source of variation can be any variation-generating mechanism, with no more weight given to planned than unplanned change. I have argued that a great deal of variation is introduced into an organization or population of organizations through error or random variation, rather than through planning or the conscious generation of alternatives. Selection is by virtue of a fit to external criterion, such as the market mechanism selecting identically producing firms under conditions of perfect competition. The environment selects the most fit organizations, and *individual* units are relatively powerless to affect the process. The basis of an organization's selection, or the reasons for the success of particular activities, may be only dimly understood by members, and they will probably attribute their good fortune to their own efforts at rational selection. Lack of knowledge of alternative forms that fail and a tendency to attribute successes to personal competence and foresight biases participants and theorists against giving much weight to environmental selection. The population ecology model does *not* assume that all selection results from the working of an impersonal "invisible hand." Selection criteria may be the result of political decisions influenced by dominant organizations, and faith in the efficiency of the established social order often depends on a person's standing in the socioeconomic hierarchy (Rueschemeyer, 1977; Huber and Form, 1973).

The time frame for analyses of environmental selection is relatively long-run, as populations of organizations are typically the relevant level of analysis and the fate of any particular organization may not have any consequences for the larger population. The possibility of innovations diffusing throughout a population, and of innovations being adopted by organizations modifying their existing practices, means that externally induced change may be fairly rapid. In this case there may be little difference between the time span of an explanation based on the rational as opposed to the environmental selection model.

WHAT IS BEING SELECTED?

Selection pressures may favor or eliminate entire organizations or forms, and the changing population distribution of organizations suggests selection is occurring at this level. Entire industries rise and fall over time, as in the rapid growth of the bicycle industry in the last quarter of the nineteenth century and its eclipse coinciding with the rise of the automobile industry in the early part of the twentieth century. The differing fate of these two organizational forms—one producing human-powered conveyances, the other motor-powered—brought in its stead the growth or decline of many associated forms: those producing ball-bearings, steel cables and chains, tubular steel, tires, and leather upholstery are examples of those that grew. Thus we may theorize about the environmental conditions promoting or inhibiting the spread of entire organizational forms: bureaucratic versus non-bureaucratic, organic versus mechanical (Burns and Stalker, 1961), and capital intensive versus labor intensive organizations.

It is also possible for organizations, as nearly decomposable systems (Simon, 1961), to change at the level of specific activities or components, such as changes in the number of subunits, styles of decision making, or type of control structure. The possibility of decomposing organizations into component parts that may be viable even when detached from the parent organization—such as individual members or coherent subgroups—complicates our analysis beyond the kind used by biological ecologists.

Organizational Forms

If an analysis is undertaken of changes in organizations *qua* organizations, or if we want to examine partial modifications of structure within various types of organizations, we must be able to identify unique organizational forms. Hannan and Freeman (1977, p. 935) suggested that "an organizational form is a blueprint for organizational action, for transforming inputs into outputs," and they listed three *ad hoc* guides to inferring differences between forms: using formal organizational structure, patterns of organizational activity, or normative orders. I suggest that organizational forms be identified by examining variations in the three dimensions used to define organizations: goals, activity systems, and boundary maintenance. These overlap substantially with Hannan and Freeman's suggested criteria, but have the advantage of being tied to a theoretically based definition of organizations, with all of its concomitant deductive properties.

All three dimensions are used to denote organizational forms examined in this book. Goals—the focal product, service, or interest of an organization—are the most common of characteristics investigators use to distinguish unique organizations: bicycle or auto manufacturers, employment security or vocational training agencies, and environmental protection or foreign tariffs lobbying groups are examples. (Simple survival is a fundamental objective of almost all organizations and thus is not helpful in differentiating among organizations.) Activity systems, especially their core technologies, can be used to distinguish between organizations that are bureaucratically or collegially organized; use craft- or assembly-line procedures; and possess loosely or tightly coupled communication networks. Boundaries may be inclusive or exclusive, controlled by organizational authorities or outsiders, and vulnerable or impervious to external pressures.

The qualitative dividing line between established and new forms is difficult to draw, given the slight attention paid to this in organizational research. Attempts at synthetic typologies of forms, combining a large number of properties in multidimensional analyses, have not been notably successful, mainly because the complexity of such typologies obscures more than it clarifies (Pugh, Hickson, and Hinings, 1969; McKelvey, 1975). Rather than go through the exercise of creating yet another typology, I point out the particular organizational form being discussed in specific examples whenever it is not implicit in the other information presented.

Fitness

Organizations competing for resources in the same environments but using different forms vary in their probability of being positively selected. Positively selected organizational forms are more *fit*, vis-à-vis that particular environment, than those not surviving. As selection pressures are also at work in situations where relative effectiveness, rather than survival, is the issue, we can consider more effective organizations as more fit than less effective organizations. In this situation, a number of variations of a form might survive in a niche in the short-run, with some more effective than others. Finally, fitness may be a question of the relative amount of change induced in an organization or a form by environmental selection pressures, in which case those forms or organizations most likely to retain their existing structure can be considered most fit for that specific environment. The term "fit" doesn't imply superiority in any sense other than the specific outcome under investigation. If a particular environment consists of a corrupt political machine opening the bidding on city contracts, then the "fit" firm is the one most free with bribes and special favors (Merton, 1957, pp. 71-82).

Hannan and Freeman (1977) argued that a clear distinction should be maintained between selection involving the selective survival of organizations and selection wherein organizations adapt by assuming a new, more fit, form. Their recommendation to investigators using the population ecology model was to study selection processes in cases where it is unlikely that organizations can ensure their survival by adopting a new form. As the empirical literature reviewed in this book makes clear, however, most research on organization-environment interaction has focused on organizations surviving by adapting, rather than on pure environmental selection. Whether the adaptations achieved represent new organizational forms is problematic, as there are no agreed-upon criteria for identifying qualitative breaks between organizational forms. In any event, we need not be so restrictive at this stage of the field's development.

ENVIRONMENTS AS INFORMATION OR RESOURCE FLOWS

The significance of environmental selection and its effect on organizational change are obscured by confusion and disagreement in the way the term "environment" is used. Two methods of dealing with this problem may be discerned in current theorizing and research on relations between organizations and their environments. One approach relies heavily on theories of perception, cognition, and decision-making, focusing on environments as seen through the eyes of organizational members. The "environment" thus consists of information serving as raw material and acted on by sentient actors. Variation in information about the environment, as filtered through members' perceptions, is the major factor explaining organizational change. A special concern of investigators adopting this perspective is the impact of uncertainty on the ability of organizational participants to make decisions, and on consequent organizational restructuring to cope with uncertainty.

A second approach treats environments as consisting of resources for which organizations compete, with the level of resources and the terms under which they are made available the critical factors in organizational change. The dimensions of environments reviewed in Chapter 3 reflect this view, and the process through which information about environments is apprehended by decision makers is not given much attention. Pure environmental selection arguments, such as the theory of the firm in microeconomics, assume resources are in the hands of a large number of actors whose individual decisions amount to a collective selection pressure against organizational inefficiency. Firms must sell to customers at a competitive price or go under. Modified environmental selection models take into account the concentration of resources in the hands of a few actors and analyze organizational attempts to avoid dependence on or achieve dominance over other organizations.

The following sections review both viewpoints on the nature of environments, and show how each has theoretical and methodological implications for the study of organization-environment interaction. The two views are predicated on different assumptions about the autonomy of actors, on concern with different stages of the process of organizational change, and ultimately on differences regarding the appropriate level of analysis in studying organizations (individuals or aggregates). Theorists leaning toward the rational selection model tend to adopt the "information" view of environments, whereas advocates of the ecological or natural selection model tend to view environments in terms of resources, but there is a continuum of positions between the extremes on each of these two dichotomies. I have not forced the two distinctions—rational versus natural selection and information versus resource view—into one dichotomy, thus permitting the inchoate nature of these competing conceptualizations to remain visible throughout.

ENVIRONMENTS AS RESOURCE FLOWS

From this perspective, the environment consists of scarce resources sought by populations of organizations that compete for as well as share them (Yuchtman and Seashore, 1967). A major difference between resource models is in the environmental dimension labelled concentration-dispersion in Chapter 3. Pure environmental selection models begin with the assumption of dispersed resources, with no environmental elements more important than any other. Modified models incorporate the concept of concentrated resources under the control of a limited number of elements.

Pure Natural Selection Model

The purest form of the resource perspective is found in the natural selection model. The environment contains limited resources. Those organizations achieving a form that is superior to others in permitting the exploitation of a scarce resource will be selected at the expense of the relatively inferior. "From a population ecology perspective, it is the environment which optimizes. Whether or not individual organizations are consciously adapting, the environment selects out optimal combinations of organizations" (Hannan and Freeman, 1977, pp. 939-40). It is the environment that "chooses" among the various alternatives presented to it by organizations, selecting the form best fitting the existing conditions.

Alchian's (1950) discussion of the relevance of the natural selection model to economic theory emphasized a central tenet of the ecological view of organizational change: It is *relative,* not absolute, superiority that matters. Among business firms in a particular industry, realized positive profits are the key to survival, not maximum profits—a firm need not "maximize profits" in order to survive, as long as it does as well as or better than its competitors. Survivors need only be the better fit, not the very best or ideal form for the given environment.

The existence of consistent environmental selection criteria in a situation of limited resources ensures directed organizational change, regardless of *how* organizations meet the selection criteria. An economic environment in which businesses must match costs with revenues allows firms showing a profit to survive, regardless of whether profit was achieved by error, chance, or hard work. Voluntary associations, not subsidized by a parent body, that recruit enough active members to support an office staff and conduct programs that satisfy members will survive, regardless of what *motivated* members to join in the first place. In a purely competitive market, organizations competing for the same resources are pushed toward adopting the same form or perishing. Scherer (1970), however, pointed out that only a minority of industries in the United States operate in *purely* competitive markets, and thus most businesses operate in environments permitting some deviation from a single "best" form.

Although some commentators have chastised organization theory for focusing on small or trivial organizations (Perrow, 1972), most organizations in industrial societies are still small enough to be subject to environmental selection pressures that could induce change. In Chapter 2, I reviewed some figures on the size of businesses in the United States indicating that in 1967, 99 percent of companies employing less than 100 people accounted for about 40 percent of all employment. Expanding markets, increased affluence, and the demand for specialized products and services provide small businesses with economic opportunities that assure the continued importance of this sector of the economy. The Bolton Committee (1971) in Great Britain, investigating the future of small business, found that even in manufacturing (the most concentrated of all industries) small firms were important employers: Small manufacturing establishments accounted for 31 percent of all manufacturing employment in Great Britain, 39 percent in the United States, 51 percent in France, and 54 percent in Japan.

Resource and niches.   In discussing environmental homogeneity-heterogeneity, I noted that two organizational forms can only coexist in equilibrium in the same environment if they depend on different resources, or there are other constraints that limit competition between them. The greater the diversity of resources, the greater the diversity possible in an organizational population. Each distinct combination of resources and other constraints that suffices to support an organization form constitutes a *niche*.

At the present stage of development of the population ecology model, it is doubtful that we can recognize a niche not occupied by an organizational form (the existence of a distinct form confirms the presence of a niche), but in theory unfilled niches do exist, waiting to be entered by some variation on an existing form. Two examples of unfilled niches that were highly profitable for the first forms to enter in the 1970s are (1) home entertainment media, exploited by firms producing electronic video games; and (2) rapid mathematical calculations required as part of office, home, and academic tasks, exploited by firms producing high speed pocket electronic calculators. Once in a niche, organizations with a specific form may hold the niche against competitors by modifying their form, accidentally or otherwise. Unfortunately, the most comprehensive treatment of niche theory in organizational sociology treated the location of new niches and the form of organizations occupying them as a single issue (Hannan and Freeman, 1977). The question of the equivalence of niches and forms thus remains problematic.

The six dimensions of environments presented in Chapter 3 describe the manner in which resources are made available to organizations and thus can be used to identify niches, once the nature of a resource is defined more precisely. Environmental capacity, homogeneity-heterogeneity, stability-instability, concentration-dispersion, domain consensus-dissensus, and degree of turbulence affect the distribution of resources in an environment, and conceivably all but the last dimension (which is a higher order dimension) could be used to *jointly* identify niches. In discussing Emery and Trist's contributions in Chapter 3, I used two of these dimensions, plus turbulence, to portray likely organizational forms that would be selected, given varying combinations of the resource dimensions. There is little point in attempting to do more than illustrate the potential of the concept of a niche in this chapter, for our ability to construct complex typologies exceeds by far the empirical literature available on organizational forms. Nevertheless, a somewhat realistic example from Hannan and Freeman (1977) on generalists and specialists conveys a sense of this line of analysis's potential.

Niches and fitness: An example of generalism versus specialism.   Some organizations are specialists, engaging in only a narrow range of activities, while others are generalists, covering a much broader range of activities. Specialists do well within that narrow band of the environment supplying their resources, as all activities and structures are explicitly oriented toward a specific state of the environment. When the environment is stable and homogeneous, in the sense that any changes represent only slight deviations from previous states, specialists have a selective advantage over generalists. Generalists do less well than specialists within any given range of the environment, but they spread their fitness over a greater number of environmental states and thus are better suited to unstable and heterogeneous environments. Specialists are more fit than generalists within that narrow range of the environment where they compete because they do not need to maintain organizational slack or excess capacity to cope with the possibility that the environment will soon be in a different state. Some specialists may still need to remain flexible within their niche and this could require a form of slack. A manufacturer of specialty goods may be unable to build a plant producing at the lowest per-unit costs because its large scale would make the firm less adaptable to changed outputs. Numerically controlled machines—controlled by preset routines electronically programmed by design engineers—were a significant development in this respect, as they substantially reduced overhead costs for specialized manufacturers.

There are several examples of the excess capacity generalist organizations must maintain in anticipation of future needs. Business firms maintain legal departments even when not in litigation because of the high probability that legal advice will be needed quickly over the course of a year. Although the delivery of babies can usually be assisted by persons with only a minimal amount of professional medical training, hospitals and clinics employ obstetricians and pediatricians in delivery rooms in case an emergency should arise that calls for professional assistance. In the short-run the amount of excess capacity in an organization may look like waste to observers, but such slack is crucial in allowing the organization to weather environmental changes that would cause highly specialized forms to fail.

If we assume that organizations cannot rapidly change their orientation from specialism to generalism and vice versa, then environmental stability and homogeneity jointly determine the fate of the two forms. "Specialists outcompete generalists over the range of outcomes to which they have specialized. . . . As long as the environmental variation remains within that interval. . . generalists have no adaptive advantage and will be selected against. Alternatively, if the environment is only occasionally within the interval, specialists will fare less well than generalists" (Hannan and Freeman, 1977, p. 950). We must know how often the environment moves to a different state (degree of stability) and how different the various states are from one another (extent of homogeneity-heterogeneity). The greater the difference between the various states the environment can assume, the less likely it is that generalists will be positively selected, as they would have to maintain excess capacity for too many contingencies. The more stable the environment, the greater the probability that specialists will be positively selected. It is also likely that an extremely unstable environment, switching back and forth between extremes, will favor specialism. Generalists will do well when differences between environmental states, even though occurring often, are fairly small and thus excess capacity is not an extreme burden on the form.

Note that these propositions are based on the assumption that environmental variation is fine-grained, meaning that the environment switches to many different short-term conditions over the lifetime of organizations. If the environment is *coarse-grained*—typical durations in varying environmental conditions are long-term—then the situation is more complex. Hannan and Freeman presented an analysis of this condition, but it is highly speculative and will only be summarized briefly here. The major difference between the analyses of fine- versus coarse-grained environments is that environments moving between states, differing greatly in their demands on organizations *but* remaining in differing states for a relatively long period, will favor generalists rather than specialists. This occurs because specialists will not encounter their optimal niche frequently enough and long enough to allow them to ride out the shocks produced by environmental instability.

Generalists, however, will survive, although they will do so inefficiently and only by carrying a great deal of excess capacity. A more efficient form would be a generalist that was loosely joined in a manner encompassing various subcomponents, each of which was optimally fit for one state of the environment. Although loosely coupled structures are more costly to operate, they have a selective advantage in unstable, heterogeneous, and coarse-grained environments. The organized anarchies discussed in the last chapter, such as universities, are examples of such forms. Another example is the diversification undertaken by large oil companies as they moved away from specializing in oil products by including natural gas, coal, and uranium in their line of products. Gulf Oil in 1977 projected capital and exploration expenditures of over $3 billion, with $100 million spent on coal and uranium projects in the United States. By creating many subcomponents oriented to different segments of the energy market, oil companies' administrators sought to insulate their firms against environmental variations threatening more specialized organizations. Coping with natural disasters has pushed disaster relief organizations—the Red Cross, police and fire departments, the national guard—into adopting a generalists' loosely coupled structure. These organizations must respond rapidly to a wide variety of disasters and thus use many subcomponents such as field command posts and specialized disaster teams (Barton, 1969).

Environmental instability, decreasing capacity, and organization failure. Aldrich and Reiss (1976) provided an empirical example of the application of the pure environmental selection model to a population of small business organizations. Their study investigated the impact of racial and economic change in urban neighborhoods on the probability of small business withdrawal and on the probability that white shopkeepers would be succeeded by blacks or Puerto Ricans. Data were obtained from a four-wave panel study of 648 businesses in inner-city neighborhoods of Boston, Chicago, and Washington, D.C., between 1966 and 1972. Each sampling area was divided into its component census tracts, and tracts were then classified as representing one of six stages of racial residential succession between 1960 and 1970 (Duncan and Duncan, 1957). The stages ranged from influx (less than 2 percent black in 1970) and low minority population (less than 2 percent black in 1960) stages to stages where blacks and other minorities were the dominant population by 1970, with the final stage labelled "succession," if a population was 97.5 percent or more black in 1960.

Two sets of indicators of environmental capacity were used. First, decreasing capacity in the study areas were reflected in both absolute population loss between 1960 and 1970 (the census years bracketing the survey years), and in declining family income, relative to surrounding suburbs. For all three metropolitan areas median family income *rose* 32 percent between 1959 and 1969, in constant dollars, compared to an average rate of increase of only 8 percent in the inner-city sample areas. This relative loss in median family income, coupled with the

TABLE 5.1   Changes in the racial composition of business owners by state of succession

	Whites Only: Businesses With Same Owner as at Previous Wave (%)			New Owners Who Are Black or Puerto Rican (%)					
Succession Stage	1968	1970	1972	1968		1970		1972	
Influx	74	82	82	10	(21)*	17	(24)	19	(21)
Low minority...............	77	70	76	[1]	(4)	57	(7)	71	(7)
High minority	80	78	79	33	(18)	50	(26)	35	(17)
Majority.....................	78	66	80	50	(8)	80	(20)	83	(12)
High majority	69	72	94	71	(7)	85	(13)	100	(7)
Succession..................	62	59	62	80	(5)	79	(14)	100	(8)
All stages	76	75	80	36	(63)	57	(104)	56	(72)

*The number of cases that the percentage is based on is given in parentheses.

Source: Howard Aldrich and Albert J. Reiss, Jr. "Continuities in the Study of Ecological Succession: Changes in the Race Composition of Neighborhoods and Their Businesses," *American Journal of Sociology, 81,* 4 (January, 1976), p. 854.

declining population of these areas in proportion to other business sites in the metropolitan areas, made these locations less desirable than suburban ones.

Second, environmental capacity was measured in three ways for individual businesses in the sample: median income in a business's census tract in 1960; change in median income between 1960 and 1970, measured by residualizing 1970 income on the corresponding figure for 1960; and profit status of the business in 1966.

The turnover rate for white-owned business was fairly stable over the four waves of the panel, as shown in Table 5.1. At the aggregate level, the proportion of businesses with the same white owner as in the previous panel was remarkably similar, except for areas of high majority succession between 1970 and 1972. Only in the later stages of race residential succession did the rate of leaving (of whites) increase significantly. Major change did occur, however, in the market for available business sites, as white businesspeople no longer viewed racially changing neighborhoods as viable business locations. The percentage of new business owners who were white decreased between 1968 and 1972 through all stages of succession. As shown in the second panel of Table 5.1, by 1972 the market of new buyers of available businesses in the high majority and succession stages was composed entirely of blacks. The same process is observed in residential succession, as whites cease purchasing homes in racially changing areas.

The fairly stable rate of white owners leaving and the increasing rate at which blacks or Puerto Ricans replaced them combined to produce a steady decrease in the proportion of white-owned businesses in all areas. The percent of white owners dropped between 1966 and 1972 from 100 to 94 in the influx stage, and in the

Table 5.2   Changes in demand for small business ownership and in business-site vacancy rate by stage of succession

Succession Stage	All Owners: Available Sites Brought by Profit-Oriented Businesses (%)			Vacant or Nonbusiness Sites (%)		
	1966–68	*1968–70*	*1970–72*	*1968*	*1970*	*1972*
Influx........................	54	60	49	12	12	15
Low minority................	40	39	35	12	23	31
High minority	45	44	26	12	18	26
Majority.....................	29	44	27	18	22	29
High majority	23	31	16	26	33	42
Succession...................	25	45	24	22	25	41
All stages	38	44	29	16	20	28

Available sites include sites vacant at the previous wave as well as those left between waves.

Source: Howard Aldrich and Albert J. Reiss, Jr. "Continuities in the Study of Ecological Succession: Changes in the Race Composition of Neighborhoods and Their Businesses," *American Journal of Sociology, 81,* 4 (January, 1976), p. 854.

remaining five stages from 92 to 75, 82 to 74, 79 to 56, 62 to 57, and 49 to 25 percent, respectively. Already in 1966, historical differences in succession between the six types of areas were reflected in differing proportions of businesses owned by whites.

Only a minority of sites vacated by businesses were reoccupied by new profit-oriented businesses, as shown in Table 5.2, because the limited amount of buying of available business sites by blacks and Puerto Ricans could not absorb the large number of sites vacated. Some former business sites were converted to nonprofit uses, especially by government-sponsored organizations and black-community-oriented organizations, reflecting changes in niches as a result of changing resources constraints. Only during the influx state was the reoccupation rate by profit-oriented businesses sufficient to absorb half or more of the available sites, and in 1972 the remaining stages exhibited a reoccupation rate of about one-third or less. Consequently, vacancy rates rose in all areas, and by 1972 the proportion of vacant or nonbusiness sites was over 40 percent in the high majority and succession stages.

Tables 5.1 and 5.2 show that the business populations of the areas examined were altered under the impact of the changing socioeconomic status and racial composition of residential populations and the decreased functional importance of central city as opposed to suburban business locations. The business population adapted, under environmental pressure, by decreasing in absolute size until it was substantially smaller than when race residential succession began. The business population also changed by undergoing an alteration in industry composition (the distribution of organizational forms) because changes in consumer and

117

labor markets had more of an impact on white-owned retail and service businesses than on predominantly white-owned industries such as construction, manufacturing, or wholesale trade. Consequently, white-owned retail and service businesses decreased in number, not only absolutely but also relative to other kinds of businesses.

The withdrawal of white-owned businesses from particular niches opened up opportunities previously closed to minorities (Light, 1972). In the early states of succession the population of black- and Puerto Rican-owned businesses increased in absolute size and in the later stages it decreased more slowly than the white-owned population, even though the individual failure rate was higher for minority-owned businesses. Most significant was that changes in the industry composition of black- and Puerto Rican-owned businesses occurred in the first four stages of succession because new businesses were being *added* in niches from which whites were withdrawing—consumer goods and retail food sales. From an ecological perspective, the form of organization used by white owners was a more efficient exploiter of resources available in the niches of consumer goods and retail food sales than forms used by blacks and Puerto Ricans, and only when competition from whites was removed did other forms manage to establish themselves. There are historical and institutional reasons why businesses owned by blacks were at a disadvantage (Cross, 1969; Light, 1972).

The study by Aldrich and Reiss of the impact of changing environmental conditons on organizational survival and changes in the distribution of organizational niches is the only large-scale longitudinal study of its kind, and so it is difficult to guage what contribution might be made to the study of organizational change by adoption of a pure environmental selection model. Hannan and Freeman's analysis and hypotheses appear promising, but the costs of conducting comparative longitudinal research on populations of organizations are such that it may be a long time before the benefits of models borrowed from biological ecology become evident. Most studies focus either on single cases or on limited cross-sectional samples.

Interorganizational Dependence and Selection

The pure environmental selection model reviewed above is apolitical in the sense that it does not take account of a prominent characteristic of organizations' relations with their environments—the fact that resources are often not dispersed, but instead concentrated and under the control of other organizations. The resource dependence perspective on interorganizational relations, emphasizing the role of external constraint on organizations' structures and activities, is a useful specification of the means by which environments affect organizational change. A major consequence of competition for scarce resources is the development of dependencies of one organization on others in its environment, with resources sought on the basis of their relevance to the organization's task and technology.

The resource dependence perspective posits that organizations attempt to avoid becoming dependent on others and seek to make others dependent on them, and that the behavior of leaders and administrators is strongly influenced by the attention they pay to interorganizational dependence.

The model of bureaucracy presented in Chapter 1 was described as a more efficient structural form than traditional structures for carrying out large-scale administrative tasks, with this relative advantage accounting for its widespread adoption in modern societies. Specialized roles of coordinating and planning, limited areas of employee competence established for easier training and evaluation, separation of instrumental tasks from purely expressive interests, and other aspects of structural differentiation are often cited in accounting for the ascendance of bureaucracy. This view is incomplete because it ignores the fact that "any judgment about efficiency hinges on a given set of ranked goals and on a given evaluation of alternative means to reach these goals. What is efficient in terms of one preference structure may be wasteful by another" (Rueschemeyer, 1977, p. 5).

A more comprehensive view of the growth of bureaucratization would acknowledge that power and domination exercised by administrative elites and the privileged classes gave them the freedom to implement differentiation in their own interests. "Efficiency" was on their terms, and they were able to disregard the disadvantages structural differentiation visits on lower-level employees: boring, repetitive tasks; no comprehension of how one's work relates to overall organizational objectives; loss of a sense of doing meaningful work; and in general, the proletarianization of labor (Braverman, 1974).

Power and domination's role in guiding selection is not as easy to ignore when the level of analysis shifts to relations between organizations and their environments. The distribution of resources in society and the terms on which they are available are clearly linked to the nature of the economy—whether it be capitalism, state socialism, or a mixed economy—and to the politics of class relations (Giddens, 1973). However, as this book represents just a beginning attempt to lay out a population ecology model, in this chapter I focus only on the immediate context of interorganizational relations rather than on the total political economy of a society.

The concept of dependence, originally developed in the context of explaining power in interpersonal relations (Emerson, 1962; Blau, 1964), was extended to interorganizational relations by Thompson (1967), Jacobs (1974), and others. Emerson (1962, p. 32) defined dependence of an actor A (which may be an individual, group, or organization) on another actor B as "directly proportional to A's *motivational investment* in goals mediated by B, and inversely proportional to the *availability* of those goals to A outside of the A-B relation." If A cannot do without the resource(s) mediated by B, and is unable to obtain them elsewhere, A becomes dependent on B. Conversely, B acquires power over A. Note that dependence is an attribute of the *relation* between A and B, and not of A or B taken in isolation. It is possible that A may be dependent upon B, while at the same time having power over C. Blau (1964, pp. 118-25) extended Emerson's work, deriving four conditions that should foster independence of an actor from others controlling potentially dependence-producing resources: (1) availability and control over strategic resources; (2) existence of alternative sources of the resource; (3) ability to use coercive power, including legal means, to compel provision of the resource; and (4) lack of a need or the possibility of reconciling oneself to doing without the resource.

Going to alternative sources and using control over strategic resources to negotiate for needed resources are the usual means organizations use to avoid becoming dependent upon others in their environment, although the use of coercion is possible under certain conditions. In Chapter 11 I will return to the concept of dependence, but the above brief description should make clear its relevance to the analysis of organizational change. Attempts to avoid dependence or enhance dominance provoke a variety of responses, including the modification of organizational structures and activities.

Levine and White (1961) argued that domain consensus is also an important determinant of the nature of interorganizational relations, but the resource dependence perspective assigns a subordinate role to domain consensus for two reasons. First, if resource acquisition is the dominant force driving interorganizational relations, it is likely that values and sentiments such as "consensus" *follow from* a pattern of interorganizational interaction that has been reached, rather than preceding it (Aldrich, 1976a; 1976b). Second, domain consensus serves chiefly as an ideology to legitimate the entrenched positions of dominant organizations. Warren, Rose, and Bergunder (1974), for example, have shown that domain consensus among social welfare organizations essentially legitimates and protects the domains of the dominant social service organizations in a community. Decision makers' *perceptions* of dependence may still play a part in determining an organization's response to a situation of dependence, and this proposition may be a way of linking the resource view of environments with the information view.

Application of the resource dependence perspective.   There are a number of examples applying the concept of interorganizational dependence to the analysis of organizational change. Benson (1975), extending Aldrich's (1972b) argument regarding the factors producing conflict and cooperation among organizations, proposed a "political economy" model of interorganizational networks. He argued that interorganizational interactions must ultimately be explained at the level of resource acquisition, with money and authority two basic kinds of resources sought by human service organizations. Control of resources in an interorganizational network is implicitly linked to interorganizational power, as a powerful organization can force others to accept its terms in negotiations of disputes or in cooperative ventures. Interorganizational networks, in turn, are affected by environmental conditions, insofar as such conditions affect the supply of resources to a network or change the organizations within the network.

Aiken and Hage (1968) argued that as social service organizations become more innovative, they develop the need for additional resources. Social service organizations typically do not charge clients for their services and have only limited opportunities for incremental state assistance, and so the major way they obtain additional resources is through joint programs with other organizations in the same field. Often this leads to dependence on the other organization, although dependence may be mutual. Aiken and Hage asserted that, as interdependence is established between organizations, internal problems of coordination and control increase. Their study of sixteen health and welfare organizations in Milwaukee indicated that organizations with more joint programs—and thus with a higher degree of interorganizational dependence—were more complex. There is no indication in their report that agency heads or members were aware of the indirect impact joint programs had on their agencies, and certainly we could not argue that agency heads would deliberately seek to restructure their agencies via the route of entering joint programs.

In research on forty-six British manufacturing and service organizations, Pugh and his colleagues (1969) identified several relationships between dependence and organizational structure. Their conceptualization of dependence was not very clear, however, and there were several problems with their measures (Mindlin and Aldrich, 1975). Using the same data set, but relying on an operational definition of interorganizational dependence based on Emerson and Blau's works, Mindlin (1974) was able to show that the higher the dependence on other organizations—excluding the parent organization—the lower the formalization and standardization of organizational structure. Pugh and his colleagues explicitly tried to avoid measures that could be affected by members' perceptions, as they based their data collection procedures on observations that could be corroborated by existing documents. Some of the measures, however, represented only the formally prescribed structure of the organization, following what Wilson (1970) called the "normative paradigm," and thus didn't take account of possible deviations from formal structure.

Much of Pfeffer's research is grounded in the resource dependence perspective, as exemplified in his studies of boards of directors and corporate mergers (Pfeffer, 1972b). In an analysis of the size and composition of boards of directors, he contended that organizations attempt to ensure future survival and growth by establishing favorable relations with other organizations controlling essential resources. Pfeffer (1972a, p. 222) hypothesized that "business organizations (and other organizations) use their boards of directors as vehicles through which they coopt, or partially absorb, important external organizations with which they are interdependent." Although this hypothesis seems to place the initiative in selecting board members in the hands of the dependent organizations themselves, Pfeffer did not analyze the actual process by which members were appointed, and it is possible to argue that the observed pattern of board composition reflects the constraining influence of demands from dominant organizations.

Research and theorizing an organizational change by persons using the resource dependence perspective permits several empirical generalizations. The generalizations are rather weak because they are based on small samples of only a tiny proportion of all possible organizational forms, study designs are typically cross-sectional rather than longitudinal, and there have been practically no attempts at replicating results. First, as interorganizational dependence increases, organizations tend to display a more flexible and open structure, characterized by less formal and standardized procedures, greater decentralization of decision making, and decreased impersonality of relationships. In addition to the studies reviewed, similar arguments were advanced in Burns and Stalker (1961), Hage and Aiken (1970), Haas and Drabek (1973), Sadler and Barry (1970), and Hasenfeld (1972). Second, dependence on external agents that control essential resources, in addition to being associated with a variety of internal changes, is also associated with such interorganizational activities as mergers, joint ventures (Pfeffer and Nowak, 1976), interlocking directorates (Dooley, 1969; Stanworth and Giddens, 1975), and cooptation (Selznick, 1949). As these actions will be examined in greater detail in other chapters, I will mention here only the major issue related to the rational versus environmental selection debate: Some of the investigators studying interorganizational dependence treat these actions as deliberate strategies used by administrators to manage dependence, while others note the pervasiveness of some practices across industries and industrial societies and attribute them to the nature of the environment within which profit-oriented organizations exist. Thus, from the latter perspective, the ubiquity of interlocking directorates and mergers is attributed to the nature of capitalist economies rather than to the wisdom of corporate managers.

ENVIRONMENTS AS INFORMATION FLOWS

From this perspective, the environment is a source of information used directly by decision makers as one basis for maintaining or modifying structures and activities. Structures and activities are indirectly affected because of differences in the way information crosses organizational boundaries. The main concerns of theorists adopting this perspective are with decision processes within organizations and with the conditions under which information is perceived and interpreted by participants. The former concern is a distinguishing mark of the rational selection model of organizational change. Theorists generally assume that decision-making processes are affected by environmental uncertainty and the consequent equivocality of information available to decision makers. This position supplements the perspective on environments as consisting of resources by including the *perception of information* as an intervening link between environments and resulting organizational activities.

The Information Perspective

The information perspective actually identifies a two-step process through which information about environments affects organizations' decision-making processes. In a statistical sense, *uncertainty* exists in environments to the extent that relationships between elements are unpredictable and there is a low degree of constraint between environmental elements. This uncertainty poses a problem for decision makers, but in addition information about environments may be *equivocal* because a source of information is unreliable or because multiple sources provide conflicting information. Unpredictability of environmental elements may be one reason why information reaching decision makers is equivocal, and persons assigned to environmental monitoring roles may increase uncertainty through incompetent or unreliable scanning and filtering (Aldrich and Herker, 1977). Moreover, perfectly reliable sources can still feed uncertainty into an organization by faithfully reproducing, in summary form, the unpredictability of environmental elements. Perhaps such a distinction is meaningful only to an omniscient observer; nevertheless, it alerts us to the fact that information processing and uncertainty pose more complicated theoretical problems than are first apparent.

Some theorists adopt the position that environmental elements—other organizations or individuals—are of no interest in themselves, but are only relevant insofar as information about such elements is attended to by organizational participants. These theorists thus ignore the first stage of the hypothesized two-step flow of environmental information into organizations. Environments, in the work of such theorists, consist of information about environmental elements rather than the characteristics of the elements themselves. At the extreme, this position is a direct challenge to the resource view of environments, as it calls into question the research methodology and causal mechanisms employed in a pure population ecology of organizations. Theorists adopting the information view often acknowledge their debt to the symbolic interactionist perspective in social psychology, asserting that the study of interaction should be from the position of actors themselves, rather than from the *a priori* assumption that persons share a system of culturally established symbols and agreed-upon meanings. Blumer (1966, p. 542) argued that "since action is forged by the actor out of what he perceives, interprets, and judges, one would have to see the operating situation as the actor sees it, perceive objects as the actor perceives them, ascertain their meaning in terms of the meaning they have for the actor, and follow the actor's line of conduct as the actor organizes it—in short, one would have to take the role of the actor and see the world from his standpoint."

Dill (1962, p. 96) was an early proponent of this view in organizational sociology: "It is not the supplier or the customer himself that counts, but the information that he makes accessible to the organization being studied about his goals, the conditions under which he will enter into a contract, or other aspects of his behavior." The environment should be treated as information made available to organizations or to which organizations, via search activity, may gain access. Investigators wishing to understand the process by which information influences organizational activities should examine three factors: the process by which organizations are exposed to different kinds of information, the readiness of participants to attend to and retain information, and organizational strategies for searching their environments. Dill's view of *how* information affects organizational activities followed March and Simon (1958), with information "triggering" preset programs, providing feedback about goal attainment and the efficacy of activities, and being used to evaluate and judge performance. Dill placed heavy emphasis on organizations as information-processing systems and on the way organizations *learn* about their environments. This is not a pure rational selection model, for Dill also stressed constraints on information processing and gaps in the learning process (Dill, 1958).

Weick (1969, p. 28) took a more extreme view than Dill, asserting that organizations "create and constitute the environment to which they react; the environment is put there by the actors within the organization and by no one else. This reasserts the argument that environment is a phenomenon tied to processes of attention, and that unless something is attended to it doesn't exist." There is strong continuity between Weick's position and that of W. I. Thomas (1928, p. 572) who advanced the argument that "if men define situations as real, they are real in their consequences."

Theorists interested in *both* stages of the two-step model of information flow between environments and organizations obviously would not agree with Weick's stand. A complete understanding of the uncertainty-equivocality dilemma requires that we know what potential information decision makers missed—what information they sought and did not seek or have available to them. This knowledge is only possible if an investigator has independent information about environmental elements. Bacharach and Lawler (1976), in their analysis of the perception of power, gave a particularly compelling argument for studying both the objective and the perceived aspects of actors' relations with their environments. Imperfect information and ambiguous cues mean that conflicting parties have a vested interest in managing the impression they make on one another. "By managing impressions of power, persons may feign power capabilities and extract concessions from an adversary greater than would be predicted from objective power capabilities" (Bacharach and Lawler, 1976, p. 123). Research can help investigators determine whether the conditions deemed important by the resource view also affect how persons *perceive* power differences in social interaction. Bacharach and Lawler's analysis found support for seven of eight hypotheses drawn from Emerson (1962) and Blau (1964), thus affirming the cognitive relevance of the resource dependence approach.

As is true of the empirical literature employing the resource dependence approach, research by Dill (1958), Lawrence and Lorsch (1967), Duncan (1972), and others taking an information view of environments permits a few weak generalizations. First, as organizations are confronted with increasing environmental uncertainty due to instability, heterogeneity, or turbulence, more flexibility is observed in their structures and activities. Second, under such conditions, there is some evidence that organizations tend to be more effective if they are more decentralized and specialized, and less formalized and standardized. The research strategy of this group of investigators is generally consistent with their theoretical focus on cognition and perception, as they examine environments through the eyes of participants rather than environmental elements taken *in situ*.

Issues Raised by the Information Flow View

Several methodological and theoretical issues have been raised by research in the past decade treating environments as information. In spite of a growing awareness of organizational constraints on information flow, little attention has been paid to the relation between participants' structural position and their perceptions. The concept of uncertainty is central to much of this work, and yet there is little agreement over how to measure it. Questions about the measurement of uncertainty are linked to the general issue of choosing objective or subjective measures of environmental properties. Finally, it is useful to ask if there are points at which the resource and information views of environments might be brought together in moving toward a more integrated sociology of organizations.

The relationship between social position and perception.   Many large-scale comparative organizational research projects have ignored the questions of whether members in different roles and hierarchical levels in organizations perceive the same organizational reality as other members, and whether relations between characteristics such as subunit size and degree of formalization are the same for all units and levels. These questions were ignored either because investigators treated persons they questioned as informants rather than respondents, or because it was assumed that individual responses could be aggregated into organizational scores if responses were first aggregated by social positions. Blau and Schoenherr (1971), Meyer (1972), Pugh *et al.* (1968), Pfeffer and Leblebici (1973a) and others relied heavily on responses from managers and administrators in providing information on structural characteristics such as size, number of departments, number of hierarchical levels, extent of formalization, and other objective properties. Hage and Aiken (1967), following Hall's (1963) procedures, ascertained structural characteristics in part by questioning each member and then aggregating their responses. They aggregated responses by hierarchical level before summing them to create organization scores. Pennings (1975) and others have simply summed all responses without using any weighting procedures.

There are many organizational properties we would expect all participants to report quite accurately, assuming they were in positions with access to the relevant information: size, number of levels of authority, major aspects of work flow processes, or the adoption of major innovations. Surprisingly, persons in different organizational roles sometimes disagree about these seemingly noncontroversial properties. Moch (1976), studying the adoption of eleven new medical technologies, asked each chief medical officer and chief administrative officer in 450 hospitals whether they had adopted the innovations. "The correlation between the adoption measures based on these independent reports was .78. In addition, the researchers visited 16 hospitals to determine for themselves whether the items were present or absent. The correlations between these observations and the reports of the chief medical and administrative officers were .86 and .75 respectively" (Moch, 1976, p. 666). Aldrich (1976a; 1976b) and Whetten (1974) found that staff members in social service agencies often did not agree in naming the significant organizations they dealt with. Ouchi and Maguire's (1975) study of five retail department stores seemed to show that supervisors and subordinates did not agree on the nature of measures used to control subordinate's behavior.

Lack of agreement between levels and subunits is even more likely regarding characteristics such as amount of influence, communication, or strictness of rule observation (Bacharach and Aiken, 1976). The more differentiated and loosely coupled an organization, and the greater the divergence between the motives and objectives of various factions and interest groups, the more likely it is that an investigator will obtain differing perceptions of the environment from members in widely separated positions (Bacharach, 1978). The impact of environmental uncertainty, for example, should be most strongly felt in an organization's boundary-spanning roles. Following Parsons's (1956) distinction between the institutional, managerial, and technical-operative levels, it is at the top and very bottom of organizations that environmental uncertainties should be most keenly perceived and measured. Resource dependence, however, is a matter of great policy concern because the avoidance of dependence is a driving force in administrators' behavior, and in this instance environmental effects should be manifest at the highest levels of an organization. We might look for such information in questioning members of the board of directors or chief executive officers.

Organizations exist in multi-dimensional and segmented environments, and loose coupling implies that different organizational units and roles are exposed to differing environments. Members can report on the environment their unit faces, but whether they can accurately report on other units' environments (or the whole organization's environment) is problematic. Differential exposure to varying environments compounds the tendency of various factions and interest groups toward biased reporting. Clearly, the problem of disparate perceptions of environmental and intraorganizational characteristics will have to be attended to more closely.

Problems in measuring environmental uncertainty.   Two studies employing the concept of environmental uncertainty captured the imagination of theorists when first published and continue to be widely cited, but both have been harshly criticized for the inadequacy of their concepts and measures. After briefly reviewing the studies, I examine the critiques and suggest that they relate to the more general issue of reliance on participant versus independent reports of environmental characteristics.

Lawrence and Lorsch (1967) examined decision makers' perceptions of environments in three different industries: foods, plastics, and containers. They were interested in the degree of integration and differentiation among production, sales, and research departments, which are three organization subsystems. They found that the more diversification perceived between the environments facing each of the three subsystems, and the more instability perceived, the greater the internal organizational differentiation required between the subsystems to achieve a high level of performance. Internal differentiation was not enough, however, to achieve effectiveness. Explicit integration subsystems that maintained organizational unity of effort were a precondition for effective performance in heterogeneous and unstable environments. Lawrence and Lorsch interpreted their findings as showing that when decision makers perceive their environments as unstable and uncertain, their organizations are more effective if they are less formalized, decentralized, and have a personal orientation in inter-member contracts. Under conditions of perceived certainty, however, a more formalized, centralized, and standardized structure will suffice.

Duncan's (1972) approach was similar to Lawrence and Lorsch in that he also relied on members' perceptions rather than objective indicators and was concerned with the structural arrangements of subunits rather than organizations as wholes. His unit of analysis was an organizational decision unit, defined as "a formally specified work group within the organization under a supervisor charged with a formally defined set of responsibilities directed toward the attainment of the goals of the organization" (Duncan, 1972, p. 313). The sample consisted of ten decision units in three manufacturing firms and twelve decision units in three research and development organizations. Units' environments were characterized as either internal or external and as composed of two basic dimensions: simple-complex, and static-dynamic, corresponding roughly to the homogeneity-heterogeneity and stable-unstable dimensions presented in Chapter 3. Both dimensions, interactively, were proposed to affect the extent to which unit members would perceive their environments as uncertain, ranging from low-perceived uncertainty under homogeneous and stable conditions to high-perceived uncertainty under heterogeneous and unstable conditions, and his analysis supported this hypothesis. He also concluded that the stable-unstable dimension was more important than the homogeneous-heterogeneous dimension.

Hall (1968) raised the first criticisms of Lawrence and Lorsch's study, pointing out that they provided no information on the causal mechanisms by which environmental influences entered organizations. In their research design they also failed to take account of other environmental pressures, original differences in structure between the firms studied, historical factors in the development of the firms, and intraindustry differences in orientation and practice. As Lawrence and Lorsch (1973) pointed out in reply to their critics, they conducted a clinical study rather than a highly quantitative, rigorously controlled field study, and their conclusions owe as much to their clinical and professional insight as to the rudimentary data analysis presented.

Tosi, Aldag, and Storey (1973) attacked the instruments Lawrence and Lorsch used to measure uncertainty, arguing that they were methodologically inadequate. They attempted to replicate the study by administering Lawrence and Lorsch's questionnaire to a group of 102 middle and top level managers who were thought to be extremely knowledgeable about conditions in their industries. The perceptions of these managers were correlated with measures of environmental volatility based on data from firms listed in the New York Stock Exchange over the previous twenty years and on corporate performance data, aggregated to an industry level by weighting firms by their sales volume. Reliability coefficients for the subjective measures of Lawrence and Lorsch were very low, inter-item correlations were low and inconsistent, and only one subscale met Nunnally's (1967) suggested criteria for research instrument reliability. A factor analysis found that three of the supposed subscales did not emerge as coherent subscales.

Perhaps most important was the finding that the scale scores of perceived environmental uncertainty were negatively or nonsignificantly correlated with industry and firm volatility measures: Subscale correlations with relevant objective data ranged between -0.29 and 0.04. Tosi *et al.* (1973, p. 33) argued that "the logic of the contingency approach. . . [is that] the degree of internal uncertainty is a function of external uncertainty. Accepting this position, one would expect at least a positive correlation between internal and external measures of uncertainty."

Obscured in this analysis, and in Lawrence and Lorsch's (1973) reply to it, was the question of which aspect of the "environment" is most relevant to assessing what Lawrence and Lorsch set out to study. Tosi *et al.*, for example, used measures of the volatility of firm outputs (sales and income) but not inputs, which may have been most important for production and research. The central issue is the extent to which organizational structures and activities respond to the types of "objective" environmental uncertainties that are partially captured in the measures of Tosi *et al.* or to the cognitive environment that decision makers spin for themselves out of information brought into the organization.

Duncan's (1972) study has been similarly faulted, but critics have overlooked a problem that the natural selection model's stress on organizational forms and niches highlights immediately. Duncan concluded that organizational type— manufacturing or research and development—is important in understanding environmental uncertainty, but not as important as environmental type. What he didn't ask was whether organizational type (form) was strongly associated with the type of internal environment facing an organizational subunit. There were ten decision groups in the manufacturing firms, and *seven* fell into the simple-static cell of a cross-tabulation of the two environmental dimensions, with *none* in the "dynamic-complex" cell. Of the twelve decision groups in the research and development firms, *seven* fell into the "dynamic-complex" cell and *none* into the "simple-static" cell. These results certainly suggest that organizational form is strongly related to the environment decision groups operate in, and that perhaps organizational form and environmental type were confounded in Duncan's analysis.

Downey, Hellriegel, and Slocum (1975) critically reviewed Lawrence and Lorsch's, as well as Duncan's, research, explicitly noting that we need not assume perceived environmental uncertainty is equivalent to uncertainty in the physical or objective environment. They administered Lawrence and Lorsch's and Duncan's research instruments to a sample of fifty-one division managers in one United States conglomerate. Lawrence and Lorsch's uncertainty measure consisted of nine items, measuring uncertainty in the three subenvironments of marketing, manufacturing, and research and development, with questions on the clarity of information, uncertainty about causal relations, and the time span for the feedback of results. Duncan's measure consisted of twelve items, with six measuring lack of information, five a respondent's lack of knowledge of the organizational consequence of a decision, and one the respondent's ability to assign probabilities for the effects of given environmental factors on organizational success or failure.

Criterion uncertainty measures were created by following Tosi et al.'s procedure, with information obtained from United States Department of Commerce publications regarding predictions about changes in industrial outputs. This was supplemented with information from respondents on perceived number of competitors, and perceived patterns of sales and price volatility. Information from the fifty-one managers was combined into four industry and eleven product groupings, and the average score for these groupings was then used as a criterion score. As in Tosi et al.'s attempted replication, Lawrence and Lorsch's uncertainty subscales failed to achieve acceptable levels of reliability, using Nunnally's alpha coefficient of reliability. Their scales were reconceptualized and Downey et al. created topic- rather than environment-centered scales, with more acceptable levels of reliability achieved. Duncan's subscales were also rescored, and two of the three achieved acceptable reliability levels.

Most distressing to investigators searching for validated uncertainty measures was Downey et al.'s discovery that there were no statistically significant relations between subscales in the revised Lawrence and Lorsch uncertainty subscales; only two of Duncan's subscales were significantly related; and relations between the uncertainty subscales and the criterion measures were either statistically or substantively insignificant, with the highest correlation only 0.24. The four criterion measures were themselves moderately or not at all correlated. Finally, the correlation between the Lawrence and Lorsch and Duncan uncertainty scales was an insignificant 0.14, and even if corrected for attentuation reached only 0.23. Duncan's hypotheses concerning the relation between uncertainty and the two environmental dimensions of stable-unstable and heterogeneous-homogeneous were also not supported.

How can we explain the lack of significant associations between perceived environmental uncertainty and the "objective" criterion measures in the Tosi *et al.* and Downey *et al.* studies? The scales themselves may be unreliable instruments for measuring perceived uncertainty, and it is not clear that it is valid to sum uncertainty scores pertaining to different parts of an organization's environment. The function relating environmental uncertainty to participants' perceptions may be much more complex than the simple linear functions specified by these investigators. The view of intraorganizational variability presented in Chapter 4 suggests that the different roles and subunits may face vastly different environments, and only some members—those in boundary-spanning roles—may have a comprehensive view of external conditions. Downey and his colleagues may well be right in concluding that a disaggregated view of organization-environment interaction, relating specific uncertainties to specific behaviors, is the better research strategy to pursue than that followed in the past. Such research would also take into account the personal characteristics of role incumbents such as tolerance for ambiguity, professional training, and previous experience.

Participant versus observer perceptions.   Sometimes a distinction is made between "hard" and "soft" measures, or "subjective" and "objective" measures, depending on whether information is obtained from participants' own accounts or from impartial observers, written records, or by the use of quantitative indicators that have a commonly agreed-upon validity. This review of the resource and information views of environments should make clear the arbitrary nature of this distinction, for the key issue is the relevance to an investigator's theoretical premises of the type of information obtained. An examination of Pfeffer and Leblebici's (1973a) analysis of the effects of competition on the structures of thirty-eight small manufacturing firms illustrates this point (Mindlin, 1974).

Pfeffer and Leblebici hypothesized that competitiveness increases the demand for control and coordination within organizations: As competitiveness increases, organizations become less specialized, develop an extended hierarchy, become more formalized and less centralized, and have more frequent reporting of subordinates to supervisors. Competition was hypothesized to interact with technology so that technological requirements for increased departmentalization and flatter hierarchies (caused by an increasing number of products and use of large-batch production techniques) would be felt only in situations of little competitiveness.

The results of their analyses were not very clear and in general did not support their hypotheses. Of the hypotheses concerning the direct effects of competitiveness on structure, only those regarding increased frequency of reporting and increased formalization were confirmed. The other correlations were either nonsignificant or in a direction opposite that predicted. Relationships for technology and structure were as expected when degree of competition was controlled, but were clearer when size was controlled.

Perhaps some of these negative findings were caused by a mixing of a resource-flow conception of environments, with perceptual indicators more clearly linked to the information view. Information about the organizations' environments—especially about competitiveness—was obtained using a questionnaire filled out by chief executives of the thirty-eight firms. The measure of competitiveness was based on the question, "What is the extent of competition in your industry?" They were instructed to choose one of the following: "Very high; moderate; low or very little competition." One interpretation of this question by respondents could be in terms of competition faced in selling a firm's products. But the question could also be interpreted to mean competition in general for the entire industry, for techonological advantages, the procurement of resources, or even from the standpoint of the industries' customers. Clearly, these interpretations are not equivalent, as the demands posed by each form of competition are quite different. Competitiveness should have been specified in terms of a specific resource, at the very least. Better still would have been a set of indicators not dependent on the perceptions of chief executives, *if* the focus of the analysis were on resource dependence and its effects on structure. The two views on environments could have been combined if independent information about the firms' environments were collected and used as a check on the quality of an organization's information-processing system, and also on the extent to which chief executives' perceptions actually influenced the restructuring of their organizations.

As Hirsch (1975a, pp. 9-10) pointed out, failure to go beyond the perceptions of managers and executives means that investigators often miss major environmental forces that shape the structures and activities of organizations studied: "When asked by professional consultants, or even the sociologist, to answer questions about their problems at any single point in time, industrial managers often stress issues internal to their organization and/or about which something can be done. . . . To the extent that respondents at the level of the single firm focus primarily on issues relating to their particular company and pass over problems confronting the entire industry (which also affect other organizations as well), this latter class of issues in the general environment must be sought out independently by the detached investigator, *whether or not respondents explicitly point out their existence.*"

Theorists and investigators subscribing to the information view of environments do so because they focus their attention on the level of individual decision makers and occasionally on organizations, rather than on industries, changes in organizational forms, and interorganizational fields. The problem in attempting to generalize from studies using Dill's (1962) or Weick's (1969) perspective to issues concerning the impact of environments on organizations is that the most important characteristics of environments may have been overlooked—the terms on which resources are made available, and the distribution and characteristics of resources in the environment. Perrow (1972, p. 199), for example, pointed out that common interests among large firms may lead to their forming coalitions to further such interests, as in the situation of large oil firms: foreign policy, tax laws, import quotas, government funding of research and development on alternative energy sources, highway expansion, and pollution control restrictions are of major concern to these companies. An analysis of environmental uncertainty in the oil industry must begin with research on the economic and political interests affecting the resources sought by oil firms, and then go on to examine decision makers' uncertainty over some of these issues as one factor in organizational change.

The view of environments as information directs our attention immediately to the role of perception. It posits a two-step flow, with information about environmental elements passing through the filtering out of equivocality, and the filtered information then integrated into the frame of reference of decision makers. The resource view of environments has not really confronted the issue of cognition and perception, either treating the flow of "correct" information as nonproblematic or as irrelevant for explaining how environments affect organizational change. Situations may arise in which a resource is not critical for an organization's survival, but decision makers view it as crucial and act on their definition of the situation. A number of studies have shown how organizations can create and act on myths and collective symbols (Clark, 1972). Such situations can only be discovered if an investigator is alert to the possibility of selective perception and information processing.

COMBINING THE VIEWS: AN EXAMPLE

The dominance of the rational selection model in organization theory, combined with the focus of the prevailing theories on perceptions and decision making, accounts for the paucity of studies using the population ecology model or treating environments as resources. The rapid rise of the resource dependence perspective in the 1970s, incorporating elements from all sides of these issues, is generating studies that will right this imbalance. Until more evidence is available, however, we cannot be sure just what the shape of organizational sociology will be in the future. Nonetheless, it is possible to propose examples of situations where investigators will have to draw on both views of environments to understand organizational change (Aldrich and Mindlin, 1978).

Consider, for example, the relationship between a manufacturing organization and its suppliers of an important raw material. The resource perspective may be brought together with the information perspective to formulate several testable hypotheses. When an organization interacts with others to obtain resources, it may face either an uncertain or certain relation, depending on the stability of the relations it has established with the interacting organization, the assurances the latter provides of supplying the resources, and the effectiveness of its information gathering and interpreting apparatus. Even if assurances are given and a reason-

TABLE 5.3 Combining the resource dependence and information uncertainty perspectives on environments: Conditions affecting organizational responsiveness.

| | | Dependence on Other Organizations | |
		Low	High
Uncertainty in Relations with Other Organizations	Low	**1** Maximum freedom from environmental constraints: lowest degree of responsiveness required (e.g., Large manufacturer dealing with a small number of large suppliers)	**3** Intermediate condition: must give into demands of others, but they are predictable (e.g., Firm agreeing to a long-term contract with a monopoly supplier)
	High	**2** Intermediate condition: freedom to switch to new organizations (e.g., A manufacturer dealing with many small, struggling suppliers)	**4** Minimal freedom from environmental constraints: greatest degree of responsiveness required (e.g., Oil refineries during the 1973 OPEC crude oil embargo)

ably stable relationship exists, the interacting organization still has potential power over the focal organization—the manufacturing firm—because it cannot substitute for the resource nor obtain it elsewhere. Thus, dependence and uncertainty may vary independently of one another, and we can theorize about their joint impact on organizational autonomy and responsiveness. Note that certainty imples neither independence nor dependence—organizations can be certain about their dependence on others, as well as their freedom from dependence.

If the manufacturing firm faces frequent and unpredictable changes in delivery schedules or in prices, uncertainty is heightened. If, in addition, there are only a small number of suppliers, each controlling a significant portion of the available supply, the firm is dependent on its suppliers and its relation with them becomes problematic (see Table 5.3). This is a situation where the focal organization faces both uncertainty and dependence, such as the situation major oil refineries in Western oil importing countries confronted vis-à-vis the OPEC oil producing cartel during the 1973 oil embargo. This type of relationship is likely to draw a considerable amount of attention, although the firm may still have a choice of exactly how to respond (Child, 1972). Stock control systems and purchase procedures may be made more complex and sophisticated, and specialized personnel may be hired to make the organization more flexible. However, management could conceivably decide that flexibility is facilitated by *ad hoc* measures and therefore they should do nothing.

In a situation where uncertainty but not dependence is present, things are not as problematic as the previous case. Lack of dependence gives organizations increased freedom in their operations—an important external constraint is less-

133

ened. A manufacturing firm may have many suppliers of a raw material, with no single supplier controlling the market. Delivery schedules and prices may vary frequently and unpredictably for some suppliers, but the firm is able to turn to others if it has problems obtaining the resource. It is very likely to obtain the material required, especially since suppliers in a competitive market will be eager to acquire new customers. This situation requires a certain amount of attention, but not as much as when both uncertainty and dependence are present. Procedures for seeking new suppliers can be standardized, and decisions can be made in advance at higher levels of the authority structure.

A similar argument can be made for situations where there is dependence but not uncertainty. An organization may rely on a few suppliers for an essential resource and be in competition with many other customers. It is thus dependent on the suppliers, but prices are firm, schedules reliable and known, and hence there is no need to constantly monitor the relationship. Potential use of power by the supplier is not ruled out, but the firm may preempt this possibility in advance by agreeing to a long-term contract that stablizes the supplier's environment. The firm is able, therefore, to rely on reasonably standardized procedures and formally established purchasing rules, without the need for specialists to handle these functions.

The example presented here is based on the hypothesis that an interactive effect exists between uncertainty and dependence, in that the effects of either will be most strongly felt when the other is present. When conditons are certain, or perceived to be certain, dependence is not as critical as when it is combined with uncertainty. There is always the danger, however, that perceptual distortions and errors of interpretation have led to a situation of uncertainty being defined as one of certainty. Uncertain conditions, within limits, are not as problematic in situations of low as opposed to high dependence as there is still the possibility of some autonomous action or of withdrawing from the relationship altogether.

SUMMARY

The rational and natural selection models rest on different assumptions about the malleability of human behavior and the tractability of organizational environments. The former model has dominated organizational analysis, although the institutional school (Perrow, 1972) of organizational sociology has challenged it with case studies of organizational transformation and unintended change. Few organizational studies have employed the population ecology model, but the emergence of the resource dependence perspective in the past decade represents a recognition of the importance of external constraints on organizational change. Part of the halting progress made toward reconciling these two models stems from a confusion over conceptualizing and measuring organizational environments. Environments have been treated as resources for organizational survival and growth or as images in participants' heads. Although at the extremes these two views are identified with the natural and rational selection models, respectively, theorists within these two traditions have not maintained a clear position in their own research. A comprehensive theory of organizational change will undoubtedly incorporate both views of the environment, but while we wait for such a model, competition between them continues to uncover other interesting issues. The role of strategic choice is one such issue, and it is taken up in the next chapter.

6 Strategic Choice: Opportunities and Constraints

Organization theorizing and research in the past decade has, more or less by default, gradually reduced the role of persons as significant decision makers in organizations. Various external constraints have been identified as sharply limiting the role that participants play in selecting organizations' structures and activities. Pure environmental selection and resource dependence models, reviewed in the previous chapter, emphasized the difficulties of accepting the rational selection model's presumption that participants' intentions make a significant contribution to organizational change. Organization size and technology, treated as imposing structural imperatives on organizations, joined environmental constraints as a triology of forces hypothesized to circumscribe prospects for purposively directed change. Child's (1972) ringing rebuttal to these pessimistic arguments, drafted in 1970, defended the concept of choice and introduced a new term—strategic choice—into the literature. Child's argument is reviewed in this chapter, together with examples of the exercise of strategic choice and limits to choice. While strategic choice is possible under certain conditions, I will argue that because of the powerlessness of most organizations, barriers to choice because of interorganizational dependence, and problems in perception and information processing, the opportunities for strategic choice are severely limited. A review of the limits to choice provides additional examples of the retention stage

136

of the natural selection model, as the review identifies sources of resistance to change in organizational forms.

ASPECTS OF STRATEGIC CHOICE

The concept of strategic choice stands squarely in the tradition of the rational selection model, positing that variation and selection are simultaneous processes dependent upon decisions made by organizational participants. Variation involves a rational search for alternative goals and methods of attaining goals, while selectivity is inherent in participants' choosing between the various alternatives. Rather than environments directly impinging on organizational structures and activities, they are mediated by the agency of participants' choices. Child (1972, p. 16) argued that the direct sources of variation in formal structural arrangements are the strategic decisions made by those persons having the power to initiate actions, and that theories proposing an environmental, technological, or economies of scale imperative were one step removed from the actual change process: "They draw attention to possible constraints upon the choice of effective structures, but fail to consider the process of choice itself in which economic and administrative exigencies are weighed by the actors concerned against the opportunities to operate a structure of their own and/or other organizational members' preferences."

Child did *not* assert that environments are "enacted" by participants or that the availability of resources is not a constraint on organizational change. Rather, he was attempting to right what he perceived as an imbalance in the field, whereby theorists were neglecting the wide range of discretion open to decision makers. Child's moderate statement of his position implies that the debate over choice versus constraint is best phrased as the *conditions under which* member discretion can have a significant impact on change and how often such conditions arise.

The concept of strategy is taken from Chandler's (1962) historical study of the evolution of General Motors, DuPont, Standard Oil of New Jersey, and Sears, Roebuck, with strategic decisions defined as those concerned with the long-run health of an organization. Chandler's (1962, p. 16) conception of strategy focused explicitly on the active role participants play in modifying structure:

> *Strategy* can be defined as the determination of the basic long-run goals and objectives of an enterprise, and the adoption of courses of action and the allocation of resources necessary for carrying out these goals. Decisions to expand the volume of activities, to set up distant plants and offices, to move into new economic functions, or become diversified along many lines of business involve the defining of new basic goals. New courses of action must be devised and resources allocated and reallocated in order to achieve these goals and to maintain and expand the firm's activities in the new areas in response to shifting demands, changing sources of supply,

fluctuating economic conditions, new technological developments, and the actions of competitors. As the adoption of a new strategy may add new types of personnel and facilities, and alter the business horizons of the men responsible for the enterprise, it can have a profound effect on the form of its organization.

The limitations to the strategic choice perspective will be taken up later, but two caveats must be noted immediately. First, Chandler's detailed study of four corporations and his cursory examination of more than seventy firms focused exclusively on very large and powerful organizations, not on a cross section of the total business population. Second, external conditions played a very important role in Chandler's explanations of why and how organizations' structures changed, and he concluded that "clearly the market was of overwhelming importance to the changing structure and strategy of American industrial enterprise. The changing American market shaped strategic initial growth, integration, and diversification" (Chandler, 1962, p. 474). Chandler's is certainly *not* a study of environmental enactment.

Strategic choice, in Child's view, is exercised by organizational elites and other members of the "dominant coalition" of an organization. The dominant coalition may be the owners or founders of an organization, but it also may be any other group in an organization that has achieved power through control over critical contingencies or essential resources. This essentially political view of the determinants of organizational activities is introduced to account for how decisions are actually made, given that environment, technology, and size are not totally responsible for organizational change or stability. "The dominant coalition concept draws attention to the question of who is making the choice" (Child, 1972, p. 14). As I noted in discussing intraorganizational variability, the assumption that organizations are highly prized objects of struggle between contending interests is perfectly compatible with an ecological model of organizations, and there can be no objections to this aspect of Child's analysis.

Child raised three arguments to counter the claim that environmental influence is an overwhelming constraint on the ability of participants to influence the course of organizational change: (1) Decision makers have more autonomy than inferred by those arguing for the dominance of environmental, technological, or other forces; (2) organizations occasionally have the power to manipulate and control their environments; and (3) perceptions and evaluations of events are an important intervening link between environments and organizations' actions. These arguments are taken up in the following sections, together with supporting evidence.

Decision Maker Autonomy and Organizational Change

Decision makers may be able to select from a wide range of viable alternatives compatible with the niche they occupy or they can choose to enter a new niche. Hospitals make decisions about what types of patients to serve, trade unions choose certain industries to organize within, and businesspeople choose to enter or leave markets. Using the concept of organizational slack, discussed earlier, Child argued that there usually is slack in operations, with few organizations operating at the limits of efficiency. If, indeed, conditions are such that environmental niches are fairly broad—perhaps because a heterogeneous environment is extremely rich in resources—then there may be a variety of organizational forms that are viable, rather than a single form.

Pennings's (1975) study of forty branch offices of the Merrill, Lynch stock brokerage firm found little support for the proposition that organizational structure was directly related to the degree of perceived uncertainty in the environment. Following arguments reviewed in the last chapter, he hypothesized that environmental uncertainty and heterogeneity would lead to structures that were decentralized and not very formalized. Instead of the expected correlations between environmental and organization structure variables, Pennings (1975, p. 401) found most correlations insignificant or in the wrong direction: "In general the relationships between the information-processing variables, that is, quality of organization intelligence, competition, uncertainty and instability, did not explain the variance in organizational structure." He also found that the goodness of fit between environmental and structural variables had little impact on the effectiveness of the branch offices, as measured by employee morale, anxiety, errors, total production, and changes in production.

One might interpret his results as supporting Child's position that organizations are not tightly bound to their environments and therefore administrators have some freedom in structuring organizations. However, we must use caution in generalizing from this study, as Pennings himself recognized. First, there were only three "objective" measures of environmental variables in the study, and two of them actually had more of an internal than an external referent: Complexity was defined as the relative magnitude of seven classes of transactions that the branch office engaged in for its clients, rather than being based on other possible indicators such as the degree of socioeconomic differentiation in the local population; demand volatility was defined as the amount of change in the number of active customers during 1967-1969, rather than being based on an independent measure of turnover in the local population.

Second, two of the three objective environmental indicators showed significant correlations with structural variables, even if the indicators based on employees' perceptions did not. Thus the greater the complexity of transactions, the lower the degree of centralization and the higher the total level of participation of employees in the operations of the local office. Resourcefulness—measured by an index combining three indicators of the level of economic affluence of an office's domain—was negatively correlated with meeting frequency, participativeness, total level of participation, and the tendency of employees to help one another. Pennings speculated that rich environments create a situation where employees need not feel pressured to produce, thus lowering the necessity of participation and providing assistance to others. This *post hoc* interpretation, if

confirmed in subsequent replications, would certainly lend support to the resource view of environments discussed in the last chapter.

Third, Pennings's sample consisted of forty minor variations on the same
basic organizational form, all using essentially the same technology. Stock
brokerage offices use a mediating technology, with all components of an organization contributing jointly to performance. Thompson (1967) called this "pooled
interdependence" to differentiate it from the sequential interdependence characterizing mass production organizations. Pennings (1975, p. 406) noted that
"perhaps all those organizations that have pooled interdependence are structur-
ally invariant with respect to environmental and technological uncertainty," because extensive collaboration between employees is not essential to effective performance. Moreover, the forty local offices are all linked to a single national
headquarters and thus have limited autonomy to adapt to local conditions.
Freeman (1978) noted that market-related environmental variation (such as variations in stock market prices, volume, and so forth) probably occurs over time
and not across offices. Whether these interpretations are correct cannot be determined unless research is designed to include a sample of heterogeneous organizational forms in varying environments.

Business, marketing, and advertising journals and magazines are filled with
advice for businesspeople on how to give their firm major advantages in the
competitive struggle. Adler (1964, p. 41) made the following observation concerning firms' attempts to achieve a wider range of discretion and gain some autonomy from the pressure of market forces: "A company's definition of itself is
at the root of marketing success. Only the company with unobstructed vision can
use the marketing weapons with maximum effect." He argued that successful
marketers have an underlying philosophy that allows them to generate and follow
through on new ideas that the average firm will not use, or at least not consistently. The traditional marketing strategy was to convince consumers that a company's product served their needs better than products of competing firms, thus
differentiating the company's product from all others. The newer strategy of
marketing segmentation involves an attempt to meet the perceived specialized
requirements of consumers in a disaggregated market.

Market segmentation is a typical strategy used by adult education programs,
which offer courses meeting the widely differing needs of an extremely
heterogeneous client population (Clark, 1956). Voluntary associations often must
choose between the differentiation and segmentation strategies—a highly
specialized association may not recruit enough members to survive, but one that
continually establishes new programs to meet the needs of different subgroups
may find that its overall objectives have been diluted (Aldrich, 1971b; Demerath
and Thiessen, 1966).

Established organizations can use their secure position to pursue strategies
capturing a wider section of the market, or even a new market. Market stretching
is a strategy of introducing new products in slightly different markets, while a

strategy of multibrand entries is a way of saturating the same market, as Bristol-Myers did with a series of differently labelled deodorants: Ban, Mum, Trig, and so on. Brand extension is another strategy for companies that have established brand recognition, as different products are used that captialize on consumer or client loyalty to the brand name. Thus we have Ivory Flakes, Ivory Snow, Ivory Soap, and so forth.

The problem with much of the business and marketing literature on organizational strategies is that it consists of a mixture of description, analysis, sage advice, and *ad hoc* rationalization. From the examples given, which are typically of *successful* firms, it is difficult to know if an investigator could have predicted the outcome *a priori*, or under what conditions a strategy is most appropriate. Adler (1963, p. 50), in contrast to Child, seemed to affirm the separation of variation and selection, as he concluded "what works well for one business will not work for another; what works well for one set of competitive circumstances will not work for another. Also, what works well at one point in time will not work at another."

Performance standards.   Child noted that traditional theories of organization treat performance as an outcome of environmental and structural factors, but that a logically prior question is what determines the particular level of performance an organization aims for. Organizations in highly competitive or demanding environments obviously do not have the luxury of contemplating a lowering of standards, but some organizations do have this option, "given the widespread prevalence of imperfections in the economics of resource allocation and competition, especially for non-business organizations" (Child, 1972, p. 11). Imperfections permit poorly performing organizations to lower their standards of efficiency and still survive. Economists disagree about the precise extent to which business firms in the United States face purely competitive markets as opposed to other types of markets that permit some managerial discretion. Scherer (1970, p. 59) estimated that "there is a modest amount of activity (not more than 6 or 7 percent of gross national product) approximating pure monopoly, most of which is subject to government regulation or control; somewhat more activity approximating pure competition; and liberal quantities of oligopoly and monopolistic competition."

Declining performance levels, if recognized, may lead decision makers to take action in order to bring their organization back to its standard operating level. Child argued, however, that there were two intervening conditions between changes in performance and changes in structure and activities. First, decision makers must believe that there is a relationship between structural arrangements and levels of performance achieved, for otherwise their choices would be irrelevant. Also, they must perceive the source of problems to be inadequate organizational structures rather than incompetent role performances by incumbents. Second, there may be alternative structures and activities that are perceived equivalent in their effects, opening up a choice situation (Child, 1977). Decision makers may also be content with varying levels of performance, as long as it does not drop below a minimally satisfactory level. If decision makers are satisfied with positive rather than optimal or maximum returns, they may decide to use any surplus beyond the satisfactory level on their own preferred projects and not strive for optimum performance.

There is a large amount of literature in economics on the question of whether decision makers in business firms strive to maximize profits, and it cannot be reviewed here (Scherer, 1970). There are some tantilizing findings, however, such as Williamson's (1963) study of the relationship between market power and executive compensation in thirty firms that lead their industries in sales. He found executive compensation was strongly correlated with a firm's market power, suggesting that decision makers had used their discretion to satisfy their own rather than organizational needs.

Organizations in lean environments may make strategic choices that are legally questionable. Staw and Szwajkowski (1975) studied 105 companies on the *Fortune* 500 list involved in possible violations of antitrust laws and the Federal Trade Commission Act between 1968 and 1972. They were attempting to determine what organizational and environmental factors led firms to use illegal strategies. Violations examined included price discrimination, price fixing, conspiracy, illegal mergers and acquisitions, tying arrangements, reciprocity, foreclosure of entry, and monopoly. Environmental capacity was measured by comparing the financial performance of the industry of a cited firm with all industries on the *Fortune* 500 list, thus using "industry" as a surrogate for environmental niche. Financial performance was assessed by using data from five years before a complaint against a firm was made, including mean return on equity, mean return on sales, change in sales, and change in profits. They noted that there were no statistically significant differences in either return on equity or sales between cited firms and their own industries, indicating that industries could be used as suitable units of analysis. The crucial comparison between cited industries and all firms on the *Fortune* 500 list showed that return on equity and sales was significantly lower for the cited industries. The cited industries were rated below average on each of the four financial indicators.

The reason cited firms performed below average apparently was not "because of such internal organizational factors as poor management or internal structure, but because of factors common to the entire industry" (Staw and Szwajkowski, 1975, p. 350). Possible industry-wide problems include shortages of raw materials, strikes and other labor disputes, and declining demand as an industry ages and its products are superceded by those of younger industries. Unfortunately, Staw and Szwajkowski did not test any of these industry-level explanations. They commented that the illegal actions they studied may be chosen by firms operating in low capacity environments where large firms still have some degree of market power, whereas firms operating in lean but highly competitive environments may have no recourse but to intensify their legal competitive practices. This example indicates that Child's idea of the exercise of strategic choice in the face of declining performance may be fruitfully integrated with the concept of environmental constraints from the ecological model. Attempts to gain additional resources from a lean environment, thus reducing organizational uncertainty regarding the maintenance of standards, may lead either to violations of laws about fair business practices or an intensification of normal competitive strategies.

Elite values and administrative discretion.   Selznick's (1957) analysis of leadership led him to conclude that leader discretion is most critical when situations call for critical, as opposed to routine, decisions. Leaders are responsible for managing crucial organizational commitments to members and outsiders that determine an organization's character or distinctive competence. The anthropomorphic notion that organizations have "characters" need not confuse us if we recognize that Selznick was simply referring to the stability of an organizational form and that critical decisions are those having the potential to transform the organization. Effective leadership requires that organizational elites be *aware* of alterations in internal and external commitments and that they have the autonomy to resist changes threatening the stability of the organization's form. Selznick's discussion of the functions of institutional leadership—leadership that self-consciously tries to preserve organizational forms—can be seen as a specification of Child's more abstract argument about the role of dominant coalitions and uses of strategic choice.

Leaders are charged with defining an organization's purpose, and with seeing that structures and activities are infused with this purpose. Robert McNamara redefined the objectives of the United States Department of Defense as not simply waging war with maximum destructive force but as one of waging war systematically and efficiently. His concept of applying cost-benefit analysis to weapons systems was instilled in all subunits, albeit with varying degrees of success. Also, leaders must defend the institutional integrity of the organization, preserving the organization's distinctive identity and avoiding damaging dependencies. As one of the major threats to organizational integrity is a high level of internal conflict, leaders must develop mechanisms to manage intraorganizational conflicts. Lawrence and Lorsch (1967) identified one such mechanism as the development of special integrative roles in firms that bridge the gap between departments otherwise differentiated because of widely differing environments.

Can organizational elites make much of a difference? Hall (1977, p. 264) concluded his review of the literature on leadership with the statement that "it is clear that top leadership is important for the organization as a whole. But we cannot specify how much more or less important, or under what conditions it is of importance when compared with some of the other factors considered, such as the existing organizational structure, informally derived power relationships, pressures from the environment, relations with other organizations, and so on."

Lieberson and O'Connor (1972) attempted to estimate the effect of leadership on organizational performance, net of other factors, by studying the sales, earnings, and profits of 167 large corporations over a twenty year period. They concluded that leadership had little impact on sales or earnings after year, industry, and company effects were taken into account, but that it did have a sizeable impact on profit margins.

Their results are highly suspect, however, because "profit margin" was defined as the ratio of net earnings to sales, and thus they were forced to argue that executives could have influence on a performance *ratio* but not on its components. In terms of their measures, a chief executive wishing to affect profits would have to increase net earnings relative to sales, and it is simply implausible that executives who failed to have an impact on sales or net earnings could nevertheless have an impact on profits. The second phase of their study was also flawed, as they were forced to use thirteen industries rather than individual firms as units of analysis because of data availability problems, and they were thus unable to control for differences in structure, technology, and other characteristics across firms.

Hage and Dewar (1973) explicitly attempted to compare the predictive power of elite values versus organizational structure in understanding organizational change. They searched for the factors associated with program innovation in sixteen health and welfare organizations between 1964 and 1967, measuring elites' values toward change with five questions assessing participants' enthusiasm for change, an evaluation of the need for organization- and community-wide change, and a commitment to the existing structure. Program innovation was positively correlated with the values of the "behavioral elite" group (the executive director and all those members who always took part in decisions). Complexity, decentralization, and low formalization were also correlated with program innovation, but were not highly correlated with elite values.

In multivariate analyses, the indicator of elite values was a slightly stronger predictor of change than was complexity, which was the most important of the structural predictors. The importance of elite values was not diminished when all structural variables were controlled, leading Hage and Dewar (1973, p. 287) to conclude that "elites are not totally determined by the kind of organization they lead, but are able to manipulate their organizations, at least for innovation." It was not possible to explore the exact causal process linking elite values with program innovation, but Hage and Dewar were able to show that elites who favored change were also more likely than others to hire specialized personnel for new projects and to seek new funds, presumably for new programs.

Organizations May Influence Their Environments

Child's second point in support of strategic choice was that organizations are not always passive recipients of environmental influence, they may also have enough power to manipulate and control their environments. Galbraith (1967) asserted that large businesses are able to create demand for their products and control their competitive environments, and Scherer (1970) and others have commented on the anticompetitive tendencies inherent in the structure of many United States industries. Theories of oligopoly were developed by economists in response to the failure of models of pure competition to cover the conditions under which groups of firms acquire the power to alter market parameters. Public and non-profit agencies also have access to a variety of tactics for warding off environmental pressures for accountability and threats to organizational dominance. Perrow (1970, pp. 92-132) cited many examples of organizations neutralizing or overcoming environmental pressures, and in subsequent chapters I present case studies of such adaptations.

If the number of firms in a particular market is small, competition can be regulated through informal interfirm arrangements (Phillips, 1960). Such informal arrangements work best when organizations have similar objectives and similar structures, but they are difficult to maintain when the number of organizations grows beyond ten or fifteen. Semiformal linkages, such as the interfirm movement of executive personnel (Pfeffer and Leblebici, 1973b), can be used when there are more, but still relatively few, organizations to be coordinated. Mergers and joint ventures are likely when more informal mechanisms fail. Organizations seeking to manage uncertainty engendered by a large and heterogeneous population of firms often turn to government regulation or other political interventions in markets.

The Commodity Standards Division of the United States Department of Commerce has issued regulations reducing the number of different products manufactured for a given market and standardizing their characteristics. These standards removed a major obstacle to interfirm collusion by ensuring product standardization, thus making it easier for firms to monitor market sharing agreements and also to indirectly standardize production characteristics of firms in an industry. Public and nonprofit organizations may form clearinghouse associations, review committees, and other centralized structures to reduce the uncertainty otherwise presented in a multi-organizational field (Warren, 1967). Private and public organizations seek assistance of various kinds from governments, ranging from direct financial assistance in the case of social welfare organizations and universities to the protection of businesses' markets from foreign competition through tariffs and quotas.

Governmental support is often a result of joint efforts by many organizations in the same industry. The United States shipping industry has been especially successful in this respect, as vast subsidies have been granted to shipyards and the merchant marine (Harriss, 1961). In 1977, the Federal Aviation Administration guaranteed loans of $61 million for the purchase of ten aircraft by six local service airlines, with Piedmont Airlines receiving the largest loan—$25 million—for the purchase of three aircraft. When world trade conditions put Danish farmers and fishermen in a difficult economic position, they took advantage of government openness and pressed for the establishment of joint pricing, special home-market prices, and the distribution of public subsidies. Agricultural coalitions were quite successful because they worked within the Danish tradition of governmental consultation with special interest organizations, and they also employed well-trained staff members with expertise in negotiating with the government. Cooperative societies of fisheries were less successful, in part because their organizations were less bureaucratized and had no internal staff to seize the opportunities that arose (Buksti, 1976).

Organizational influence: An example.   Hirsch's (1975b) study of the pharmaceutical and phonograph record industries revealed substantial differences in the ability of firms to control or resist environmental forces, particularly in the three areas of pricing and distribution of products, patent and copyright law, and the cooptation of external opinion leaders. Although differing markedly in profitability, the two industries are quite similar in many respects: technologies are highly mechanized around batch production; dependence on external gatekeepers (doctors and disk jockeys) to reach consumers is high; greatest profits come from the sale of new products and there are strong incentives for product innovation; legal environments are extremely complex, built on patents, trademarks, and copyrights; and the development and production of new products involve many stages in a very long sequence. Hirsch obtained information about firms in the two industries by interviewing executives and managers, attending trade association meetings, consulting records of congressional hearings, and reviewing published secondary material.

Large firms in the pharmaceutical industry turned to government legislation for protection when they found their dominant position threatened after World War II by the growing number of companies producing drugs chemically equivalent ("generic") to their own products. In 1954 the large manufacturers formed the National Pharmaceutical Council (NPC), which, in turn, campaigned before state Boards of Pharmacy to have the rules governing drug substitution changed. Traditionally, illegal substitution had been defined as substituting a different *type* of drug for the one prescribed, whereas the NPC argued that substitution should be defined in terms of the *brand name* of the drug prescribed. Thus, if a prescription called for Bayer aspirin, Rexall or Bufferin aspirins could not be substituted. The NPC's campaign was enormously successful, and within eight years, thirty-eight state Boards of Pharmacy had adopted the new definition of substitution. This helped the large pharmaceutical firms to preserve their already captive markets and to substantially increase the costs of entry into the industry for new firms.

The record manufacturing industry was not successful in attempting to retain control over distribution and pricing. The widespread adoption of 33 and 45 rpm unbreakable records, coupled with the United States copyright law *requiring* song owners to license songs to any manufacturer who wishes to record them, created an unmanageable environment. Major manufacturers attempted to sell only through "authorized" distributors, but the growth of the mail-order record business, mass merchandising operations with central purchasing offices, and local high volume dealers specializing in "hit" records were developments they could not legally control. It was comparatively easy for new record manufacturers to enter the industry, and no company could withhold a "hit" song from others wishing to record it. Absolute sales in the record industry grew, but profit margins and profits for firms fell. Some of the largest manufacturers adapted by moving into the mail-order business and by setting up their own chains of record stores. Price competition remains keen in the industry today, and "list" prices on records are only rough guides to what a consumer will pay in a discount record shop.

Patent and copyright protection is a second area in which pharmaceuticals did much better than record companies in influencing important environmental actors. Until the pharmaceutical firms brought pressure on the United States Patent Office to relax its traditional interpretation of the law, no "naturally occurring" substances were patentable, including antibiotics. Prices of antibiotics fell drastically in the 1940s and early 1950s, as new firms entered the production of standard antibiotics such as penicillin, whose price in 1955 was only 6 percent of its price in 1945. Industry representatives argued that patent protection was needed to encourage firms to invest in research and in the development of new drugs, for otherwise there was no economic reward for innovating firms. The large pharmaceutical firms were successful, and the new interpretation allowed firms to patent nearly 2,000 variations on antibiotics between 1950 and 1958, with 6,107 new prescription drugs introduced. "The price differential between patented and unpatented antibiotics produced by the same firms yielded a gross profit of 75 percent or more on patented products, but only 20 percent on the others" (Hirsch, 1975b, p. 335).

Record manufacturers were unable to obtain an exclusive license for recording and promoting a new song, given the provisions of the United States Copyright Act of 1909. While manufacturers must pay a fixed royalty to a song's composer on every recorded version of the song they sell, they are not allowed exclusive rights to it, thus depriving companies of control over the core of their product. Instead, competition between record companies is over particular singers or groups, access to radio air time, and coverage of retail outlets. Record companies and performers lobbied unsuccessfully for a change in the copyright law, arguing "that they were entitled to a performance fee or royalty for the public performance of their product by other profit-seeking organizations" (Hirsch, 1975b, p. 337). Radio stations, however, opposed such claims, for they had access to a "free" product that they could play as often as they chose, without cost.

A third area where pharmaceutical firms were highly successful was the cooptation of institutional gatekeepers, and in particular the American Medical Association (AMA). Pharmaceutical firms and the AMA moved from an adversarial relationship in the 1940s to the complete cooptation of the AMA by the drug industry in the 1960s. During the 1950s the AMA dropped its strict stand on drug advertising in its journals and permitted any drug approved by the United States Food and Drug Adminstration (FDA) to be listed by brand name. The AMA's Council on Drugs was replaced by a committee with more lenient standards, and "between 1953 and 1960, the income of the AMA from advertisements tripled, while revenues from membership dues and subscriptions increased 20 percent; as a proportion of total revenues, income from advertising rose from less than one-third to approximately one-half" (Hirsch, 1975b, p. 338). Hirsch recorded an unusual degree of job mobility between the AMA and the Pharmaceutical Manufacturer's Association, formed in 1958. The AMA also lobbied against new federal legislation that would have given the FDA power to rule on the effectiveness of a new drug and thus control a manufacturer's access to the retail market.

The record industry failed in its attempt to coopt the gatekeepers that counted—radio station disk jockeys. As radio stations lost listeners and advertisers to television during the 1950s, they adopted new formats that included playing more popular music, This amounted to free advertising for those record firms whose records were played, but so many new firms entered the industry and so many new records were released that by 1963 fewer than one-quarter of the newly released 45 rpm recordings were played in any city in the nation. Bribery of radio station staff—called "payola" in the 1950s—was attempted, but competition was too intense, and the payola scandals of the late 1950s closed off that illegal tactic.

Hirsch's analysis documented the pharmaceutical industry's success in controlling its environment and the phonograph record industry's dismal failure, but it did not permit him to answer unequivocally the question of *why* one industry was so much more successful. He suggested that an answer be sought in either functional theory (stressing the greater prestige and societal importance of the pharmaceutical industry), or conflict theory (stressing the larger size of the pharmaceutical industry, which gave it the ability to expend resources on lawyers, lobbyists, and other boundary-spanning personnel to deal with important external agents and agencies). However, there are difficulties with each approach. For our purposes, what is important is the fact that, under certain conditions, organizations have the power to manipulate and control their environments, fending off pressures that others succumb to or are transformed by.

Role of Perception in Strategic Choice

Child's third argument against environmental determinism was that theories stressing the importance of environments have frequently blurred the distinction between characteristics of the environment and the perception and evaluation of these characteristics by organization members. We need to distinguish between "variability and an experience of uncertainty, between complexity and an experience of cognitive profusion, between illiberality and an experience of stress"

(Child, 1972, pp. 4-5). This issue was covered extensively in the previous chapter, in the discussion of the resource and information views of environments, and so it will not be reviewed again here. The distinction is important for strategic choice because if people do not always accurately perceive environmental characteristics, and if perceptions are the intervening link between environments and organizational structure and activities, then the dominant coalition's view becomes stronger. In spite of the importance of this issue, the causes and consequences of the extent to which members accurately perceive their environments has gone largely unexplored. Pennings's (1973) examination of problems in the measurement of intraorganizational characteristics found only minimal correlations between "objective" and "subjective" measures. In the last chapter a review of research by Tosi et al. (1973) and Downey et al. (1975) indicated the same may be the case for environmental characteristics.

LIMITS TO STRATEGIC CHOICE

The arguments raised by Child against the universal applicability and "metaphysical pathos" (Gouldner, 1955) of the environmental selection model are persuasive, but his points also have their limitations. I will argue in this section that opportunities for strategic choice are much more limited than Child's discussion would imply, and that external constraints heavily influence nearly all organization-environment interaction. Three general constraints are examined: (1) constraints on the capacity of decision makers to make optimal choices of new environmental niches; (2) limits on the power of organizations to influence their environments; and (3) the limits to choice implied by a logical extension of Child's distinction between environments and perceptions of environments. The argument is *not* that strategic choice is impossible, but rather that external constraints severely limit its impact.

Constraints on Choosing New Environments

New environments may occasionally be selected by organizational decision makers, but there are significant constraints on the operation of this process. Potential environments may be excluded by law, because of funding restrictions, or by legal barriers to entry. Economists have identified three barriers to entry that prevent potential entrants from gaining a position in a market already served by existing organizations (Caves, 1972). Although developed to explain barriers to entry facing profit-oriented organizations, the arguments can be generalized to other kinds of organizations as well.

Scale economy barriers to entry.   Economy-of-scale barriers exist when an organization's unit production costs remain higher than those of competitors until the organization accounts for a substantial share of the market. Until its costs are competitive, the firm must absorb higher costs and hope that a larger share of the market is obtained before the firm exhausts its capital. Alternatively, a firm could build a large plant of efficient size at the outset and hope to achieve enough market share to dispose of all it produced. Assume, for example, that companies making automobiles experience significant economies-of-scale up to the million automobile point, after which their cost curve levels off and there is little advantage to larger volume. Assume further that the national market for automobiles is four million units, and that four firms split the market, each producing one million autos.

What choice do aspiring auto manufacturers have? First, they can attempt to build an efficient factory at the start (which means making one million units per year), but this means either completely dispossessing a current firm of its market share or knocking each of the present firms down from 25 percent to 20 percent of the market. Could the new manufacturer do this quickly enough to survive? Second, they can begin with a small plant and try to grow, but costs will be higher than competitors' and the new firm will either have to charge more or accept a lower profit margin. Could the new firm ever grow larger?

Scale economies are present in many industries, but two points should be noted. First, scale economies apply primarily to plant size rather than firm size. Bain's (1956) investigation of economies-of-scale factors in moderately to highly concentrated manufacturing industries in the United States found little or no economic gains for large multiplant firms. Second, Bain found that the factor of economies-of-scale could not account for the large size of many major industrial corporations; their size is a consequence of other corporate considerations. Scale economies are typically not great and are achieved at a scale of operations far smaller than that which prevails in many industries. In sixteen of the twenty industries studied by Bain, the percentage of national industry capacity contained in one optimal plant was 6 percent or less. Absolute capital requirements were quite substantial, however, in all but a handful of the industries.

The concept of economies-of-scale can be extended to other forms of organization, as well as to profit-oriented businesses. State and federal legislation may only grant a place on the ballot or allot campaign subsidies to political parties that achieve a given level of self-financing or votes, thus effectively limiting the growth of new political parties. One special issue political party—one concerned exclusively with the "right to life" issue—managed to overcome all the legal hurdles and qualify for federal subsidy of its campaign in the United States 1976 presidential election. Subsequently, representatives of the two major political parties began examining means to raise barriers to new parties still higher. The United Fund requires new applicants for funds to demonstrate the existence of a large market for their services, and universities only subsidize those student associations that are able to demonstrate sufficient student interest. Maintaining a consistently nationally competitive intercollegiate football program is almost impossible except for the two dozen or so universities whose large student body and alumni following, plus geographic location, allow them to generate the huge attendance necessary to fund a competitive program—Notre Dame, Michigan, Southern California, and the University of Oklahoma are examples. Economies-of-scale are also cumulative, in that a winning record and national reputation bring in additional revenue from televised games and post-season bowl appearances.

Absolute cost barriers to entry.   Absolute cost barriers to entry exist when a new firm's costs are higher than those of existing firms, regardless of the firm's output, or when the cost of entry to achieve economies-of-scale or market acceptance is so great as to exclude most potential entrants. Existing organizations may possess knowledge or technology not available to new entrants, perhaps because of patents or the prohibitive expense involved in research necessary to gain the knowledge. Hirsch's (1975b) analysis documented the role of patents in protecting the position of dominant pharmaceutical firms. He also found that when several companies claimed patents on the same new drug, the United States Patent Office allowed them to settle the dispute among themselves to save the time and expense of litigation. Settlement typically took the form of one firm obtaining the patent and then licensing it to the "losers" in the dispute, effectively shutting out other firms from the lucrative profits involved in producing the new drug.

Existing firms may have acquired control over the supply of an important resource, thus denying its use to a new firm. This is especially likely in industries based on minerals or metallic ores, as in copper refining. Until the end of World War II, the Aluminum Company of America maintained its position as the single supplier of aluminum through its monopolization of the bauxite supply. After the war, government aluminum plants that were built at public expense were sold to Kaiser and Reynolds, which were then also able to gain access to bauxite supplies. The aluminum industry is still dominated by these three giants, accounting for about 90 percent of aluminum capacity. In the copper industry, four firms produce 90 percent of United States copper: Kennecott Copper, Anaconda, Phelps Dodge, and American Smelting and Refining.

The amount of capital required to start a new firm may be so enormous as to be prohibitive. Bain (1956) estimated that building an efficient automobile plant would require from $250 to $500 million. It is not surprising that there have been no new major domestic entries into the automobile market. Other minimum capital requirements to build new efficient plants, as of 1950, were as follows: cigarettes, $125 million; viscose rayon, $90 million; distilled liquor, $30 million; and tires and tubes, $25 million (Bain, 1956). At the other extreme, a new flour milling, shoe manufacturing, or meat packing plant could be built for less than one million dollars.

Most local nonprofit associations require only a small amount of resources in their initial stages, and publicly supported organizations and agencies have the vast borrowing power of the state to draw on. New nonprofit associations with aspirations for a national constituency, however, confront sizeable absolute cost barriers. The costs of mounting a national advertising campaign, generally through direct mailings, require such aspirants to seek funding from philanthropic foundations or wealthy individuals. Common Cause, founded by John Gardner, and Public Citizen, founded by Ralph Nader, had the benefit of such support. At the very least, new special interest organizations must turn to sympathetic established organizations in similar niches for mailing lists of possible supporters. Black-oriented special interest associations, such as the National Negro College Fund, the NAACP Legal Defense Fund, and the Voter Registration Project can turn to the NAACP for assistance. American agricultural associations historically have had substantial assistance at their founding from nonagrarian interest groups (Salisbury, 1969).

Product differentiation barriers to entry.   Product differentiation barriers to entry exist when established firms have acheived high visibility and their brands have gained wide recognition. For a new business to enter the market, regardless of the production economies involved, it must spend an enormous amount on advertising to develop brand recognition and market acceptance. The existing competitor need spend only enough to maintain an image developed over a long period of time. The new entrant's advertising expenses give it a cost disadvantage that must be absorbed or reflected in higher selling prices. The new firm could try to compete by spending less on advertising and cutting prices below the established competitors, but it still has to fight to overcome the advantages of the accepted firms. Cutting prices or absorbing extra advertising expenses lower the new entrant's profit margin, and in a competitive market could seal its doom.

Voluntary associations face similar problems, as particular objectives or social issues become identified with particular special interest groups and associations (McCarthy and Zald, 1977). Consider, for example, the problem a new group working in the environmental protection field would have winning members away from the Sierra Club. The new group would have to find some basis for differentiating itself from the established organization. Some special interest groups have achieved such strong public acceptance that they are able to ignore local United Funds (designed to rationalize fund raising for social welfare groups) and go directly to the public with their own campaigns, such as the American Cancer Society, the American Red Cross, and the Muscular Dystrophy Association have done. Many public sector organizations further raise barriers to entry for new organizations by being recognized legally or socially as monopolies for a particular constituency they represent, The National Rifle Association, the American Legion, Veterans of Foreign Wars, the National Council of Churches, and the National Conference of Mayors all enjoy semiofficial status in their lobbying of the United States Congress, and are treated as the representatives of the constituencies they claim in their titles.

Limits on choice of environments—summary. The existence of barriers to entry makes clear organizations' limits to choices of environments. Barriers to entry have a more general relevance for the natural selection model, as they are an example of forces leading to the *retention* of forms in an organizational population. Barriers to entry limit the range of variation in a population and are a negative selective force operating against new organizations and new forms. The higher the barriers to entry, the lower the pressure for change in the structure or activities of existing organizations. Thus, barriers to entry provide a partial explanation of why rates of organizational change are slower in some populations than others. (Large firms are sometimes able to overcome barriers to entry by acquiring a small firm in an industry they wish to enter.)

Child's concept of decision makers exercising "choice" in picking environments appears to be an overstatement of the actual degree of planning and rationality exercised by organizations in moving into new niches. Behavioral theories of the firm assume that decision makers critically examine their environments only when they are under pressure to do so (Cyert and March, 1963) or that the search for new opportunities occurs only when failures or crises occur. These are not the most opportune times to make such momentous decisions as moving to a new niche or merging with another organization. Field studies of managers have found that they often operate on the basis of folk theories or conventional wisdom, taking their environment as given and working within its constraints (Mintzberg, 1973). Even fairly large organizations sometimes make colossal mistakes, such as RCA's short-lived entry into the computer business, IBM's entry into the office copier market, or the United States government's involvement in the Viet Nam War.

Limits to Organizational Influence Over Environments

Child's second criticism of the environmental selection model—that organizations have the power to strategically influence their environments—is true chiefly for the largest organizations or those politically well connected. In Chapter 2, I presented a great deal of evidence documenting that the vast majority of organizations in the United States, and probably other countries, are quite small. The list of business organizations compiled by the United States Social Security Administration shows that only slightly more than 3 percent of all businesses employ more than fifty people. In 1972, about two-thirds of all businesses took in less than $25,000 in receipts, and slightly less than three-fifths of all corporations had less than $100,000 in assets. It is unlikely that businesses as small as these have much power to affect their environments, although this could vary by local circumstances. Many of the examples cited in subsequent chapters concern the attempts of organizations to buffer themselves from environmental pressures, rather than change external conditions.

We must recognize, however, that concentration of resources in fewer large organizations is increasing. There is no denying that the 6 percent of corporations with assets over one million dollars or the 11 percent with sales over one million dollars—accounting for almost 90 percent of all corporate sales—dominate many aspects of life in the United States. Their economic and political power has a major influence on the legal framework within which organizations must adapt. Large corporations managed to pressure the United States Congress into reducing the penalties under the Federal Trade Commission and Clayton Act bills from criminal to merely civil sanctions. This preserved the image of corporations being within the law, while still allowing regulatory agencies to mete out civil penalties, cease and desist orders, and so forth. Comparable organizations in the public sector have similar impacts on social conditions, a situation duplicated in all industrialized nations (Child, 1976).

The issue we must address, however, is whether it is fruitful to build a sociology of organizations on exceptional organizations. Political sociology, theories of state and society, and industrial sociology clearly must make large organizations the center of their analyses. In spite of their unrepresentativeness, large and powerful organizations figure quite heavily in topics covered in this book. Nonetheless, their social, political, and economic significance should not blind us to the fact that the great majority of organizations are not large or powerful. Dominant organizations set conditions of existence for the small and powerless, and they must be incorporated in any analysis of organizational change. Typically, however, they are not themselves the objects of analysis.

Center and periphery firms.   Averitt (1968) made a useful distinction between center firms (those with the power to shape their environments), and periphery firms (those only able to respond to, rather than influence, their environments). Center firms are large in terms of employees, assets, and receipts, they operate in national and international markets, they are diversified and decentralized, and such firms tend toward vertical integration. Cash flows are large and credit is excellent. Decentralization allows top management to concentrate on long-range planning, while lower levels of the managerial hierarchy handle short-range operating problems. Center firms can be recognized by their dominance of key industries. In steel, twelve firms control about 80 percent of the productive capacity in the United States; the electrical industry is dominated by four firms—GE, Westinghouse, RCA, and Sylvania Electric, which is a branch of General Telephone; farm machinery is dominated by three firms; and the petroleum industry is controlled by twenty major producers.

Periphery firms are small, not integrated vertically, and serve local or perhaps regional markets. They produce only a limited range of products, and may be tied in a dependence relationship to a center firm. Management is centralized and lower levels of management are not as competent as those in center firms. Financial problems are paramount, as cash flows are small and credit ratings low, forcing them to pay higher interest than center firms. Management has little time to consider long-range problems, as short-range problems are overwhelming. The bulk of business firms in the United States are, by definition, on the periphery, with little if any prospect of making a significant impact on their environments.

Averitt (1968, p. 16) argued that the largest corporations at the center were virtually invulnerable to attack:

> They present a spongy target to possible attacks by environmental enemies. Their strongest protection against future threat comes from having successfully met past threats. When the demand for a major commodity falters, center firms can concentrate their energies on other products while experimenting with new lines. When a new technology portends revolutionary potential for home industries, center firms use their financial and technical resources to embrace it. If raw material prices began to rise, center firms can integrate backward, and supply themselves. When rising labor costs pose a substantial threat, automation, cybernation or self-service may provide long-run relief, depending on the industry. Expensive production labor must now contend with easily financed capital substitution in industries where center firms dwell.

Averitt's view has been disputed by Karpik, on the basis of his studies of large corporations in France.

Karpik (1972, pp. 45-46) asserted that even large corporations spend much of their effort on reacting to environmental changes:

> Although Galbraith states that the large enterprise controls its environment and can therefore develop private planning, direct observation indicates that the large technological enterprise operates within a situation marked by a high degree of uncertainty, which results mainly from the composition of the world of competition, from the overall evolution of science and technology, and from their effects on methods and products, from industrial relations, politico-economic phenomena, etc. This uncertainty is experienced in concrete terms in the present phenomenon of private "deplanning" in favor of strategic action combined with forecasting.

This description may fit France or England better than the United States or West Germany. For the moment we can only take note of the existence of such powerful firms, for they inhabit a different world from the one sociologists and other organization theorists usually investigate. Perhaps in ten years a textbook on organizational sociology will be able to do justice to their importance, based on empirical studies.

Legal limits to organizational influence: Examples.   A society's legal system sets constraints that limit the impact organizations may have on their environments. The legal system includes national laws, state and local laws, and perhaps most important, the legal structure and its agents who enforce the law, including prosecuting attorneys and courts. The evolving nature of legal environments results from relations between legislatures or Congress, which enact legislation, and the structure that monitors compliance and sanctions violators. Two areas illustrating the significance of national legislation are labor and industrial relations and the medical and health care system in the United States.

Legislative history in the field of industrial and labor relations has fluctuated between prounion and promanagement legislation, beginning with the union-oriented National Labor Relations Act of 1935 that resulted in the creation of the National Labor Relations Board. The Taft-Hartley Act of 1947 made the unfair practices aspects of the 1935 act applicable to unions as well as management, and the 1959 Landrum-Griffin Act extended governmental protection against undemocratic union practices to individual union members. Running parallel to the laws enacted were a series of Supreme Court decisions interpreting and extending the legislation.

Especially important were a series of decisions giving federal courts the general power to oversee collective bargaining agreements but eliminating the courts from the substantive arrangements between unions and management. Court decisions in the *Steelworkers' Trilogy* and *Lincoln Mills* cases solidified the legal rationale for the emergence and legitimacy of a United States industrial relations "common law." The courts were instructed to lean toward the principle of allowing arbitrators to fashion awards in industrial relations disputes on the basis of industry tradition and *without* becoming involved in the "correctness" of the awards. Even with the major role played by federal legislation and the courts, the United States system of labor relations is unlike that of many nations of Western Europe, where the state is even more heavily involved in dispute settlements.

National legislation affecting the medical profession and hospitals in the United States involves the state deeply in community health care systems (Freidson, 1970). The Medicare and Medicaid legislation in 1965 committed the federal government to subsidizing aged and indigent health care consumers, adding a third party to the doctor-patient relation. The Professional Standard Review Organization Act of 1972 represented a challenge to professional self-regulation, and the National Health Planning and Resources Development Act of 1974 affected the ability of communities to expand their hospitals. It attempted to control rapidly escalating health care costs by regulating capital expansion and renovation programs and by promoting the regionalization of health care.

Hospitals' relations with their employees were sharply affected by a 1974 amendment to the Taft-Hartley Act, extending the right of collective bargaining to hospital employees. The proportion of hospital employees unionized went from 6 to 18 percent by 1977. Another interrelation between the legal and health care systems occurs through malpractice suits, sparked in part by the high ratio of lawyers per capita in the United States. The costs of legal insurance have raised hospital operating costs, and lawsuits have brought the courts into the health care system.

Participants' Perceptions of Reality as Limits to Choice

Participants' perceptions play some role in their actions, but there are a variety of social forces that limit the possibility for really "strategic" choices, contrary to Child's third argument. Difficulties in discovering reality inductively, the dependence of perceptual interpretations on previous experiences, the heightened role of social influence in conditions of uncertainty, and a host of collective socialization processes reinforce strong commitments to existing, socially approved perceptions (Starbuck, 1976). Members rarely examine the existential basis of their everyday actions, as perceptual inertia and habitual behavior suffice to see most people through the day. Occasions for non-routine or critical decisions often pass unrecognized, but because conceptions of the environment are widely shared, no organization is disadvantaged by such slips. As the following discussion will indicate, the frequency of truly strategic choices may be quite small.

Difficulties in discovering reality.   Learning about environments by observing them is extremely difficult, as the example of the naive observer at the beginning of Chapter 3 made clear. Individuals have too limited a view and things are happening too quickly to permit reliability checks on accumulated information. "Consequently, a perceiver's ability to organize and interpret his observations depends very strongly on the theories and beliefs he holds *a priori,* and he tends to learn what he already believed" (Starbuck, 1976, p. 1080). There is usually a relationship between perceptions and environmental characteristics, however, as resource constraints and negative feedback from misperceptions direct perceptions toward congruence with reality. The gap between an omnisicent observer's view of "reality" and that of participants may still be quite wide, as it is relative rather than absolute accuracy that guides environmental selection.

Uncertainty and social influences on perception.   Given difficulties in discovering reality inductively and an awareness that an uncertain situation has been encountered, individuals may feel uncomfortable at not being able to resolve their uncertainty. Festinger (1954) argued that persons unable to validate their perceptions using their own resources turn to their social environments for guidance. Social and cultural factors affect cognitions and perceptions in two ways. First, social and cultural factors affect members' perceptual sets—their readiness to attend to and interpret environmental stimuli—by shaping values, beliefs, and attitudes. Second, social forces affect cognitions and perceptions directly in situations where stimuli are ambiguous and individuals either lack confidence in their own responses or are dominated by the outlook of other members of their unit.

A variety of social and cultural forces combine to induce a common perception of the environment within subpopulations of organizations. Organizations tend to hire management personnel from within the same industry or subpopulation (Pfeffer and Leblecici, 1973b; Baty, Evan, and Rothermel, 1971). Wall Street law firms traditionally sought white upper-class graduates from prestigious

Eastern law schools to fill their need for associate members, and only broadened their recruitment search when competition for such lawyers increased (Smigel, 1964). College fraternities and sororities seek members who are "compatible" with the group's image of itself; socioeconomic status, personality, and appearance are the major selection criteria. Personal contacts are evidently a major source of job information for white-collar workers, increasing the tendency for organizations to hire like-minded individuals as they recruit "friends of friends" (Granovetter, 1974). Salaman (1974, p. 82) noted that the process of recruitment and selection is "an important method of organizational control, since senior members of organizations will attempt to select those persons who, in their eyes, display evidence that they will be amenable to methods of organizational control and who appear to hold some commitment to organizational "goals" and the organizational culture." Evan's (1976, p. 162) study of the United States Federal Trade Commission found that "in recruiting attorneys the FTC evidently attaches more significance to regional background, old school ties, and political endorsement of applicants than to their ability as reflected in grades or in the quality of the law schools they attended."

Imitation and borrowing are important sources of new ideas, and business, trade, and professional publications promote the development of a common frame of reference in an industry. Managers and staff are sent to the same training institutions, and various types of coalitions depend on shared perceptions for the coordination of interorganizational behavior (Starbuck, 1976). The professional training of scientists and lawyers creates a bond to a professional community that makes them partially insensitive to the interests of other groups, and this has been a vexing problem for federal regulatory agencies. The professional training and organizational experience of scientists in agencies such as the Food and Drug Administration (FDA) makes them valuable to the industries they are supposed to regulate. Between 1959 and 1963, about 10 percent of the 813 scientific, medical, and technical employees who left the FDA accepted employment in companies regulated by the FDA (Evan, 1976, p. 161). The Interstate Commerce Commission enjoys a similarly tight coupling to the transportation industry it regulates.

The effect of these processes is to homogenize perceptions across organizations, making each organization less sensitive to the unique characteristics of its local environment (Starbuck, 1976). If a local environment is benign and has a wide tolerance for deviations from the ideal structure or performance, then socially induced misperceptions are not fatal. No single organization is at a relative disadvantage in resource acquisition when perceptions are universally shared. In unstable or lean environments, however, deviant organizations not sharing the common misperceptions may have an adaptive advantage. If they stumble onto a more effective form, they will be positively selected and could take over the niche before the others modify their perceptual sets.

Situational forces also affect the probability that individual participants will be able to make strategic, as opposed to routine, choices under conditions of uncertainty. The more ambiguous the stimulus confronting participants, the more un-certain they will be about how to interpret it and what action to take. There is not a one-to-one relationship between situational ambiguity and participants' uncer-tainty, however, as the nature of individuals' relations to the group within their unit or organization can heighten or dampen the impact of uncertainty (Wiener, 1958; Taijfel, 1969). The greater the confidence members have in the group's overall reliability of judgment and in its judgment in the particular situation call-ing for a choice, the more likely they are to acquiesce in its judgment and sus-pend their own. Conversely, the less confidence they have in the group and the more they have in their own judgment, the more likely they are to make a distinc-tively personal judgment.

A substantial amount of empirical literature has accumulated in social psy-chology on the conditions under which social influence is most likely to affect individuals' judgments (Taijfel, 1969). Social influence is greatest when the am-biguity of the stimulus is great, group cohesion is high, the individual has a high need for social approval, the individual is in a minority, and the judgment is not of great importance to the person. Social influence is least effective when a per-son has made a public or private precommitment to a position, the judgment is of great value, the individual has someone to agree with him or her, the judgment is kept anonymous, there is the possibility of independent checks being made on the validity of the group's judgment, and the situation is so uncertain that the indi-vidual doesn't think that others are any better than he or she at guessing the cor-rect response.

Many of these factors are open to manipulation by the dominant coalition in organizations, such as increasing group cohesion, isolating individuals with de-viant views, reducing ambiguity by prescreening information transmitted to members, and controlling access to information so that independent checks are not possible. The more successful the dominant coalition is at manipulating these factors, the less uncertainty participants will report experiencing in their tasks. An investigator should not accept their reports, however, as reports on the state of the environment. Instead, following the research prescriptions advanced in the previous chapter, we must always distinguish between perceptions of environ-ments and the actual conditions existing in environments.

SUMMARY

The concept of strategic choice is an essential addition to the analysis of organi-zational change, for it directs our attention to the role of dominant coalitions in organizations and the conditions under which organizations can influence their environments. Decision makers have some autonomy in selecting strategies and setting performance standards, but there are severe restrictions on their ability to select new environments. Barriers to entry make it extremely difficult for new business organizations to enter many manufacturing industries, whereas the lack of barriers to entry in the retail and service industries allows the formation of thousands of businesses each year. Voluntary associations and other forms of nonbusiness organizations also confront barriers to their entry into new niches. Barriers to entry are theoretically significant because they limit the range of variation in a population and increase the likelihood of the retention of existing organizational forms.

Some organizations have the power to manipulate and control their environments, but this is much more likely in one small subpopulation than among all organizations. The fortunate subpopulation, consisting of very large organizations, associations, and public agencies, contains organizations that are unlikely to fail and frequently have the power to alter their environments. Tactics and strategies used by these fortunate organizations are discussed in later chapters on interorganizational relations and networks. The larger, remaining subpopulation consists of smaller organizations that have a significant probability of failure and a high rate of turnover. This group is much larger in number than the fortunate few, although the subpopulation of large organizations is of greater social, economic, and political significance than the subpopulation of smaller organizations. Even though large firms and public agencies seldom fail, this does not mean that they are immune to environmental effects on structures or activities. The review of constraints on the exercise of strategic choice indicates that autonomous choice is problematic even for very large organizations.

The relevance of participants' perceptions of their environments is stressed by the strategic choice argument, but the critical issues to consider are the extent to which organizational perceptions vary from objective indicators of environments, and the forces causing such variations. The more critical the divergence between the two types of indicators, the greater its significance for organizational change.

Environmental selection processes set the limits within which rational selection among alternatives takes place. Prior limits and constraints on available options leave little room for maneuvering by most organizations, and strategic choice may be a luxury open only to the largest and most powerful organizations. Whether strategic choice operates only at the margins of change (producing small effects of little consequence) or at the forefront of change (remaking environments in the organization's image) is ultimately an empirical question, open to resolution only through the cumulation of historical research.

7   The Creation
of Organizations

Under what conditions are new forms of organizations or new organizations using current forms most likely to emerge? What environmental opportunities increase the likelihood of success, and what constraints limit the viability of new forms? If the environmental selection model is to prove useful for the study of organizational change, it must suggest answers to these questions. All three stages of the model are relevant to understanding the emergence of new forms and the reproduction of existing ones. First, the likelihood of new forms emerging or new organizations being founded increases with increasing *variability* in a population. Increasing exposure to ideas from other societies or regions, the spread of a secular world view and faith in science, improved communication and transportation technologies, and other forces can lead to more attempts at innovation, planned or otherwise. Second, environmental *selection criteria* are altered as the distribution of resources, and the terms on which they are made available, change. Changing patterns of resource availability (due perhaps to political revolution, state intervention, or the expanding size of markets) open new niches. Third, *retention mechanisms* that protected old organizational forms may break down or dissolve because of rising levels of competence in the labor force, changes in government regulation, or successful assaults on barriers to entry protecting a particular form.

Precise distinctions between the consequences of changes in any of the three stages are fairly easy to make analytically, but extremely difficult to apply in practice. Many of the social changes and specific historical events covered in this chapter overlap all three stages, such as the increasing importance of powerful nation-states or the transition from the feudal to the agricultural and then industrial capitalist modes of production. Moreover, giving all relevant forces their due would require a much more comprehensive treatment than can be accomplished in this book, and so I will only sketch a general outline that can be filled in by consulting the literature cited. I will not try to keep the three stages separate, but rather will focus on five interrelated substantive areas: (1) the motives and incentives of organizational entrepreneurs and their significance in the emergence of new forms; (2) the role of the state in facilitating or inhibiting organizational change; (3) major historical forces affecting environmental variability and niche generation; (4) patterns of founding new forms and several examples of the emergence of new forms; and (5) constraints on the viability of new forms.

ORGANIZATIONAL ENTREPRENEURS: MOTIVES AND INCENTIVES

The rational selection model of organizational change emphasizes the role of organizational entrepreneurs—persons who discover opportunities for combining resources in novel ways, recruit others to join them, and thus found new organizations. The concept of "organizational entrepreneur" is not limited to persons founding business organizations, as a similar function is evident in the creation of social movements, voluntary associations, or public agencies. The theory of the firm in economics uses the term "entrepreneur" as a useful abstraction, covering a type of behavior expected of risk-taking economic actors when they are afforded an opportunity to profit by founding a new business. Management science and decision-making theorists are more interested in the personal characteristics of entrepreneurs, asking questions such as whether they differ from others in their degree of aversion to risk, need for achievement, and so forth. This concern for the motives of persons founding organizations is difficult to incorporate into a straightforward sociological theory of organizations, which focuses on social structural conditions rather than individuals' characteristics.

Even Stinchcombe (1965, p. 146) began an essay entitled "Social Structure and Organizations" with a section on "motivations to organize," noting that people found organizations when they learn of new and better ways to accomplish tasks, they can assemble the required resources, they are reasonably certain of keeping some of the organization's benefits for themselves or their friends and relatives, and they can protect their new organizations from predatory outsiders. But Stinchcombe was not really interested in motivations as such, for he added that the probability that people will be motivated to start an organization is dependent on the social structure and on their position within it. His argument was not about the motives of specific individuals, but rather about the conditions that make it easier for them to fulfill whatever self-interested ends they might have.

We might question whether we really require a theory of "motives to organize," given the difficulties involved in applying the concept. The danger of tautology is ever-present, as we typically will not know peoples' "motives" until we observe a new organization or organizational form, introducing an undesirable circularity into the analysis. Thus, someone founded an eschatological social movement *because* he or she wanted to spread the word that the end of the world was near, someone founded a bridge club *because* his or her friends were enthusiasts, and a business was founded *because* its owner perceived a chance to make a profit. Moreover, some organizational entrepreneurs are active across a wide range of forms, especially in the business sector. Profit-oriented entrepreneurs are generalists, seeking opportunities anywhere and founding businesses in a variety of niches.

A better formulation of the issue is to ask what environmental conditions raise or lower the salience of certain *incentives* people may have to found organizations (Clark and Wilson, 1961). Three types of incentives appear to be present in all societies and also to vary with time and individuals' social positions: material incentives, which are the tangible rewards such as money that result from organized action; solidary incentives, which are the intangible rewards resulting from the act of associating with others in organized social interaction; and purposive incentives, which are the intangible rewards resulting from the sense of satisfaction of attaining a worthwhile cause, as in ideological or "cause" oriented social movements. The salience of these incentives—the extent to which they attract the attention of entrepreneurs—rises and falls as conditions permitting their realization change. The salience of purposive incentives decreases during major wars, except for those organizations related directly to the war effort. None of the fifty-three challenging groups studied by Gamson (1975) was formed during a major war. Gamson (1975, p.112) also found that thirty-nine of the fifty-three groups "began during relatively turbulent periods, periods characterized by major social movements and many new and diversified challenges. In particular, the 1830s, the period from 1880 until the eve of World War I (including the popularist and progressive eras), and the 1930s" were significant eras for the founding of challenging groups.

Not all members of a society respond to organizing opportunities or to changes in the salience of incentives to organize, and so a complete explanation of the origins of any given organization will have to include a consideration of founders' characteristics. Members of socially marginal ethnic or religious groups, such as Jews and Quakers, are a much greater proportion of industrial entrepreneurs than their proportion in the population would imply. Persons from these groups were often forced into entrepreneurship because they were barred from some occupations or they encountered prejudice against mobility in professional careers (Francis, 1977). However, for our purposes little is lost by focusing on the structural and historical conditions that make possible the fulfillment of individuals' motives. Most of the social structural conditions and changes discussed in this chapter are impervious to the actions of individual entrepreneurs, no matter how dedicated they are. Organizational entrepreneurs can only work with the resources their environments make available to them, and major innovations in organizational forms are inevitably linked to significant changes in environmental conditions.

THE ROLE OF THE STATE

Sovereign nation-states affect the creation of organizations by establishing necessary preconditions, such as political stability and calculable law, and by supporting institutional arrangements regarding the allocation of resources, such as state-supported corporations or banks. Political stability and ideological legitimation are affected by the strength of the state, but even weak states may facilitate and protect new forms. Educational systems, improvements in transportation and communication networks, and national economic planning and other state investments affect the terms on which resources are made available to organizational entrepreneurs. Political repression raises the cost of organizing and may block it altogether. Indeed, the state must surely be the *major* force affecting organizational formation in the twentieth century. Only a rough indication of the state's power is possible in the following discussion, and readers are referred to the literature cited for a more extensive treatment of the issues raised.

Levels of Analysis:
World System or Nation-States?

Controversy exists over the relevant level of analysis for studying the historical evolution of modes of economic production and political systems: Should it be individual nation-states or what Wallerstein (1974) called the "world system"? This controversy is important for theories of organizational change because of its bearing on the allocation and redistribution of resources within nations. Outside economic competition or intervention may preexempt certain niches, denying entrepreneurs the opportunity to form certain types of organizations. Frank (1966), for example, asserted that "underdeveloped nations" were underdeveloped in part because of the subordinate role they played in the world capitalist system, with local industries confined to niches that served rather than challenged industries in dominant nations.

The world-scale economic system prespective has been most forcefully argued by Immanuel Wallerstein (1974). He asserted that the transformation of feudal Europe into a capitalist world economy occurred in the "long sixteenth century" (1450 to 1640), and that once this transformation was accomplished, national states became of lesser importance. Nation-states played roles within an international division of labor, as in the role eastern Europe played in producing raw materials for the industrializing West. The process of differentiation of the world economy resulted in nations taking on roles in the core, semiperiphery, or periphery of the system. While political or economic elites within a particular nation could affect the redistribution of resources at the margins, the major conflicts were played out in international markets and patterns of trade.

The *traditional* unit of analysis for studies of economic and political evolution was the nation-state and not the world system, and theories of "development" and "modernization" in the 1950s and 1960s implicitly assumed the integrity of state boundaries. Whether arguing for the convergence or divergence of nations under the impact of industrialization, such theories treated nation-states as independent entities. Recent work by Anderson (1974a), Brenner (1977), and others, while not following the developmentalist bias of modernization theorists, has emphasized the continuing importance of the political autonomy of nation-states. Even within a world economy dominated by a capitalist mode of production, political boundaries still have an impact on organizations and institutions within nations. Skocpol (1977, p. 1087), for example, argued that "we should investigate the world-historical emergence and development of capitalism in terms of hypotheses about variations in both (1) institutionalized class relations of production and exchange, and (2) patterns of state structures and interstate relationships, without simply reducing the latter to the former. To be sure, markets and patterns of trade are bound to be part of the picture, but it seems unlikely that they can be understood in their origin, functioning, or effects except with reference to changes in class and political structures." Economic growth and modernization are characteristic of most societies today, but the paths nations have followed to these ends differ according to historical circumstances peculiar to each country.

Meyer *et al.* (1975, p. 229), after noting that the pattern of convergence toward economic growth and modernization among nations in the twentieth century is too rapid to be explained by the independent evolution of autonomous societies, made a strong argument for the relevance of a world system view, although not necessarily the one proposed by Wallerstein. Societies participating in the world economy are strongly pressured by the forces of economic rationalization, with many societal institutions modified as a result: money and banking, advanced technical education, corporate and labor law, and the growth of a market in wage-labor. The inability of the United Nations to establish itself as the governing body of a world state has increased pressures on smaller nations. Many nations that were insulated from international pressures in their dependent status as colonies of an imperial power were thrust center-stage after World War II as independent nations. Their new international position was both an opportunity and a threat: They were free to engage in economic competition, but their economic weakness left them open to exploitation by dominant powers. Internally, mobilization of a newly enfranchised citizenry raised demands on leaders, which were difficult to fulfill with the nation's own resources. Both external and internal pressures thus pushed nations into joining the world-scale economic system that was emerging, including adopting many of its institutional and organizational forms.

Observers agree that a convergence toward modern institutions is occurring among almost all nations of the world. It is not yet possible to ascertain whether the observed convergence results from nations responding to the exigencies of an industrial economy, to the rapid diffusion of modernity, to the incorporation of independent nation-states into the world economy, or perhaps a combination of the three.

Political Stability

Even though economic and social conditions may be changing, political stability allows organizational entrepreneurs to indulge in *future* oriented behavior. Obviously this is most critical in the business sector, where entrepreneurs are required to risk their capital and that of investors on the chance that they will receive a return on their investments. Given political stability, entrepreneurs can be more certain that they will be repaid for the effort of creating organizations and investing in them than under conditions of instability (Stinchcombe, 1965). Even if the founders are not able to benefit, they can foresee that others with whom they are associated—family or communal groupings—eventually will. This may be one reason why even some of the rather strict eastern European socialist countries set a size limit below which they do not expropriate privately held firms. The economies of these countries still depend upon small businesses (generally with less than five employees) for many essential services and products, including especially the agricultural sector. Removing the threat of state expropriation lessens the uncertainty organizational entrepreneurs would otherwise face in deciding whether to establish their own businesses.

Weber (1947), in his historical analysis of economic systems, stressed that future-oriented behavior was facilitated by state action ensuring calculable law, calculable taxation, and military security. In the feudal mode of production, political sovereignty was fragmented among various lords, each of whom, in turn, owed loyalty to a feudal superior (Anderson, 1974b). These superiors might be linked into another level of dependency, with a king holding nominal title to all lands. There was no overarching dominant political center in such a system, and law, taxes, and security depended very much on local circumstances. Long distance trade was a hazardous enterprise, and while individual feudal cities grew fairly strong, the lack of a unifying center held back large-scale trade until stronger states emerged in the "long sixteenth century." With the transition to more powerful and politically stable nation-states, political sovereignty was centralized and conditions much improved for the rise of a capitalist mode of production.

Whether a state is defined as politically stable depends, in part, on whose interests the state is perceived as protecting. Zeitlin *et al.* (1974) argued that the short-lived socialist government of Chile was perceived by the business community as a threat to its existence, despite the relatively small number of expropriations carried out. I shall return to political stability and also the role of the state in ensuring continuity of key societal institutions in a subsequent section.

Ideological Legitimation

Major transformations in economic systems, bringing with them wholesale across-the-board changes in the form of economic enterprises, require a change in the ideologies of management if the new form is to survive. Bendix (1956, p. 2), whose analysis I am summarizing here, defined "ideologies of management" as "all ideas which are espoused by or for those who exercise authority in economic enterprises and which seek to explain and justify that authority." More succinctly put, ideologies are ideas used as weapons for social interests (Mannheim, 1936). In the early stages of industrialization, economic ideologies focus on justifying the position of the entrepreneur, while in later stages the position of managers is legitimated. Ideologies, whatever their substantive content, serve three functions. First, they legitimate the particular system of productive enterprises in terms of its relations to the state and to the general "public welfare" of the society. Second, they legitimate the manner in which enterprises control their employees. Third, they provide a system of beliefs allowing entrepreneurs and managers to achieve a sense of self-justification for their roles in the system.

A crisis of legitimacy occurs when the fundamental nature of a society's economic system changes and the old ideology is no longer relevant. This occurred with the onset of the industrial revolution in eighteenth century England and with the coming to fruition of Tsar Peter the Great's forcible industrialization of Russia, also in the eighteenth century. A crisis occurred because the new economic system disrupted the established social order, generating conflict between the various social classes and status groups in the society. Industrialization in England produced conflict between the politically powerful landed aristocracy and the newly formed entrepreneur and merchant classes. A similar conflict arose in Russia. The resolution of these conflicts and the subsequent content of the ideology legitimating the new economic system were contingent upon three factors. First, conflict was affected by the extent to which entrepreneurs and managers formed an autonomous class in the society or were subordinate to the power of the state. In England, the rising entrepreneurial class had a great deal of autonomy from government intervention. They were free to innovate and develop their enterprises as they chose. In Russia, industrialization was directed and controlled by the state from the very beginning, and Peter the Great single-handedly introduced many industrial innovations into Russia in the early eighteenth century. Industrialization was controlled by the state in the name of the state's interests, and the state intervened at the local level whenever entrepreneurs seemed in danger of losing control, as in local labor disputes.

Second, the intensity of the conflict depends on the nature and extent of previous class conflict in the society. The same conflict occurred in all societies during the initial period of industrialization, as entrepreneurs had to win acceptance from two hostile groups for the new form of economic activity. The politically dominant aristocracy viewed industrialization as a threat to their political dominance and traditional way of life, and rightly so, for the size of their fortunes was quickly dwarfed by those of the *nouveau riche*. The lords and landed gentry in England and the boyars in Russia gained their income from the agricultural labor of landless workers and serfs, who were needed in the factories of the industrialists. This new work force was hostile, for industrialization was also a threat to their traditional way of life. New demands were made upon them, as production for the market demanded a different set of work routines than did personal production.

Third, the content of the resulting ideology depends upon the historical development of religious and political ideologies in a society. During the initial period of industrialization, major differences appeared between England and Russia. In England, ideological developments were dominated by the growth of the evangelical movement and the spread of Malthus's arguments about the state's limited ability to alter the condition of the poor. Political ideology in Russia, however, stressed the absolute authority of the Tsar, together with his responsibility to manage relations among contending social groups. The strongly centralized state of Russia could not extricate itself from the continuous resolution of conflicts, and so became mired deeper and deeper in them. The state lost legitimacy in the eyes of workers and employers, dissatisfaction and dissidence increased, and "the revolution of 1905 signalized the failure of Tsarist autocracy" (Bendix, 1956, p. 190).

Once the initial conflict is resolved in favor of the continued industrialization of a society, ideological justification of the relations between industrial enterprises and the state are no longer problematic. The form of economic activity and the role of the state are taken for granted, and attention turns inward, to the internal structure of business organizations. Problems with internal coordination and control within firms might require occasional state intervention, but the economic system itself is stable. Bendix's work on the changing content of entrepreneurial and managerial ideologies shows that investigators examining only one historical era would have been unable to document the tentativeness of belief systems created. The changes occurring over time in the form of social organization—the nature of relations between social units—mean that theories of organizational change must be firmly grounded in knowledge of historical trends.

Direct Nation-State Support and Protection of Organizations

The power of the state has increased in almost all modern societies, but there is disagreement over whether state power in peripheral states of the world economy has increased as much as in the core states (Meyer *et al.*, 1975). One argument is that the extraordinary power of the core states has allowed them to extend civil liberties and political participation to their citizens to a much greater extent than peripheral states, which must be more concerned with mobilizing their populations in the pursuit of economic growth and independence. There are also disagreements over whose interests the state serves, and whether the state has interests of its own, apart from those of the dominant classes or political parties. Increasing state power permits governments to respond to the needs of organizational entrepreneurs directly by measures such as import quotas and subsidies, and indirectly by investing in educational, transportation, and communication improvements that benefit most organizational forms.

Increasing state power, and its implications for the creation of organizations, can be documented via a myriad of indicators (Meyer *et al.*, 1975, pp. 238-39). The percent of the gross national product (GNP) appropriated by central governments increased from 20.5 percent to 23.7 percent during the years 1951-1969 for fifty-nine non-Socialist countries, at the same time that GNPs were growing larger. Total taxing power also increased during this period. The post-World War II period witnessed the emergence of national planning systems in a majority of sovereign states—before 1945, only 8 states engaged in national planning, but by 1965, 136 states established national planning agencies. Elites in all countries are committed to social and economic modernization, thus making them highly receptive to the adoption of organizational forms diffusing from more industrialized to less industrialized countries. State power has expanded into all sectors of society, especially those of welfare and education, and the growing number of ministries and departments oriented to a specific societal sector is reflected in the increasing size of each government's cabinet. States are collecting more and more information in the form of "social indicators" that are required for the national planning process and also are extremely useful for those industries that must do long-range planning. These developments indicate that state power is increasingly oriented to centralized planning and regulation of the economy. Some increases in state power have added external constraints while others have removed them, which is why the overall impact on the number and diversity of organizational forms is difficult to summarize.

State investment in education increases environmental capacity by raising the information-processing capacity of a society and of the people within it. Increased information-processing capacity facilitates the spread of ideas about new forms and also increases the organizing capacity of the work force. Literacy breaks down barriers to communication and thus can effectively link persons and organizations in widely scattered sectors of a loosely coupled system. To the extent that the spread of information creates a more homogeneous world-view within a population, it may promote political stability. Deutsch (1953) noted that one of the first items on the agenda of governments in developing nations is standardization of a national language and the creation of a communication network through which the population can be mobilized.

For new organizational forms, a heightened ability to process information makes learning new roles easier, and enables participants to record past transactions and experience, thus promoting organizational efficiency. Monitoring the environment is less difficult, and opportunities for long-range planning are enhanced. The drive toward industrialization in the latter half of the nineteenth century in the United States was preceded by the introduction of free education, with the system implemented more fully in the North and West than in the South. After the 1910 political revolution in Mexico, the state made massive investments in education, and in post-revolutionary Russia, the state "wrote grammars in the minority languages, herded everyone into schools, and increased literacy almost as fast as steel production" (Stinchcombe, 1965, p. 151).

The degree to which states monitor and control their national boundaries also affects the rate of formation of new organizations. In societies with highly permeable boundaries there is a fairly high rate of information flow into the country from external sources (Caplow and Finsterbush, 1968). Innovation and diffusion of new forms are facilitated, and creative entrepreneurs can match borrowed organizational forms to opportunities in their own societies. The inability of Chinese authorities to defend the integrity of China's boundaries against foreign intervention in the nineteenth century opened Chinese coastal cities to rapid organizational change. In the twentieth century, Western and Japanese educated elites have played an important role in introducing innovations in organizational forms into their native societies. Developing nations face a serious dilemma by opening their borders and permitting easy access to foreigners, however, as they may also expose their nascent industries to the withering effects of competition from multinational corporations based in dominant nations.

McCullough and Shannon (1977) argued that the protective functions of states are clearly evident in the historical record, and that all organizational transactions have been conditioned by state protective power. The state came into existence as a monopolizer of protection, and the building of powerful states in the fifteenth and sixteenth centuries enabled princes and nobles to solidify their monopoly over the means of violence. Economic activity, such as international trade, was conducted under rights bought from the state, and organized bureaucracies were necessary to administer the sale of rights and protection. The state had an interest in creating monopolies in the various lines of trade, as they were easiest to control with a rudimentary state administrative apparatus. European states had interests of their own vis-à-vis other states, quite apart from whatever interests merchants and traders might have had. Competition for the expansion of overseas empires and the enhancement of state power through amassing national wealth gave states an interest in protecting national enterprises.

State protection of monopolies was a cornerstone of sixteenth- and seventeenth-century national policies. The Navigation Acts, which caused a great deal of conflict between England and her American colonies, gave English shipping companies a monopoly on colonial trade. State power created a national monopoly sheltering privately held companies (Davis, 1966). The growth of a state-protected English trading and shipping sector reduced England's dependence on the Spaniards and the Dutch who otherwise dominated international trade, and the trained seamen and warships involved in the protection of commerce were also useful in the defense of the nation.

The modern state has a much more fully developed administrative apparatus with which to support and protect the creation and growth of organizations (O'Connor, 1973). At the local level, communities compete with one another to attract industry by offering tax rebates, exemption from zoning ordinances, publicly owned industrial parks and buildings, and employment training programs. At the national level, states use tariff barriers, import quotas, export subsidies, tax laws favoring certain types of investments, direct subsidies to industries deemed vital to the national interest (such as airlines and shipping firms), loan guarantees, and in extreme cases, military protection. I noted earlier that the United States federal regulatory commissions have had the latent effect of stabilizing conditions in regulated industries, reducing environmental uncertainty. Clearly the role of the state in the creation of organizations deserves major attention in a theory of organizational change, and no doubt research in the next decade will reflect this need.

The Role of the State: Summary

There is controversy over whether the world economy or the nation-state is the relevant level of analysis in analyzing economic development. Until more cross-national comparative organizational research is completed, we will not know whether the patterns of convergence found at the state level are mirrored by similar patterns of organizational structure and activities. Similar distributions of forms by industries are evident in industrialized countries, rankings of occupational prestige are quite similar, and preliminary attempts at cross-national comparisons of organizational structure seem to indicate similarity there also (Horvath et al., 1974). Political stability and ideological legitimacy reduce environmental uncertainty and thus encourage future-oriented behavior, giving organizational entrepreneurs the confidence to found new organizations. Nation-states facilitate and protect organizations both directly and indirectly, and whether these efforts ultimately increase or decrease organizational diversity is not yet known.

ENVIRONMENTAL VARIABILITY AND
NICHE GENERATION

Three major factors affect the rate of formation of new organizational forms, in addition to those discussed in the chapter on variability. One is historically unique: the transformation of the world economy from a feudal to a capitalist base, representing a shift toward the allocation of resources within a market-oriented economy. The other two factors—the urbanization of all societies and the occurrence of political revolutions—are continuous processes. I will not attempt to explain *why* urbanization, political revolutions, or the transition to capitalism occurred, but I will take them as given and discuss their implications for the founding of organizations.

Market-Oriented Economy

The transformation of feudal Europe into a capitalist world economy—to a system where production is for an impersonal market rather than individual or group needs and where economic behavior is oriented toward the accumulation of value—was accompanied by two essential processes that severed the link between economic resources and traditional uses. The emergence of *formally free labor*, not bound by custom or traditional authority to fixed social roles, occupations, or a feudal lord, made possible the rational allocation of a critical resource. The proletarianization of labor threw many laborers (heretofore employed in agricultural production for their own use and that of their traditional superior) into grinding poverty. Laborers no longer could live a marginal but assured existence in traditional agricultural pursuits, but instead were forced into selling their labor power to the highest bidder. Most workers remained on the land, but with an altered status; freed from the constraints that previously bound them, laborers were available to be recruited by entrepreneurs for employment in agricultural contract labor and later in industrial production in shops and factories. As capitalism insinuated itself in modern societies, even "education" became a commodity, falling from its earlier status as preparation for political or religious careers to training for purely material pursuits.

Land as well as labor became a commodity, and the *commercialization* of land allowed it to be put to new uses (Moore, 1966). Agricultural resources could thus be shifted more easily to the production of whatever crops were in greatest demand at the moment. Land could also be diverted to industrial uses. As Wallerstein (1976, p. 279) pointed out, the transformation from a feudal to a capitalist mode of production did not mean the elimination of other forms of labor and of land ownership, and he asserted that "the existence of non-proletarianized labor and non-commercialized land is quite essential for the optimization of opportunities for overall profit in a capitalist world-market . . . ." For our purposes, it is enough to note that the rise of formally free labor and the alienability of land—the ability of owners to sell their lands without regard to traditional restric-

172

tions—freed resources and made them available for new combinations and investments in new organizational forms.

Ecologists have treated the alienability of land as a central feature of urban growth and organizational change even in the twentieth century (Form, 1954). Hughes's (1928) study of the Chicago Real Estate Board dealt with the secularization of land as it became valuable during Chicago's rapid spurt of growth from 1860 through the turn of the century. The value of land could be expressed in monetary terms and thus organizations and occupations (the real estate profession in particular) were created that formed a cash nexus with land and its uses. Conditions of cutthroat competition and disorganization in the real estate industry spurred the formation of the Real Estate Board in 1883. By standardizing norms and procedures, the Board played a social control function, limiting the impact of environmental turbulence on the real estate field (Burns, 1977).

Although it antedated the rise of the capitalist world economy, the development of a *money economy,* with its universally accepted standards of value, made an important contribution to the creation of new organizational forms. A money economy freed resources from particularistic ties to traditional uses, thus allowing their transfer to new organizations. Customers could switch loyalties between businesses more easily, creating a truly "free" market of totally impersonal economic relations. A universalistic standard of value "simplifies calculation of the advantages of alternative ways of doing things, and allows more precise anticipation of the consequences of future conditions on the organization" (Stinchcombe, 1965, p. 152). Marx (1973) in the "Chapter on Money" from the *Grundrisse,* analyzed the importance of a money economy quite thoroughly, showing its relevance to a capitalist mode of production.

Banks and other financial institutions played a key adminstrative coordination function in the early stages of American industrialization. Chandler (1977, p. 31) reviewed the history of banking in the United States from the late 1790s to the 1840s, showing how banks helped coordinate international trade by supporting American commodity producers: "Payments made by the British and Europeans for American cotton and other commodities were deposited, normally with London merchant bankers, and became the source of funds and credit for American merchants purchasing goods abroad." Prior to this, international trade was hindered because transactions were almost on a barter basis—goods exchanged for goods. The Second Bank of the United States of America was highly successful in coordinating monetary flows, growing at a rapid rate during the 1830s and dominating the foreign exchange business of the United States, but its charter was not renewed in 1836 because of President Andrew Jackson's veto.

Urbanization

Urbanization removes some constraints on the likelihood of ideas attracting enough interest to be turned into new organizational forms; also it increases the diversity of the organizational population by generating environmental heterogeneity and new niches (Fischer, 1975). Stinchcombe (1965, p. 151) stressed the consequences of urban social heterogeneity for the acceptance of new ideas: "Socially differentiated urban populations present alternatives to each other, and most innovations can find a home in some social segment." The secular city, with its universalistic standards and high rates of social mobility, is a favorable atmosphere for nurturing and sheltering new ideas until they can become forms. In this respect urbanization has the same effect as an increase in societal information-processing capacity (see Tilly, 1973).

Urban economists and geographers (Thompson, 1965; Pred, 1966) emphasize the increasing heterogeneity of resources and markets resulting from increases in the scale of urban areas. Increases in environmental capacity and heterogeneity, in turn, increase the number of different constraints and thus the number of different organizational forms. Agglomeration economies—advantages of spatial concentration resulting from the scale of an urban area—make new forms possible in cities, which could not survive in towns and villages. A simple example of agglomeration economies is the meat packing industry and the associated industries that follow when the scale of the slaughtering process is large enough; the byproducts from slaughtering can support leather tanning, the production of fatty oils and soaps, and then indirectly the industries using these products, such as the shoe manufacturing or cooking oil industries. The larger market in urban areas supports more organizations in the same or related industries, and the urban infrastructure makes interfirm communication easier, permits the sharing of facilities, and allows firms to keep abreast of the latest technological changes. In analyzing reasons for the selective growth of the leading eastern port cities of the United States during the nineteenth century, Pred (1966, p. 195) pointed out the importance of agglomeration economies: "Extension of credit, reduction of risk, and other services attainable from banking and insurance institutions augmented the lure of the major ports, and also encouraged hinterland aggrandizement (selective urban growth) because these identical services could not mature fully where the aggregate scale of wholesaling and trading activities was relatively small."

The "central place" function of larger urban areas—the functions cities fulfill because they are in the center of a trading area—means that the flow of resources through the city is large enough to support fairly esoteric and specialized organizational forms (Ullman, 1941). Ecological studies have found a strong relationship between the size of a community and the diversity of its business population, but this effect is not limited to the business sector. The diversity of voluntary associations and interest groups also increases with increasing urban growth. A study of Mensa (Aldrich, 1971b), a voluntary association for people of exceptional intelligence, found that the number of special interest groups within the association increased systematically with city size, ranging from none in Ann Arbor to over twenty-five in Los Angeles.

Political Revolution

Political revolutions break the ties that bind societal resources to certain vested interests and set the stage for possible new combinations of organizations and resources. Revolutions remove barriers to the entry of new interests into existing organizational activities, and permit the winning side to redirect resources into new organizational forms, if they so choose. Skocpol's (1976) historical analysis of the Communist revolution in China illustrates the manner in which societal resources are reallocated as a result of revolutions. Industrialization in China did not really begin until the successful revolution of 1949. In the nineteenth century, China was exploited by Western nations, but lacked the resources to fight off this imperialism, as "the Chinese central government could not wield significant leverage over the Chinese society and economy as a whole" (Skocpol, 1976, p. 297). Even though Chinese authorities recognized the importance of industrialization, they were in no position to promote it. This obvious weakness encouraged further foreign penetration, and in the 1930s Manchuria was lost to the Japanese. Industrialization, when it did occur, was limited to those port cities where foreign intervention and influence were strongest. One estimate is that through 1949 almost 90 percent of China's traditional marketing system remained intact.

After the successful 1949 revolution, which drove the Nationalists to Taiwan, the Communists had to begin from a very elementary level of development in their attempt at industrializing China's economy. Agricultural production was much more efficient, for example, than in Russia after the 1917 revolution, and so there was no prospect of reaping large surpluses by squeezing the peasants still further. However, they were able to use the peasants as a positive force, since peasants were accustomed to being involved in projects that extended beyond the village (due to the persistence of the multi-village market unit from the pre-1911 regime). Moreover, during the period of the Chinese civil war and Japanese occupation, the Communists had acquired experience and developed fundamental political organizations and techniques for directly mobilizing peasants in efforts to increase agricultural and small-scale industrial production.

There was a struggle between two factions of the Communist party. One wanted to follow the Soviet model and stress heavy industrialization, whereas the other, under Chairman Mao, wanted to stress the more gradual method of actively involving the peasants and developing rural and light industry. Chairman Mao and his faction won the battle, with the great proletarian cultural revolution of 1965-68 the culminating point of this struggle. Resources were mobilized in support of Mao's objectives, and China began to industrialize, following a rather different path than the one taken by the Soviet Union. Since Mao's death, it appears that Chinese leaders have partially reversed his objectives. Skocpol noted that the differences between China and the Soviet Union reflect the strong continuity of certain structural patterns from the pre-revolutionary regimes.

Revolution does not only free resources for novel uses; military defeat can also lead to the wholesale replacement of state bureaucrats and other important institutional leaders. After the defeat of Germany in 1945, the four Allied Powers moved swiftly to remove all Nazis from power. Government officials—regional and local—were chosen with one criterion in mind: having been anti-Nazi. Later, in East Germany, the Soviet Union applied another test: evidence of commitment to socialist or communist organizations. These new recruitment and selection policies substantially changed the social composition of the bureaucratic class in East Germany, as many more officials than before were chosen from the agricultural and working classes (Harden, 1976).

Environmental Variability and Niche Generation: Summary

The transformation of the world economy from a feudal to a capitalist mode of production overshadows all other environmental changes in the past millennium as the major change affecting the creation of new organizational forms. However, we now take the capitalist world economy as given, and thus our attention turns to more limited changes. Urbanization and political revolution are recurring forces that have freed resources and permitted new organizational forms to emerge, although urbanization has been displaced by suburbanization in Western industrial societies in the past several decades (Hawley, 1971.)

The population ecology model leads to the expectation of finding highly similar forms of organizations in similar environments, even though the forms may be arrived at through rather different routes. Similar social structural conditions, resource distributions, and environmental exigencies should lead to convergence of highly adaptive forms. Campbell (1969, p. 81), citing Julian Steward's research, noted that "where storable grains made a division of labor possible and where the tillage conditions made cooperation profitable, agriculturally based urban communities have repeatedly independently emerged." A common role in societies with centrally controlled agricultural systems were warriors, whose function was to guard the seed stores. If the grain put away for the next growing season's planting were eaten instead, the society would perish of starvation. Thus, societies with such roles had a selective advantage over those without them. Rotating credit associations developed independently in Japan and the West Indies (transported from Africa) to fill a niche giving its occupants a substantial selective advantage: the ability to amass capital rapidly and at low interest rates, so that participants could buy houses or start small businesses. In a world where efficient transportation and communication networks link nearly all parts of the globe, independent invention of forms is less important than their diffusion from one society to another. Nevertheless, it is still an hypothesis to be entertained whenever similar forms are found at widely separated locations.

PATTERNS OF ORGANIZATIONAL CREATION

An examination of the historical evolution of organizational forms reveals two interesting trends: (1) the generation of new organizational forms occurs in waves, and (2) some forms, once established, remain viable with their original form intact for a considerable length of time, whereas others change rapidly. The first trend will be examined in this section, while the second will be reviewed in the next chapter. The central issue is to determine what factors account for the appearance of different organizational forms at different points in history—or, What determines the origin of organizational niches? New organizational forms have occurred on the crest of waves of historical conditions over the past two centuries in the United States, and Table 7.1 lists selected forms associated with specific periods. Ideally information should be presented on the rate of formation of organizational types over time, but such information is simply not available. The internal structural form of many types of organizations persisted for long periods after their original founding, and the reasons for this will be explored in the next chapter.

Table 7.1   Patterns of organizational creation: Waves of new forms

Type	Date of Emergence
Men's national social fraternities	
a) Northern liberal arts colleges	1840–1850
b) Southern colleges	1865–1870
c) "anti-fraternities" for Jews, blacks, Catholics, teacher's colleges	1900–1920
Savings banks	1830s
Textile factories (imported to the U.S. from England)	1800–1830
Railroads and steel companies	1850s & 1870s
New universities in the U.S.	1870–1900
National craft unions	1860–1900
Streetcar companies and electricity producing companies	1887–1910
Reorganization of retail trade:	1858–1900
department stores, chain stores, mail-order houses	
Mass communication industries	1920s
New federal agencies: Securities and Exchange Commission,	
Federal Communications Commission, Federal Housing Authority,	
National Labor Relations Board, Social Security Administration,	
Rural Electrification Administration	1934–1935
Air transportation	1945–1950
Record producing and distributing companies	1955–1970
"Pure" conglomerate corporations	1960s
Junior colleges	1960s

Source: Adapted from Stinchcombe, Arthur L., "Social Structure and Organizations," in J. G. March (ed.), *Handbook of Organizations*, © 1965 Rand McNally College Publishing Company. Reprinted by permission, with additions.

In addition to the obvious differences in goals and technology among the organizational forms listed in Table 7.1, there are also differences in internal structural characteristics. Stinchcombe (1965) observed that organizational types differed in their use of family labor, the proportion of administrative workers employed as clerks, and the proportion of administrators who are professionals. How does the population ecology model account for differences in forms over time? Clearly, the environment must have been changing in ways that gave a selective advantage to particular forms at particular times *and* organizations founded during a particular period must have been limited to the use of technologies and structures available at the time (Coleman, 1970). Stinchcombe (1965, p. 160) noted that "certain kinds of organizations (and consequently the technical systems which require them) could not be invented before the social structure was appropriate to them." This seemingly tautological statement contains the seeds of an ecological argument, although as noted in Chapter 2, the retrospective causal analysis required for historical analyses always carries the danger of circularity.

Organizational forms depend on the nature and distribution of the resources available in a specific environment. The changing role of the state, the development of a market-oriented economy, urbanization, political revolution, technological innovations, and other forces affecting the distribution of resources account for the major waves of differing organizational forms. Within a given historical epoch, three factors are especially useful in explaining the emergence of new forms: (1) technological innovations and social structural support for new technical developments; (2) entrepreneurs' access to power and wealth; and (3) the changing structure of labor markets.

Technological Innovations

Organizational forms are limited by the nature of the existing technology. The mass circulation daily newspaper was made possible by technical innovations in the first four decades of the nineteenth century: Newspaper presses were made of iron instead of wood, the revolving impression cylinder was substituted for the platen, steam power was substituted for hand power, and the typecasting machine replaced hand typesetting (Pred, 1966, pp. 202-3). As I noted in discussing the technological importance of the machine tool industry in the latter half of the nineteenth century, the invention of an efficient sewing machine in the 1860s made possible the vast shoe and ready-to-wear clothing industries.

Technological change is sometimes treated as the result of many inventors working over a long number of years, with the invention then exerting an independent influence on social structure: "In the past in many important cases the change occurred first in the technology, which changed the economic institutions, which in turn changed the social and governmental organizations, which finally changed the social beliefs and philosophies" (Ogburn, 1937, p. 10). Social structural factors, however, also affect receptivity to and investment in the development of new technologies. England squandered its early lead in the industrial revolution by failing to support organizations and institutions that would have made further technological development possible. In contrast, Napolean created the *Grande Ecoles* to train administrators and engineers, and Germany took the lead from France in the middle of the nineteenth century because of heavy state support for technical research.

"By 1870, the German university system could boast a considerable number of professors and lecturers, especially in the sciences, who, favored by light duties and well-equipped laboratories, could pursue basic research. Industrial research laboratories, such as that maintained by Krupp at Essen were to become models for corporate research everywhere" (Braverman, 1974, pp. 160-61). Polytechnic Institutes, created in the 1830s and 1840s as alternatives to universities, evolved into the *Technische Hochschulen* with a higher status than the universities. In the United Kingdom, Colleges of Advanced Technology were not upgraded to the status of "technological universities" until 1964 (Francis, 1977).

Access to Wealth and Power

Organizational forms are limited by the access of organizational entrepreneurs to sufficient wealth and power. The amount of wealth and power determines how well new forms compete with the old. The enormous expansion of the railroad industry in the United States—from about 30,000 miles of track in 1860 to over 166,000 miles in 1890—was made possible through capital furnished by major eastern bankers and investment houses and by government grants of land for railroad rights of way. Capital was not amassed in the name of an individual but rather in the name of a *corporation*. Indeed, a major milestone in the development of new organizational forms in industrial societies was reached with the evolution of the corporate, limited liability form of organization. The concept of a "corporation" depended upon the development of role-based rather than person-based forms of organization (Coleman, 1970). New sets of rights and responsibilities were created to take into account the abstract nature of the corporation—it has no physical corpus, as such, but exists only in the abstract as a set of relations and obligations between roles.

In England, joint-stock and limited liability legislation developed from 1844 to 1862 created the legal basis for the growth of the large industrial corporation, although it was not heavily used until almost thirty years later. The liberalization of laws of incorporation in New Jersey, New York, and Delaware permitted a widespread merger movement in the United States in the dwindling years of the nineteenth century, making possible the growth of truly giant corporations. Inaccessibility to wealth and power limited the development of industrial firms in England. The split between the landed gentry (and later the combination of the gentry and merchants) and industrialists was a severe handicap in the latter's efforts to raise money for investment (Francis, 1977). Financial institutions in England *preceded* the development of industry and were created to serve the needs of merchants, not industrialists. The historical precedence of merchants over industrial interests was reinforced by the low social status of the "new" economic activity and merchant elites' desires to reinvest in land or opportunities abroad. Much of the capital used to build railroads in nineteenth century America came from England, with United States railroad owners then using their profits to create national financial institutions in New York.

In the United States, the major financial institutions were created during the period of large-scale industrialization rather than before (Chandler, 1962; 1977). Industrialists in the United States were "new men" in most cases, but in England the original landed class transformed itself into a capitalist class while retaining its anti-industrialist bias. Mercantile as opposed to industrial capitalism was thus favored by the English gentry, whereas the closest equivalent in the United States to a landed gentry—the Southern aristocracy—was decisively defeated by the industrialized North in the Civil War. Mercantile and financial interests, which were the largest potential investors in nineteenth century England, did not invest very heavily in new industries. Potential industrialists were forced to raise money by mortgaging their homes or borrowing from relatives during the early critical period of industrialization, and expansion was through reinvesting profits (Francis, 1977).

Banks and financial institutions are not the only sources of wealth and power supporting the creation of new organizations. Kinship groups, ethnic associations, fraternal and religious associations, territorially based groups, and wealthy individuals may provide resources to organizational entrepreneurs. McCarthy and Zald (1977) noted that conscience constituents—persons supporting an organization even though they don't benefit directly from its success—may provide money, facilities, and labor to social movement organizations, as well as political legitimacy. Professional external support has been significant in spawning new organizations in the alternative institutions and self-help movement (Rothschild-Whitt, 1976). The New School for Democratic Management in San Francisco has offered inexpensive courses in accounting, finance, bookkeeping, and other subjects for people in organizations with a participatory ideology. Sessions in 1977 had enrollments of over 100 participants, learning skills to increase their organizations' effectiveness. The social movement industry, comprised of all the organizations committed to the alternative institutions movement, could thus be sustained even though the probability of failure for individual organizations was quite high (McCarthy and Zald, 1977, p. 1219).

Labor Market Characteristics

The structure of labor markets changes over time, and since labor is a crucial resource, changes in workers' competence, motivation, and degree of organization have had a major impact on organizational forms. In comparing labor markets for their impact on the form of organizations created, we would need to consider how persons are prepared for work roles, whether workers are organized into unions and professional associations, and how governmental regulations or self-regulations are related to occupational standards and licensing (Stinchcombe, 1965, p. 164). Some theorists argue that the public schools' major contribution to the labor force quality is not in teaching students specific skills but rather in instilling discipline and obedience to authority (Bowles, Gintis, and Meyer, 1975). Controversy also exists over whether the high educational qualifications employers require for entry-level jobs accurately reflect the level of skills necessary to do the job (Berg, 1969).

Immigrant labor has played a very important historical role in industrialization and economic growth. The demand for immigrant labor has resulted from several factors: (1) shortages of appropriately skilled labor in a society because of wars, natural disasters, emigration, and so forth; and (2) shortages of labor due to an economic system expanding more rapidly than population growth. Almost one million able-bodied men were killed in the United States Civil War between 1861 and 1865, thus substantially reducing the work force at the point when the drive to industrialization was beginning. Their places were taken by European immigrants, and toward the end of the century almost one-third of American manufacturing employees were foreign born.

Restrictions on international immigration to the United States produced by World War I and the events leading up to it meant that industrialists lost access to an important labor pool. Foreign immigrants were replaced by blacks migrating from the South—eventually over one million per decade—and the upgrading of blacks already in the North. Western European industry in the past few decades has benefitted from vast temporary movements of southern Europeans into the lowest paying and least desirable jobs. Migrants from Turkey, Greece, Italy, and North Africa partially alleviated the labor shortage in Germany, France, and other northern countries, while at the same time easing the problem of a labor surplus in their home countries. From the world system's perspective, the international division of labor places some countries in the role of exporting labor rather than goods. The foreign exchange earned abroad by immigrants enables labor-exporting countries to partially right their imbalance of payments with the more industrialized nations.

An Example of Creation: Credit Reporting Agencies

The emergence of commercial credit reporting agencies in the United States during the mid-1800s is an excellent example of the convergence of social structural conditions, technological innovations, and changing resource availability in the creation of a new organizational form. Madison's (1974) historical analysis of the development of two credit reporting agencies—Mercantile (later Dun) and Bradstreet—documents the origin and continued viability of the new form. Traditionally, merchants in early nineteenth-century America relied on their personal knowledge or on information from friends and associates concerning the credit-worthiness of their customers. As long as markets served were small and the volume of trade was low, informal methods worked fairly well. However, "as population and the volume of trade increased in the antebellum years and as the market area expanded with construction of canals and especially railroads, merchants began to trade with customers and towns that they did not and could not know personally" (Madison, 1974, p. 166). Larger merchants could afford to hire their own credit agents to check on prospective customers, and groups of merchants sometimes financed traveling agents, but these mechanisms were not financially feasible for most businesspeople. The economic crises of the 1830s and 1840s showed businesspeople that they had been extending credit to poor credit risks because of faulty or incomplete information.

A niche was thus open and the selective advantages gained by any entrepreneur creating a form to fill it were substantial. In 1841, Lewis Tappan founded the Mercantile Agency and began recruiting correspondents to submit reports to his agency from across the nation. Correspondents submitted reports twice a year to the New York office, where clerks copied them into the agency's forms, and merchants then could call at the office and have a clerk read the report to them. It contained the estimated wealth and business standing of the businesses reported on, together with a rather mixed lot of miscellaneous information, character reports, and gossip. The demand for the Mercantile Agency's services was so great that within ten years it employed almost 2,000 correspondents, with 30 clerks in the New York office and with around 700 of the largest merchants in the New York City area as subscribers. By 1870 the agency had twenty-eight branch offices around the nation and almost 8,000 subscribers. Mercantile's major competitor, Bradstreet, was founded in 1849 and the two agencies dominated the commercial credit reporting industry from that point. The two agencies merged in 1933 to become Dun and Bradstreet.

Two types of changes increased the viability of the credit agencies: a change to using full-time, professional credit reporters, and a series of changes in the technology of recording and reporting credit information. Improvements in the work force began in the 1860s, and by the 1870s both agencies employed full-time, paid, and trained reporters in most cities. The reliability of credit reports improved, as they were no longer based on second-hand information and chance gossip picked up by part-time reporters. Professional reporters interviewed businesspeople and asked them to fill out and sign agency reporting forms. Formalized methods were introduced for monitoring employee performance, including an operations manual and traveling reporters who conducted reliability checks on the reports of local correspondents. Branch offices were added so that some of the work could be decentralized, and local offices were given reponsibility for credit reporting and servicing subscribers in their areas. As for technological innovations, the telegraph and the typewriter made it much easier to transmit vast quantities of information between the various branches and the head office. The telegraph was too expensive to be used for routine communications, but it was valuable for emergency reports, such as the failure of large businesses. The typewriter and the development of carbon paper proved more widely applicable, as they eliminated the ncesssity for hand copying reports whenever copies were required.

The emergence of commercial credit reporting agencies illustrates all three major factors affecting the generation of new niches. Technological changes, such as the development of the telegraph, typewriter, and practical carbon paper, allowed the agencies to bureaucratize their information-processing procedures and thus expand their operations. The recruitment of full-time, professional employees gave the agencies a skilled labor force that turned in more accurate reports and improved the reputation of the agencies for reliable service. The exercise of power, in the form of the cooptation of state legislatures and the fending off of legal challenges, enabled the agencies to remove major uncertainties in their environments. In a series of lawsuits in the two decades after the Civil War, the agencies won significantly favorable decisions "as the courts restricted the agencies' obligations to subscribers and to persons they reported, while enlarging the liability of businessmen providing false information to credit reporters" (Madison, 1974, p. 180). Attempts by state legislatures to regulate the agencies were defeated, with the last major battle fought in Pennsylvania in 1874, after which no further challenges arose. Madison's analysis is an example of the carefully detailed historical studies required to furnish the cases necessary for a full-fledged understanding of the conditions under which new organizational forms emerge.

CONSTRAINTS ON THE VIABILITY OF NEW FORMS

The rate of formation of new organizations is fairly high, as noted in previous chapters, and while information on the rate of formation of new organizational forms is less complete, scattered evidence suggests that it has increased during this century. Failure rates are also high, however, inhibiting net growth of the organizational population. Stinchcombe (1965) wrote of the "liability of newness" of new organizations, especially those with new forms, identifying characteristics of work forces and markets as posing the primary problems for emerging organizations. Government regulation and other legal constraints also affect new forms. As I have already discussed the role of the state in supporting and protecting new ogranizations and the importance of increasing environmental variability in generating new niches, this section will focus only on work force characteristics, markets, and legal constraints. Nevertheless, almost all of the social, political, and economic conditions considered in this chapter have some relevance to the viability of new organizations or forms.

Work Force Characteristics

Members of new organizations must learn new roles, and in recruiting members, organizational entrepreneurs have to rely either on the possibility that skills have been learned elsewhere or they must retrain people. New organizations have an advantage to the extent that they are recruiting in areas where skills learned outside the organization can be generalized. Free universal education, especially in systems including advanced technical training, generates a work force with such characteristics, and nearly all developing countries in this century have copied the educational systems of industrialized nations. Urban economists often note that cities are germination centers for new forms of organizations because of the availability of a high-skill, heterogeneous labor force. After asserting that generalized skills in the labor force are important in reducing the liability of newness, Stinchcombe (1965, p. 149) argued that norms and attitudes are even more important: "probably more important still is the degree of initiative—the sense of responsibility for getting the job done rather than doing as they are told—in the labor force as a whole. Such a disciplined and responsible work force, combined with social routines for letting them exercise initiative, greatly reduces the liability of newness."

In organizational forms representing really radical departures from prevailing forms, members must learn new values, behaviors, and motivations. Socialization practices and external work roles represent patterns that must be broken if the new forms are to survive. Mao Tse Tung's efforts at a cultural revolution in China and the anti-hierarchy ideology of the new alternatives movement in the United States are examples of attempts to break away from established work force characteristics.

In developing countries, or isolated regions within developed nations, two force problems are likely to be critical. First, as Bendix (1956) noted, industrialization is a threat to the way of life of the newly recruited work force, as adapting to the demands of daily routines takes time to learn. New organizations involve the intermeshing of new roles and a new structure of relations, and there is a high cost in time and resources if things are not done properly. Some theorists argue that industrialization demands workers adopt a "modern" personality, characterized by openness to change, faith in science and technology, tolerance of diversity, and a more secular outlook on nature (Inkeles and Smith, 1974). Second, "new organizations must rely heavily on social relations among strangers" (Stinchcombe, 1965, p. 149), and participants must learn to trust one another if a complex structure is to function efficiently. Increasing the mobility of resources and populations brings strangers into contact with one another in situations where they cannot rely on particularistic ties, such as kinship or ethnicity, for assurances that promises will be kept. The liability of newness is lessened to the extent that a society already prossesses institutions operating on universalistic standards, such as legal institutions or universalistic religions.

Market Characteristics and Economic Concentration

New organizations or organizational forms must overcome the barriers to entry discussed in the last chapter: economy-of-scale barriers, absolute cost barriers, and product differentiation barriers. New organizations typically start small and must win members or customers away from established organizations. This task is made doubly difficult if existing organizations are more efficient users of resources because they use a technology with significant returns to scale, or if they control a critical resource or access to wealth that gives them an absolute advantage over all new entrants. Product differentiation barriers, as explained in the last chapter, exist when established organizations have gained a loyal following and have formed stable relations with their customers or participants. New organizations must overcome such loyalties, and they are assisted in this competition to the extent that existing organizations do not enjoy protected markets because of legal or traditional authoritative sanctions. In the business sector, the transformation to capitalism—accompanied by the growth of formally free labor and the commercialization of land—disrupted traditional ties between organizations, sponsors, and clients, and created a context within which transfers of patronage are legitimated.

Coercive conduct by existing firms, especially in highly concentrated industries, constitutes a severe handicap that new organizations have difficulty overcoming. Once we have drawn industry boundaries, we can use the concept of *seller concentration* to describe an industry's structure and thus the likelihood of firms within it engaging in certain kinds of restraints on competition. The concentration ratio is based on the number and size of the firms within an industry. To compute the ratio for an industry, we rank firms in order by size, starting from the largest in the industry and measuring size either by sales or number of employees. (In assessing not-for-profit organizations we might use total membership.) We then compute what percent of total industry sales or employment are accounted for by the top N number of firms. In the United States, published figures usually give concentration ratios for the largest four, eight, or sometimes twenty firms. For example, in 1953 the four-firm sales concentration ratios for the following industries were: passenger cars, 99 percent; electric lamps, 92 percent; cigarettes, 80 percent; tires and inner tubes, 70 percent; textile machinery, 35 percent; bread and related products, 23 percent; men's and boy's suits and coats, 14 percent; and screw machine products, 5 percent (Scherer, 1970, p. 55). Eight-firm ratios for these industries would, of course, be higher.

There are four problems with published concentration ratios that we must be aware of. First, the ratios are highly sensitive to how widely or narrowly an industry is defined. Ideally, an "industry" should be defined as all those firms within the same niche which are competing for the same resources, meaning that customers or clients treat their products as interchangeable or as equivalent substitutes. The United States Census Bureau developed the Standard Industrial Classification (SIC) system as a method for categorizing the output of business establishments, using a series of seven digit numbers, with each successive digit indicating a finer degree of classification (Scherer, 1970, p. 53). While some industries are defined using all seven digits, concentration ratios are published at the four- and five-digit level, and some "industries" thus defined are still rather heterogeneous. Second, within the top four or eight firms there may be an uneven size distribution, as in the passenger car industry where the top firm produces about half the autos sold and the fourth struggles to hold on to its less than three percent share. Third, concentration ratios are computed on the assumption of national markets, whereas many firms compete on a local or regional level. Regional concentration ratios could well indicate a much higher degree of concentration within an industry. Finally, the role of foreign trade is neglected, as the ratios are based on domestic producers only.

In spite of these problems, concentration ratios are a good shorthand indicator of the potential for concerted action and the exercise of power and dominance within an industry. Cross-national studies have found a very high degree of similarity between concentration ratios within the same industries in Western industrialized nations. In a study of the United Kingdom, West Germany, France, and Italy, George and Silberton (1974) found correlations ranging from 0.56 to 0.77 between concentration ratios for the same industries in the four countries, taken two at a time. A study of sixteen industries in the United States, Canada, and the United Kingdom also found a high degree of similarity between concentration ratios (Caves, 1972).

If the concentration ratio of an industry is high and if the number of firms in the industry is relatively small, new organizations may be kept out by agreements among the firms, ranging from price-fixing arrangements and cartels to tacit collusion. Dominant firms can use predatory price-cutting to frighten off potential entrants or drive new organizations out of business. Firms operating in more than one geographic market can use profits from one area to subsidize cutthroat competitive practices in another, raising still further the barriers to entry of new organizations. Vertically integrated firms can shut out new organizations by integrating backward to control sources of raw material and forward to tie up retail outlets. During the period of intensified industrial mergers in England and the United States, around the turn of the century, British manufacturers could use methods of market control that were closed to Americans. Networks of trade associations covered the industrial field, and there were numerous "gentlemen's agreements" and understandings in restraint of trade. Manufacturers in England didn't need to worry about judicial or legislative hostility toward pools and cartels, as Americans did, and one consequence was less pressure toward mergers than in the United States (Payne, 1967).

Government Regulation

Just as the state plays an important role in supporting and protecting organizations, so it also acts occasionally to limit the viability of new organizations by restricting their entry into new markets. In previous chapters I presented a number of examples of the importance of government regulation or protection in smoothing the way for interfirm collaboration or sustaining industry profit rates, such as in the pharmaceutical industry or publicly chartered monopolies. Pfeffer (1974) presented additional examples of federal regulatory agencies' policies having an adverse effect on entry into an industry. In the trucking industry, the number of carriers has consistently declined, falling from 18,036 in 1957 to 15,426 in 1966. This decline occurred in spite of the Interstate Commerce Commission receiving thousands of applications from new firms or existing firms desiring new routes, and in spite of a steady increase in the volume of freight shipped. The concentration of business receipts increased: In 1957, 2.32 percent of the general carriers had more than one million dollars in receipts and accounted for about 50 percent of total receipts, whereas by 1964, 3.47 percent of the carriers took in more than five million dollars apiece and accounted for about 66 percent of all receipts. The trucking industry, needless to say, is quite profitable. In the commercial banking industry, some observers estimate that without legal restrictions, there would be nearly two times as many banks as there are now.

Although airline profits have not been boosted by government regulation, until 1978 the Civil Aeronautics Board (CAB) was effectively restricting the entry of new airlines into the industry. "The only carriers providing trunk service [were] the sixteen carriers in existence when the CAB was created in 1938. . . ; and the only local service carriers were the 21 airlines that received certificates in the period of 1943 through 1950, during a special experiment with local service. Yet . . . just within California 16 intrastate carriers entered during the period from 1946 through 1965" (Pfeffer, 1974, pp. 472-73).

Wiley and Zald (1968) pointed out that private certifying associations perform a similar function, in that certification by the association determines whether an organization will be perceived as legitimately entitled to access to needed resources. The North Central Association of Colleges and Secondary Schools and the Southern Association of Colleges and Schools "have not had the coercive power of the state behind them, nor have they directly controlled economic incentives. However, the major sanction of the organization, admission to membership, has affected the ability of the colleges to recruit faculty and students" (Wiley and Zald, 1968, p. 39). In the medical sector, the American Hospital Association and the American Medical Association perform a similar sanctioning function. They can remove the certification of hospitals, thus denying them access to government funds in programs such as Medicaid and Medicare. The American Bar Association's guidelines for advertising by law firms (prohibiting advertising services by price) has limited the ability of newly created law firms to break into the market for legal services, as established firms are more visible and have stable ties to clients. Price competition, which might persuade clients to change law firms, has been ruled out, although the ABA's guidelines are now under challenge in a number of states as an illegal restriction on competition.

Constraints on Viability: Summary

New organizations, especially those adopting a new form, must overcome many obstacles if they are to survive and carve out a new niche for themselves. Work force characteristics, such as levels of skill and literacy, affect the type of control and communication structures that new organizations can adopt, and unionized labor forces may raise firms' costs to a point where firms must move to survive. Market characteristics, such as barriers to entry and the level of concentration in an industry, also affect new organizations' viability by making access to required resources more difficult. Legal constraints, whether government- or self-enforced, severely limit entry or restrict it to only those organizations complying with the practices of existing organizations. Constraints on viability are similar to constraints on variability, in that they limit the range of variation in a population and thus slow the rate of organizational change.

SUMMARY

New organizations and new organizational forms are most likely to emerge when environmental variability and attempts at innovation increase, selection parameters change and previous patterns of resource distribution are disrupted, and forces retaining existing forms of organizations break down. The motives of organizational entrepreneurs are important in constructing a comprehensive explanation of the creation of organizations, but I have argued in this chapter that they are much less important for a theory of organizational change than is an understanding of structural, political, and economic conditions. Several historical forces and changes were reviewed, including the transformation of the world economy from a feudal to a capitalist mode of production, the long-term trend toward increasing urbanization in all societies, and the frequent occurrence of political revolutions. The role of the state is perhaps the single most important factor in accounting for patterns of organizational creation, for state support and protection constitute an overwhelming advantage for organizations receiving state blessing, directly or indirectly. Several case studies described in this chapter illustrate the potential for an application of the natural selection model to the study of organizational creation, but most organizational studies continue to use ahistorical, cross-sectional methods that fail to capture the rich contextual details required by the ecological approach.

8 Persistence and Transformation of Organizations

Many new organizations, especially those with a new form, succumb to the liabilities of newness and survive for only a short time. Others succeed to such an extent that their form spreads throughout the population, occupying a particular niche and persisting over many generations of organizational births and deaths. Some organizations, buffeted by external forces or faced with irresistible internal pressures, experience a transformation of form instead of extinction. What external and organizational forces account for persistence and transformation of organizations and organizational forms? The answer to this question builds upon the models and concepts of the preceding chapters, following Hernes's (1976) suggestions for the explanation of change: (1) the same model and concepts should be used to explain constancy and change; (2) intrinsic sources of change should be included in the model, as in Chapter 4; and (3) the explanation should recognize the importance of individual actors in the change process, as in the preceding chapter's discussion of motives and incentives of organizational entrepreneurs. Only a small number of new concepts will be introduced to explain persistence and transformation. The variation, selection, and retention stages of the natural selection model provide the overarching framework within which the necessary arguments can be introduced.

189

PRELIMINARY ISSUES

The distinction between forms and niches, explained in Chapter 5, is important for the analysis of organizational forms' persistence and transformation because niches can remain the same while forms change. Forms may also persist in niches that are steadily shrinking as adjacent niches expand. The transportation industry, for example, includes water, rail, highway, and air transport, with each type of transportation at one time enjoying a selective advantage over previous types. Organizations still use transportation technologies of all four types, but long-distance passenger traffic (by passenger-miles) is now dominated by airlines. Stinchcombe (1965) noted that railroads persist in using an organizational form developed in the last century, but he did not note that railroads have been pushed out of part of their traditional market by newer forms of transport, such as buses and airplanes. Thus the persistence of an organizational form does not necessarily mean that the niche it occupies has been stable as well.

Persistence and transformation can be analyzed at either the level of populations or individual organizations. The population ecology model's emphasis on population level analyses reminds us that the persistence of organizational forms does not depend on the fate of any particular organization. Stable selection criteria and effective retention mechanisms preserve forms at the population level, regardless of the failure of individual organizations, as in the construction or retail trade industries, social fraternities, and private universities. Similarly, the same forces that promote the creation of new organizational forms may lead to changes that transform the population of organizations occupying a niche, as in the transportation or machine tool industries. At the population level, then, the analysis of transformation is identical to the explanation of the creation of new forms, covered in the last chapter.

Individual organizations may be transformed in their own lifetime, and most organizational sociology studies of transformation are of single organizations. Changes in goals, technologies, and activity systems have been attributed to internal and external forces, but the underlying similarity of the study of persistence and transformation has passed almost unnoticed—the nonpersistence of an organization implies either its demise or its transformation.

Types of Change

Hernes (1976), in his discussion of structural models of social change processes, provided a number of concepts useful in understanding organizational persistence and transformation. An observed structure is a consequence of social forces that may be constant or changing, and three distinct aspects of the change process may be distinguished: an output structure, a process structure, and a parameter structure. These concepts are best grasped in the context of the example dealing with environmental capacity, presented in Chapter 3. A logistic equation for growth in a population of organizations was defined as follows:

190

$$\frac{dx}{dt} = ax - bx^2$$

In the equation a equals the instrinsic rate of increase in the population, in the absence of resource constraints; b equals the inhibiting effect of intrapopulation competition resulting from organizations with the same needs competing for a limited supply of resources; and a/b equals the carrying capacity of the environment, given a fixed organization size.

The *output structure* in this example is the population in a given time period that results from organizations being added (at rate dx/dt) to the existing population. The population's characteristics include the total number and the age and size distribution of all organizations. The *process structure* is defined by the forces producing change in the population: the intrinsic rate of increase and the inhibiting effect of competition. These two forces are represented by the two coefficients a and b in the equation. The *parameter structure* is the precise way in which the forces producing change have an effect on the output structure. The parameters are the *values* of the two coefficients in the equation—in Table 3.1, a was given a value of 0.5 and b equaled 0.01. Both parameters in this example are affected by the level and distribution of resources in the environment inhabited by the "x's" and accordingly may change if the environment changes.

The concepts of output, process, and parameter structures may be used to define four types of change processes, as shown in Table 8.1: (1) simple reproduction, (2) extended reproduction, (3) transition, and (4) transformation. The four types of change are arranged in the manner of a Guttman scale, with no change in any of the three structures defining simple reproduction and change in all structures defining transformation.

Under *simple reproduction*, the output structure is fixed, the process structure is unchanged, and parameter values are such that the system is in equilibrium. In the example in Table 3.1, simple reproduction is achieved when the population of organizations reaches fifty in number, for then no further growth is possible and new additions are matched by the demise of existing organizations. A state of

Table 8.1   Four possibilities for change or stability at three levels

| | Types of Change Processes | | | |
Structure	Simple Reproduction	Extended Reproduction	Transition	Transformation
Does the output structure change?	NO	YES	YES	YES
Do the parameter values change?	NO	NO	YES	YES
Does the process structure change?	NO	NO	NO	YES

Source: Gudmund Hernes, "Structural Change in Social Processes," *American Journal of Sociology*, 82, 3 (November, 1976), p. 524.

simple reproduction in a population is reached when selection criteria are stable and retention mechanisms effectively preserve current structures and activities. I noted in Chapter 3 that lack of strategic advantages and restrictions on technological innovation would ensure that the population of fifty organizations of equal size would remain that way. Marx (1967) used the concept of reproduction to refer to the capitalist economic system's dependence upon the continued production of the resources required for its operation, especially labor power. In an economic system where workers must sell their own labor power as a commodity so that they can purchase the means for daily subsistence, persons are constrained to take wage-labor jobs. "Self-preservation requires daily consumption, which in a money economy requires payment and hence wage labor—but . . . wage labor tends to maintain these very conditions" (Hernes, 1976, p. 524). Simple reproduction in the case of a single organization would consist of an organization successfully reproducing the conditions required for persistence of its form.

Extended reproduction is defined as a situation where process and parameter structures remain the same but the output structure changes. In the example from Table 3.1, output structure changes until the environment's carrying capacity is reached, and if organizations are added beyond carrying capacity, the population rapidly adjusts downward as the less fit are eliminated. Occasionally economic systems experience a condition of rapidly rising expectations that cannot be met with available resources. Organizational entrepreneurs found new organizations on the false hope that a new level of prosperity will be reached, and the failure of these aggregate expectations leads to a system-wide crash. At the level of individual organizations, organizational growth may result in a changed output structure, raising the costs of communication and control, but it can also lead to changes more properly characterized as transformation.

Transition is defined as a change not only in output structure but also in parameter values. Hernes (1976, p. 527) cited the example of the theory of demographic transition, describing how changes in the two components of the rate of natural increase in populations led to substantial demographic changes in Europe in the eighteenth and nineteenth centuries. A falling death rate but a stable high birth led to a population explosion, slowed only when birth rates fell as well. Note that the process structure did not change—by definition, natural increase is a result of the excess of births over deaths—but that parameter values (the rates) changed and thus affected the output structure. The previous chapter described a number of forces affecting parameter values of otherwise fairly stable process structures: Increases in state tax power raise the proportion of business income set aside for the government, increased investment in education produces a more skilled labor force, and ideological legitimation—although a basic requirement of all economic systems—is achieved differently under different regimes. Changes in government regulation are an ever-present source of changes in parameter values within a constant process structure.

Transformation involves changes in all three structures—outputs, parameters, and processes. The transformation of the world economy from a feudal to a capitalist mode of production was the most far-reaching transformation in the current millenium, but many other types of transformations have occurred. Technological changes are continually altering process structures in organizational populations and making new forms possible. Commercial credit agencies gained a secure niche only after the development of efficient typewriters and the telegraph service cut their communication costs enough to allow decentralization of their operations. The machine tool industry continually fed new technological innovations into American industry in the nineteenth century, changing process structures by allowing the mechanization of production processes. Individual organizations often face resource pressures, forcing them to adopt new processes and hence new forms, as in the example of ACME Vegetable in Chapter 1, and in several other examples discussed later in this chapter.

Of the four types of processes listed by Hernes, two receive direct attention in the remainder of this chapter—simple reproduction and transformation. Extended reproduction is discussed indirectly in a consideration of the effects of growth on organizational structure, and transition is treated indirectly in the discussion of transformation. Persistence of forms, or simple reproduction, is examined at both the population and organizational levels, as it has not been treated in previous chapters. Transformation, however, is analyzed only at the level of single organizations, because it was treated extensively in discussing the creation of new organizations and organizational forms in Chapter 7.

PERSISTENCE: A POPULATION PERSPECTIVE

The specific characteristics of a new organizational form depend upon the nature and distribution of resources available in the environment, technological development, access of organizational entrepreneurs to wealth and power, and the structure of labor markets, as discussed in the previous chapter. Some forms, once created, persist over time with the same structural characteristics as at the point of their founding. An entire organizational population, such as the apparel or coal mining industries, may continue with the same level of bureaucratization or technological development, as new organizations founded in the industry adopt the traditional form. In Hernes's terms, this is a situation of simple reproduction, and in terms of the natural selection model, the situation can be analyzed by examining what forces affect the *retention* of selected forms in a population. Stinchcombe's approach to the problem is examined first, and then his argument is recast to fit the natural selection model.

Stinchcombe's Examples

As evidence for the stability of organizational forms over time at the population level, Stinchcombe (1965) presented United States Census data on the work force characteristics of four groups of industries: prefactory, early nineteenth century, railroad age, and modern. A number of differences are apparent between these groups of industries. Prefactory industries, such as agriculture and retail trade, still use more unpaid family labor than industries founded later. Early nineteenth-century industries, such as woodworking and apparel, are still family firms, but differ from earlier forms in that they are bureaucratized below the top management level. Railroad age industries, such as railroads and coal mining, have career officials rather than family members at the very top, but their staff departments are not as professionalized as modern industries. Modern industries, such as motor vehicles and air transport, are extensively bureaucratized, with a high proportion of clerical and professional workers at the top and almost no family labor or management. All comparisons are based on the 1952 Bureau of the Census report, although Stinchcombe noted that figures from the 1960 Census showed a similar ranking of industries. Where comparable data were available for 1950 and 1960, he noted that all industries but one (out of fourteen) had become more professionalized, and all but one (out of five) prefactory industries had become more bureaucratic. Thus the relative stability of forms does not mean that no changes are occurring.

Stinchcombe derived an *ad hoc* set of three hypotheses to account for the persistence of these historical differences. First, the original form may still be the most efficient. Second, institutionalization may have preserved the form through traditionalizing forces, protection by vested interests, or a strongly legitimated ideological position. Third, the original form may have no competitors because it is a natural monopoly or is assured of a stable funding base. These explanations were not tested empirically. However, they appear plausible and I will show that they can be deduced from the natural selection model.

Before considering the ecological model's explanation of persistence, we should note the presence of a problem previously cited—the arbitrary nature of definitions of organizational forms. Following the practice of the United States Bureau of the Census, Stinchcombe classified railroads and air transport as different industries. His analysis would have been different had he classified industries by their functional niche in the interorganizational division of labor. The natural selection model implies that innovative organizations and new forms will appear in niches adjacent to existing niches, perhaps exploiting different resources at first, but with the potential of expanding to take over the adjacent niches. The trucking industry, for example, has made inroads into the market for long-haul shipments once served by the railroad industry. If new forms are classified as occupying different niches, then Stinchcombe's analysis remains unchanged. However, it is questionable whether many of the industries separated by Stinchcombe actually occupy different niches. Water, rail, and air transport might be considered evolving forms of transportation, and printing and publishing might be considered the forerunners of telecommunications. Coal mining, crude petroleum, and natural gas might be considered alternatives within the energy industry.

If industries are reclassified by functional niche, different inferences emerge from Stinchcombe's data. The new classification scheme would show evolution toward more bureaucratic structures as each new form ascends to prominence within the niche. This argument could be tested by examining rates of growth in each of the component industries within the larger functional classifications, as it implies that newer forms should be gradually displacing older forms and achieving a larger share of the market. At some point the new form might completely eliminate the older form, as for example electronic means of communication—telephone, telex, telecopying, and other forms of telecommunication—have cut deeply into the market traditionally served by the postal service. The stability of forms uncovered by Stinchcombe may not be an accurate portrayal of the extent to which forms within a niche have changed over time. An investigator might still choose to focus on the reasons for the persistence of declining forms, but the implications of this type of analysis would be quite different from Stinchcombe's.

Explanations for Persistence

Persistence, or the simple reproduction of forms, can be treated under the more general issue of the selective retention of organizational forms. The natural selection model directs our attention to three conditions under which the liklihood of stable forms is quite high: (1) environmental selection operates freely and the original form continues to be selected because the environmental parameter structure has not changed and the original form is still the most efficient; (2) environmental selection operates freely and environmental selection parameters might have changed, but constraints on organizational variation prevent new entrants from developing a more advantageous form; and (3) environmental selection is severely restricted because organizations are insulated from environmental effects. Note again that whether forms are treated as stable or evolving depends in part on how widely an environmental niche is defined.

In some industries environmental selection parameters change only slowly, if at all, and the most efficient form is still the original one. The garment business in London's East End—the "rag trade"—has persisted with virtually the same organizational forms from the 1870s. The system of small shops and homework first employed Jews and then Indians and Pakistanis as workers and shopowners. Forms persisted because of a lack of space for expansion to realize economies-of-scale in production and technological change, seasonal variations in demand and style changes, competition from goods produced abroad by cheap labor, and the presence of an immigrant population that could be exploited at low wage rates. The stability of the family farm in the agricultural industry, until the fairly recent advent of agri-business, was due in part to the efficiency and productivity improvements of the traditional form.

If variation is constrained within an industry, then changing environmental conditions are not as likely to induce changes in forms. Environmental selection has a maximum effect when the rate of variation is high and the life span of any one unit is relatively short. An industry's form may be stable because the length of a generation is relatively long or there are few failures or new starts. These conditions, in turn, may be due to barriers to entry, a slow rate of technological change, or a high proportion of owner-controlled firms. Owner-controlled businesses are relatively well protected from takeover by outside acquisition or management coups from within. Some evidence indicates that owner-controlled firms can survive for a long time in spite of relatively poor economic performance (Hindley, 1970). Variation may be suppressed because businesses are passed between successive generations of the family, as when a son takes over his father's firm, a practice especially prevalent in agriculture (Boswell, 1973).

The lower the degree of variation across organizations within a niche, the less likely are drastic changes in forms. The environment might have had a powerful effect at one time in selecting a homogeneous population of organizations, and environmental stability or a high degree of risk-aversiveness by entrepreneurs then perpetuated the form. Variation may be relatively infrequent because there are few entrepreneurs willing to undertake the risk of starting a new organization with a form differing from traditional ones. Without variation, which is most likely to be introduced by new organizations, environmental selection criteria are largely irrelevant in affecting organizational change and simple reproduction is assured.

Organizational forms may be insulated against environmental pressures because of government protection or regulation, support from powerful elites, or shared beliefs and values that selectively screen out potentially disruptive external events. All three factors have been discussed in previous chapters and they are discussed again in the section on the persistence of individual organizations. In the United States, federal price supports and subsidies to agriculture have helped keep alive the family farm, even though most of the benefits have gone to the largest operators. Some critics allege that the Civil Aeronautics Board's regulation of the United States airline industry reduced competitive pressures that otherwise would have produced major changes in operating characteristics. Private universities with substantial endowments have been able to resist pressures to modify their traditional practices regarding student-teacher ratios, course offerings, and use of the summer session's slack time more easily than publicly supported universities.

Forms may persist because they are still the most fit, the range of organizational variation is constrained, or environmental selection criteria do not operate freely. Clearly some organizations attempt to create the conditions that will ensure their reproduction, and creating barriers to entry—either through interorganizational arrangements or seeking governmental protection—is probably the most common strategy for large and powerful organizations. Less powerful organizations do not have access to such tactics, and their survival is contingent upon their responding to environmental selection criteria. Note that the persistence of forms in a population does not depend upon the fate of any particular organization. Organizations do not give birth directly to succeeding generations in their niches, and so continuity in forms depends upon retention mechanisms that permit new organizations to copy their predecessors and on stability in environmental selection criteria that constrain new organizations to use the traditional form.

PERSISTENCE: INDIVIDUAL ORGANIZATIONS

An explanation for the persistence of particular organizations can be constructed using the same arguments as for the persistence of forms in a population, but more attention must be paid to tactics and strategies of an organization's dominant coalition. As noted in Chapter 2, most studies of organization structure focus on internal retention mechanisms—the forces that perpetuate a particular organization's structure and activities—even though investigators themselves do not frame their analyses in these terms. Bureaucratization is the key internal characteristic facilitating structural persistence, and professionalized management—another consequence of the rationalization of organizational life—increasingly protects large organizations from radical change, although it may increase the rate of piecemeal modifications. External forces are a more significant factor of persistence for most organizations, as interorganizational arrangements, government support, and elite social and political support benefit smaller as well as larger organizations.

Internal Factors in Persistence

The characteristics of bureaucracy have attracted sociologists' attention precisely because they are factors intrinsic to the organizing process that help account for the persistence of an individual organization's form. Written documents and office files are readily available guides from the past to appropriate practices for the present and, together with specialization and standardization of roles, ensure continuity in participants' role behaviors. In organizations large enough to possess an internal career ladder for members, performance sanctions reward them for adhering to prescribed duties.

Role discretion, which carries the potential for deviation from past practices, is limited by formalization and an official hierarchy of authority that restricts the range of opportunities open to any member for random deviation. Standardized selection procedures for leaders and members contribute to organizational continuity, and socialization activities instill a sense of respect for the past in new recruits. If an organization achieves a successful fit to environmental criteria, bureaucratic administrative structure and activities increase the likelihood of the organization's persistence, as long as selection criteria do not change drastically.

Gamson (1975) found that challenging groups (groups seeking to mobilize an unmobilized constituency against an outside antagonist) possessing a bureaucratic structure were more likely than others to gain acceptance and new advantages from the antagonist and to survive for a longer period. Bureaucratization was measured by the existence of a written document stating the purposes of the organization, a formal list of members, and three or more levels or internal divisions. Challenging groups in the sample included the American Free Trade League, the National Urban League, the American Federation of Labor, and the Tobacco Night Riders. Bureaucracy enabled challenging groups to be more successful because "by creating a structure of roles with defined expectations in the place of diffuse commitments, a challenging group can better assure that certain necessary tasks will be routinely performed. It gives the challenging group a higher readiness for action" (Gamson, 1975, p. 91). Some of the groups began with highly bureaucratized structures, with others adopting them over their lifetime. Centralization of power, either in the form of a dominant personal leader or a strong executive committee, made an added contribution to a group's probability of success, as did the absence of internal factionalism.

Sixteen groups had a period of challenge lasting twenty years or more, and 75 percent were bureaucratized, whereas of the thirty-one groups that had a challenge period of ten years or less, only 29 percent were bureaucratized. After noting that bureaucracy had a strong relationship to the gaining of acceptance, Gamson (1975, p. 122) suggested that "bureaucracy helps a group to survive for a longer period in the absence of tangible results; a system-wide crisis then occurs and outside pressures push the group's antagonist to make some accommodation with it." Bureaucratic structure, by contributing to organizational persistence, thus contributed to the likelihood that a group would be successful in its challenge.

Professionalized management.   In reviewing Collins and Preston's (1961) study showing that the rate of turnover in the list of the top 100 manufacturing, mining, and distribution industries has declined over time, Scherer (1970, p. 50) concluded that managers in very large corporations have adopted a more professionalized, long-range view of their functions. They no longer see their role as preserving the specific products of their firms, but rather as ensuring the survival of the firm as an organization, meaning that they are willing to adopt new products and technologies when necessary. He noted that "as a by-product of their more professional managerial outlook and increased size, large corporations may have become more diversified, hedging against shifts in demand." Evidence Scherer reviewed in his book indicates that this is, indeed, the case. McCarthy and Zald (1977, pp. 1233-34) made a similar point about social movement organizations, noting that older, established organizations developed professionalized staffs and a clear image of themselves, enabling them to survive while newer organizations failed.

The rate of turnover among large firms has never been very substantial, as pointed out in Chapter 2. Collins and Preston (1961) compiled a list of the top 100 firms, ranked by assets for five time periods: 1909–19, 1919–29, 1929–35, 1935–48, and 1948–58. They then computed the number of firms dropping out of the top 100 firms for each year during these periods, identifying two types of exits: firms dropping off for any reason, and "natural" exits, which excludes the effects of mergers and antitrust actions. The average exits per year for the five periods were 4.0, 3.1, 2.7, 1.5, and 1.6, respectively; for only "natural" exits, rates per year were 2.6, 2.1, 2.0, 1.5, and 1.7.

There are no absolute standards for judging whether these rates are high or low, but they do show a fairly high degree of stability when compared to the turnover among small businesses. Moreover, these rates are only for exits from the top 100 firms, not failures. Few, if any, of these firms went out of business. Whittington's (1972) study of the top 100 manufacturing companies in the United Kingdom between 1948 and 1968 showed similar results; the only total disappearances were due to mergers, take-overs, or nationalization. Depending upon the circumstances, a merger or take-over might represent "failure" from the perspective of the acquired firm. Whatever the reason—professionalized management, market power, political connections, diversification, and so on—the very largest firms persist, evidently adapting to or creating the necessary environmental conditions for their survival.

External Forces in Persistence

External resource constraints are a major threat to organizational persistence, and it is difficult for organizations to resist being transformed by such pressures. Three conditions shielding organizations from pressures toward transformation are examined in this section: (1) interorganizational arrangements; (2) government support; and (3) support from social or political elites.

Interorganizational arrangements.   A variety of relations with other organizations may be used to resist external pressures, including mergers, joint ventures, cartels, price-fixing agreements, interlocking directorates, sponsorship, and other types of cooperative agreements. Insofar as organizations avoid sacrificing control over their own affairs in return for the resources made available by such arrangements, their prospects for structural stability are enhanced. The conditions under which these types of interorganizational relations are entered into will be examined in subsequent chapters; therefore, only a few examples will be presented in this section.

Many organizations, primarily voluntary associations, survive because they are attached to other organizations that sponsor them. The sponsoring organizations provide resources, legitimacy, and absorb the administrative overhead that would pose a major burden for the voluntary association. Public school systems provide essential services for many organizations, ranging from outright sponsorship to a meeting place for otherwise homeless groups. Many national special interest associations for youths operate through the schools, such as the National Honor Society, Junior Achievement, Boy Scouts, and foreign language clubs. The national 4-H organization relies on local cooperative extension agents of the Department of Agriculture and local schools for advisers and meeting places. In the 1960s, Community Action Agencies (CAA) served as a focal point for many local liberal or radical movements, providing facilities for meetings, machinery for typing and duplicating leaflets and newsletters, and a convenient source of new recruits. CAAs are now under local political control, but in their new form and under a variety of local names they are still the major sponsor of the Head Start Program, one of the most popular of the "Great Society" programs.

Kunz (1969) examined the effect of sponsorship on Boy Scout troops, using information on the stability of troop sponsorship between 1959 and 1966. He found that troop sponsorship was most stable when sponsors were youth oriented and were relatively rich in organizational resources. Organizations whose major purpose was directed toward youths, such as schools, were classified as "youth oriented." Organizations with a subunit serving youth were classified as "partially youth oriented," such as Rotary Clubs, and organizations with no youth programs, such as fire departments, were classified as "non-youth oriented." Over the seven year period, 64 percent of the troops whose original sponsor was non-youth oriented changed sponsors, compared to only 38 percent of the partially- and 31 percent of the totally-youth oriented sponsored troops. Resources of the sponsoring organization were assumed high when it was part of a national organization (and especially a religious organization) and low when it was solely a local organization. Lack of organizational resources was directly related to the percent of troops *changing* sponsors: national religious denomination, 21 percent; national civic and service organizations, 38 percent; school and PTA sponsors, 34 percent; locally autonomous religious denominations, 50 percent; and the most volatile of all, local civic and parent groups, 65 percent.

The more committed the national religious denomination to the policy of local units sponsoring Boy Scout troops—as measured by a denomination's relative share of all religion-sponsored troops—the less likely was discontinuation of a troop or turnover in its sponsorship. There was also a tendency for troops whose sponsorship was discontinued to acquire a new sponsor with greater organizational resources than its previous sponsor, suggesting that local troop leaders were exercising strategic choice in their search for a new sponsor. The policy of the national headquarters of Boy Scouts of America from 1915 to 1966 also reflected an implicit objective of obtaining national-affiliated rather than purely local sponsors, as indicated by the rapid growth in the number of troops with nationally-affiliated sponsors.

Government support.   The state's role in supporting and protecting organizations was discussed in previous chapters, and many of the arguments are applicable in considering organizational persistence. Just as entire industries benefit from certain kinds of state action, so do individual organizations: Tariff barriers and import quotas shield existing firms against foreign competition and pressures to innovate; export subsidies and indirect assistance give businesses a competitive edge in the world market; tax laws favoring certain types of investments help channel funds into particular industries and businesses; loan guarantees—as in the United States government's guarantees to Lockheed Aircraft or the British government's underwriting of Chrysler Corporation's operations—keep struggling firms afloat; and military intervention may be requested to protect a company's foreign investments. Regulatory commissions may promulgate rules that effectively block the entry of competitors to existing organizations, as in the airline and pharmaceutical industries of the United States. The United States Interstate Commerce Commission's regulations regarding railroads, such as disallowing the sloughing off of passenger trade and unprofitable routes, had the unintended consequence of preserving not only the existing railroads but also inefficient technological and organizational practices.

Elite social and political support.   Support from elites is a third means of increasing the likelihood of organizational persistence. Selznick (1957) argued that a major function of organizational elites is to defend an organization's integrity while at the same time justifying the organization to external elites. Modern industrial societies are thoroughly permeated by business values and actions and so elite support is usually not problematic for business organizations (Child, 1969). Trade and professional associations, in their promotion of a shared world-view among members, set standards of legitimate business practices and also lobby to have their standards accepted or even given force of law by governments. Private accrediting associations, such as the American Hospital Association or the North Central Association of Universities, Colleges, and Secondary Schools, grant legitimacy to organizations meeting their standards. Many local voluntary associations, public sector organizations, and other nonprofit organizations, however, cannot rely on automatic acceptance from community or societal elites and thus their persistence is problematic. Organizations with precarious values— objectives not accepted or understood by non-members—are highly vulnerable to external pressures, and elite support is one way of gaining legitimacy (Clark, 1956).

Whether elites will be able to protect vulnerable organizations and meet challenges to their hegemony depends upon three conditions: (1) the amount of power and resources controlled by elites and their ability to create new controls or shape regulatory institutions, thus preserving their own position and undermining their opponents; (2) the extent to which the elite is unified and thus capable of rapid collective action; and (3) "the extent to which opposition to the elite is unified and commands substantial resources inside or outside the system" (Alker, Buckley, and Burns, 1976, p. 8; see also Banfield, 1961). Examining how and why these conditions vary across communities and societies is beyond the scope of this book, but several examples of the consequences of elite support are available.

Colleges and universities traditionally defining themselves as producing "elites"—training children of upper-class parents and preparing them for positions of societal leadership—must preserve a different image than colleges oriented to "mass education." Elite colleges such as Harvard and Yale have "developed a tradition of producing leaders of government, business and the professions, notably high finance and corporate law . . . and this 'saga' becomes a central definition of the rights and meanings attached to graduates" (Kamens, 1977, p. 217). Schools claiming to train elites must preserve the myth by their high selectivity, small size, residential character, broad curriculum and semi-isolated location. They give up these characteristics at the peril of losing their image and elite support. Pressure from wealthy alumni, prestigious donors, and concerned recruiters for elite organizations thus helps preserve the form of "elite" colleges.

Elite control of public social control agencies, especially the police, has always been a key element in the protection of the elite's property (Silver, 1967). In his analysis of the persistence of the police control board in St. Louis, Maniha (1974a) argued that the major factor in the board's survival was the cooperation and approval of the city's business elite. In 1861, control of the police force in St. Louis was removed from the city and given to the state government, and this form of control continues to the present despite its abandonment in almost all other major cities in the United States. Why did this form persist, despite the odds against it? State control was adopted in 1861 for two reasons: (1) city control of the police was perceived as inefficient and corrupt, and (2) the Democrats who controlled the state legislature wanted to place Republican-controlled St. Louis firmly under their control in anticipation of the impending civil war and the struggle to enlist the state in the Confederate cause. The Metropolitan Police Act of 1861 created a Board of Police Commissioners comprised of four people with total administrative and financial power over the St. Louis police, with all four members appointed by the governor.

The creation of the board was accompanied by intense political conflict and it continued sporadically for the next seventy years. However, "state control as an organizational form both persisted despite opposition, and even underwent further legal consolidation. There is also evidence that the system was undergoing operational consolidation, as indicated by a gradual smoothing out of the tenure, turnover, and succession of police commissioners, and the depoliticization of their social involvements and commission activities" (Maniha, 1974a, pp. 802–3). In short, the board adopted an increasingly bureaucratized mode of operation and recruitment.

The crucial point in the consolidation of the elite's support came in the Great Strike of 1877, when city officials appeared not equal to the task of coping with the perceived threat to the city. Although there were strikes in other cities, only in St. Louis was the strike so successful as to constitute a true "general strike" and only in St. Louis were socialists the undisputed strike leaders. The governor of Missouri was perceived as more capable of coping with the threat than the mayor or other city administrators.

The depth of the business elite's anxiety was illustrated by the formation of a paramilitary force called the St. Louis Police Reserves in 1873, set up by businesspeople. Several historians have asserted that the St. Louis business and social elites were in general conservative and predominantly interested in stability. "Here was a commercial elite predisposed to favor the removal of the police budget from the vagaries of fickle city councilmen who might have other fiscal priorities" (Maniha, 1974a, p. 808). The election of socialists to city offices did nothing to allay their fears.

The governor's appointments to the Police Board were from the commercial and propertied elite, with an increasing tendency over time to appoint lawyers and bureaucrats. Between 1861 and 1880, only two of twenty-five commissioners whose birthplaces could be traced were natives of St. Louis, but gradually more natives were appointed, until they constituted slightly more than half of the appointments in the 1921–1961 period. In spite of an obvious class bias in the appointments, major ethnic and religious groups were fairly well represented. Maniha (1974a, pp. 812–13) concluded that "not only would commissioners be acceptable to elites but increasingly, appointees came from the city's major ethnic and religious minorities as well, a factor that undoubtedly strengthened the base of support for state control among elites in the various minority communities." State control of the St. Louis police was supported by the city's business elite and the form persisted despite some local opposition because (1) elites perceived that their interests were best served by state-appointed police commissioners who (2) were recruited from the nonlocal economic elite.

TRANSFORMATION: SINGLE ORGANIZATIONS

Nonpersistence of a given organization implies either its failure or transformation, and in this section I consider the internal and external forces that result in transformation. The discussion is limited to single organizations, as transformation of forms at the population level was treated in the previous chapter. The concept of organizational transformation encompasses major changes in goals, technologies, and activity systems, but it is extremely difficult to identify precisely what degree of change from a previous form constitutes a qualitative break sharp enough to justify being labelled a "transformation." Most sociological studies of organizational transformation are of voluntary associations, social movements, or public sector organizations, except for studies of the impact of growth on organizational differentiation. As most of these studies are analyses of single organizations, investigators have not been forced to make explicit how they distinguished transformation from extended reproduction and transition. The concept of transformation has been only implicit in analyses of the impact of size on organizational structure and activities, and investigators have not linked their work to ecological issues, with the exception of Freeman and Hannan (1975). Much of the discussion in this section is thus rather tentative.

Internal Forces: Growth, Power, and Goals

Intraorganizational variability may strain the capacity of an existing form and lead to organizational transformation, either because the dominant coalition could not foresee the effects of apparently harmless developments or because some factions sought the transformation. Three internal forces are examined in this section: (1) growth; (2) oligarchical tendencies among elites; and (3) changes in goals. Growth is an intrinsic source of change with potentially unintended effects, and some subunits are better positioned than others to protect themselves against such effects. Oligarchical tendencies are present in almost all membership-based organizations, such as unions and voluntary associations, and if unchecked can lead to transformation. Organizations with diffuse goals or innovative leadership are sometimes able to survive the crisis of completing their original mission by moving on to other goals.

Growth.   Are large organizations qualitatively different from small ones? Hannan and Freeman (1977) suggested that, at some point, growing organizations differ so sharply from their earlier forms that they are indeed "new" organizations. In small organizations, problems of communication and coordination can be managed by leaders or administrators fairly easily, and structure tends toward tight coupling. Founding entrepreneurs may run organizations by themselves or with the assistance of only a small staff, as there are few barriers to communication and participants' actions are highly visible and therefore easily monitored. Increasing size generates pressures toward a more bureaucratized and loosely coupled structure, especially if tasks are complex and administrative resources are limited.

Blau (1972) created a formal theory of the impact of increasing size on organizational differentiation and the administrative component, based on his analysis of five types of work organizations: government employment security offices; government finance departments; department stores; universities and colleges; and hospitals. He was interested in the impact of an increasing volume of work rather than number of members, but as the two indicators of size were highly correlated, he used number of employees as the operational indicator of size in his analyses. I will summarize only his theoretical argument rather than report his empirical results, but the findings were compatible with his theory. Blau's empirical analyses have been subjected to criticisms (Argyris, 1972; Freeman and Kronenfeld, 1973), but his conceptual scheme appears plausible nonetheless.

Functional differentiation and administrative hierarchies are the central concepts in Blau's theory, with growth affecting each differently and thus transforming simple into complex structures. *Functional differentiation* refers to three aspects of organization structure: (1) occupational specialization, as analyzed by Durkheim (1933); (2) the presence of separate subunits or divisions, indicating that a common enterprise has been differentiated into units with distinct responsibilities, as discussed earlier in the chapter on variability and loose coupling—an auto factory, for example, is differentiated into separate divisions for chassis, bodies, and accessories; (3) the distinction between operations actually producing goods or services and persons in administration organizing the work of others or maintaining the organization itself. *Administrative hierarchy* refers to two ways of subdividing administrative work: (1) administrative duties that depend on the exercise of managerial authority are separated from those that do not, such as recruitment and bookkeeping—this is the familiar distinction in management textbooks between "line" and "staff" functions; (2) administrative responsibilities for management and supervision are differentiated vertically into hierarchical levels that vary in their span of control and type of major responsibilities, linked to subunit or departmental differentiation. An "administrative ratio" can be constructed for an organization by computing the ratio of administrative personnel to all employees.

Blau's first proposition was that the administrative ratio is proportionately smaller in large organizations than in small ones, and that as organizations grow, proportionately fewer persons are added to administration than to operations. Thus, the proportion of administrators becomes smaller as organizations grow larger, up to a point. This occurs because of economies-of-scale in administrative work, as "organizing work entails initial investments largely independent of the volume of work to be carried out" (Blau, 1972, p. 17). Designing structures and procedures is time-consuming, but once operations are functioning smoothly they can be expanded with little additional administrative work. Setting up an assembly line, designing and administering wage and compensation plans, planning a sales campaign, and organizing a stock control system involve the same minimal amount of administrative work, regardless of the size of the organization.

The second proposition was that increasing size produces an increase in structural differentiation, although at a decreasing rate, as work is subdivided into more specialized segments and assigned to separate units in an organization. Blau (1972, p. 14) made explicit note of the qualitative difference between the organization of work in small as opposed to large organizations:

> Whereas work in small groups tends to become organized, subdivided, and coordinated in the course of direct social interaction without formalized procedures, explicit formal procedures are necessary to organize and coordinate the work of a collectivity too large for every member to have direct contacts with all others. A work organization is simply an explicit system for organizing the work of many persons in a common enterprise. A sheer

increase in the volume of work, by determining whether its accomplishment requires only one person or a small group or a large collectivity, alters the principle in terms of which the work is organized (by subdivision in time, among individuals, or among subgroups).

Blau argued that differentiation is necessary to ensure the social integration of complex enterprises, as the heterogeneity of the total operation is reduced to manageable dimensions through subdividing work into homogeneous subunits. Homogeneity of tasks within subunits reduces intraorganizational conflict, and smaller units are easier to control than larger ones. Classic management theory was preoccupied with determining the proper degree of differentiation for achieving optimal use of managerial time and effort.

Obviously, the degree of differentiation is limited by an organization's size, as highly specialized functions cannot request subunit status until the volume of work is large enough to justify it. The positive impact of size on structural differentiation declines as an organization grows *very* large, because the administrative problems of managing a large number of subunits become overwhelming. Controlling an extremely large number of heterogeneous departments increases administrative costs, requiring a more fundamental transformation of an organization's structure that Blau did not mention: the adoption of a divisional structure. Chandler (1962, pp. 53-54) argued that "by placing an increasing intolerable strain on existing administrative structures, territorial expansion and to a much greater extent product diversification brought the multidivisional form. Du Pont, General Motors, Jersey Standard, and Sears, Roebuck first devised the new type in the 1920s." This new form was not widely copied by other large firms until after World War II, but its use is now widespread.

Chandler (1962, p. 2) described the divisional form as one in which

a general office plans, coordinates, and appraises the work of a number of operating divisions and allocates to them the necessary personnel, facilities, funds, and other resources. The executives in charge of these divisions, in turn, have under their command most of the functions necessary for handling one major line of products or set of services over a wide geographical area and each of these executives is responsible for the financial results of his division and for its success in the marketplace.

A divisional form is also called a "decentralized" structure in management science.

Argyris (1972), responding to two earlier articles by Blau that reported results from studies of government agencies, argued that the association between size and structural differentiation was due to external factors. First, if administrators in government bureaus follow traditional administrative management principles regarding principles of task specialization, unity of command, span of control, and so forth, then we would expect to find that an increase in the number of employees was accompanied by an increase in structural differentiation. Argyris implied that differentiation is not a result of internal organizing problems but rather a consequence of administrators' beliefs in the appropriateness of management science's advice. One could still ask, however, *why* these principles gained the status of received wisdom if they do not contain some element of validity. Second, resource pressures account for the decreasing rate at which growth generates structural differentiation in government agencies. As budget limitations arise, new positions must be squeezed into existing departments rather than into new ones because the domain served and services offered by the agency are constrained by law.

Blau's third proposition was that increases in structural differentiation lead to increases in an organization's administrative ratio, because "structural differentiation increases the heterogeneity of responsibilities in an organization among managerial levels as well as functional divisions and sections" (Blau, 1972, p. 19). Heterogeneity, in turn, creates problems of communication and control. Increasing vertical differentiation intensifies problems of communication because the qualitative gaps between levels of authority hamper the free flow of information and it becomes easier for subordinates to use secrecy and information distortion as weapons to enhance their positions. Increasing horizontal differentiation—the proliferation of subunits, departments, and divisions—creates problems of control because all units must still be coordinated toward a common purpose. These pressures result in an increase in the volume of administrative work and hence in the administrative ratio.

Growth thus has contradictory effects on organizational structure in Blau's model, as the direct effect of growth *decreases* the administrative ratio but the indirect effect, through growth's effect on structural differentiation, *increases* the administrative ratio. On the one hand, increasing organization size leads to a reduction in the administrative component because of economies-of-scale in administration, greater homogeneity resulting from larger subunits, and more efficient use of specialists. On the other hand, increasing organization size leads to an increase in the administrative component because it generates greater heterogeneity among the subunits and raises the costs of communication and control. As Freeman and Hannan (1975) pointed out, the elegance of Blau's model is not matched by a comparable sophistication in methods for studying the effects of growth. Most studies have been cross-sectional, plagued by problems of definitional dependence between independent and dependent variables, and have been based on the tenuous assumption that administrative ratios behave the same in both growing and declining organizations. Nevertheless, Blau's model highlights the qualitative differences between small and large organizations and the processes of growth that transform organizations.

Power and political factors.   The victorious faction in a struggle for control may use its newly acquired power to transform an organization. Michels (1962) argued that all mass-based organizations—political parties, unions, voluntary associations, and even nations—were susceptible to the "Iron Law of Oligarchy," which is the tendency toward tyranny and unresponsiveness by leaders toward the membership. Michels, a German sociologist, wrote *Political Parties* in 1911 on the basis of his observations of the German Social Democratic Party and the socialist parties in France, Italy, and elsewhere. These parties were ideologically committed to the extension of democracy to the working class, yet in their own internal structure they were highly undemocratic. Rather than completely devoting their actions and resources to achieving the manifest purposes of the organization, the leadership was concerned with defending itself in office and preserving its position against internal challengers. Michel's analysis of oligarchy was the stimulus to Lipset, Trow, and Coleman's (1956) study of union democracy, as they examined an exceptional case where the "Iron Law" did not seem to apply: the International Typographical Union.

Michels (1962, p. 61) recognized the importance of organizations in the achievement of complex economic or political objectives by a class or other interest group: "Organization, based as it is upon the principle of least effort, that is to say, upon the greatest possible economy of energy, is the weapon of the weak in their struggle with the strong." The strengths of organization, however, also contain a danger, for the rewards and privileges of office eventually create a bifurcation of interest between the leaders and the led. Selznick (1943) summarized Michel's argument quite well and I shall follow his summary here.

Action on a large-scale requires that participants organize their efforts, and this necessitates the creation of an administrative apparatus, as Weber pointed out. Leaders and bureaucrats become the agents of the collectivity and in mass-based organizations, such as the challenging groups Gamson (1975) studied or the political parties Michels examined, the agent's actions are presumably directed toward the organizations' stated goals. Ordinary members cannot devote much of their time to the work of organizing action, and many do not have the temperament or ability to perform administrative duties. The delegation of functions creates the opportunity for a conflict of interest to arise between the full-time officials and the rank and file membership.

A bifurcation of interest develops because leaders find the actions required to preserve their positions sometimes conflicting with the actions they should take for achieving collective goals. Selznick identified three sources of conflicts between officials and members. First, members find it difficult to understand or appreciate the mundane day-to-day tasks required to sustain an organization, not realizing that the essential character of the organization is shaped by such tasks. Members turn out for "big" events, such as strike votes or political rallies, but the bureaucrats must handle other jobs. Second, officials become attached to their positions and committed to remaining in office because the job of "official" is more prestigious or pays more than their previous jobs, gives officials access to important officials in other organizations and agencies, and provides them with a sense of personal power and efficacy. Union officials, for example, may prefer white collar work in an office to blue collar work on the shop floor, especially if there is a large contrast between the two in working conditions. The longer officials remain in office, the more skilled they become at the job and the less fit they are for their previous work. Third, officials begin to believe in their own indispensability and worthiness in office, with their personal fate becoming inextricably intertwined with that of the organization.

The bifurcation of interest between officials and members results in a struggle for control of the organizational apparatus, with officials desiring to maintain themselves against the rank and file who perceive the organization's original goals have been abandoned. Bureaucrats and officials almost inevitably gain the upper hand in this contest, as they control the means of administration and can use a number of tactics unavailable to the membership. First, members are dependent on officials because of the latter's greater skill and knowledge concerning rules, regulations, and procedures. Dependence is increased to the extent that officials' jobs, or more likely those of their staff, are professionalized—officials can argue that only they understand the lawyer's or accountant's reports. Second, many members may believe that the continued existence of the organization is dependent on the current leadership, and thus do not respond to calls from dissident members to organize against the officials. Even if established procedures exist for replacing leaders, "they are relatively harmless to the entrenched leaders (because functionless) so long as the ranks fear the consequences of using them" (Selznick, 1943, p. 52).

Third, officials seek an external source of power that reduces their dependence on the rank and file. The head of a challenging group may seek some sort of accommodation with officials in the target organization, or may form a coalition with other organizations seeking similar objectives. In either case, the officials can claim they have a responsibility to a wider constituency than just the membership, and that the external tie is so important that it justifies their retention in office. In the United Mine Workers, under Tony Boyle, union officials cultivated the support of management, using the above argument, and relations of the British labor union's officials with the Labor Party, through the Trades Union Congress, give them an external base. Fourth, officials also seek an internal base of support from a subsegment of the membership, establishing a personal base of supporters loyal only to them. Political factions in trade unions, an elite guard or secret police force in political parties, an "inner circle" in local voluntary associations, and kinship ties in organized criminal gangs are examples of this tactic. A major internal source of power is control over the organization's communication system—newsletter, magazine, posters, office telephone—and without access to it, dissidents must expend most of their resources just publicizing their existence.

Fifth, the incumbent leadership creates an ideology justifying its domination, using it as a weapon against challengers. Officials link their personal fate to that of the organization and argue that dissidents are threatening the viability of the group by attacking the leadership. In Arnold Miller's campaign to wrest control of the United Mine Workers from Tony Boyle in 1972, Boyle labelled the students who went to West Virginia and other states to aid Miller as "communists," "outside agitators," and enemies of the UMW. Richard Nixon invoked "national security" arguments against investigators trying to untangle the Watergate conspiracy, and in the struggle for control with the Chinese government after Mao Tse Tung's death, his wife and her supporters were labelled the "group of four" and condemned as enemies of the state.

The overwhelming advantages of incumbent officials typically result in their success in the competition for control, and organizational resources are diverted to their objectives. As Selznick (1943, p. 51) noted, "The action of the officials tends to have an increasingly *internal relevance*, which may result in the deflection of the organization from its original path, which, however, usually remains as the formally professed aim of the organization." Officials' actions and policies reflect as much of their concern for internal power relations as for the manifest goals of the organization. Leaders and bureaucrats must assess new programs in terms of their effects on support for the incumbent leadership and the possibility of the program provoking a challenge to their dominance. The latter possibility may keep the leadership more responsive than otherwise, but it may also lead to a strengthening of incumbent domination as a counter-measure. Reform groups, such as those within the Democratic Party in the United States, may influence the leadership but pose no substantial threat because they do not seek the overthrow of the incumbents.

Although the development of organizational oligarchies is usually described as leading to a more conservative stance by officials, Zald and Ash (1966, p. 339) noted that in social movement organizations this is not always so: "If a leadership cadre are committed to radical goals to a greater extent than the membership-at-large, member apathy and oligarchical tendencies lead to greater rather than less radicalism." Leaders with a strong commitment to the social movement's goals may take actions that are more extreme than the members would support, if they had more effective means of controlling the leaders' behavior. Wood (1972) reported that the Commission on Religion and Race of the National Council of Churches (NCC) adopted a more radical stand on civil rights in the 1960s than many of its member denominations would have liked. The NCC's radical stand on civil rights and integration issues affected the positions taken by some of the predominantly white denominations to such an extent that an appreciable number of their local members and churches dropped out. This was particularly the case in the South, where church members objected to the NCC's "call for participation in demonstrations; the use of money to support 'questionable movements' such as NAACP and CORE; sending ministers into southern cities against the wishes of the local ministerial associations; and controversial pronouncements which presume to represent the member denominations" (Wood, 1972, p. 515).

Southern denominations suffered heavily from their affiliation to the NCC, yet none resigned from it. Instead, individual members and local congregations quit, some affiliating with denominations not affiliated with the NCC, such as the Southern Methodist Church. Others cooperated to found new denominations, such as the Association of Independent Methodists and the Anglican Orthodox Church, which promised not to contribute money to "causes which are alien and dangerous to our Christian way of life." The NCC's Commission on Religion and Race was pressured into its radical stand by two denominations whose leaders did not have to worry about losing southern members, since they had so few congregations in the South. Wood hypothesized that NCC-affiliated southern denominations did not drop their membership because they accepted, at least partially, the beliefs and values of the northern denominations and the arguments of the NCC concerning the need for ecumenical cooperation. Leaders of the southern denominations were able to defend their own relatively radical stand by asserting that it was the NCC's doing, and that the other goals of the NCC justified accepting its stand on civil rights. "In this sense, the NCC could even be considered a coalition of leaders against their members" (Wood, 1972, p. 520). The example of the NCC demonstrates that not all organizational transformations because of triumphant oligarchy result in a deflection of activities from original goals.

Goal succession.   Some purposively oriented organizations achieve their goals and go out of existence, while others are transformed by shifting to new goals. The best known case is the transformation of the National Foundation for Infantile Paralysis into simply the National Foundation (Sills, 1957). The Foundation was established in 1938 and by 1953 had over 3,000 local chapters, raising over $51 million in its annual March of Dimes campaign staffed by approximately three million volunteers. With the successful development of the Foundation-sponsored Salk polio vaccine (1952–54), it became clear that the Foundation's original mission was nearly completed. Anticipating the crisis that would occur when the large and effective structure created by the Foundation no longer had a meaningful objective, Foundation leaders commissioned research to learn more about the volunteers and the public that supported it. Public and volunteer support was quite high, and the Foundation's staff, in consultation with scientists and medical personnel, searched for a means to keep the organization alive. By 1958, the leadership decided on a new set of goals, and the renamed Foundation began to support research and patient care in arthritis and congenital malformations among youth. Later, the arthritis program was taken over by the Arthritis Foundation. Clearly, major factors in the Foundation's success in transforming itself were its (1) extremely high degree of acceptance by the American public; (2) high degree of professionalization; (3) early decision to search for new goals; and (4) a high level of slack resources—80,000 volunteers available during the year and a multi-million dollar budget.

The Planned Parenthood Federation evolved out of the Birth Control Federation in the 1940s by adopting a broader set of programs. The American National Red Cross survived the crisis of increased governmental intervention in disaster relief by adopting its highly successful national blood donor program. As we are limited to case studies of a few spectacular successes and failures of voluntary associations attempting organizational transformation, it is difficult to assess how important an innovative and far-sighted leadership is in affecting the outcome. The extent of external support enjoyed by an organization is obviously important, and in the next section I will review studies of transformation where environmental forces were an apparently dominant factor in the process.

External Forces in Transformation

The failure of an organization to obtain resources and support from its environment may lead to failure, but survival is sometimes possible through organizational transformation. Some organizations are more vulnerable than others to pressures for transformation, such as those with diffuse goals, uncertain support, precarious or illegitimate values, and those facing a declining market for their products or services. In the business sector, market forces are the most general explanation for transformations, when they occur, although business failures are more common. Among voluntary associations and public sector organizations, the problems of recruiting members or clients and maintaining precarious values often lead to transformation of structures and activities. Subsequent chapters— on boundary control problems and managing relations with other organizations—will examine various consequences of organizations attempting to manage environmental selection pressures. Three examples of transformations are examined in this section: changes in products by businesses, the movement from specialism to generalism by organizations with an enrollment economy, and decay and deterioration in social movements.

Market forces.   Most businesses that offer a product or service nobody wants go out of business, but some survive by offering new products or services. No systematic information is available as to how often this occurs, but it is clear that the largest corporations are particularly adept at diversification and surviving changes in product markets. Some industrial economists attribute the immense staying power of the largest firms (recall the low drop-out rate for the largest 100 firms in the United States since 1909) to their ability to shift to new products, either by growing internally or acquiring other firms. In the past several decades, American oil companies have adapted to changing conditions by acquiring coal mining firms and investing in research on nuclear power and other energy sources.

Some of the transformations occuring in the United States during the period of rapid industrialization between the Civil War and World War I are nothing short of remarkable (Rosenberg, 1963). Beginning with the Civil War, Pratt and Whitney introduced machinery for the production of firearms, followed in succession by machinery for producing sewing machines, bicycles, and automobiles, as well as other high-precision machinery. In Hartford, Connecticut, a plant under a series of owners produced machine tools, guns, sewing machines, bicycles, motorcycles, and automobiles. Perhaps the most striking of all was the experience of the Leland, Faulconer, and Norton Company, which later became the Cadillac Auto Company. It "was founded in 1890 as a producer of machine tools and special machinery, introduced machinery for producing bicycle gears during the brief heyday of the bicycle, switched to building gasoline engines for motor boats when the bicycle industry began to decline, and by 1902 had undertaken the production of automobile engines" (Rosenberg, 1963, p. 443). One implication of the population ecology model's emphasis on the importance of chance or accidental factors in organizational variability is that we should be cautious in attributing these transformations to entrepreneurial ingenuity. For every firm that succeeded, there were many more that failed.

Specialists to generalists: Pressures of an enrollment economy.   Some organizations that are unable to acquire enough resources by specializing in a limited range of products or services manage to survive by becoming generalists. By offering a wider range of products and services, a generalist is able to appeal to the diverse segments of a heterogeneous population and compensate for the low environmental capacity supporting its original form. Adult education in California (Clark, 1956) and the YMCA in the United States (Zald and Denton, 1963) began as rather marginal organizations serving a specialized clientele and heavily dependent on local support for their survival. Both evolved into generalists serving a wide range of clientele and successfully meeting the pressures of an enrollment economy, wherein their continued existence depended on the *number* of clients they served.

Clark (1956), analyzing changes in adult education programs in California from the 1920s until the early 1950s, illustrated two points about organizational transformation. First, some organizational forms do not retain the same structural features as when they were created because they are unable to obtain protection from external pressures. Second, the structure of the adult education program was transformed mainly because of resource pressures—after the transformation, an ideological position was developed that legitimated the "adaptation" that had been made. Three types of pressures affected adult education programs in California: (1) changes in the declared goals of adult education; (2) organizational marginality; and (3) operating pressures arising from an enrollment economy funding scheme.

The declared goals of adult education changed over time as a response to internal and external factors. Before 1925, adult education emphasized night school, with programs restricted chiefly to elementary and high school remedial education, vocational training, and programs for socializing immigrants. After 1925, two divergent themes emerged. First, adult education was justified in the name of "enlightenment" and a more general education that would meet the diverse needs of adults. Second, grass-roots administrators began to stress the uniqueness of adult learning, rather than applying the traditional student-teacher model to adult education. Clark did not make clear the source of these changes, but they were probably related to the trend in the United States in this century toward a service-society ideology.

The organizational marginality of adult education was a result of the precariousness of "adult education" as a valued activity in California. The output target of adult education evidently has never been a strong constituency. Adult education was forced to compete for education funds with other organizations seen as more legitimate in the eyes of the public, such as elementary and high schools, and junior colleges. No politically powerful group came to the aid of the program.

Operating pressures were the third external force affecting adult education. It operated in an enrollment economy situation in which its support depended upon the number of students it enrolled, rather than on the quality of the program or its staff. School income was largely set by student attendance, most money came from the state, and local school districts only rarely used local funds to support the program. Thus, the program had to attempt paying its own way. Students were only marginally linked to the program, as most were part-time; by definition, voluntary; and were "highly susceptible to casual attendance and easy termination" (Clark, 1956, p. 332).

Changing goals, organizational marginality, and pressures from an enrollment economy made adult education highly sensitive to its environment. The program's extreme vulnerability to short-run changes in student interest shaped the nature of its transformation from a specialist to a generalist. The program adapted by becoming more diversified, flexible, and highly sensitive to the concentration of environmental resources. Courses were created that would attract a large number of students, especially in the area of vocational interests and hobbies— the much-maligned "underwater basket weaving" is an example. Student demand was monitored closely by means of sign-up lists and group petitions, so that courses could be added whenever the demand justified it. Classes were provided for organized interest groups—city agencies, private firms, and voluntary association—as the program responded to such concentrations of valuable resources (students).

Adult education administrators attempted to keep the program flexible by retaining the teaching force on a part-time status, so that teachers could be added and dropped rapidly. In Los Angeles in 1952, over 90 percent of the teachers were hired on a part-time basis. "Adaptation to a heterogeneous clientele involves considerable specialization in subject-matter and the hiring of the part-time specialist, e.g., a welder, a gardner, a dental technician, a housewife skilled in lampshade making" (Clark, 1956, p. 334). Offering whatever course tickles students' fancies was not a way of maintaining academic respectability, and occasionally the program came under fire from state legislators and economy-minded interest groups. However, resource pressures were too great to permit the priority of academic respectability over that of service to the adult community. Administrators developed an ideology to justify and legitimize their activities, emphasizing the value of adult education as a public relations vehicle for the schools and the orientation of the program to serving the "people's" needs.

The YMCA was founded in England in 1844 and was brought to the United States shortly thereafter. It began as an evangelical organization to convert young men who had migrated to the city to Christianity, but within a few years young men were allowed to join even though they had not converted. Several of the YMCA's permanent characteristics were established soon after its founding; "members paid dues; wealthy businessmen contributed to its support; it was interdenominational; and . . . control was reserved to the laity" (Zald and Denton, 1963, p. 217). Originally the organization stressed its Christian orientation and its programs were heavily religious in nature. Local YMCAs were established in a community only upon local initiative, and local control made the YMCA highly sensitive to environmental trends. This federated structure (emphasizing local rather than national office initiative), combined with the dominance of local YMCA boards by lay persons rather than YMCA professionals or ministers, meant that the organization was not as vulnerable to oligarchical tendencies as other national organizations.

Between the 1860s and the early 1900s, the YMCA was transformed from an organization with a highly specialized evangelical base, stressing religious activities, to one emphasizing general programs to develop "the whole man," without regard to religious affiliation. The increasing secularization of American society could have led to the YMCA's isolation and extinction, but the YMCA's openness to external influence allowed it to keep pace with the times. Zald and Denton do not dwell on the forces producing the transformation, but local control and an enrollment economy appear to have been primarily responsible. Americans developed an interest in physical fitness and organized sports in the late nineteenth century, and the YMCA's programs gained ready acceptance. At the same time, the YMCA's religious programs were reduced because public response was poor and local churches were developing their own religious programs, obviating the need for the YMCA's programs.

The organization's base was broadened when persons who were not members of evangelical churches were admitted, and women were allowed to attend public lectures, although not given formal membership until 1934. Inclusiveness of membership enabled the YMCA to grow quite rapidly, and by the late 1950s, 96 percent of cities with populations of over 50,000 boasted of at least one YMCA. The interdenominational character and dominance by laymen of the organization meant that it was not strongly tied to a set religious ideology and thus not constrained from adapting to local needs, as perceived by YMCA boards. The YMCA was similar to the adult education programs in that membership fees were an important part of its income. Most programs offered were expected to generate part of the income required to operate them, but support was also obtained from community sources, such as the United Fund and local businesspeople.

The YMCA responded to resource pressures and large-scale changes in American society, such as increasing secularization and increasing leisure time for persons of all ages, by becoming an all-purpose service organization. Zald and Denton concluded their analysis with a discussion of four factors affecting organizational change. First, the federated structure of the YMCA gave local programs a great deal of autonomy and allowed them to adapt quickly to local needs. Second, broadly defined goals—a commitment to the "whole man"—allowed the YMCA to add or drop programs as they waxed or waned in popular appeal. Third, the lack of development of a professional ideology among YMCA full-time local secretaries facilitated organizational change. Fourth, "an enrollment economy is immediately sensitive to the changed demands of the market place" (Zald and Denton, 1963, p. 234). If programs were expected to pay part of their own way, then (just as in the adult education program) client wishes must be catered to. The culmination of these forces transformed the YMCA from a specialist into a generalist, just as organizational marginality and an enrollment economy transformed adult education programs in California.

Decay and deterioration. The Townsend Organization and the Women's Christian Temperance Union (WCTU) are examples of organizations whose transformation led to organizational decay and drift, rather than growth. Both achieved success, of sorts, but it was short-lived and neither found a niche within which it could use the experience and membership resources previously accumulated. The Townsend Movement was founded by Dr. Francis Townsend, who proposed to end the Great Depression of the 1930s by allowing persons to retire at age 60 with a monthly pension of $200 a month. The organization was founded in late 1933, and by 1936 it had over two million members. The passage of the Social Security Act in 1935 undercut the urgency of the Townsend Movement's goals, and by 1951 it had less than 60,000 members (Messinger, 1955). Extensions to the Social Security Act and the end of the depression with the onset of World War II gradually eliminated the rationale of the movement. The Townsend Movement survived, but in a much different form, by adapting in two ways: (1) it obtained financial support by selling vitamin pills and other consumer goods; and (2) it became a sociable organization (Aldrich, 1971b), with members gathering for various social events, such as card parties and bingo games. The original goals were abandoned and the leadership concentrated solely on organizational maintenance and survival.

The WCTU was founded in the nineteenth century to save the working class from the dangers of drinking. The temperance movement was staffed by middle-class women expressing a concern for the welfare of the working class, and they achieved their greatest success with the passage of the Eighteenth Amendment to the Constitution in 1919, prohibiting the sale of alcohol in the United States. However, the WCTU was fighting a losing battle, and the repeal of the Prohibition Amendment in 1933 was a sign that the temperance movement was in decline. Gusfield (1963) showed that the WCTU gradually abandoned its goal of winning over the working class and redirected its efforts toward the middle class. The class composition of the WCTU also changed, as it became more lower middle and working class. Instead of the activism of the late nineteenth and early twentieth centuries, it switched to the tactic of "moral indignation." Clearly the WCTU, like the Townsend Movement, failed to achieve its original goal. However, unlike the YMCA or adult education programs in California, the WCTU and the Townsend Movement failed to achieve a successful transformation— membership in both dropped precipitously and they turned inward, away from their original purposes. One organization had its original goal coopted by government action, while the other was foiled by changing social attitudes toward drinking. Both succumbed to environmental pressures, as thousands of smaller organizations do every year.

Transformation: Summary

Analyses of transformation raise the issue of the role of strategic choice in organizational decision making. Is transformation an adaptive strategy used by leaders and administrators to ensure organizational survival, even at the cost of compromising original goals, or is transformation simply a more extreme instance of change induced by environmental pressures selectively affecting organizational variability? Large organizations appear to accept some types of transformation willingly, as diversification and expansion are long-run strategies of administrators in the biggest firms and agencies. Smaller organizations are not as well placed, and some are clearly transformed in spite of their obvious resistance.

Transformation, as opposed to incremental change, is not an option open to all organizations because opportunities within niches are limited by the availability of resources and the state of existing technology. It is also questionable whether transformation through internal growth or tendencies toward oligarchy is a result of planned change—it is unlikely that administrators or leaders can foresee all the changes accompanying rapid growth or the increasing bifurcation of interest between members and leaders in mature organizations. The greater the identification of leaders or managers with the rewards of their position, as opposed to the goals or outputs of the organization, the more open they are to changes enhancing the survival of their organization. Transformation is one possible outcome from this commitment, and it thus need not be a "planned" change.

SUMMARY

The creation, persistence, and transformation of organizations can be analyzed at either the population or organizational level, using the population ecology model. Constraints on variation, changing selection parameters, and the efficacy of retention mechanisms enter into the explanation of all three phenomena. Forms and niches must be examined separately, as forms may change in quite stable niches or niches may change while forms remain stable. The significance of this issue is highlighted in a reexamination of Stinchcombe's (1965) attempt to construct a general explanation of organizational persistence.

Hernes's (1976) distinction between output, process, and parameters holds great promise for the study of organizational change, as it enables us to differentiate between four types of processes: simple reproduction or persistence, extended reproduction, transition, and transformation. The empirical literature on organizations, however, does not yet contain the longitudinal and comparative studies required to fully apply Hernes's model. Note that Hernes's model complements the population ecology model, in that he has specified *types* of change, whereas the ecological model provides the overarching framework within which any type of change can be examined.

218

9 Boundaries and Organizational Responsiveness

Organizations are defined as boundary-maintaining systems of human interaction, and examples in previous chapters show that boundary control is a problem for many organizations. The rational selection model has traditionally been concerned with methods for maintaining organizational boundaries, especially in recruiting and selecting new members and in discovering ways to protect an organization's core technology from external influence (Thompson, 1967). Boundaries are also a central concern of the population ecology model, from the viewpoint of understanding how boundaries change in response to environmental conditions and how authorities' freedom of action is circumscribed by external influence over their organizations' boundaries. Whereas previous chapters dealt with the broad historical conditions under which organizations were created and transformed, this chapter focuses specifically on the more immediate environment affecting organizational persistence and change after an organization is founded.

The conceptual scheme defining organizations in terms of boundaries, presented in Chapter 1, relates to the population ecology model at each of its three stages. Organizations' inability to control their boundaries leads to *variation*, as organizations are opened to external influence and authorities seek means of clos-

219

ing off vulnerable segments and coping with heterogeneous and varying demands from clients, members, and others. Boundary control is a defining characteristic of organizational forms, and variations in forms can be related to varying environmental conditions. Issues of *selection criteria* arise because theorists wish to know how much choice authorities have in designing internal structures, as well as interorganizational arrangements, given problems in controlling boundaries. Strategies of boundary control and the conditions under which they are used are thus investigated in this chapter. In returning to the theme of the conditions under which authorities have opportunities to exercise choice, this chapter builds on the discussion of strategic choice and its limitations in Chapter 6.

Retention of organizational activities and structures is an underlying theme of this chapter because being retained requires organizations to continually monitor, adjust, and maintain their boundaries. In many cases, an organization's ability to retain its established form depends upon satisfying members and clients, and such responsiveness is more important for certain types of organizations than others. Organizational persistence and retention of form become more difficult and boundary-maintaining activities become more important as environments tend toward instability and turbulence. I present an example of changes in Wall Street law firms' recruiting practices under the impact of such pressures.

Weber's (1947) definition of a formal organization is used to derive a unified conceptualization of boundaries, authorities, and members. Members' reactions to deteriorating organizational performance may take the form of exit, voice, or silence (Hirschman, 1972), and conditions of member entry and exit—boundary-crossing phenomena—constrain members' choices among these alternatives. Entry and exit are everyday organizational occurrences, and the permeability of boundaries highlights the role played by persons occupying boundary-spanning positions. The functions and structural correlates of boundary-spanning roles are examined in the next chapter.

DEFINING BOUNDARIES, AUTHORITIES, AND MEMBERS

In everyday discourse, people take the existence of organizational boundaries for granted; they talk about groups, voluntary associations, and other organizations as if they were corporate actors (Coleman, 1974). The ACME Canning Corporation, the Midville Anti-Pornography Movement, and the local university are discussed as if these organizations had clearly defined identities and their members were easily recognized. Some theorists argue that we should not readily accept this taken-for-granted assumption without at least investigating its theoretical implications. Consider, for example, the question of how to define the boundaries of your college or university—how would you set the limits? Would you include students, staff, trustees, and alumni; make a distinction between full- and part-time members; or create different definitions for different purposes? Other types of organizations (hospitals, police departments, and welfare agencies) appear equally challenging, as we would have to decide whether to include clients, public officials, taxpayers, and so forth.

Starbuck (1976) argued that organizations have different shapes and boundaries, depending upon which components are observed and who is observing. He created an example using four different dimensions to measure the distance of various persons from the hypothetical "center" of a private business firm: psychological job investment, social visibility, influence on resource allocation, and speed with which the person's actions affect the organization. In his hypothetical example, based on organizations he had known, Starbuck found that some roles were central on one dimension but peripheral on others. He concluded that organizational boundaries are essentially arbitrary creations, depending on an observer's frame of reference. Overlooked in his discussion of the simulated organization, however, was the fact that all the roles he placed along the central-peripheral dimension—switchboard operator, plant manager, unskilled worker, sales manager, typist, influential customer—were *organizationally defined*. None of the roles would exist without an organization controlling who enters them and, indeed, defining the nature of the roles themselves. The observation that organizations set the conditions under which people enter roles associated with organizational action is the basis for the definition of boundaries offered in the next section.

Boundaries and Organizational Authorities

The minimal defining characteristic of a formal organization is the distinction made between members and non-members, with an organization existing to the extent that entry into and exit out of the organization are limited. This concept of boundaries is presented in Weber's (1947, pp. 139-46) definition of a formal organization:

> a [social] relationship will . . . be called "closed" against outsiders so far as, according to its subjective meaning and the binding rules of its order, participation of certain persons is excluded, limited or subjected to conditions. . . . A social relationship which is either closed or limits the outsiders by rules, will be called a "corporate group" so far as its order is enforced by the action of specific individuals. . . .

Formal organizations admit some persons while excluding others, thus allowing an observer to draw a boundary around the organization.

Defining organizations in terms of boundaries to interaction suggests a parsimonious definition of the role of formal authority in organizations: Authorities are those persons who are given the task of applying organizational rules in making decisions about entry and expulsion of members. This definition also follows Weber's (1947, p. 146), as he defined a *formal* organization as one with a person in authority present: *Authorities* are those persons who "act in such a way as to tend to carry out the order governing the group." The definition and location of a specific boundary is problematic, and may only be possible given a specific organizational context. Nonetheless, these definitions allow a theoretical integration of several concepts hitherto treated separately, and they emphasize the importance of power and authority in the maintenance of organizational boundaries.

Organizational membership can be defined in the same terms as authority and at the same level of generality, again following Weber (1947, p. 140): "A party to a closed social relationship will be called a 'member'." Thus, a member is a person whose entry and exit into and from an organization is controlled by the authorities of the organization. Authorities set the conditions for member entry, controlling wages or salaries, hours of work, amount of work expected, and the allocation of a member's organizational time. As for controlling exit, authorities can terminate the association of a member with the organization at will, or with certain contractual restrictions. Outsiders are not subject to these types of controls.

This definition emphasizes that the membership is a matter of degree rather than an "either-or" distinction. Considering only entry and exit, it is evident that suppliers, customers, inmates, and others in an organization's domain are potential members insofar as the organization gains control over their actions at some point. The reason for distinguishing members from other parts of an organization's environment is that their behavior can be predicted with greater certainty by authorities, and aggressive authorities may seek this degree of control over important outsiders. Barnard (1928, p. 112-13) used a very similar definition of members in his work:

> Thus I rejected the concept of organization as comprising a rather definite group of people whose behavior is coordinated with reference to some explicit goal or goals. On the contrary, I included in organization the actions of investors, suppliers, and customers or clients. Thus the material of organization is personal service, i.e. actions contributing to its purposes.

Barnard, however, had a much more harmonious and benign view of organizations and authorities' motives than portrayed in this book.

Many persons are affected by organizations' actions but have little or no chance of ever falling under the direct control of organizational authorities. The environmental and consumer protection movements of the 1970s called attention to the negative externalities generated by businesses and that plagued the general public: air, water, and noise pollution; unsafe automobiles, appliances, and other consumer products posing a hazard not just to their users but also to those around them; and other actions affecting the quality of life for persons with little likelihood of taking counteraction by themselves. Prior to the 1970s, persons suffering these consequences might simply have endured them, but new organizations arose copying the structure and tactics of the civil rights movement to aggregate public complaints into a force with economic and political power. Although this development is not treated extensively in this book, it is clear that the *external constituency* of organizations—persons and organizations indirectly affected by organizations' actions—deserves greater attention in research on organizational change.

Limits to Organizational Authority

Organizations vary widely in the extent to which they have control over their own boundaries, as implied by the population ecology model's stress on external selection parameters. Boundaries are not immutable, and change over time occurs in response to changing opportunities and constraints facing organizational authorities. The extent to which authorities manage to control entry and exit has a major impact on organizational responsiveness to environmental forces, such as the potential threat to survival posed by dissatisfied customers and clients. Three factors affect the degree to which authorities are limited in their authority and autonomy vis-à-vis their organization's boundaries: control over entry, control over exit, and members' or clients' control over their own participation. Taken together, these factors indicate an organization's extent of dependence on other organizations, and on members, customers, or clients. The greater the dependence, the less an organization's fate lies in the hands of its authorities and the greater the likelihood of externally induced changes.

Control over entry.   The exercise of authority often takes the form of setting conditions for entry into an organization and consequently for access to organizational resources. Employees and members are distinguished from customers or clients primarily in terms of their direct access to using organizational resources. As almost all organizations have a great deal of autonomy in choosing their own employees, the following discussion focuses on customers and clients.

Students must take entrance examinations, pay tuition, and adhere to course requirements as a condition for their membership in a college or university. Fraternities require pledges to learn the organization's history and go through elaborate initiation rituals. In capitalist societies, with formally free labor, business organizations use the acceptance of a proffered wage or salary rate as a condition of entry. In a nation-state, denial of entrance or of continued membership takes the form of immigration laws or loss of citizenship, imprisonment, and deportation. Organizations able to control entry are often quite exclusive, such as radical social movements or elite social clubs, whereas others are inclusive and admit just about anybody wishing to join, such as political parties or evangelical churches (Zald and Ash, 1966). Businesses normally fall into the inclusive category, admitting all who can afford the asking price for their product or service.

Some organizations lack the authority to control entry, as entry conditions are set by charter, legal restrictions, or parent bodies. Prisons receive their inmates from the criminal justice system, and are obliged to accept all "clients" sent to them. Public utilities and government agencies must make their services available to anyone from the general public, and some state universities must accept all high school graduates in their state. At one time, the United States Army was dependent upon the Selective Service System for new recruits, although inductees were screened by army examiners before final acceptance. These examples show that organizations dependent upon others for resources, for whatever reason, may lose some of their authority to control entry. Other organizations' ability to set selection criteria for new clients or members deprives the dependent organization of control over an essential part of its environment.

Control over exit.   Control over exit is also a defining characteristic of an organization's authority. Authorities have the power to sanction deviants or remove undesirables, and the ultimate sanction they wield is expulsion from the organization. Authorities hold this power through delegation from the membership or sponsoring authorities, or through rights of ownership. For voluntary associations, the ability to control exit is crucial to the maintenance of organization integrity and cohesion. As I noted in discussing the effects of organizational growth in the last chapter, small organizations are not highly differentiated, vertically or horizontally, and thus persons with different motives and perspectives cannot be shielded from one another in different subunits or levels of the organization. Voluntary associations and other small organizations, such as communes, can use expulsion as a functional alternative to structural differentiation in coping with extreme member heterogeneity.

Organizations vary in the ease with which they can expel clients or members. Most private businesses have a great deal of authority over their employees, but it is increasingly shared with or monitored by other organizations: Labor unions bargain with organizational authorities regarding the conditions under which an employee may be laid off or discharged, and civil liberties groups defend employees' rights to varying standards of dress and demeanor. Children must attend school until they reach a certain age, although expulsion is possible in extreme cases. The courts and civil liberties groups have begun to exercise a restraining influence in the authority of the schools to expel troublesome students, just as courts in a number of states have reduced the discretion of mental hospitals to retain patients indefinitely. Prisons are probably the archetype of an organizational form with almost no authority to control exit, except for the recommendations prison staff can make to parole boards.

The inability of authorities to control exit indicates that they must search for other means of handling difficult or disruptive clients and members. Public schools, for example, use physical segregation of disruptive pupils and preferential treatment of gifted children to compensate for their lack of exit control (Carlson, 1964). However, to the extent that clients' or members' exit is inhibited—whether through external constraints or lack of alternatives—the development of internal hierarchy and domination is made easier. Organizations are then free to use repressive measures against difficult clients and to suppress dissident movements, just as authoritarian state regimes without an independent judiciary can violate citizens' civil liberties with impunity.

Member and client autonomy.   Organizations differ in the degree to which members or clients control their own participation, ranging from situations where they have no choice in affiliating to situations of maximum discretion. Under competitive conditions, with many organizations offering the same product or service, clients or customers are limited in choice only by resource constraints affecting their access to communication and transportation. At the other extreme, in situations of achieved or government-approved monopolies, clients or customers have little or no choice. Government bureaus that issue permits and licenses; telephone and utility companies with a legal monopoly over a domain; "company stores"; and public schools all count on a captive population for their services. The implication of this dimension of organizations' relations with outsiders is that the greater the degree of member autonomy, the more organizations must modify their activities to attract and keep potential clients and members. Thus, the greater the autonomy of members, the more organizations are dependent upon them.

Boundary control and responsiveness.   Control over entry and exit and member autonomy must be considered jointly in assessing the extent to which boundary control is a potential problem for authorities. The typology presented in Table 9.1 can be used to classify organizations according to the degree of difficulty authorities face in maintaining boundaries and the severity of pressures for organizational responsiveness to client or member interests. Organizations in cell *I* were labelled "wild" organizations by Carlson (1964) to emphasize their lack of dependence on other organizations and their need to compete in the marketplace for clients or members. Most voluntary associations, special interest groups, and social movements are free to set entrance requirements and to expel unwanted members, and potential members are free to choose whether to join the organization. This combination means that authorities must concern themselves with incentives for attracting members, but need not worry that deviant members will have a long-term impact. Organizations in cell *II* are those controlling exit but not entry, and in which members enter of their own free will. Being unable to control entry, such organizations must find other ways of dealing with problem clients and members. Publicly supported universities in some states in the United

Table 9.1 Limits of organizational authority and autonomy: Organizational control over entry and exit, and member or client control over participation

		Member or Client Autonomy: Choice in Participation			
		YES *Does the organization control entry?*		*NO* *Does the organization control entry?*	
		YES	NO	YES	NO
Does the organization control exit?	YES	*I* Social movement	*II* Public university with open enrollment	*III* Private monopoly	*IV* Public elementary school
	NO	*V* Fraternal association	*VI* Business's customers in a competitive market	*VII* Craft union	*VIII* Public monopoly

States admit all high school graduates, which is an extremely heterogeneous population. University systems have responded in several ways: Less qualified students take "pre-university" preparation courses the summer before enrolling; learning centers and other tutorial procedures provide remedial education services; and units are differentiated by expectations concerning students' aptitude—universities, four-year colleges, two-year colleges, and vocational or technical institutes.

Organizations having entry and exit control over clients or members having no choice of participation need not be highly responsive to clients' interests, as is implied by the example of "private monopolies" in cell *III*. Grocery stores and other shops catering to a captive population are free to charge higher prices than otherwise, as many students in college towns discover to their dismay. Before the abolition of the draft, the United States Army relied upon the Selective Service System to furnish its recruits, and draftee induction centers could treat young men as so much "meat on the hoof" in their processing, with draftees forced to accept a series of degrading routines with no prospect of exit. Organizations in cell *IV* possess exit but not entry control and deal with clients or members who have no choice of participation. Lacking entry control and faced with a captive population, such organizations face a more severe problem than organizations in cell *II*, which deal with a voluntary clientele or membership. Public elementary and high schools cannot assume that most pupils are willing clients and must make greater efforts to motivate them than colleges and universities. Tracking systems are used to separate students by aptitude and interest, and the most disruptive students are expelled or subtly coerced into private schooling.

Organizations in cells *V* through *VIII* lack control over exit, and thus differ sharply from those in cells *I* through *IV*. When clients or members have a choice of participation and the organization possesses entry control, as in cell *V*, lack of exit control is not problematic. Many fraternal associations, such as college fraternities and sororities, induct members for life and "de-activating" a noncontributing member is an extremely serious matter. Although expulsion is possible in principle, few fraternities or sororities ever resort to this drastic step, as high entrance standards and free choice of participation mean that a reasonably high level of performance can be expected of members most of the time. Organizations classified in cell *VI* are in more serious difficulty, as they are totally dependent upon clients or members choosing them and thus must invest substantial resources in attracting or motivating them. The classic example is, of course, businesses scrambling for customers in a freely competitive market.

When clients lack autonomy concerning their own participation, lack of exit control is not as serious as when clients can exit to viable alternatives, as shown by the example for cell *VII*. Persons wishing to pursue careers in a craft-based occupation, such as plumbing or carpentry, must join a craft union if they desire steady, well-paid work, especially in large cities. After serving an apprenticeship and being admitted to the journeyman list, members of craft unions gain seniority and are typically immune to expulsion from the union. The long apprenticeship and union reliance on personal references for new members mitigates the impact of lack of control over exit.

Organizations classified in cell *VIII* are highly dependent on their environments in terms of lacking entry and exit control, but dependence is vis-à-vis other agencies and organizations, not clients or members. Other agencies and organizations supply clients or members to such organizations (such as prisons and public mental hospitals), or define classes of customers that must be served (such as the New York State Public Service Commission defining persons who must be served by telephone companies in the state). The fate of clients or customers depends on the standards set by these controlling agencies, and prison inmates typically have a low priority in most state correctional systems whereas public utilities' clients occasionally are treated quite attentively by regulatory bodies. Thus, organizations in cell *VIII* are responsive not to clients or members directly, but instead to the agencies or organizations with regulatory power over them.

Several implications follow from this examination of limits to organizational authority and autonomy over boundaries. First, some organizations sacrifice autonomy for survival—they give up control over entry or exit in exchange for an assured existence. Organizations with no control over entry because of public subsidy are guaranteed a minimally steady flow of clients in cases of low client autonomy. Expansion of government's role in the human services sector has probably increased the number of organizations relying on a protected existence. In the short-run, retention of the organization's established form is guaranteed, but a subsidized existence often means losing control over key decisions to sponsors who have their own selection criteria. Department of Labor funding supported New York City's Mobilization for Youth (MFY) employment training program, but MFY had to give up its interpretation of unemployment as a structural problem in the economy and concentrate instead on remedying the individual "deficiencies" of the unemployed (Helfgot, 1974).

Second, under conditions of member or client autonomy, organizations must develop methods for attracting and motivating persons, as is the case in social movements, state universities, and firms in competitive markets. The greater the responsiveness to the market's characteristics, the more organizations develop activities or products isomorphic with the interests of the population served. The adult education programs in California (Clark, 1956) described in a previous chapter were almost totally dependent upon meeting clients' interests and thus provided course offerings matching the changing fads and fashions of their clients. Similarly, grocery stores serving ethnic neighborhoods carry foods catering to the special tastes of the clientele (Light, 1972). When clients or members have little or no choice, organizational authorities are freer to ignore or discount their interests, as in many prisons and public monopolies. In portraying a telephone company employee during a satirical sketch on public utilities' unresponsiveness to customers, Lily Tomlin remarked, "We're the phone company. We don't care [about you]. We don't have to!" However, when freedom of choice is lacking, there is always the prospect of protest by disgruntled clients or members. The impact of dissent is then magnified by the lack of an exit option.

Third, internal organizational variability should be highest in cells *I*, *II*, *V*, and *VI*, and lowest in cells *III*, *IV*, *VII*, and *VIII*. Variability should be lowest in organizations in cell *VIII*, as they are in an environment of assured resources and can disregard the desires of potential members or clients. In contrast, variability should be highest among organizations in cell *I*, as they are in highly uncertain environments and pressures for responsiveness are great. This typology could thus be used to examine the likelihood of organizational transformation or persistence in conjunction with the other factors discussed in previous chapters.

Pressures for Responsiveness in Recruiting Employees

The creation of an organization with a particular technology, a set of goals, and an established structure involves, by definition, the necessity of selecting persons from the environment as members or employees. Recruiting and retaining members or employees are boundary-crossing and boundary-defining activities, and an organization's distinctive competence is based upon which persons are admitted and which are excluded. Depending upon environmental conditions, authorities may have to expand or constrict organizational boundaries, add special boundary-spanning roles or units, modify goals, or take other steps to obtain members or employees. In examining the creation of organizations, I discussed how the nature of labor markets affects the types of organizations founded in particular environments. In this section most of the characteristics of labor markets will be taken as given. I examine here a case study of how a group of organizations adapted to environmental changes causing a scarcity of potential employees. These changes are examples of environments moving from rich to lean capacity with regard to the availability of staff.

Either environmental changes or changes in goals and technology may lead to problems in recruiting an appropriate labor force. At the environmental level, competition from new organizational forms may drain off the best qualified workers in the labor market, or legal changes may require the recruitment of previously ignored segments of the labor market. The expansion of a public university system with a higher pay scale and better fringe benefits than private universities may deplete the supply of the best qualified teachers previously recruited by private colleges. In the 1960s, the expansion of the aerospace industry attracted engineers and other highly skilled technical workers away from traditional industries. In the 1970s, the United States government directives that organizations take affirmative action to recruit more women and minority group members heightened the competition for competent persons with these categories. One effect of requirements for affirmative action was the creation of the role of an affirmative action officer in corporate personnel departments and the growth of private consulting firms specializing in offering advice to firms on how to meet affirmative action guidelines.

At the organizational level, new goals or technologies, which may themselves be externally induced, sometimes render the old labor force obsolete or no longer as easy to recruit as before. In the United States, the change to a volunteer army in the post-Viet Nam War era made recruitment problematic. The Department of Defense responded by paying more attention to the recruiting function, conducting national advertising campaigns, publicizing the relaxation of traditional army discipline, and increasing compensation for enlisted men and women. The Gar Wood Company found that a change in the type of product it produced required a change in its labor force (Perrow, 1970, p. 167). The company originally built high-quality custom boats, but executives decided to shift to producing mass-produced, lower-quality boats to expand its share of the market. Employees had trouble meeting the changed work standards—producing more boats with less attention to detail—and the company eventually had to move to a new location and start over with a new labor force, not socialized in traditional Gar Wood procedures.

Externally induced changes in the recruiting function: An example.   Smigel (1964) conducted one of the classic analyses of how environmental changes can affect organizations' recruiting activities. He examined changes in the recruiting activities of large law firms in New York City in the 1950s, relying on interviews with lawyers from twenty-one large law firms, law school placement officers, and law school students, as well as a content analysis of job announcements. Traditionally, Wall Street law firms had a fixed image of the type of law school graduate they wished to recruit, seeking men with three attributes: upper-class lineage, ability, and personality. Desirable candidates were those from elite Eastern law schools who were at the top of their class and who worked on their school's law review. Also, their families were listed in the Social Register and they maintained pleasing, clean-cut appearances. Before World War II, law firms could wait until a prospective recruit came to them, and not much attention was paid to the recruiting function. As the ecological model would predict, the lack of environmental pressures on the organizations' boundaries meant that the recruitment function was not very complex and there was little variation among firms.

After World War II, a number of changes occurred that brought selective pressures to bear on law firms' recruiting practices and led to a series of organizational changes. First, there was an increase in the number and size of law firms. Growth in the economy and an increasing number of federal and state laws caused an expansion in the volume of legal work, with the increased volume met by old firms growing larger and new firms being founded, also seeking "Ivy League" lawyers. Second, there was an increase in exits from Wall Street law firms, in addition to the normal level of turnover. Some lawyers were discontented because of working conditions in large firms and left to take jobs in smaller firms. Some firms adopted an "up or out" policy to weed out associates—beginning members—who were not going to be made partners in the firm. The clients of large law firms had increasing legal needs, and many created their own internal legal departments or increased the size of the old one, hiring lawyers away from the large firms. Third, other organizations were also recruiting the preferred candidates, as the increasing legal complexity of the environment put them in the market for lawyers. Government agencies, the courts, corporations, and universities had to cope with an increasing volume of legal work and they attempted to hire lawyers fitting the image of the Wall Street lawyer.

Fourth, the number of lawyers graduated did not keep pace with the demand, especially at the Ivy League schools. The rate of admission to the bar in 1930 was 81 per million population, and only 57 per million in 1958. Large firms' discrimination against women, Jews, and other minorities made it difficult for them to fill their needs with these readily available substitutes. Fifth, two types of changes took place in law school graduates' aspirations about their careers: More graduates looked to locations outside of New York City as favorable locations for practicing law, and more graduates were deciding against practicing in Wall Street law firms because of their negative image. The consequence of these five changes was that Wall Street law firms found it increasingly difficult to recruit their preferred candidates.

Large law firms responded to changing environmental conditions by modifying their recruiting practices and internal structure in a number of ways. First, the firms collaborated in creating a cartel arrangement to restrain two types of competition. Firms agreed not to "pirate" other firms' employees away by offering higher salaries or other inducements. Firms also agreed to pay the same beginning salary, and, as in other oligopolistic situations, this led to nonprice competition between firms for new recruits. Second, Wall Street law firms intensified their public relations efforts to create a more favorable image of themselves in the eyes of law school graduates. They tried to overcome the dislike and fear many students had of working in a large law firm, and thus the Harvard Law School Association of New York City held a meeting during Christmas holidays for Harvard Law School students at which invited speakers defended large firms against their critics. Firms attempted to improve their images by sending carefully written brochures to law schools' placement offices, stressing that their firm was not like other large firms, that new lawyers were given several years of training before being asked to specialize, and that lawyers who were not promoted were assisted in finding jobs elsewhere.

Third, increasing environmental pressures caused some firms to create a new role, the *hiring partner*, thus increasing their internal division of labor. Specializing and formalizing the hiring partner's role brought a number of advantages to the large firm. The person in the role was chosen for his personal attractiveness so that he would make a favorable impression on candidates. In this respect, the role of hiring partner was very much like that of rush chairperson in fraternities and sororities. The hiring partner held the role full time and thus was able to see *all* the candidates, permitting an accurate comparison to be made between them. Formalization of the hiring process extended to having the hiring partner visit the various law schools and weed out all but the most promising candidates, with only this select group invited to the firm for interviews.

Fourth, the recruiting process was *standardized* to ensure that the process was as bureaucratically rational as possible. As a large firm might interview 300 to 400 candidates per year, the potential economies-of-scale in a rationalized administration of the process were very great. One law firm used fourteen partners in the hiring process, with three different partners responsible for each day of the week. Fifth, internal operating procedures were modified to formalize the hiring function, as normal routines were changed and used as another recruiting mechanism. Second-year students were invited to clerk with the firm during the summer before their third year—the student could learn about the firm, the firm obtained a preview of the student's ability, and the student returned to his law school to share his (hopefully) favorable impressions of the firm with his peers. Increased opportunities for on-the-job training were provided by rotating associates to new responsibilities within the firm on a regular schedule. Sixth, some large law firms began to drop their discriminatory barriers against Jews and other minorities. These Jewish lawyers were at the top of their classes, and Smigel implied that eventually Jews would be recruited no differently from gentiles. Women were still discriminated against, and in 1977 some Wall Street law firms had no female partners, although they had female associate members.

Changes in recruitment: Summary. Large Wall Street firms adapted to a scarcity of an important resource—law school graduates from elite law schools—by changes in their structures and procedures. Whether the adaptations were the result of strategic choices made by administrators is difficult to determine, as Smigel presented only the successful rather than the attempted changes. The recruitment function became more specialized, standardized, and formalized; in short, law firms became more bureaucratized in response to environmental pressures. The adaptations were retained because of continued environmental pressures, chiefly from other organizations recruiting lawyers and from changes in the aspirations of law school graduates. The magnitude of the unforeseen side effects resulting from the changes leads us to believe that not all law firms accepted them willingly. The hiring partner role was formalized and the person occupying it was forced to give up some of his law practice. Some partners were unhappy with this development, but many found they gained power within the firm as a result of controlling a strategic contingency. The commitment to place associates elsewhere if the "up-or-out" decision was "out" led to the growth of placement as a major function, requiring an additional investment of organizational resources. Educational procedures for new lawyers were formalized, adding managerial and tutorial duties to partners' responsibilities and increasing the complexity of a firm's administrative structure. Wall Street law firms thus regained some control over an important resource, but at the cost of increasing bureaucratization and paying more attention to lower-level participants.

MEMBER AUTONOMY AND ORGANIZATIONAL RESPONSIVENESS

The previous section considered entry and exit primarily from an organization's point of view, treating control over boundaries as problematic for organizational authorities. An underlying assumption was that authorities seek stability and control in maintaining boundaries. A different way to treat boundary-crossing is to examine it from the viewpoint of disgruntled members and clients who are responding to deteriorating or unsatisfactory performance (Kolarska and Aldrich, 1978).

Albert Hirschman's (1972) contribution was to provide a conceptual framework within which investigators could simultaneously examine people's responses to deteriorating organizational performance *and* administrators' responses to members' or customers' attempts to put organizations back on a more desirable course. Deteriorating performance or failures to perform up to expected standards are continual problems for all organziations. Traditional economic analyses have focused on customers ceasing to buy a firm's product and rigorous competition as remedies for declining organizational performance. Hirschman added a second general response: "voice," or customers and members expressing their dissatisfaction directly to management or to some other authority to which management is subordinate. By bringing "voice" into the analysis, Hirschman supplemented the market forces usually examined by economists with an explicitly political dimension.

Responses to Declining Organizational Performance

Hirschman's analysis covered firms producing saleable goods for customers, and organizations providing services to their members, such as political parties and voluntary associatios. An organization's performance was assumed to be subject to deterioration for unspecified and random causes that may be corrected *if* management responds quickly enough. Decline need not be absolute; relative decline may result from the creation of new organizations providing a higher quality product or service, or innovations occurring in established organizations. The result is the same: Management must respond or go under.

What does a person do when faced with declining performance in a business, public agency, voluntary association, or other organization? Hirschman presented an essentially rationalistic model of individual decision making in such situations, with persons weighing the costs and benefits of various options and taking opportunities and constraints into account.

Choice of response.   The first consideration is whether people believe that performance can be improved—that the quality of the product or service can be restored or increased to meet their expectations. If people believe in the possibility of improvement, then they will stay put (Barry, 1974). If not, they will exit. After the first choice is made (between exit versus nonexit), then a second choice must be made: Should the dissatisfied person remain silent or protest? Figure 9.1 diagrams the decision situations facing a disgruntled member or customer. As

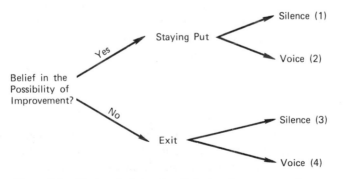

Figure 9.1.   Choices facing a dissatisfied customer or member.

Source: A. H. Birch, "Economic Models in Political Science: The Case of 'Exit, Voice, and Loyalty.' " *British Journal of Political Science*, 5 (January 1975): 65-82.

Barry (1974) pointed out, Hirschman collapsed these two distinct choices into only one—exit or voice. As shown in Figure 9.1, the two decisions lead to four possible outcomes: (1) stay and be silent; (2) stay and be vocal; (3) exit and remain silent; and (4) exit and be vocal. Hirschman focused on the second and third options, considering only marginally the options of staying silently and exiting noisily (Laver, 1976).

Four options.   *Exit* from a deteriorating or inefficient organization is one response open to dissatisfied members and customers. Customers stop buying a firm's product, patients switch to another clinic, and members resign from their organization. Some of these responses are conscious attempts to punish the organization, but most are simply signs that discontented persons are taking the path of least resistance in adapting to an undesirable situation. Regardless of the objectives of persons using the exit option, the consequences are similar: A business's revenue drops or an organization's membership declines, leading authorities to search for ways of correcting deficiencies. Not all administrators and leaders are alert enough to immediately perceive what is happening, and deterioration may reach a point where recovery is no longer possible.

Most persons who choose to exit do so *silently*, with contradictory consequences for the organization's future. The real reason for silent exist may go undetected by authorities for some time, leading to a false sense that nothing is wrong. Were departing members or customers to articulate their grievances, authorities would have a clearer picture of the organization's failings. A second consequence is that persons exiting silently do not spread discontent within the organization or publicize its problems to the public. As a result, mass exit may be delayed while authorities use the time gained to bring the organization's performance back to standard.

Some persons who choose exit also use *voice*, attempting to convince others in the organization to join them, appealing to leaders to correct problems, and publicly condemning the organization. Hirschman treated exit and voice as exclusive alternatives and thus devoted only passing attention to this option. He did discuss the case of officials resigning and publicly protesting against government policies, and he lamented the fact that such overt protests are so rare. Most government officials choose to exit silently, as was the case in the United States during the Viet Nam War.

Persons choosing to remain with a deteriorating organization, as members or customers, may choose to voice their complaints or remain silent. Hirschman treated voice as an alternative to exit, focusing on the use of voice by persons choosing to stay and consequently neglecting the category of persons who remain but are silent.

Voice refers to members or customers expressing their dissatisfaction to authorities either directly or indirectly. *Direct voice* is the direct vocalization of grievances to authorities within an organization, whereas *indirect voice* is exercised by appealing to an outside authority or interest group. Indirect voice is typi-cally used only after direct voice fails. Direct voice may be used by disgruntled customers or members to express their discontent to authorities, perhaps through complaints at meetings, the circulation of petitions, or by public protests.

In the 1960s, the use of voice by clients of social service agencies in the United States was so widespread that Haug and Sussman (1969) referred to it as the "revolt of the clients." In schools, hospitals, colleges, welfare agencies, police departments, and other social service agencies, clients began to question the autonomy of the professionals claiming to have the expertise and humanita-rian commitment to make decisions for clients. Whereas in previous years dis-contented clients simply chose exit, clients in the 1960s used voice to protest their treatment. The use of voice was accentuated by the bureaucratization of pro-fessional services, as clients increasingly met professionals in an organizational rather than individual practice context. Professionals' goals were seen as subor-dinate to organizational objectives, and clients identified professionals with their organizations, rather than the "higher calling" claimed by professionals.

Indirect voice may involve appealing to an external authority with power over the poorly performing organization. Appeals typically are made to government agencies or officials: A legislature is asked to pass a law setting safety standards in coal mines, or state courts are asked to enjoin an employer from requiring employees to work around dangerous machinery. Indirect voice may involve appeals to outside organizations *without* formal authority over the declining or-ganization. The mass media—radio, newspapers, and television—are often ap-proached for aid by customers or members who have been rebuffed by their own organizations and government agencies (Kolarska, 1977). The major weapon of the media is moral persuasion and the creation of a climate within which the re-calcitrant organization feels pressured to defend its actions.

Doing nothing is the option chosen by those who remain in the organization and do not use voice. Hirschman devoted little space to this possibility, and yet it is probably the most common response by discontented members. Exit or voice require at least a minimal degree of effort, whereas doing nothing is often the path of least resistance. Lack of response may be due to feelings of loyalty, apathy, withdrawal, the lack of structural means for aggregating discontent, or contentment with overall conditions. Distinguishing genuine satisfaction from other causes of non-response is extremely difficult in the absence of some persons exiting or using voice.

"Doing nothing" is more than a residual category. Managers, leaders, and other authorities seek the freedom from constraint that follows from a quiescent membership or clientele. Staying silently is assumed to be the standard against which authorities judge other responses by discontented members and clients.

Exit and voice are important for the study of organizational change because they are sources of pressure that may disrupt established structures and activities. For business organizations, exit is one means through which authorities discover their lack of fit to a niche, and exit need not be announced to authorities for it to have an effect. Declining revenues and falling membership speak for themselves, although misinformation and perceptual distortions may lead authorities to disregard danger signs until it is too late. Voice can be a pressure promoting the maintenance of internal complexity, especially in voluntary associations perceived by members as departing from their original goals. Exit and voice are pressures toward the selective elimination of certain organizational structures and activities (or even entire organizations), as well as examples of intraorganizational variability. Lack of member and client response allows the persistence of the established form.

Under What Conditions Are Options Chosen?

Hirschman discussed a number of conditions under which exit or voice would be chosen, and most of his original analysis is still relevant when the revised model of Figure 9.1 is taken into account. Combining ideas developed by Hirschman with suggestions made by his critics yields four conditions affecting the probability of exit (versus remaining) and voice (versus keeping silent): the availability of alternatives, loyalty to the organization, the availability of structural means to channel discontent, and the likelihood of retaliation.

Availability of alternatives.   Exit is most readily chosen when alternatives of better quality are available from other organizations. Exit to alternatives is only possible, of course, when members or customers have control over their own involvement in the organization—they are not coerced into membership or unable to choose an alternative because of an achieved or state-protected monopoly. For customers of business firms, these conditions for exit are met when substitute goods or services of comparable quality are available elsewhere and thus the demand for a particular firm's products is quality elastic.

The availability of alternatives appears at first glance to make exit less costly than voice, as a simpler action is involved. However, there are conditions under which exit actually can be quite costly. For example, an organization may rely on a supplier for an important resource and may have invested a great deal of time and effort in negotiating the production of a good or service satisfying its specific needs. If the organization were to immediately switch to another firm because of declining quality from its current supplier, it would incur these costs once again in training the new supplier (Hirschman, 1973). Similarly, customers wishing to switch to higher quality alternatives will need to spend time searching for a reliable supplier and adjusting to the new product's idiosyncratic characteristics. There are thus often strong incentives for dissatisfied firms and customers to use voice before attempting exit.

Lack of alternatives closes off the option of exit and hence raises the likelihood that voice will be considered by discontented members and customers. Organizations in which persons lack control over their own participation are thus likely to face voice rather than exit from dissidents. Under conditions of monopoly (when a customer has no prospects of choosing among alternatives), voicing dissatisfaction is the only avenue open to persons upset by poor performance. Prison inmates cannot exit, and thus overt protest is the only mechanism for expressing the intensity of their grievances. Similarly, sailors on ships at sea must mutiny, whereas soldiers on land can desert. Protestant church members can break away to found new sects, whereas Roman Catholics are tied into a unique organizational structure in which the central authorities own the premises (Zald and Berger, 1978).

"Almost monopolists" have an interest in leaving open the possibility of exit, as exit relieves them of the major problem of dealing with a highly vocal, organized opposition that is committed to voice because exit is foreclosed (Hirschman, 1972). The United States Postal Service accepts the existence of private business-oriented parcel delivery services, partially because these private services are a safety valve. They provide dissatisfied Post Office clients with the possibility of exit rather than the necessity of voice in responding to inadequate services.

Loyalty.   Hirschman argued that voice is most likely when members or customers feel some loyalty to an organization. His argument was that the higher the loyalty to an organization, the longer persons wait to use exit and the higher their perceived investment in resolving the difficulty. If loyalty inhibits exit and allows time for voice to develop, then we would expect to find the most loyal customers or members leading a protest against declining performance, while the less loyal choose to exit. Hirschman treated loyalty, then, as a commitment to a "higher value" representing the original goals of the organization.

Critics noted several problems with Hirschman's concept of loyalty. Barry (1974) argued that loyalty may inhibit exit, but that isn't sufficient to predict voice—silent nonexit is another alternative. Indeed, Birch (1975) wrote that the term "loyalty" seems most appropriate for those people who are so loyal that they accept whatever their leaders do, thus choosing silence rather than voice. This is contrary to the spirit of Hirschman's book, but this view is encouraged by his relative neglect of people who choose silent nonexit.

A suggested redefinition of loyalty proposed by Laver (1976) partially meets these objections. In general, a loyalist is a person who stays when others would have left. However, we should omit people who are apathetic or coerced from this category. Optimists, people who are future-oriented and who perceive the decline is short-term, and people who are generally confident persons will remain with the organization. These people are assuming the organization will be able to recover from its current difficulties, but future-oriented or optimistic people will probably perceive no need to use voice. Only generally confident persons would be expected to consider voice as an action necessary to force the organization back on course.

Structural means to aggregate discontent.   Structural means for communicating complaints cut the costs of voice and permit persons to consider using it before taking the options of exiting or staying silently. Voice often loses out to exit because its effectiveness depends on the discovery of new methods of exerting influence on an organization. Any organizational form that enables discontented activists to more easily mobilize dissatisfied members and customers increases the probability that voice will be used (Gamson, 1967). The growth of labor unions in industrialized nations during the past century has given disaffected workers a structural means through which they can influence employers, and reformist groups within political parties have played a similar role.

Three conditions increase the likelihood that dissidents will search for new forms of communicating dissatisfaction before exiting. First, confident loyalty pushes persons toward searching for new means of communication, as loyalists are reluctant to exit until exhausting all available avenues of protest. Second, a lack of alternatives raises people's perceived investments in an organization and increases the potential payoff of voice. Third, the cost of voice may become a benefit when people can join a movement or crusade that gives them the satisfaction of associating with like-minded persons to act against unsatisfactory organizational performance.

The significance of crusades and movements in promoting the exercise of voice demonstrates that the issue cannot be treated solely in instrumental, individualistic terms. Voice often appears to be a result of expressive or solidary-purposive incentives (Clark and Wilson, 1961) rather than of individual calculations regarding costs and benefits. For example, Ralph Nader's campaigns can't be explained by arguing that he was motivated by the increase in the quality of the goods he buys for himself (Barry, 1974). This way of phrasing the argument emphasizes the fundamental rationality of those persons who choose to remain silent (whether they exit or not) in the face of organizational deterioration, for only on rare occasions does quality deterioration evoke the level of expressive solidarity among persons necessary to motivate them to exercise collective voice.

Citing Olson's (1968) work on the logic of collective action, Barry (1974, p. 92) remarked that "only in very small groups—of less than a dozen, say—is the expected benefit *to oneself* from the exercise of voice in pursuit of the 'public good' of an improvement in general quality likely to outweigh the costs of exercising it." In larger organizations, individuals perceive that the marginal value of their contributions to the success of a protest is minor, and it is more rational to simply sit back and collect the benefits of others' actions on one's behalf. Barry argued that the rarity of voice is one reason why economists have neglected it in favor of studying exit. Nonetheless, issues do arise that cause large numbers of people to overcome their reservations about the cost of voice. Such issues typically involve questions of the public interest: protests against the war in Viet Nam, corporate investment in South Africa, building of nuclear power stations, and attempts to reform abortion laws.

Retaliation.   People who use voice while remaining in an organization are vulnerable to retaliation from management or leaders (Hirschman, 1976). Retaliation and reprisals may therefore inhibit the use of voice, although there are some mechanisms used to protect people, even in the absence of exit: a secret vote in voluntary associations, an ombudsman in government agencies, and trade unions in factories. Birch (1975) noted that the possibility of retaliation may cause people to use voice only if exit is available.

Management's Responses to Exit and Voice

Measured against the baseline of an inactive membership or clientele (people who "stay silently"), exit and voice are problems requiring administrative attention. Hirschman assumed that managers are usually sensitive to exit and voice, and therefore it is enough for members or customers to make their wishes known in order to change management policies (Kolarska, 1977). He recognized situations in which mangement repressed voice or ignored exit; but, as a rule, he treated insensitivity to voice or exit as a pathological reaction by management. From the resource dependence perspective, insensitivity to exit and voice are not pathological phenomena but rather perfectly rational behavior, when viewed from leaders' or managers' viewpoints. If leaders and managers seek autonomy and shun dependence, repressing or controlling exit and voice increases the range of activities over which the dominant coalition is free from constraint.

Sensitivity to options.   Administrators' sensitivity to exit ultimately depends upon their organizations' openness to market forces and the extent to which members or customers have control over their own participation. Exit is likely to have little effect on organizations protected by state subsidies or by a private monopoly position. Hirschman (1972, p. 45) gave an example of the decline in performance of the publicly owned railroad in Nigeria, relative to the privately owned trucking industry: "exit did not have its usual attention-focusing effect because the loss of revenue was not a matter of the utmost gravity for management."

Sensitivity to voice depends on management's perceptions of the answers to two questions: Will voice ultimately lead to exit, and, if exit is impossible (because of lack of alternatives), will voice escalate and interfere with the organization's essential activities? If exit is not a problem for the organization, and if persons using voice can be persuaded or forced to exit, managers and leaders need not fear voice. In cases where exit will have a damaging effect on the organization, the threat of exit as expressed in voice will attract management's attention. When exit is impossible or unlikely, management will respond to voice to the extent that persons protesting deterioration cannot be isolated or silenced.

Hirschman's analysis of the differential sensitivity to exit and voice of private as opposed to public schools illustrates several of the above points. If a community's public schools decline in quality and private schools are available but expensive, the first parents to move their children into private schools are those either most concerned about educational quality, regardless of what it costs, or the most affluent, who can afford to move their children into private schools whenever they are slightly dissatisfied. The exit of these groups might evoke some response by the publicly supported schools, but not nearly as much as if they had remained within the school system to fight deterioration. Being committed to high-quality education, parents of private school children will respond quickly if the private schools begin to deteriorate. The threat of exit is much more powerful in the case of market-oriented private schools than in public schools, and so private school authorities will respond vigorously to both voice and the possibility of exit by disgruntled parents. Consequently, the gap between the quality of private and public schools is likely to widen further.

The sensitivity of authorities might be increased if discontented members and customers appeal to outside groups via indirect voice (Kolarska, 1977). Administrators must protect their organization's claim to legitimacy, as they exist within a context of scarce resources that other organizations are also competing for. Organizations gain legitimacy to the extent that their activities are congruent with the institutional values of the larger society (Parsons, 1966). Powerful outside organizations—public agencies, the mass media, political parties—might succeed in interceding on behalf of members and customers ignored by their own organizations.

Attempts at controlling voice.   Managers and leaders attempt to free themselves from constraints that they perceive to hamper their organization's efficiency. From this perspective, voice (and threats to exit) can be a very troublesome constraint. Rather than divert resources to correcting organizational deficiencies, authorities might calculate that a cheaper strategy is simply to expel discontented members, stop serving complaining customers, and control or suppress voice. In a nonmarket context, where administrators can essentially ignore the costs of exit, controlling or managing voice may be a rational short-run strategy.

Hirschman argued that the higher the loyalty to an organization, the longer persons wait to use exit, which allows time for voice to develop. Instead of encouraging voice, however, loyalty may cloud members' visions and lead to their ignoring events and policies that objectively deserve a response. Rather than using voice as performance declines, loyal members and customers may simply do nothing. Authorities can play upon this possibility by promoting identification and commitment to the organization, thus raising member or customer tolerance of inefficient performance.

Members and customers may have difficulty separating loyalty to the organization from loyalty to what it once stood for: the official goals or advertised products of the organization. Authorities would therefore be expected to encourage beliefs in "tradition," spread distorted information and do everything possible to blur the distinction between the two kinds of loyalty. If such manipulations are successful, the threat of voice or exit by long-time members and customers is lessened and administrators achieve the quiet life they are seeking.

Professionals in social service organizations in the United States responded to the revolt of the clients in the 1960s with tactics designed to raise client loyalty to their organizations (Haug and Sussman, 1969). Organizations adapted to increased voice by devising strategies for incorporating protestors into the organization (Aldrich, 1971b). Voice was thus muted through the promotion and encouragement of loyalty. Hospitals created patients' councils, colleges added students to curriculum committees and boards of trustees, and poverty agencies appointed community representatives to advisory boards. The objective of authorities was to "socialize the dissidents into the special organizational knowledge of the inner professional circle" (Haug and Sussman, 1969, p. 158) while retaining actual power in the hands of professionals and administrators.

If efforts at manipulating loyalty fail, authorities can use retaliation or special inducements to silence protestors. Retaliation and reprisals may be counter to organizational or societal norms, and so authorities may have to turn to singling out persons for special favors—buying off or co-opting them. Organizations thus avoid having to deal with the general problem of decline by silencing the most vocal dissenters. Hirschman recognized this flaw in his argument when it was pointed out by critics of his over-optimistic view of voice's potential. Writing of the use of co-optation, Hirschman (1976, p. 388) noted that "this managerial strategy is present when firms extend 'gold plated service' to their more important customers; it is also often practiced by administrative agencies rationing out goods and services to applicants according to nonmarket criteria."

Member Autonomy and Organizational Responsiveness: Summary

Exit, voice, and doing nothing are responses by members and clients to declining organizational performance, and the major condition affecting their use is environmental: Are there alternatives available from other organizations or agencies to supply the required product or service? Differences between members and clients are also important, as some are more sensitive to deteriorating performance or more loyal to the organization than others. When the exit option is available, feelings of loyalty are the major force inhibiting exit, and knowledgeable authorities attempt to manipulate commitment and loyalty to their organization so that exit is impeded further. Dissident organizational entrepreneurs can combat authorities' attempts at controlling loyalty and channels of communication by developing structural means for aggregating individuals' grievances and mobilizing dissidents. Ironically, in an era of heightened demands for citizen involvement and participation, the extension of the public sector and of government support to segments of the private sector is rendering the exit option less powerful.

Voice, not surprisingly, is growing in importance, but it is very much dependent upon the availability of information and means for communicating with other dissidents, both of which are subject to manipulation and control by organizational authorities.

Organizational actions have many consequences and large organizations are highly differentiated by function, market area, and so forth. Hirschman's analysis implicitly treats organizations as single-purpose entities, with members and clients reacting as a single body to changes in performance. Recognizing the complexity of organizational outputs complicates an analysis of exit and voice considerably, because heterogeneity in organizations' output constituencies means there is probably never a point at which *all* people are dissatisfied. Authorities must therefore weigh the importance of the various interest groups and their discontent. Similarly, individuals may be happy with some aspects of organizational performance, while not with others. They also face the problem of weighing their preferences and deciding at what point to act. Perceptual distortions, lack of information, ambiguous goals, and other factors affect the weighing of preferences by authorities and members or clients, and it is doubtful that the process is as rationalistic as described above.

SUMMARY

Organizations are boundary-maintaining systems of human interaction, and a minimal defining characteristic of formal organizations is the distinction made between members and non-members. Authorities attempt to preserve the integrity of an organization's boundaries and the stability of its structure by controlling entry and exit, but some organizations lack control over these processes. Dependence on other organizations or on members having free choice of entry and exit limits organizational autonomy and makes authorities responsive to the wishes of outsiders. The rational selection model of organizational change works best when applied to situations where member autonomy is limited and organizations control entry and exit, but these conditions are lacking for many types of organizations. Boundary-control problems open organizations to external influence and may generate variation, either through strategic maneuvers by authorities or actions taken by outsiders.

Dissatisfied clients or members have several alternative courses of action in seeking greater responsiveness by authorities, although they need not be *consciously* chosen as strategies. Exit, voice, offering inducements, and doing nothing are possible responses by unhappy members. Their use depends on several limiting conditions, the primary ones being the availability of other alternatives and members' or clients' loyalty to the organization. Authorities may encourage limited exit or manipulate loyalty as ways of avoiding more responsive behavior.

10 Spanning Organizational Boundaries

Organizations are boundary-maintaining systems, but they are obviously not closed to external influence. In conflict situations, members constitute strategic resources for organizations, and authorities seek methods of varying boundaries for making the best use of members' contributions. Boundaries might be expanded or constricted, depending on the nature of the conflict and the organization's internal compliance structure. Boundary-crossing processes involving entry and exit are also critical under nonconflict conditions, and some members are delegated special responsibilities as they assume boundary-spanning roles. Locating a specific organization's boundaries can be problematic, and the existence of boundary-spanning roles is an important guide to environmental contingencies perceived as significant by authorities. Boundary-spanning roles also result from external selection of those activities that have contributed in adaptive ways to the flow of information and influence across organizational boundaries.

The first section of this chapter focuses on variations in organizational boundaries as responses to conflict between focal organizations and persons or organizations in their environments. Looking at boundaries from the perspective of strategic choice, I examine the conditions under which authorities are able to use boundary expansion or constriction as a conflict-resolution strategy. The remaining sections take the existence of boundaries as given and focus on variation in boundary-spanning activities by members. I examine the functions served by boundary roles and sources of variation in the structure of such roles, with the final section examining boundary-role specificity, discretion, and power. Effective boundary-spanning contributes to the retention of positively-selected forms, and also allows rapid organizational responses to changing environmental selection parameters.

INTERORGANIZATIONAL CONFLICT AND MEMBER COMPLIANCE

Member participation is important to authorities in normal circumstances because the maintenance of organizations depends upon member contributions to the activity system. In conflict situations, the more actively members participate, the higher the likelihood of success. From the perspective of authorities, then, member compliance both sustains an organization in normal times and provides critical resources in conflict situations. In this section, two organizational strategies for dealing with member compliance are discussed, and the probability of using one or the other is related to problems of boundary maintenance during interorganizational conflict.

Expanding or Constricting Boundaries

Two strategies may be used by authorities to heighten the contribution of member participation in interorganizational conflicts. Pressures to use either strategy arise from authorities' desires to minimize the uncertainty of conflict situations, with uncertainty caused by their lack of knowledge as to how members will respond to conflict and by their lack of control over many external elements in the conflict. One method of girding organizations for conflict is to tighten organizational boundaries, and the other is to expand them. Organizational strategy may take the form of constricting boundaries by strengthening the requirements of participation, with more asked of each member by way of conformity to organizational rules and ideology. Organizational strategy may also take the form of expanding organizational boundaries in order to take in persons from competing groups or organizations to make them members of the focal organization.

Tightening and strengthening an organization's boundaries means either raising performance standards or appealing to members' loyalty to the organization. Increased centralization gives authorities more direct control over members' energy and time, allowing them to reallocate resources rapidly. Simmel (1955, p. 92) pointed out two ways for organizations to achieve consensus in the face of an external threat: "either to forget internal counter-currents or to bring them to unadulterated expression by expelling certain members." If an organization is able to amend internal rifts, then all members can be counted on in the struggle. After their nominating convention, political party members are expected to forget internal differences as they prepare for the election campaign. In the heat of preparing for the election, standards for participation are raised and members put in much more time than during the rest of the year, when party officials control day-to-day activities.

A second strategy for dealing with member compliance during conflict is to take persons from the challenging groups and organizations inside organizational boundaries. They may be absorbed, co-opted, or amalgamated into the focal organization (Etzioni, 1961, pp. 103-4). These methods generate additional costs for an organization, as they necessitate taking on new, unsocialized members; this adds an element of uncertainty to organizational activities. An attempted solution to a conflict can thus have the unintended effect of increasing the problem of member compliance for authorities. The Tennessee Valley Authority (TVA) used co-optation to neutralize potential opposition to its program. This tactic increased the problem of member compliance because members came into the organization with values and goals opposed in many ways to those of the TVA (Selznick, 1949).

Constraints on choices of strategies.   Limits on organizational autonomy determine which of the two strategies will be used by authorities. The central dimension is the system an organization uses to control its members, with the control system affected by the degree of member autonomy and loyalty. (Note that this discussion focuses on members only, not customers or clients.) At one extreme organizations are freely chosen by members, while at the other members are coerced into organizational membership. These two extremes are reflected in the two halves of Table 9.1. A mid-point between the extremes can be distinguished, allowing the classification of three types of organizational control structures: normative, utilitarian, and coercive (Etzioni, 1961). Normative control structures achieve compliance by appealing to members' beliefs and values, making use of solidary and purposive incentives. Solidary incentives are the intangible rewards resulting from the act of associating with others, and purposive incentives are the intangible rewards resulting from the sense of satisfaction in working for a worthwhile cause (Clark and Wilson, 1961). Potential members have complete freedom in choosing organizations with normative control structures, as the initiative for membership is expected to result from congruence between a person's beliefs and values and those of the organization.

Utilitarian control structures achieve compliance by offering members material incentives, which are tangible rewards such as money and material possessions. Membership in a utilitarian organization is required in a society where one's economic rewards depend on association with a wage- or salary-paying organization. Only the independently wealthy are not constrained to become members of utilitarian organizations. Finally, organizations with coercive control structures are not usually entered by choice, and the typical incentives offered are negative ones—punishment for not carrying out duties or conforming to regulations as ordered.

The type of control structure affects an organization's capacity for varying its boundaries and also influences the cost of such actions; the control structure is therefore associated with the type of conflict strategy chosen by authorities. An organization's capacity for varying its boundaries can be considered along two dimensions: (1) the degree to which an organization's boundaries include the life-space of members (Lefton and Rosengren, 1966); and (2) the degree of loyalty and commitment members feel toward the organization, as discussed in Chapter 9. The degree of inclusion of a member's personality or life-space is an indication of the member's dependence on the organization. In normative and coercive control structures, the degree of inclusion is quite high, although for quite different reasons. Members of normatively structured organizations are committed to their objectives, whereas members of coercively structured organizations have no alternatives. In these types of organizations additional claims upon the members meet with less resistance than in utilitarian organizations, where the degree of inclusion is much less, except for top administrators. However, the extensive inclusion of members' life-spaces poses a difficult problem for the socialization of new members, and the introduction of new members is therefore more of a risk than in utilitarian organizations.

The degree of loyalty and commitment of members affects the likelihood that membership itself will be perceived as a reward by members. The possibility of increasing demands upon members is directly related to their degree of loyalty. In normative organizations, loyalty and commitment are high for nearly all members, whereas in utilitarian organizations the degree of member commitment is directly related to the economic benefits received. In organizations with coercive control structures the degree of inclusion is quite high, but the degree of loyalty and commitment is rather low for most members, except for those whom Goffman labelled "colonizers" (Goffman, 1961).

The *cost* of boundary expansion or constriction is also related to an organization's control structure. In normative organizations, expansion of an organization's boundaries carries the potential cost of seriously compromising original goals by contaminating the "purity" of the organization's character. Utilitarian organizations expand at the cost of added complexity and increased administrative overhead costs. Coercive organizations' tenuous control over their members would be seriously threatened by expansion. The major cost of boundary constriction is the loss of potential contributors to an organization's activity system, but this loss is probably not significant for coercive organizations. The structural complexity of most utilitarian organizations implies that a reduction in membership could require a structural reorganization that might be costly.

Conflict Strategies and Boundary Control

Several predictions can be derived from the above discussion of the relationship between conflict strategies and an organization's degree of boundary control, considered in terms of the three internal control structures. Organizations with normative control structures are more likely to follow the tightening-up rather than the expansion strategy, as admission to the good graces of the organization constitutes a major control mechanism. Expansion to take in new members is undesirable because it raises the prospect of hordes of unsocialized members who will be difficult to control. Moreover, performance standards for members are ordinarily slight and many of them are likely to desert when confronted with a true test of their convictions. Conflict is likely to increase the visibility of ideological divisions within exclusive normative organizations, with the various factions attempting to purge the others. Divisions within the Communist party in the Soviet Union and China, the split in the Social Democratic party in Germany in the latter half of the nineteenth century, and purges within radical student organizations in the United States in the 1960s are examples of this pattern.

One factor that might lead inclusive normative organizations to employ an expansion strategy is the absence of a rigid ideology to which all members must subscribe. Political parties in the United States are known for their ability to encompass within themselves a wide variety of positions, and this is particularly true of the Labor party in Great Britain. Normative organizations with purely sociable goals sometimes face conflicts over member loyalty, but lacking a highly specific belief system, they are able to resolve the conflict by using the expansion strategy and adding new interest groups or auxiliaries. The Los Angeles branch of Mensa International expanded to over thirty special interest groups in the early 1970s, all peacefully coexisting despite extreme heterogeneity of members' interests (Aldrich, 1971b). Member compliance is retained in ideologically loose organizations by incorporating potential conflicting relationships into the organization.

Organizations with utilitarian control structures have a very wide range of tolerance of member behavior. Competition and conflict between utilitarian organizations—mainly businesses—is ordinarily so benign that only a minimal degree of member loyalty and commitment is required of lower level participants. Given the prevailing business values of size and growth, it is very unlikely that a utilitarian organization will use the constriction strategy except as a short-run tactic of absolute necessity. Expansion through mergers, acquisitions, joint ventures, cartel arrangements, and other boundary-expansion strategies are more likely responses to competition and conflict.

Firms often attempt to combat employee militancy and union organizers by absorbing them into a company union or even into the company "family" (Blauner, 1964). Industrial espionage is common, as is the pirating away of a competitor's skilled workers (Wilensky, 1967). Such actions are possible because a utilitarian organization's control over its boundaries is highly uncertain, with entry and exit of members depending ultimately on the financial health of the organization. If another organization is able to make a lucrative offer to a high-level employee, his or her low level of organizational loyalty is easily broken.

Organizations with coercive control structures are a different case, as they are continually oriented to minimal member participation. The primary type of conflict they face is inadequate control of their inmates by staff who are under utilitarian control structure. Although authorities in coercive organizations are unlikely to use expansion as a conflict strategy, expansion is often used by the opposition to co-opt or capture the lower-level functionaries of such organizations. Sykes (1956) described the process by which prison inmates achieve some influence over guards' behavior as the "corruption of authority." The case of organized crime and urban police departments is instructive. Organized crime is in conflict with police departments, and yet this conflict leads in many cases to decreased compliance by officers. Traditional social theory would predict increased compliance because officers are battling an external foe, but the opposite occurs. Even though police departments have quasi-coercive command structures, we might have expected corruption to occur, as police officers are recruited and held on a utilitarian basis and may transfer their loyalty to the highest bidder, whether inside or outside the organization. The process does, however, involve a *de facto* co-optation of the "syndicate" in exchange for a certain degree of ordered criminality (Whyte, 1955). In this sense, organized crime becomes a part of the police organization, following the definition of *membership* presented earlier in Chapter 9.

Conflict and Compliance: Summary

Members are resources for organizations, but several factors may make authorities uncertain about the response of members to interorganizational conflict. Member autonomy, loyalty and commitment, and control over entry and exit permit some organizations the luxury of normative control structures. Such organizations are likely to follow a boundary constriction strategy in interorganizational conflict, in contrast to organizations attracting members with purely material incentives. Organizations with utilitarian control structures are likely to use boundary expansion as a strategy. Organizations with coercive control strategies present authorities with a unique problem, for they must assume that members have no commitment to organizational objectives. Administrators of reform schools, prisons, prisoner-of-war camps, some mental hospitals, and concentration camps must devote most of their resources to social control, and growth poses severe problems of administration.

BOUNDARY-SPANNING ROLES

Certain organizational members are more tightly linked to the environment than others, regardless of whether the linkage is one of conflict or cooperation. Interorganizational conflict heightens the visibility of boundary-spanning roles, as labor negotiators, community relations specialists, tactical squad officers, and other persons are mobilized by the organizations affected. However, the functions of internal information dissemination and establishing linkages to important external elements are essential to *all* types of organizational environments. External conditions affect the extent to which boundary-spanning roles are differentiated from other roles, formalized, and given authorization to act in the organization's name.

Functions of Boundary Roles

Two types of functions are filled by boundary roles: information processing and external representation. Information from external sources enters an organization through boundary roles, and boundary roles link structures and activities to environmental conditions in the form of buffering, moderating, and influencing external events. Any given boundary role can serve multiple functions, and so the following should not be taken as a classification of boundary roles but rather of their functions. The responsibilities and potential impact of boundary-spanning roles varies with different hierarchical levels in an organization, but as so few studies have examined this relationship it is treated only briefly in this chapter.

The information processing function.   As discussed in Chapter 5, it is possible to treat the environment as a source of information used directly by decision makers as a basis for maintaining or modifying structures and activities, or used indirectly because of the way information selectively filters across organizational boundaries. Theorists taking an information perspective on environments are chiefly concerned with decision processes within organizations and the conditions under which information is perceived and interpreted by members (Allison, 1971). Not all decisions depend on external information, and not all information available is actually used, but the rational selection model alerts us to the potential importance of decision-maker access to valid information. Authorities require information so that they can judge the amount and sources of support for their goals, and the trend toward increasing environmental turbulence puts a premium on participants' abilities to monitor changing environmental contingencies.

Boundary-role incumbents are exposed to large amounts of potentially relevant information by virtue of their strategic position. Not all this information is passed on to persons within the organization, and the situation would be overburdening if all information originating in the environment required immediate attention. Boundary roles are a main line of organizational defense against information overload, as boundary-spanners are selective in the information they pass on. Some information has strategic value, some is relevant to short-run tactical managerial decisions, and other information concerns technical developments that may affect an organization's technological core.

The process by which information filters through boundary positions is as important as the kinds of information attended to by boundary-spanners. Boundary roles serve a dual function in information transmittal, acting as filters and facilitators. Considering only information selected as relevant to an organization, information overload would still be a problem if all relevant information were immediately communicated to internal members. Accordingly, boundary-role personnel act selectively on relevant information, filtering out unnecessary or lower priority items before communicating their interpretations to others. Persons in boundary roles act autonomously on some information, and consolidate, delay, or store other information. The filtering process alleviates the problem of overloading communication channels, although an organization may incur other costs if crucial information is mistakenly filtered out. Boundary personnel thus facilitate information entry by summarizing and directing it to the organizational units that need and can act on the information.

Boundary-role personnel may act on information requiring an immediate response, such as sales representative responding to an inquiry from a customer about product specifications. In this case, the boundary-spanner is authorized to act autonomously, without checking with other units or supervisors. Boundary-spanners may store some information for possible future use, such as a purchasing department does by filing information on a new supplier's prices so that it can be referred to when reordering is necessary and a more systematic search is undertaken for the lowest-priced supplier of an important product. People in the marketing department may uncover trends in the demand for their organization's products that will have a major impact on the mix of resources required in the near future, and this information will be communicated to the purchasing department. Boundary units may summarize information about competitors' actions and communicate it to other units on a regularized basis. In small organizations a great deal of useful information is obtained by lower level participants, such as delivery and repair people, through their visits to customers' premises and observations of changes from previous visits.

The expertise of boundary-role occupants in summarizing and interpreting information may be as important to organizational success as expertise in determining who gets what information, depending upon the uncertainty in the information processed. Information often does not consist of simple verifiable "facts," especially if conditions beyond the boundary are complexly interrelated and not easily quantified. Under these conditions, boundary-spanning personnel may engage in *uncertainty absorption*—the process by which inferences are drawn from perceived facts and only the inferences passed on to others (March and Simon, 1958, p. 165). Recipients of summarized information are in no position to check the original sources and therefore must trust the ability of boundary-spanners to correctly interpret the raw information.

Consider the case of lobbyists formulating reports on bills and on a series of amendments that will differentially affect the operations of their organizations. They will not only have to summarize information about the progress of the bill, the testimony in committee hearings, and the apparent predispositions and sentiments of committee members and other legislators, but they also will have to make the entire situation meaningful to their superiors. Their superiors would probably not be able to understand all of the interrelationships and implications of the raw information and would, therefore, not be able to use it. To convey information and meaning, some simplification is necessary and the relationships of events in the legislature to organizational operations will have to be clearly specified. The lobbyists will have to put their information in usable form. This example illustrates that boundary personnel must be quite skilled at sifting information and drawing inferences that adequately represent environmental events but at the same time they must be able to summarize them in terminology other members can understand.

Boundary-spanners may generate or sustain internal organizational variation by channeling information about external developments to relevant parts of their organizations. Innovation and structural change are sometimes mentioned as consequences of information brought into an organization by boundary personnel (Hage and Aiken, 1970). Organizations have a tendency to move toward an internal state of compatibility and compromise between units, with a resultant isolation from important external influences. This trend may jeopardize the effectiveness and perhaps the survival of an organization, unless it is effectively linked to its environment through active boundary personnel. By scanning environments for new technological developments, innovations in organizational design, relevant trends in related fields, and so forth, boundary personnel can prevent organizations from becoming prematurely ossified and no longer matched with their environments. (Of course, some organizations can afford to be ossified, especially subsidized and protected ones.) In their study of program change among sixteen welfare agencies providing services involving physical or mental rehabilitation or psychiatry, Hage and Aiken (1967) found that the greater the degree of professionalism in an agency, the higher the rate of program change. Number of occupational specialties, length of professional training, and involvement in professional societies all had positive effects on program change, presumably because of the additional information professionals possessed or were exposed to in their outside activities (*see also* Whetten and Aldrich [1978]).

From an information processing point of view, then, boundary roles serve a number of functions for an organization. They are the points of contact with the environment for information monitoring and intelligence gathering, and because they absorb uncertainty they protect the core of an organization from information overload. They make information relevant to the rest of an organization's members, and by importing new developments into an organization they make possible its continued renewal and adjustment to changing environmental conditions. Conversely, mistakes and errors by boundary-spanners can trigger organizational disasters and inappropriate moves that result in an organization's elimination from a population.

The external representation function. The second major function of boundary-spanning roles—that of external representation—can be viewed in terms of an organization's response to environmental influence. Environmental pressures sometimes produce internal organizational differentiation to match the pattern of the relevant environment, and this adaptation requires boundary-spanners to provide information about the resulting segmented environment. Some organizations manage to gain power over relevant elements of their environment so that they are manipulated to conform to organizational needs, a process which by definition requires the use of boundary-spanning agents. Between two extremes of lack of power and total power is the more typical case of marginal adjustments in structure and activities on a day-to-day basis, with boundary personnel appearing in normal boundary-spanning roles. Included under the external representation function are all boundary roles that involve resource acquisition and disposal, political legitimacy and hegemony, and social legitimacy and organizational image management.

Boundary roles concerned with resource acquisition and disposal include purchasing agents and buyers, marketing and sales representatives, personnel recruiters, admissions officers, and shipping and receiving agents. With these roles an organization is represented to its environment and the normal flow of authoritative commands is from the core of the organization to boundary-role personnel. The behavior of personnel in these roles is supposed to reflect the policy decisions of authorities in line roles. The one-sided flow of directives to boundary personnel from authorities poses two problems for boundary spanners. First, they are at points where much of the information attended to is of external origin and where it occasionally becomes apparent that policy directives flowing to the boundaries are based on out-dated information, given currently available information. The conscientious boundary-spanner is faced with a dilemma, especially in highly decentralized organizations: Should behavior be immediately modified to correspond with latest developments, or should action be delayed until the information has been processed through the proper channels? This problem is heightened for boundary personnel who are geographically distant from the core of their organizations, such as foreign ambassadors, field sales representatives, and regional directors of international corporations.

Second, as Strauss (1962) observed in his study of purchasing agents, some boundary personnel are dissatisfied with their subordinate position in the organizational hierarchy, given their self-evident strategic importance to other departments. Dissatisfied boundary-spanners may take the initiative to increase their power vis-à-vis other units. Personnel officers suggest changes in job descriptions before agreeing to post them, social service departments' intake staff develop their own criteria of "worthy" applicants, and purchasing agents make mutually beneficial informal compacts with salespeople from outside firms to support certain products. Gordon's (1975) study of a New York City public assistance center found a large degree of discretion delegated to staff in determining clients' eligibility for benefits. She found that caseworkers exercised their discretion in ways that benefitted clients who had "bureaucratic competence"—the ability to relate to bureaucratic rules and regulations and to give the appearance of respecting them. It appears that caseworkers were rewarding those clients who made their job easier by going along with regulations, knowing how to fill out forms, and knowing how to present their cases.

Boundary roles involved with maintaining or improving the political legitimacy or hegemony of an organization not only represents the organization but also mediate between it and important outside organizations. The term "mediate" refers to those aspects of a boundary-spanner's negotiations that will eventually affect the power of the focal organization vis-à-vis another group or organization. Kochan (1975) noted that city governments have created collective bargaining units as a response to threats to their control over employees, and have only entered into collective bargaining when forced to do so by the growth of public employee union pressures. The role of the corporate lawyer is perhaps the most clear example of both the necessity and the difficulty of preserving an equal balance of rights and responsibilities between business organizations. Third-party negotiators and arbitrators are often called in when boundary-spanners cannot come to an agreement on the obligations of their organizations.

Boundary-spanning personnel can help maintain the legitimacy of their organizations by providing information to important client groups that is specifically adapted for them. Aldrich and Reiss (1971) found that police officers on their beats transmitted an image of city law enforcement capabilities to small businesspeople that was independent of the businesspeople's attitudes toward the police themselves. The division of labor between the police and small business owners caused businesspeople to seek aid from the police and made them dependent on the police not only for protection, but also for much of their information about law enforcement. Business personnel saw police officers much more often than judges or other law enforcement officials. Interaction between the two groups was fairly high, as 30 percent of the businesspeople in the sample claimed they talked to a police officer at least once a day, and another 30 percent said they did so several times per week. About a third of them reported helping the police by giving them information, and at least a fourth said they did favors for the police. The study showed that police officers developed a shared set of beliefs with regard to the efficacy of their city's government, and this was communicated to citizens with whom they interacted. Information transmittal was facilitated because police officers and small businesspeople were exposed to environmental forces that made their commonality of interest highly salient—crime is an occupational hazard for both groups. Many police chiefs are aware of police officers' boundary-spanning function, as shown by their use of "human relations training" and other preparations designed to turn police officers into organizational assets in the field.

Adair (1960) studied the use of Navaho Indians as health aides for their native communities, with the aides serving as mediators in a boundary-spanning role that brought white doctors and native patients closer together. Health aides who had little formal schooling were selected from Navahos who had previous contact with doctors from the health team. They were taught English and put into the field to report illness, give simple medications, and carry on an immunization program. The program worked because the Indian health worker offered a different side to each of the parties involved—white doctors and native patients—and managed to find a middle ground to settle discords between them. The health aide was able to overcome the natives' suspicions of "white medicine" and to make doctors more sensitive to Navaho culture. As a result of working within two different sets of reference groups, health aides experienced some role strain. Detached school workers perform a similar representation function for school systems, linking family groups with school officials.

The functions of maintaining an organization's image and enhancing its social legitimacy are less a matter of attempting to mediate between the organization and outsiders than of simply trying to make the organization visible. Advertising and public relations specialists try to make an organization visible by influencing the behavior of groups in ways that benefit their organization, without bargaining or negotiating with the target. Successful product differentiation through enhanced organizational visibility can be an extremely significant asset, as was pointed out in the discussion of barriers to entry, especially for organizations in niches where all products are actually quite similar. For advertising and public relations roles the flow of intraorganizational influence to them is much more one-sided than for other types of boundary roles, and one apparent consequence is a high rate of turnover in such roles. Indeed, in the advertising industry as a whole, there is a high turnover of clients between advertising agencies, even in the midst of successful campaigns.

One of the functions of boards of directors and public advisory commissions is to link organizations to target groups in a highly visible way so that they will feel their interests are being represented. As was pointed out in examining the "revolt of the client" in the 1960s, women and blacks are being appointed in increasing numbers to corporate boards, and students now serve as trustees on the boards of some universities. Fulfilling this function requires recruiting people who are already members of or in contact with specific target groups. Maniha and Perrow (1965) described the formation of the Ann Arbor Youth Commission's Board in terms of the various community interests represented: Catholics, the university, youth-oriented voluntary associations, and so on. The mayor made certain he appointed persons from the most powerful agencies involved with youth—the high school and the YMCA—so that the existing agencies would realize he did not want the new commission to challenge their authority.

Three varieties of external representation functions have been identified. First, resource acquisition and disposal roles are directly linked to the work flow processes of organizations, such as the roles of purchasing agents and buyers, and admissions officers. Second, boundary roles concerned with maintaining or improving the political legitimacy of an organization serve a mediating function and thus are empowered to negotiate for the organization. Third, maintenance of the "image" of an organization can be accomplished either through boundary roles that seek to influence targets through direct persuasion, or by selective recruitment of boundary personnel.

The Creation of Boundary Roles

All organizations have some boundary-spanning roles, if only at the level of the organization head or top administrators. Some organizations, however, have an elaborate set of boundary roles while others have only a few. In some organizations boundary roles are formalized into full-time positions, while in others they are only part-time activities for their incumbents. This section examines the generation and formalization of boundary roles as explicit organizational roles, relating these processes to organizational size and environments. An understanding of the *process* of boundary-spanning behavior would require an interactive model of the kind developed by Adams (1976), but such models are highly specific to the particular pair-wise relationship examined. I am concerned only with the general features of boundary roles, recognizing that actual behavior in such roles will vary from context to context.

Organizational positions vary a great deal in the extent to which they involve interaction with elements outside of a focal organization. Many positions outside of the technical core involve some extra organizational interaction, but only a few positions require intensive interaction. A thorough study of boundary-spanning roles requires a measure that provides better than a "yes-no" categorization of roles as either boundary-spanning or not. Such a measure would include the proportion of time spent with outsiders, the number of outside contacts, and importance of each contact, and reasons for the contact (Whetten, 1974).

The number of formally designated boundary-spanning roles is partially dependent on organizational size. Small organizations are able to survive with a fairly simple structure, using relatively few differentiated roles and functions (Blau, 1972; Child, 1973). Being only slightly formalized, small organizations are much more amenable to restructuring to adapt to changing environmental conditions. Authorities in small organizations might be willing and able to rely on information brought into the organization informally by members. This tendency is more prevalent among organizations with very loyal members or among those that are not highly dependent on day-to-day monitoring of their environment for survival. A small religious sect, corner grocery store, and local voluntary association are examples of such organizations. As organizational and environmental complexity increases, organizations can no longer afford nondifferentiated boundary-spanning activities.

Environment and boundary-role differentiation. Environmental pressures or demands are responsible for much of the observed boundary-role differentiation in organizations, and the environmental dimensions presented in Chapter 3 can be used to formulate several generalizations concerning the impact of environmental conditions on boundary role differentiation. The general principle underlying these generalizations is that of isomorphism between environmental characteristics and organizations structure: As environments become more complex or differentiated, so do the relevant boundary roles.

As previously dispersed resources are *concentrated* in a single organization or one of its departments, other organizations affected by the concentrated resources must modify their boundary roles. Concentration may thus evoke a similar concentration of power in the relevant boundary-spanning role of an affected organization, or a new unit may be created with expanded powers. Specialized labor relations units have sprung up in city governments in response to the concentration of employee power in public employee unions. Growth in the power of federal agencies has provoked the growth of intensive lobbying efforts by unions, trade associations, and other organizations representing vested interests affected by governmental action.

The consumer, environmental protection, and other public-interest movements brought pressure on corporations, which responded by establishing special public relations units to deal with pressure groups. A similar response occurred within public agencies, as exemplified by the President's Office for Consumer Affairs, and similar offices in HEW, HUD, and other federal departments (Nadel, 1971). Given the degree of ignorance surrounding proposed solutions to problems of consumer and environmental protection, race and sex discrimination, and social welfare programs, it has typically been sufficient for organizations to show that they are doing something about a problem, rather than proving that what they are doing is effective. A visible effort has often muted the voice of pressure groups, but lobbying groups large enough to follow through on an issue have kept the pressure on, such as Common Cause's efforts regarding reforming Congressional practices.

Environmental heterogeneity evokes more boundary-spanning units and roles, following the principle of structural isomorphism, as organizations "seek to identify homogeneous segments and establish structural units to deal with each" (Thompson, 1967, p. 70). Separate units, whether established on the basis of heterogeneity in a client population or in a geographical domain served, lead to a higher proportion of boundary roles than in organizations of comparable size serving homogeneous domains. This occurs because each unit duplicates the boundary-spanning functions of the others in tailoring its information-collecting and external-representation functions to its own needs. Auto manufacturing firms have responded to heterogeneity in their client population's income distribution by divisionalizing their operations around products with different selling prices, but not necessarily different costs. Each division has its own sales force and marketing operation, although they receive other services in common from the parent company. Some community health care systems have decentralized out-patient services to small neighborhood clinics, each with its own intake and patient registration procedures.

Environmental stability presumably requires less frequent monitoring and therefore evokes fewer boundary roles than unstable environments, although much depends on whether change occurs at a constant or variable rate. In the cultural industry—books, records, films—where styles and fashions change rapidly, we find the proliferation of boundary roles for the acquisition of raw materials and the disposal of cultural products (Hirsch, 1972). In organizations producing for a stable market, most roles will be directly related to the production process, although an unexpected shift in the market can change the situation drastically. The example of ACME Vegetable Company, reviewed in Chapter 1, illustrates the disaster awaiting an organization that neglects to pay careful attention to its environment on the assumption that everything is stable. Terreberry (1968) argued that the most salient characteristic of organizational environments today is their rate of change, which should lead to an increase in the proportion of boundary-spanning roles in most organizations.

In rich environments—those with *high environmental capacity*—we would expect to find fewer boundary roles than in lean environments, as environmental search and monitoring are less critical for survival than in environments where lack of resources prevents the accumulation of organizational slack. During periods of interorganizational or international hostility, environments become less rich in information and so organizations and nations must allocate more roles to their boundaries if they are to make use of what little information is available. Note that there is nothing inevitable about this development—the ecological model predicts only that organizations able to allocate more resources to boundary-spanning, or that already have a high proportion of boundary roles, will have a selective advantage over those that do not. If *no* organizations respond to an environmental transition from rich to lean capacity by adding more boundary-spanning roles, then the selective advantage will lie with those organizations already making use of a high proportion of boundary-spanners.

Environment and boundary-role formalization.   Arguments reviewed to this point posit that the proportion of an organization's roles allocated to boundary-spanning activities will vary directly with concentration, heterogeneity, instability, and lack of wealth in the environment. To the extent that increasing internal complexity is associated with these pressures and demands, boundary roles will be officially designated full-time roles, especially if authorities recognize the existence of such contingencies. Recognition by authorities of potentially costly environmental contingencies need not be based on the intelligence an organization has accumulated itself. Professional education, professional and trade publications, and informal interfirm contact keep authorities abreast of new developments in the design and administration of formal organizations. Not all leaders and administrators attend to even these indirect sources, however, and this accounts for the selective significance of boundary-spanning roles.

Most large organizations formally designate the roles of labor negotiators and corporate lawyers responsible for transactions in the labor relations sector, because strikes and lawsuits could potentially cripple their organization. Labor contracts are negotiated for fairly long periods and the costs to an organization of mistakes made in boundary-spanning negotiations with unions are therefore high. Mergers and acquisitions have given large corporations a strong asset base, enabling them to employ large teams of lawyers and bargaining specialists. Industrial unions have responded by creating the Industrial Union Department (IUD), in the AFL-CIO, to bridge the boundaries between the various unions that deal with a common employer. Coordinated bargaining committees, created with the assistance of the IUD, involve boundary-spanning efforts between unions that wish to counter the power of large, multiple-site corporations.

The more critical the environmental selection pressures, the greater the probability that boundary roles will be explicitly formalized and the process of selecting incumbents rationalized. This is particularly evident in the composition of boards of directors for large corporations, and some investigators argue that boards of directors are used by organizations to co-opt or partially absorb external groups and organizations controlling required resources (Pfeffer, 1972a). A study of state wildlife governing boards found that one major function of the board members was to serve as buffer group between the full-time staff and the public (Price, 1963). Zald (1969, p. 99) also argued that boards of directors serve an external representation function: "They promote and represent the organization to major elements of the organizational set, for example, customers, suppliers, stockholders, interested agencies of the state, and the like. That is, they defend and support the growth, autonomy, and effectiveness of their agencies vis-à-vis the outside world."

A critical contingency for large corporations involves managing reciprocal relations with other large firms, and the role of the trade relations person was created to meet this pressure. A trade relations person searches for opportunities to cooperate with other firms when it would be to their mutual advantage. In the late 1960s, the practice of reciprocity was so extensive that about 60 percent of the top 500 corporations had staff members in trade relations roles (Perrow, 1970, p. 122). Undoubtedly there were many executives and managers who could have fulfilled this role, but trade relations were considered important enough to deserve full-time attention from a specialist.

Pursuing leads on the possible acquisition of other companies is an important function explicitly assigned to members of corporate development units. Aguiler (1967, p. 47) noted that the high volume of acquisition leads generated by corporate development staff demonstrated "how the formalization of a search procedure can significantly increase a company's relative involvement with a particular kind of information." Large firms are the most active in pursuing merger leads, and between 1950 and 1961, the largest 500 industrial corporations acquired 3,401 firms. Merger activity was heavily concentrated among the largest firms, as the top twenty absorbed 1,943 firms. Smaller firms are much less active—typically they are targets rather than initiators of merger activity—and so they have no staff assigned to merger activities.

Role Specificity, Discretion, and Power

The degree of role specificity of boundary roles varies considerably, with some boundary roles highly formalized and others not. Role specificity refers to the extent of formalization of role behavior by authorities, and ranges from extreme lack of specificity, where "prescription is in general terms and goes no further than outlining the boundaries of legitimate discretion to roles where all but a fraction of role behavior is minutely described" (Hickson, 1966, p. 225). Thompson (1962, 1967) identified three conditions that caused authorities to increase their specificity of control over boundary-role personnel. First, organizations that provide services for large numbers of people and thus face many nonmembers at their boundaries must either substantially increase the number of personnel in boundary positions or else routinize the tasks so existing staff can handle a higher work load. Purchasing agents and salespeople interact frequently with suppliers and buyers and usually deal with fairly homogeneous groups of individuals and organizations. A high frequency of interaction and homogeneity of elements at the boundary allows a high degree of routinization in these roles. A high degree of specificity is reflected in the existence of standard purchase and sales forms or contracts, standard operating procedures for soliciting and accepting bids, and standard operating procedures for calling on customers and closing sales. The classic example of this kind of role is the government clerk who can only accept one type of form, properly filled out in triplicate, and signed in all the right places.

Second, organizations using a mechanized production technology that places a premium on large runs of standardized products depend upon a large volume of standardized transactions per member at their output boundaries. Pressures for role formalization are somewhat lessened when the non-members dealt with have little or no discretion to participate in a relationship. Third, stable environments are likely to produce boundary roles governed by rules, whereas unstable environments are likely to require increased flexibility in boundary-role routines. In the cultural industry, tastes in books, records, and films change rapidly and boundary personnel responsible for acquiring new "products" are delegated a great deal of discretion in their activities. Salespersons for companies producing custom-built products, such as heavy machinery or buildings, have more discretion than salespersons for magazines and vacuum cleaners.

Routinization of roles at an organization's boundary not only increases efficiency in handling predictable relationships and large numbers of repetitive transactions, but also serves a local control function. The programmed nature of these activities is partial insurance of boundary-spanner consistency with the procedures of an organization. Members who interact frequently with non-member groups are likely to develop attitudes consistent with those of non-members, rather than with those of their focal organization. This possibility is often mentioned in discussing relations between the staff of federal regulatory agencies and persons from regulated firms. Standard operating procedures and limits to boundary-spanners' discretion partially protect organizations against attitudes and behaviors not consistent with organizational objectives.

Macauley (1963) noted the existence of different behavioral orientations among boundary and nonboundary personnel in his study of the use of contracts among business firms. Sales departments tended to accept nonorganizational norms that made them willing to conduct transactions without legally binding contracts. The controller and members of legal departments upheld the organizational norm of using contracts, which not coincidentally happened to be the norms of their professional reference groups.

A study of staff members at two Scandanavian prisons identified the boundary role of "social worker" as the position most difficult to routinize: "Though almost all staff members claimed there were few or no specific rules or regulations guiding their communications, the social workers appeared particularly vehement about it, and included relations to official organizations. They stressed that there they had to be extremely flexible; that they had to organize the work on a day-to-day basis and according to the unique circumstances of the individual case" (Mathiesen, 1972, p. 76). Telephoning was preferred to the use of letters, and when complex cases arose, face-to-face meetings were arranged. Boundary roles proliferate in heterogeneous environments, and dealing with a heterogeneous client mixture has a similar effect. Boundary personnel working with streams of heterogeneous elements require a minimal degree of routinization in their roles so as to maximize flexibility in dealing with exceptional cases.

The degree to which boundary roles are routinized is thus a function of both pressures to adapt to environmental contingencies and constraints and the necessity of controlling the behavior of potentially deviant members. Role formalization can be a useful social control mechanism when authorities cannot assume a normative commitment of members to organizational procedures or goals. Similar social control mechanisms include the use of uniforms to reinforce organizational identification, or the frequent shifting of employees between boundary and core roles to prevent their developing an identification with environmental elements.

Power in boundary roles. When environments are heterogeneous and unstable and pose critical contingencies for an organization, boundary personnel are often expected to exercise discretion and develop an expertise for interpreting external events to members. To the extent that boundary-spanners are perceived as successful in their jobs, they acquire power within the organization (Thompson, 1967). The potential power of boundary-spanners is illustrated by the importance of their information processing function. Information filtering into organizations through boundary positions is not raw data but the inferences of boundary personnel. This type of information is very difficult for anyone at some distance from the boundary to verify. The process of uncertainty absorption by boundary-spanners involves the creation of organizational intelligence, and once created, intelligence tends to be accepted (Wilensky, 1967). Reliability checks are expensive and the urgency of daily pressures on members leaves little time for consideration of alternative interpretations.

Organizations therefore rely on the expertise and discretion of their boundary personnel. Boundary-spanning personnel play the role of *external gatekeepers* in their organizations, and may become even more powerful if they make correct inferences and the information they pass on is vital for organizational activities. Allen and Cohen's (1969) study of information flow in two research and development laboratories found that external technical information was brought into the laboratories by a relatively small number of scientists. Gatekeepers held more patents, published more papers, and were in positions of higher authority than their colleagues, and served as sources of information for them. Pettigrew (1972) showed how the self-interested filtering of information during a decision process by a gatekeeper enabled a boundary-spanner to consolidate and enhance his power. He passed on only favorable information about his preferred choice to others in the organization, and suppressed information about other choices. Access to information and control over its dissemination is a power resource in organizations, and boundary-spanners are in excellent structural positions to convert this resource into actual power.

The boundary role of labor negotiators is an example of a position with duties that are difficult to routinize, leading to the *de facto* concentration of power in the role. Even though negotiators may deal with fairly homogeneous groups, outcomes are highly unpredictable and potential costs are also high. Negotiators are therefore able to demand a high degree of flexibility and discretionary power in carrying out negotiations. Their power is further enhanced to the extent that the group they are negotiating with is perceived as powerful by authorities. Kochan (1975) found that tactics that increased the power of a public employee union—involvement in city elections, the use of strike threats in bargaining—also increased the power of the labor negotiating unit within the city government.

An organization's dependence on boundary-spanning personnel raises the question of their loyalty and integration into the organization, and authorities typically search for ways to control their behavior. If possible, the least costly monitoring mechanism is to rely on the professional identification and ethics of the boundary-spanners. More obtrusive strategies include attempts to indoctrinate boundary personnel in organizational policies and goals prior to their engaging in interorganizational transactions. Rotation of members among boundary roles is another active strategy, although it has costs in terms of disruptions of local adaptations made by persons serving a local clientele. Some companies have a general policy of rotating staff geographically and through various divisions as a means of breaking up overly strong commitments to local environments. Another control strategy is to grant powerful boundary personnel higher positions within the organization to reinforce commitment. However, such promotions may result from the power boundary-spanners have gained through successful interaction on behalf of the organization, such as the common practice of picking top management out of the sales division of consumer-goods oriented companies.

Conflict and satisfaction in boundary roles.   Many studies emphasize the strain and conflict felt by persons in boundary roles (Kahn *et al.*, 1964; Snoek, 1966), but tend to overlook the positive potential inherent in the role. Sieber (1974) argued that multiple relationships with diverse role partners provide numerous sources of gratification as well as strain. Role rights and privileges may accumulate more rapidly than duties, and overall status security may be enhanced by means of buffer roles. "An individual with a wide array of role partners, some of whom might be located in disparate groups or social circles, is able to compensate for failure in any particular social sphere or relationship by falling back on other relationships" (Sieber, 1974, p. 573). Boundary-spanners deal with a large number of outsiders, some of whom might furnish essential moral support and feelings of worth that compensate for the lack of positive feedback within the organization. "Insiders" have fewer role partners to turn to for such support.

Multiple roles can serve as resources for status enhancement and role performance, in addition to the institutionalized role rights and privileges accompanying the official definition of a position. Boundary-spanners have access to third parties who can advance their career interests through their connections and potential recommendations. They may use their role discretion to divert company property to their own use, and their contacts may provide them with inside tips on valuable business investments. Graft and bribes are also available in some boundary positions, and their greater freedom from organizational supervision makes it more likely that boundary-spanners will be free to enjoy these perquisites of office. Finally, multiple roles may enrich the personality and self-conception of boundary-spanners, offering them a diversity of experience closed off to other members.

Two studies of boundary roles in a research and development organization and a large manufacturing company report positive correlations between boundary-spanning activity and several dimensions of job satisfaction (Keller and Holland, 1975; Keller *et al.*, 1976). In the research and development organization these correlations were quite high, but they were more modest in the manufacturing company. These studies also found very small or insignificant correlations between boundary-spanning activity and role conflict and ambiguity. Keller *et al.* argued that boundary-spanning roles, to the extent that they enable persons to reduce uncertainties for others, have a positive impact on their incumbents. They permit boundary-spanners to gain power, improve their bargaining position, and hence increase their job satisfaction and perhaps even gain better jobs. Miles's (1977) research in nine governmental research and development organizations did not support Keller *et al.*'s findings, as he found that boundary-spanners reported more role conflict than others. However, he also found that boundary-spanners were better able to deal with potentially stressful external relations than "internals," experienced fewer problems with role ambiguities in handling external contacts, and were put under less strain when working under persons having considerably more authority than themselves. Thus the evidence is highly limited and mixed, but it appears that theorists may have overemphasized the degree of role stress felt by persons in boundary-spanning roles.

SUMMARY

The existence of organizational boundaries is the key to identifying independent organizations, and a number of other organizational phenomena are directly linked to boundary maintenance—authorities, membership, and conflict strategies. Interorganizational conflict causes authorities to pay more attention to member compliance and boundary maintenance, as boundary expansion or constriction are alternative strategies for girding an organization for conflict. Organizational control structures reflect in part the degree of member autonomy and commitment to an organization, and these factors constrain authorities' choices between the expansion and restriction strategies.

Boundary-spanning roles link organizations to their environments and fill either information processing or external representation functions. Information-processing functions include scanning the environment, intelligence gathering, and protecting an organization against information overload. Boundary-role personnel make information relevant to other members, and may aid adaptation to the environment by importing innovations into the organization. External representation functions include resource acquisition and disposal, maintaining or improving the political legitimacy of an organization, and enhancing its "image" and social legitimacy. Boundary roles are expected to proliferate when organizations are in concentrated, heterogeneous, unstable, and lean environments.

Boundary roles vary in the degree to which they permit incumbent discretion according to the tasks, environment, and social control needs of an organization. Routinization is greatest when tasks are simple, volume of output is low, the environment is stable and homogeneous, and managers cannot assume members are normatively committed to organizational standards. The greater the discretion afforded boundary personnel, the more powerful they are likely to become because of their control over information and the mediation of critical contingencies for their organizations. Many investigators have stressed the strain of role conflict built into boundary-spanning roles, while neglecting the opportunities for power aggrandizement and resource accumulation available to boundary-spanners. We are limited in our knowledge of boundary-spanning roles because of a paucity of research on how boundary-spanners actually go about their duties. More observational studies and detailed firsthand reporting are needed to allow us to understand the process by which boundary-spanning roles are generated, elaborated, and made use of by their incumbents.

11   Interorganizational Relations

The major factors that organizations must take account of in their environments are other organizations. Organizations control the flow of capital, personnel, information, and other essential resources through a social system and they represent concentrations of resources that administrators cannot ignore. Regardless of the niche an organization occupies, it must deal with other organizations in obtaining resources it needs. Some interorganizational transactions are simple exchanges, involving equal value given for value received, but others are grossly imbalanced in favor of one party. The resource dependence perspective discussed in previous chapters posits that most administrators and leaders search for opportunities to exploit imbalanced situations. Avoiding or exploiting dependence relationships is a central dynamic of interorganizational fields. Concepts of power and dependence are crucial to interorganizational analyses, but other concepts are also necessary in creating schemes to monitor interorganizational relations; such concepts are formalization, standardization, reciprocity, and intensity of relations. Similarly, aggregating pair-wise relations for analyzing other than simple dyadic interorganizational transactions requires new concepts: organization sets, action sets, and networks. Several examples of organization set analyses are presented to show how this concept illuminates the study of organizational change,

265

with examples of action set and network analyses presented in subsequent chapters.

EXCHANGE AND DEPENDENCE

Organizations are not able to generate internally all the resources and functions required to sustain themselves, and thus administrators must enter into transactions with environmental elements supplying such requirements. Leaders and administrators also must find ways of adapting to the pressures from organizations competing for the same resource. These fundamental facts of organizational life are the basis for the science of economics and a useful starting point for the analysis of interorganizational relations. Hawley (1950) noted that these two relations—with dissimilar and similar environmental elements—are the fundamental building blocks of the interrelatedness of life in all communities. Mutual dependence between unlike elements represents a *symbiotic* relationship, and "because they make dissimilar demands on the environment, members of different species may supplement the efforts of one another" (Hawley, 1950, pp. 36-37). Species that make similar demands on the environment are in a *commensalistic* relation, and commensalism, "literally interpreted, means eating from the same table" (Hawley, 1950, p. 39). The most common commensalistic relation is competition, which is a relation based on members of a species attempting to exploit the same resource supply.

Relations between organizations are not as easy to classify as those between biological organisms, as multiple purposes and multiple consequences of organizational actions defy straightforward categorization as leading to symbiotic or commensalistic relations. The particular resources sought by organizations depend upon their goals and technologies, and, as the population ecology model implies, in large populations there is usually a great deal of diversity in resource needs. The evolutionary model asserts that populations become diverse when organizations specialize in the resources they require, and that new organizational forms are successful to the extent that they enter niches previously unoccupied (or occupied inefficiently). A distinguishing characteristic of modern organizations is that they serve multiple functions and relate to their environments in complex ways. A large corporation appears to stand in a commensalistic relation with its employees over the allocation of profits between wages and dividends, but in a symbiotic relation—mutual dependency—with regard to the production process, after-work benefits provided, occupational prestige conferred, and so forth (Sturmthal, 1977). Organizational analysts should be highly sensitive to the dangers of assuming that a relation between organizations and environmental elements is either symbiotic or commensalistic; typically, it contains characteristics of both.

The population ecology model of survival through specialization explains the degree of differentiation and interorganizational division of labor we observe in populations of organizations. This same process accounts for the necessity of transactions between organizations, with the specific characteristics of a transaction dependent on organizational goals, technologies, and other factors. The term "exchange" can be used as a label for the processes through which resources and services flow between organizations as a result of the "normal" interdependencies between organizations. Levine and White's (1961) definition of *exchange* captures this "normal" aspect of interorganizational relations: Exchange is any voluntary activity between two organizations that effects the realization of their goals. This definition explicitly excludes relationships involving coercion or domination, and the stress in Levine and White's discussion is on the word "voluntary." Current organization theory, however, sensitizes us to another way of looking at interdependencies.

Dependence

Beyond the normal interdependencies based on the interorganizational division of labor, some interdependencies are sought (or avoided) because of the power and control possibilities inherent in the state of dependence. Organizational differentiation and specialization of function are likely to lead to interorganizational dependencies whenever organizations manage to acquire monopoly control over important resources and are able to defend their position. The attempt to avoid dependencies may take the form of minor adjustments to internal structure, such as reducing the impact of uncertain supply schedules by increasing stockpiles. More long-range strategies may be undertaken, such as mergers that are entered to restrain interorganizational competition.

The resource dependence perspective thus goes beyond the idea of simple exchange in arguing that one consequence of competition and sharing of scarce resources is the development of dependencies of some organizations on others. This proposition is the basis for Yuchtman and Seashore's (1967) definition of organizational effectiveness: the ability of an organization to exploit its environment in obtaining resources, while at the same time maintaining an autonomous bargaining position. The implicit assumption made regarding managerial and administrative behavior is that major goals of organizational leaders are avoiding dependence on others and making others dependent upon one's own organization (Benson, 1975). The general picture conveyed is one of decision makers attempting to manage their environments as well as their organizations. Note that the resource dependence perspective is *not* an alternative to the population ecology model but rather a specification of how authorities and members behave within the constraints set by their environments.

The population ecology model stresses the importance of environmental constraints on the activities of organizations, but we must not lose sight of the orientation of decision makers as they maneuver to avoid or create dependencies.

There may, in fact, be a conflict between administrative and organizational rationality, as the dependence that administrators try to avoid may be a fairly certain method for insuring organizational survival. Smaller organizations have the best chance for survival if they are under the protective wing of a dominant organization, as is true of the small manufacturing companies that supply parts to major automobile manufacturing companies, or social service agencies wholly supported by the United Fund. Selection criteria may thus favor organizations that develop the very thing administrators supposedly avoid—dependence on dominant organizations.

Dependence and power.   Emerson's (1962, 1972) articles on dependence provided the spark for the subsequent development of his concept and its incorporation into organization theory. His general point was that one's *power* resides implicitly in another's dependency: The parties in a power relationship are tied to each other by the dependence of one on the other, or perhaps by mutual dependence. Emerson (1962, p. 32) defined dependence of an actor A (an individual, group, or organization) on another actor B as "directly proportional to A's *motivational investment* in goals mediated by B, and inversely proportional to the *availability* of those goals to A outside of the A-B relation." The dependence of A on B provides the basis for B's power over A, as B is in control or otherwise has influence over goods or services A desires. To the extent that A can't do without the resources and is unable to obtain them elsewhere, A is dependent on B. The power to control or influence others thus resides in control over the things they value, ranging from iron ore to love and affection.

Dependence is a characteristic of the *relation* between two parties, and therefore it is possible that A is dependent on B, but in turn, A has power over C because of C's independence on A. B, in turn, may be dependent upon C. Power is a relational concept and is not necessarily transitive; that is, knowing B has power over A and A has power over C does not allow us to deduce that B has power over C. We must be careful of using phrases such as "the" power of A or B; rather, A or B has power only within the context of a particular relationship. Rather than theorizing about amounts of power, we should theorize about organizations' control over resources that form a possible basis for power in particular relationships. From this perspective, power is equivalent to the possession of resources (including legitimated authority) and influence is the use of resources in attempts to gain the compliance of others (Burt, 1977).

Recall that Weber defined power as the probability that one actor within a social relationship will be in a position to carry out his or her will despite resistance. This seems to imply something left out of Emerson's definition; the implication of sanctions being used. However, Weber did not write solely about coercive power (negative sanctions) of a physical nature, as there is an implied element of voluntarism in his definition. Actors being subjected to the exercise of power have a choice—the punishment could be chosen in preference to compliance, but this will hardly do if one's will is to be carried out (Blau, 1964, p. 117). Thus, ordinarily the exercise of power must be tempered with the realization that future demands may be jeopardized by current harshness.

Emerson's concept of dependence actually incorporates Levine and White's concept of exchange in all but one respect. Levine and White (1961) listed three determinants of exchange. The first, the objectives of an organization and its resource needs, is simply a restatement of a necessary result of the interorganizational division of labor: Organizations cannot generate internally all the resources and services they require. The second, an organization's accessibility to required resources from external sources, is the same condition Emerson refers to as the availability of alternative sources of supply. The third determinant—the degree of domain consensus among organizations—has no direct parallel in the resource dependence perspective, and deliberately so. The population ecology model treats competition for resources as the driving force behind organizational change. As explicated in the resource dependence perspective on administrators' behavior, values and sentiments are treated as either resulting from a pattern of resource flows already established or created to justify such a pattern.

Conditions of dependence and independence. Blau (1964) generalized Emerson's ideas by considering the conditions under which actors will be able to maintain their independence in a situation of potential dependence, the conditions that actors must meet to ensure the dependence of autonomy-seeking actors, and the system level implications of the moves and countermoves of the two groups. Blau argued that by supplying services to others, a person establishes power over them. By regularly supplying services that people can't obtain elsewhere, or can obtain only at great cost, a supplier obligates people to him and they must search for ways to repay him. "Unless they can furnish other benefits to him that produce interdependence by making him equally dependent on them, their unilateral dependence obligates them to comply with his requests lest he cease to continue to meet their needs" (Blau, 1964, p. 118). Arab nations used their control over a scarce resource—oil—to coerce Western nations into a more pro-Arab stance on the Arab-Israeli conflict, and they used the threat of cutting off lucrative contracts to induce business firms into complying with the Arab boycott of Israeli commercial transactions.

From the viewpoint of a potentially dependent organization, what alternatives are there to becoming dependent upon another organization? Blau identified four conditions that should foster the independence of one organization from another that controls potentially dependence-producing resources (see Table 11.1). First, independence is facilitated through access to and control over strategic resources, as this allows the possibility of an exchange relation in which neither organization gives up more than it receives. A social service agency may be potentially dependent upon another agency for counseling and rehabilitative services, but avoids dependence because it controls access to a large supply of clients required

Table 11.1. Conditions facilitating independence and dependence between organizations.

Conditions for the Independence of A from B	Conditions for B's Retaining Power	Implications for Interorganizational Structure
Control over Strategic Resources	Indifference to A's Resources	Potential Exchange and Bargaining- Barter
Existence of Alternative Sources	Control over the Alternative Sources	Potential Competitive System-Exchange Rates
Use of Coercive Power	Control over Law and Order	Coalition Formation
Lack of Need for B's Resources	Ability to Manipulate Values and Control Innovation	Increased Innovation and Formation of Ideologies
A Has None of the Above	B Has All of the Above	Dependence of A on B

Source: Peter M. Blau, *Exchange and Power in Social Life* (New York: John Wiley & Sons, 1964), p. 124, with modifications.

by the counseling and rehabilitation agency. Second, the existence of alternative sources for needed resources enhances an organization's independence, as it improves its bargaining position and "exit" can be the ultimate negotiating point. If there is only one potential supplier (a situation of monopoly), that supplier may have great power vis-à-vis its customers. If there are few suppliers, each controlling a sizeable share of the resource, the situation is an oligopolistic one and the power of each supplier is lessened unless they come to a collective agreement on controlling the market. If there are many small suppliers, the power of any one is very small and there is little likelihood of customers being pushed into a condition of dependence.

Third, independence may be achieved by using coercive power to force the other organization into providing the required resource without complying with its demands. Coercion includes the use of the law and administrative sanctions, as well as thuggery and violence. Organizations in the human services' sector often attempt to achieve a legislatively or administratively defined status as the only supplier of a particular service or the only receiver of certain types of clients, thus forcing other organizations to deal with them. Legislation monitored by the United States Department of Commerce requires that a certain proportion of federal contracts to be "set aside" for bidding from small businesses only, thus excluding larger and more powerful corporations. Until labor unions achieved a federally protected status in the United States, employers often dealt with employee organizations' demands by intimidation and violence, hiring private protective forces to harass and injure union leaders.

Fourth, lack of a need for the resources controlled by the supplying organization facilitates independence, and this is achieved by modifying the organization's goals or technology so as to be able to do without the resource or use a substitute. This is more difficult, the more critical the resource is to the organization. The greater the possibility of substituting for or doing without the resource, the lower its *essentiality*.

Jacobs (1974) related the concept of essentiality to the potential variability and flexibility an organization has in responding to dependence. Essentiality is a function of the extent to which an organization's goals, technology, and activity system are limited to a narrow or wide range by environmental pressures and by its pattern of historical development. Generalists, for example, might have an easier time substituting for a resource than would specialists. Organizations with a labor-intensive technology may have trouble responding to labor problems, whereas a capital-intensive organization could simply substitute more equipment for recalcitrant laborers. Essentiality is partly a matter of administrators' time perspectives, however, varying with their willingness to take a short- or long-run view of problems. In the short-run, a union in a labor-intensive organization may have great power because automation takes time to implement. However, automation, if feasible, will curb the union's power in the long-run and an organization with slack resources may be able to sit out short-term disruptions as it adapts to automation.

Just as it is possible to identify conditions for the independence of organization *A* from *B*, so it is also possible to list the conditions under which organization *B* retains power by countering *A*'s strategies with moves of its own. These four conditions are listed in the middle column of Table 11.1, matched by rows describing *A*'s initial attempts to overcome its dependence on *B*. First, organization *B* can retain power if it has sufficient means to remain indifferent to the strategic resources *A* controls. Blau (1964) noted that an organization could encourage competition among the potential suppliers of an essential resource, such as business firms encouraging the formation of rival unions (or company unions) so that potential union power is fragmented. Second, *B* can block *A*'s access to alternative sources by monopolizing control over all sources. Industrial firms sometimes use vertical integration, forward and backward, to deny essential resources to competitors and to avoid paying a higher price to independent suppliers or charging lower prices to independent retailers. In the early part of the twentieth century, oil refineries integrated backward by buying up sources of crude oil and integrated forward by establishing their own distribution chain, in time making smaller refineries and independent distributors dependent upon their largess.

Third, if *B* gains control over the forces of law and order, it can prevent *A*'s use of coercive power, such as an appeal to political parties or the state itself. After the overthrow of the Portugese dictatorship in 1974, communist-led peasant and working-class groups were able to occupy and expropriate large, privately owned agricultural estates because the power of the state was no longer being used to defend large land owners. As the Socialist party and other moderate groups gained power in a few years, the power of the state was used to oust a few groups and to restrain further "unauthorized" occupations. Influence over public police forces was essential to the ability of private businesses to thwart union organizing drives in the first third of this century.

Fourth, organization B can block organization A's attempt to do without or substitute for essential resources if it can manipulate key values and control the flow of innovations. "Materialistic values, which make money and what it can buy of great significance, strengthen the power of employers. Patriotic ideals, which identify people with the success of their country in war and peace, fortify the power of the government" (Blau, 1964, p. 122). Revolutionary movements must develop an ideology to counter the impact of such values or risk losing members to dominant groups. Large corporations are always alert for innovations with the potential for making their own products obsolete, and many buy up new patents or enter into exclusive licensing agreements with inventors so that other organizations cannot escape their dependence on the large firm.

Organization A's attempt to avoid dependence and B's attempt to maintain its dominance have a number of implications for change in interorganizational structures. First, to the extent that A is successful in achieving control over strategic resources, forcing B to negotiate over the transfer process, an elementary exchange and bargaining structure is created. If only two organizations are involved, they will need to barter over the terms of the exchange, as the lack of alternatives inhibits the development of realistic exchange rates. Second, if A is successful in finding other sources of supply, then a potentially competitive system will develop. Multiple alternatives indicate that a market exists for the resource, and exchange rates will develop that reflect the essentiality of the resource to organizations.

Third, A's attempt to use coercive power and B's attempt to prevent it will result in a struggle over political power, as each seeks legitimation of its cause from state authorities. A's subordinate position may drive its leaders to seek a mobilization of power through coalition formation with other organizations. Such coalitions may change the terms on which power and wealth are available in a society. Fourth, A's efforts to do without the essential resource or to find a substitute for it may lead to increased rates of innovation in the organizational population, especially if such conflict is common among many forms. The challenging group's need to construct a value system legitimating its doing without an essential resource, and the dominant organization's counter-ideology, may increase value diversity in a society and lay the groundwork for further change.

An interorganizational relationship may objectively be one of dependence of a subordinate on a dominant organization, but this may be only a potential problem for the dependent organization. The effects of dependence may only be felt when the dominant organization makes demands upon the subordinate organization. In this case, no effects of interorganizational dependence are visible unless the subordinate organization reacts to its situation of *potential* dependence. The perception of dependence and one's power position, and the extent to which accurate information is available, are thus critical variables in the analysis of interorganizational dependence (Bacharach and Lawler, 1976).

DIMENSIONS OF INTERORGANIZATIONAL RELATIONS

A condition of dependence is the most important relation between organizations because of its potential impact on a dependent organization's activities. It is probable that most interorganizational networks are bound together by dependence rather than pure exchange relations; leaders and administrators must be sensitive to the dangers in such relations. However, dependence is not usually at stake in most interorganizational transactions, and thus it is necessary to consider the more mundane aspects of everyday transactions and relations. The dimensions discussed in this section are useful as an accounting scheme for monitoring and analyzing interorganizational relations, and are adapted from Marrett (1971) and Aldrich (1972b). Dimensions are illustrated with examples from the social services sector and business organizations, and I point out the relevance of the dimensions to the resource dependence perspective.

Formalization

Traditional theories of bureaucratic structure emphasize the importance of formalization in stabilizing activities and ensuring continuity in staff behavior. Formalization of relations between organizations has similar consequences.

Agreement formalization. This is the extent to which a transaction between two organizations is given official recognition and legislatively or administratively sanctioned. An interorganizational relation is formalized if it is legislatively mandated, as if often true in the social services sector. Less formalized relations are represented by the *ad hoc* transactions entered into with other organizations on a temporary or chance basis, such as an occasional referral from a social services department to a local Planned Parenthood Agency. The resource dependence perspective treats authority as a resource that is sought by organizations seeking control over their environments. Authority over other organizations is sometimes achieved through the strategies mentioned in the previous section, but in the social services sector it is most often attained through legislative mandates or bureaucratic directives from supraordinate authority (Hall *et al.*, 1977).

Research on the manpower training system in the United States has shown the importance of mandated relations in bringing organizations together that might otherwise ignore one another. Prior to the 1973 national reorganization of federally funded manpower programs, the Employment Service occupied a central role in local manpower training systems because many manpower programs were administratively mandated to use it for referrals and placements. The scope and intensity of relations between the Employment Service and manpower organizations formally linked to it were much greater than for organizations whose ties were based only on needs generated by the interorganizational division of labor (Aldrich, 1976a, 1976b). Currently, mandated interaction between social services departments and the Employment Service exists under the 131.5 program, which requires employable welfare recipients to pick up their checks at Employment Service offices. This program brings welfare clients into contact periodically with another important social services agency, even though it may only be a perfunctory visit.

Among business firms, a relationship is formalized if it is embodied in a written contract, such as the agreement a Christmas wrapping paper manufacturer signs during the summer to deliver a certain quantity of goods to a department store in the fall. Many business contacts are not formalized, and contractual conditions are often ignored in business transactions (Macaulay, 1963). Legal and accounting departments press for formalized relations that sales departments sometimes ignore in the interest of hastening a transaction's completion.

Structural formalization.   This mode of formalization can be identified as the extent to which an intermediary organization coordinates the relationship between two or more organizations. Adding a third party usually changes the nature of a relationship, as Simmel (1950) noted in discussing the differences between dyads and triads. A relation is nonformalized if contact between two social service agencies takes place solely through mutual clients rather than through an intermediary. Referrals between people-processing organizations and their organizational clients, such as transactions between executive recruitment agencies (so-called "head-hunters") and their corporate clients, are typical examples of this. A high degree of structural formalization existed in community manpower training systems of the 1960s, as many federally supported manpower programs were required to use the Employment Service to make placements, rather than making them directly. This requirement made the Employment Service a primary element in the social services network.

The offering of corporate bonds through an underwriter (or group of underwriters) to potential purchasers, rather than direct corporation-investor contact, is an example of structural formalization. Structural formalization of interorganizational relations is of special significance in societies where the role of the state is expanding. At the national level in the United States, an elaborate system of regulatory agencies (SEC, FCC, ICC, and so forth); intergovernmental bodies; Office of Management and the Budget directives; federal programs; and other mechanisms set conditions for interorganizational relations. Third parties have been inserted into interorganizational transactions, requiring the consideration of new interests and values, and thus adding new constraints to organizational environments.

Intensity

The concept of intensity refers both to interorganizational transactions and relations—both the process and the context of transactions. The level of intensity indicates the amount of *investment* an organization has in its relations with other organizations.

Amount of resources involved.   The magnitude of an organization's resources that are committed to a relation indicates its intensity. Among human service organizations, the number of services, referrals, and staff support provided to another organization are common indicators of the intensity of a relation. For people-processing organizations, the number of "bodies" sent to another organization is a highly visible indicator of interorganizational commitment. The intensity of an organization's relations with particular kinds of organizations is often an unobtrusive indicator of its commitment to specific programs, such as the Ford Foundation's grants to international studies programs of universities in the 1960s.

Measuring the magnitude of resource flows is easier in the private profit-oriented sector because we can measure resources in the standardized currency units of a nation. Goods and services can be converted into their monetary value, and comparisons can be made across different organizational forms. The ability to evaluate interorganizational transactions in standardized units gives private sector managers a substantial advantage over administrators in the public sector, as organizational performance is easier to document and the cost of adding new activities is easier to assess.

Frequency of interaction.   Frequency of interaction is the amount of contact between organizations, measured in either absolute or relative (to total frequency) terms. The nature of contacts and the authority level at which they take place need to be distinguished, as one meeting per year with a sponsoring body to renew an organization's budget ranks as an extremely infrequent but highly essential contact. Most contacts in the social services sector involve boundary-spanning personnel who arrange referrals of clients and these contacts are not critical to the organization's survival. Formalization of relations between agencies leads to more frequent interaction, and frequent interaction is likely to lead to further efforts toward formalizing relations.

For the sales department of a firm, intensity is usually indexed by number of calls per period on regular customers. This is one of the major "sales effort" variables controlled by department heads. When the organization begins an intensified drive, a department head may instruct his or her sales force to increase their frequency of contact with marginal customers or to push on into new markets.

to be highly standardized. Transactions between retailers and wholesalers are more standardized than those between producers and consumers of specialty goods, such as heavy machinery and plant equipment. If standardized procedures are more efficient than unstandardized procedures, environmental selection pressures would favor them. This is probably the case in the business sector, which possesses sophisticated means for assessing the costs of employees' activities. It is less likely in the social services sector, which stresses an inherently ambiguous standard of "quality" in service delivery. Thus, unstandardized transactions persist because there are no effective environmental criteria selecting against them. Attempts to introduce cost accounting, management by objectives, and other cost-control strategies developed in the private sector have not proved notably successful in the human services field.

Summary

The four dimensions of interorganizational relations, together with the concept of interorganizational dependence, provide the beginnings of an interorganizational relations accounting scheme. The dimensions do not stand by themselves, but fit into the resource dependence perspective on administrators' behavior, which is one component of the population ecology model. Several examples at the end of this chapter illustrate how the dimensions may be used in an analysis of organizational change. Table 11.2 summarizes the definitions of the four dimensions.

TABLE 11.2   Dimensions of interorganizational relations

1. Formalization

   a. *Agreement formalization:*   the extent to which a transaction between two organizations is given official recognition and legislatively or administratively sanctioned.

   b. *Structural formalization:*   the extent to which an intermediary organization coordinates the relationship between two or more organizations.

2. Intensity

   a. *Amount of resources involved:*   the magnitude of an organization's resource committed to a transaction or relation.

   b. *Frequency of interaction:*   the amount of contact between two organizations, in either absolute or relative terms.

3. Reciprocity

   a. *Resource reciprocity:*   the extent to which resources in a transaction flow to both parties equally or benefit one unilaterally.

   b. *Definitional reciprocity:*   the extent to which the terms of a transaction are mutually agreed upon.

4. Standardization

   a. *Unit standardization:*   the extent of similarity between individual units of the resources in a transaction.

   b. *Procedural standardization:*   the degree of similarity over time in the procedures for transactions with another organization, ranging from standardized to case-by-case interaction.

INTERORGANIZATIONAL RELATIONS
AT THE POPULATION LEVEL

Interorganizational relations, up to this point, have been dealt with in terms of transactions or relations between pairs of organizations—organization *A* interacting with organization *B*. Such analyses provide a little information about the environment of organizations, but obviously organizations are involved in more than one relation at any given time. An understanding of the totality of environmental conditions affecting organizations is obtained only when we consider the aggregate of all the relations and transactions involved. Expanding the study of organizational change beyond the pair-wise level requires the development of concepts allowing theorists to set meaningful limits to the scope of an interorganizational aggregate. Without guides to bounding aggregates, relations between pairs of organizations could be extended and organizations included that would expand an aggregate indefinitely. The concepts of organization set, action set, and network furnish a rationale for setting boundaries to our analyses.

Organization Sets

An organization set consists of those organizations with which a focal organization has direct links. Usually only single-step links are considered, but indirect links can be included by specifying how many steps removed an interacting organization can be from the focal organization and still be treated as being in the set (Evan, 1966). The concept of an organization set is taken from the concept of role set, as defined by Merton (1957, p. 369): "that complement of role relationships which persons have by virtue of occupying a particular social status." Merton based his discussion on Linton's (1936) concepts of social status and social roles. According to these concepts *social status* refers to a position in a social system that carries certain expectations about performance in that social position and *social role* refers to the "behavioral enacting of the patterned expectations attributed to that position" (Merton, 1957, p. 368). He gave an example of the status of the public school teacher and the teacher's role set, relating the teacher to: pupils, colleagues, school principal and superintendent, Board of Education, and professional organizations of teachers. An organization set might be defined as an organization's suppliers, customers, unions, distributors, and trade associations, but this gross definition fails to distinguish between the various statuses an organization occupies.

Role sets are different from status sets, as a status set refers to the various statuses that an individual occupies, such as the statuses of teacher, husband, Democrat, and club president. Each of these statuses has a distinctive role set associated with it. There are as many organization sets as there are different statuses for an organization: the status of retailer in relation to customers, the status of buyer in relation to suppliers, or the status of employer with respect to unions representing an organization's employees.

279

constructed nature—but rather in what ways network concepts are useful in studying interorganizational relations. As represented in graph or matrix form, a network is a static entity, and its usefulness stems from an investigator's ability to link network structures to the processes that sustain or are empirically correlated with them. Three kinds of studies are particularly promising for the application of network analysis. First, the diffusion of innovations is often facilitated through the use of interorganizational networks. The spread of educational innovations (Clark, 1965), the adoption of new medical techniques and products (Becker, 1970; Coleman et al., 1957), and innovations in human service delivery systems (Aldrich, 1978) are three types of network-facilitated innovations examined in previous research.

Second, although networks are not themselves boundary-maintaining systems, they may create the conditions under which organizations and action sets arise. Powerful organizations can use their central position in networks to mobilize coalitions around specific issues, and the prior existence of ties between organizations facing similar environmental pressures may interact with the perception of the rewards of joint action to produce a cohesive action set. Third, network concepts help clarify concepts of interorganizational environments, such as the concept of market structure. Pennings (1978), borrowing from Leontif's (1966) model of input-output analyses of interindustry transactions, has shown that relations between buyers and sellers in a given market can be conceptualized as a matrix of resource-exchange transactions.

The typical forms for representing data from a network analysis are directed graphs and matrices, as shown in Figure 11.1 and Table 11.3. An interorganizational network can be represented in the form of a graph, with arrows connecting

TABLE 11.3.   Adjacency matrix of presence of influence relations among ten organizations, shown graphically in Figure 11.1

Organization Number		To									
		1	2	3	4	5	6	7	8	9	10
	1	0	1	1	1	0	0	0	0	0	0
	2	1	0	1	0	1	0	0	0	0	0
	3	1	1	0	0	0	1	0	0	0	1
	4	0	0	0	0	1	0	1	0	0	0
From	5	0	0	0	0	0	1	0	0	0	0
	6	0	0	0	0	1	0	0	1	0	0
	7	0	0	0	0	0	0	0	1	0	0
	8	0	0	0	0	0	0	0	0	1	1
	9	0	0	0	0	0	0	0	1	0	1
	10	0	0	1	0	0	0	0	1	1	0

Key: Organizations are numbered from 1 to 10; a "1" in a cell indicates that organization i has an influence on organization j, e.g. "1" in a cell a_{12} indicates organization 1 can influence organization 2.

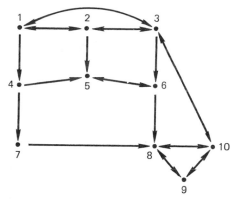

Key: Arrows indicate influence relations are present between organizations, with the direction of influence indicated by the head of the arrow. Mutual influence is portrayed by double-headed arrows.

FIGURE 11.1   Graphic representation of influence relations among ten organizations. The network is also portrayed in Table 11.3.

organizations having a relationship and with the directionality of the relation indicated by the head of the arrow, as shown in Figure 11.1. A network can also be represented in the form of a matrix, and Table 11.3 was constructed from the network portrayed in Figure 11.1. The a_{ij} cell contains a "1" (or other number) if organization i reports a relation with organization j, and a "0" otherwise. The content of cell a_{ij} does not have to be the same as cell a_{ji}, unless symmetry is assumed in all relations. Organization i might report a relation with j, which j refuses to acknowledge. Or, if network analysis is used to study power and influence relations among organizations, then ties of dependence and unequal influence will appear in matrices as asymmetric links, and cells a_{ij} and a_{ji} will be different.

Three problems limit the confidence we can place in the result of graph or matrix manipulations, and investigators must address them in the early stages of their research. First, the content of links in a graph or a matrix can be as simple as whether persons in two organizations know one another or as complex as a summary measure of interorganizational dependence. Most quantitative network analyses use relatively simple links, whereas more complex links are dealt with in mainly qualitative analyses (Boissevain, 1974). Analytic complexity is compounded if multiplex relations are introduced, with multiplexity referring to the simultaneous existence of several different kinds of relations between organizations. Most successful network analyses rely heavily upon an investigator's intimate knowledge of the context and history of the network studied.

Second, social psychological studies of networks within small groups are only partially relevant to interorganizational analysis because studies work with fairly small populations under conditions where boundaries are tightly controlled and the links examined are primarily affective ones. Concepts of "balance" and "dissonance reduction," referring to the emotional investments people have in relationships, are of questionable applicability to relations based on resource flows and dependence between organizations. Authorities undoubtedly attempt to balance inequitable relationships with other organizations, but cognitive balance or reduction of dissonance are not the primary issues. Anthropologists have been highly successful at uncovering problems involved in empirical research on large networks, as many difficulties only become apparent in the actual field work of collecting network data (Mitchell, 1969, 1973).

Third, investigators must use explicit criteria, theoretically derived, to bound networks under investigation. All operations on graphs and matrices assume that the initial population is a theoretically meaningful one. In practice, defining the population of organizations within which a network analysis is conducted often appears quite arbitrary, as in Allen's (1974) decision to trace out the corporate interlocks within only the largest 200 nonfinancial and 50 financial corporations. Levine (1972) selected for study only those industrial corporations interlocked with a bank in one of three cities and included in Fortune magazine's list of the top 100 corporations. Allen and Levine were constrained in their choices by the availability of data, a problem common to all archival studies but especially troublesome for network analysis.

USING THE CONCEPT OF ORGANIZATION SET IN STUDYING CHANGE

The concept of organization set has been used in a number of studies to illuminate the process of organizational change. Investigators have used the concept as an aid in bounding the population of organizations studied and in organizing the data collected. The actual principles employed for explaining change were derived from traditional organization theory. Two case studies are summarized here—Evan's (1972) study of the Interstate Commerce Commission and Hirsch's (1972) study of organizations in the "culture" industry. Action sets and networks are examined in subsequent chapters.

The Interstate Commerce Commission's Capture by Special Interests

The Interstate Commerce Commission (ICC) was created in 1887 to regulate interstate commerce in the area of transportation: rail, shipping, trucking, and pipelines (Evan, 1972). (The air transportation industry was assigned to the Civil Aeronautics Board, rather than the ICC.) As of 1969, the ICC employed 1,906 people. By law, the ICC's input set—those organizations furnishing resources, legitimacy, and policy direction to the agency—includes the Congress, the executive branch, the courts, and other government agencies.

The ICC's output set—the targets of its rulings—consisted in 1970 of 17,000 companies in the rail, trucking, shipping, and pipeline industries. None of these industries had organized a self-regulatory body of the kind found, for example, in the securities industry (the National Association of Securities Dealers) or the medical industry (the American Hospital Association). These self-regulatory bodies claimed to have the interests of their clients as their primary concern and they set standards of ethical conduct for their members. In contrast to the securities and medical industries, the ICC's output set was well-organized into a variety of trade and professional associations whose primary concern was looking after the self-interests of their members: the American Association of Railroads, the American Trucking Association, the Water Carriers Association, the Motor Carrier Lawyers Association, and the ICC Practitioners. There was no large organization representing the interests of consumers of industry services, whereas the trade and professional associations employed a large number of company lawyers and lobbyists to represent their industries' interests.

ICC employees had intensive formal and informal contacts with members of the regulated industries, with such contacts permeating the regulatory process. Critics alleged that the ICC had established a reciprocal relationship with the industry it was supposed to monitor. First, ICC employees accepted personal favors from companies they regulated: "industry regularly pays for luncheons, hotel rooms. . . . Commissioners and upper staff are commonly transported around at their convenience by corporate jets, private rail cars, and pleasure yachts" (Fellmeth, 1970, pp. 16-19). Note that most of these practices have ceased in the aftermath of the Watergate scandal and the closer Congressional attention being given to potential governmental corruption. Second, regular conferences were held between ICC employees and seventeen transportation industry interest groups, with no group present to represent consumer interests. Third, former ICC employees were hired by companies in the transportation industry. Of the last eleven ICC Commissioners to quit as of 1972, six were hired as top transportation company executives, three became ICC practitioners, and two retired.

The consequences of these environmental pressures on changes in the ICC were predictable. Members of the ICC's output set became members of the input set, with a major influence in ICC regulatory policy. The lack of a strong consumer-interest voice among members of the input and output sets meant that only one set of role expectations was being reinforced—the industry viewpoint. Inadequate representation of consumer interests is quite common in proceedings before federal regulatory agencies. In 1975, the American Telephone and Telegraph Company (AT&T) spent $2.2 million in hearings before the Federal Communications Commission on increasing AT&T's rate of return, whereas consumers were not represented at all. The eleven United States trunk airlines "spent $2.8 million on outside legal counsel to represent them before the Civil Aeronautics Board in 1976. The only consumer group dealing with such matters had a total budget of $40,000 that year, about half of which went toward the agency proceedings'' (Cerra, 1977, p. 24).

Role conflict between regulating and defending the industries was resolved in favor of the organizations with the most intensive interaction with the ICC. ICC staff reciprocated industry favors by only passively enforcing ICC statutes. The intensity and scope of industry relations with ICC boundary-spanning personnel led to the development of a shared perspective in problems, to the benefit of the regulated industries. In the trucking industry, for example, the number of carriers declined in spite of an increase in trucking volume and in applications to the ICC from new companies. Evan's example illustrates the effect of external pressures on a vulnerable organization—members of the ICC's organization set representing industry interests outweighed other interests and thus were able to subvert the original reason for the existence of the agency. Similar analyses of other federal regulatory agencies led members of Congress in the late 1970s to call for abolishing or reducing the power of such agencies.

Organizational Change in the "Culture" Industry

Hirsch (1972) conducted what he called an "organization set analysis" of organizations engaged in the production and mass distribution of cultural items. However, much of his analysis also dealt with action sets, as will be clear in the following summary. Hirsch's analysis treated both aspects of organization-environment relations: organizations constrained by selection pressures to adapt to their environments, and organizations responding aggressively to constraints by efforts to neutralize or overcome them.

Cultural products are produced to satisfy the expressive rather than utilitarian needs of customers. Unit standard is relatively low, compared to consumer durables or hard goods. Clearly, many consumer goods contain an "expressive" element, but movies, plays, books, art prints, records, and spectator sports are primarily cultural products: "each is non-material in the sense that it embodies a live, one-of-a-kind performance and/or contains a unique set of ideas" (Hirsch, 1972, p. 642). The focal organizations in Hirsch's analysis, insofar as they can be singled out, are the profit-seeking organizations that produce cultural products for national markets. However, many local organizations are eventually involved in the action sets within which national firms move.

A large number of different organizational forms are involved in the production and distribution of cultural products. Individual entrepreneurs and artists are also important, particularly in the generation of potential new products, and they are a primary source of variation in the organizational population. The three industries examined were book publishing, phonograph records, and motion pictures, and the focal organizations were publishing houses, record companies, and movie studios.

On the input side, each focal organization must obtain raw material from artists, authors, agents, talent scouts, and others, and then invest in the creation of a product. Producing organizations must then attempt to market their products by making effective use of mass distribution channels controlled by other organizations and autonomous gatekeepers, such as disc jockeys, film critics, and book reviewers. All three industries utilize a technology that Stinchcombe (1959) called the "craft administration of production." Such a system is made up of many autonomous operating units coming together for the duration of a job and then going their separate ways when the job is finished. The major benefit of craft systems is that they minimize fixed overhead costs, since no single organization is responsible for the maintenance of all the components required to produce a finished product.

Book publishers, record companies, and movie studios are capable of producing a product, but they rely on other organizations or individuals to discover ideas worthy of being produced. They also rely on other organizations and individuals for the marketing of their products. Innovations that *might* be turned into products are brought to a focal organization by boundary-spanning personnel, such as book acquisitions editors and record or film producers. Few organizations can afford a permanent stable of artists of the type maintained by Hollywood movie studios in the 1930s and 1940s, or some record companies in the 1950s and 1960s, such as Detroit's Motown Records.

Relations with artists, writers, and singers are temporary and on a royalty basis, and an artist makes money only if the product does well. Overhead is minimized by subcontracting for services as they are needed: Film studios rent sets and costumes on a picture-by-picture basis, and publishers and record companies subcontract out standard printing and record-pressing jobs. Structural formalization is high, as marketing and distribution of products is through intermediary distributors, although the largest organizations usually have their own sales forces. Many publishers and movie studios rely on intermediaries to distribute their products, with jobbers distributing books to bookstores and regional film distributors bringing films to local theaters. The record industry is also beginning to be dominated on the distribution side by huge, multistore discount houses.

All three industries are thus characterized by a loosely coupled structure, as described in earlier chapters. Clearly, because of so many uncontrolled steps in the innovation-production-distribution sequence, producing organizations must cope with a high level of uncertainty. In searching for an explanation for the loosely coupled structure, Hirsch identified an environmental characteristic and a technological characteristic: (1) uncertainty of demand for an organization's products, and (2) an inexpensive technology that makes overproduction a viable adaptive strategy.

Demand uncertainty. Demand uncertainty in cultural industries is a function of volatile consumer preferences, legal and normative constraints on vertical in-

advertise films almost a year before they were released; indeed, before they were even edited. *Close Encounters of a Third Kind* cost almost $30 million to produce and Columbia Pictures allocated over one-quarter of the budget to promotional activities, which included flying hundreds of journalists to a press conference promoting the picture.

Gatekeepers are critical external selectors because they can facilitate or block the generation of consumer demand. Moreover, with more direct means of attempting to influence gatekeepers blocked, extremely subtle means to promote reciprocity have been developed. One method used is to publicize an organization's high expectations for a new product by running full page ads in the trade press, inviting gatekeepers to cocktail parties to "meet the author," and suggesting that a television talk show use a particular actor or singer. Personal visits by boundary-spanners are also used in attempting to persuade gatekeepers of the superiority of a product.

Organizational change: Summary.   Organizations in the cultural products industry are loosely coupled in a "craft" system because of environmental and technological factors. Producing organizations must cope with expectations from a highly diverse organization set, and when relations with organizations in their sets are examined, certain dependencies and uncertainties stand out. Producing organizations have not accepted these constraints and contingencies passively, as a number of strategies are open to them. Additionally, certain actions—such as overproduction—appear not so much as exercises in strategic choice as simply following a course of least resistance.

SUMMARY

Other organizations are the key elements in most organizations' environments, as they control the flow of resources in a society. The interorganizational division of labor, under the pressure of resource competition, ensures that most organizations must seek out others with the specialized resources they require. If an organization seeking resources from another controls strategic resources, has access to alternative sources, can use coercive power, or can modify its goals and technologies to do without the resource, it can avoid becoming dependent on the supplier. If, however, these conditions are not met or if the supplying organization makes effective countermoves to blunt attempts at independence, an organization in need may find itself in a dependent relationship. An organization in a dependent position vis-à-vis a dominant organization might be forced to comply with requests inimical to its own interests. Dependence is thus the most important interorganizational relation, and the resource dependence perspective on administrators' behavior gives a primary role to the concepts of dependence and power. Most interorganizational transactions do not raise issues of power and dependence, at least explicitly, and other dimensions are required to describe typical transactions and relations: formalization, intensity, reciprocity, and standardization.

Moving from dyadic relations to multi-organizational aggregates of organizations requires the development of concepts appropriate to analyzing aggregates: organization set, action set, and network. The latter two concepts will be discussed subsequently, and in this chapter I have focused on the usefulness of the organization set concept for examining organizational change. Organization set analyses of organizations adapting to or modifying their environments pose a major problem of observer arbitrariness because an organization set is not an organization with boundaries fixed by formal authority. It is neither a corporate body nor a coordinating association, and therefore by definition cannot act in ways that an organization or an action set can. In the Evan and Hirsch studies, most of the activities analyzed were pair-wise interactions between focal organizations and specific, interacting organizations, and not interactions involving the entire organization set. As a purposively derived construct, defined specifically for the analysis of a particular situation, the concept of the organization set proves useful chiefly as a scheme for classifying data.

were internal to the firms (Smigel, 1964). DuPont, General Motors, Jersey, and Sears, Roebuck adapted to increasing problems of control and communication by adopting divisionalized structures, which created new problems requiring intraorganizational relations, but not increasing interorganizational dependence (Chandler, 1962).

Aggressive Actions

In spite of the risks, some organizations take aggressive actions aimed at reducing uncertainty or increasing influence over environmental elements. Hiring employees away from competitors' organizations is a standard method for obtaining information on industry trends (Wilensky, 1967). Pfeffer and Leblebici (1973b), in a sample of 100 firms from twenty randomly selected industries, found that the proportion of executives whose last job was in the same industry was highest in industries with high sales growth rates and high increases in productivity. Larger firms were more likely to hire from within the same industry than smaller firms, supporting again an implicit assumption of the population ecology model: Small organizations generally take opportunities where they find them, whereas large organizations make their own.

Businesses sometimes engage in actions designed to change the structure of their environments—the market. By using coercive practices, they try to drive out or weaken existing rivals and prevent new firms from entering the market. Predatory price cutting was a common tactic in the nineteenth and early twentieth centuries, as financially strong businesses attempted to weaken or eliminate their rivals. Strong firms undercut the prices of their weak rivals in markets where they competed, and made up for the price cuts by charging higher prices in noncompetitive markets. Railroads used this tactic effectively, establishing different prices for cities and regions, depending on the degree of competition they faced. Independent grocers in the 1930s accused supermarket chains, such as the Atlantic and Pacific Tea Company, of driving neighborhood grocers out of business by offering certain items below cost to attract customers. The passage of the Clayton Act and the establishment of the Federal Trade Commission in 1914 made it more difficult for firms to use such blatantly coercive tactics.

A more subtle proprietary strategy involves acquiring control over raw materials or distribution channels through expansion or vertical integration. Existing firms in an industry can substantially increase barriers to entry for potential firms by integrating backwards to control sources of raw material, such as oil, or forward to tie up retail outlets, such as buying up choice gasoline station sites. Product differentiation is another proprietary strategy that organizations may use in seeking to escape competitive pressures. It exists when consumers form different preferences among the individual brands of products or varieties of services organizations offer.

Product differentiation removes pressures on organizations to sell at a single market price, allowing fortunate firms to set their own pricing policies and therefore changing the nature of the market. This strategy is most prevalent in consumer goods industries and is least often found in manufacturing industries that sell to other producers. Its success depends on the degree to which buyers are uninformed about essential product characteristics. In the consumer goods industries, the durable goods sector—refrigerators, washing machines, or automobiles—display the greatest amount of product differentiation and sophisticated consumer choice, while basic household necessities industries display the least. Organizations in the public and nonprofit sectors often establish product differentiation through negotiating domain consensus with other organizations, although typically some form of action set is created to enforce the consensus (Warren, 1973).

The list of potential proprietary strategies for managing interdependencies is endless, limited only by the imagination of managers and employees, constraints on internal variation, and legal and normative sanctions. Growth, internal differentiation, predatory practices, bribery of government officials, management-by-objectives, cost-accounting schemes, and other strategies and programs may allow organizations some breathing space from environmental pressures. Indeed, anything that contributes to intraorganizational variation has the potential for selection as a proprietary "strategy," although this way of phrasing the possibility renders the line between "strategies" and "lucky hits" difficult to draw. When we turn to consideration of activities involving direct cooperation with other organizations, the role of managerial choice and participant involvement comes into sharper focus.

DYADIC STRATEGIES

After proprietary strategies, the next most preferred strategies are those requiring cooperation or negotiation with isolated or small numbers of other organizations. Dyadic strategies require giving up some autonomy to win a greater measure of control over essential resources or an environmental contingency. This strategy is more problem-laden than the proprietary strategy because it involves negotiation and bargaining with other organizations, which are also attempting to preserve their independence and exploit their bargaining positions. Whether a focal organization will play a dominant, equal, or subordinate role in a dyad depends on whether it has access to the conditions promoting independence, as examined in the discussion of dependence relations in the previous chapter. Two dyadic strategies are examined: choosing representatives for the board of directors, and entering into mergers and joint ventures.

Choosing Boards of Directors

The composition of an organization's board of directors can be viewed as both a response to environmental pressures and as an instrument for managing environmental dependence and uncertainty. Critical interdependencies with other or-

and the central role played by financial institutions (Mintz, 1977). The arguments of both sides imply that boards of directors cannot be studied in isolation from the networks of economic interests and power relations in the surrounding society.

Regardless of the resolution of the debate between the various factions, one fact concerning boards of directors is clear: the thesis of overwhelming "managerial control" of large corporations in the United States is premature. Berle and Means (1932) argued that stock ownership was so dispersed into a myriad of small holdings that the chief operating officers of corporations could gain control of corporate policy. Using their insider's knowledge, top management could use the lack of an effective stockholder's voice to set policy and control the selection of directors to the board. Subsequent studies seemed to confirm Berle and Means' argument, as their finding that 44 percent of the 200 largest nonfinancial corporations were under management control was expanded to a claim that, in 1963, 84 percent of the 200 largest firms were management controlled (Larner, 1970). However, problems of definition and data availability have plagued investigators in this area. Responding to Larner's analysis, Chevalier (1970) and Burch (1972) concluded that only between 40 and 43 percent of the largest corporations were under management control. Burch extended his investigation to the 300 largest corporations, and concluded that "contrary to most professional and popular opinion, family interests still play a fairly prominent role in the conduct of big business affairs in the United States" (Burch, 1972, p. 10).

As Mintz (1977) pointed out, most proponents and opponents of the thesis of managerial control have based their conclusions on analyses of the dispersion of corporate stock ownership. Rather than directly addressing the question of who controls coprorations, all they have investigated is whether stock ownership is the basis for control. Discovering that no single person or interest group owns more than 5, 10, or 15 percent of a corporation's stock only allows an investigator to conclude that evidently stock ownership is not the basis for control of that corporation. It does *not* permit the conclusion, though; that a corporation is managerially controlled. There are other bases for control, such as that exercised by financial institutions in granting loans, and the only reliable way to determine effective control is to investigate, on a case-by-case basis, the circumstances of each corporation. As there is no consensus on which interests control United States corporations—except for the point that family or single-interest control appears more widespread than previously acknowledged—I will move on to research findings about the composition of boards themselves, returning in the next chapter to the issue of networks of economic interests.

Research on Boards of Directors

A number of systematic studies of boards of directors were conducted in the past decade, although most have been concerned with the extent of interlocking directorships rather than the boards themselves. In studying interlocking directorships (or "the interlocking directorate"), an investigator's focus is on the characteristics of the organizations linked by sharing a common director. As most directors sit on the board of only one company, studies of interlocking directorates thus exclude the majority of board members. Dooley (1969, p. 315) reported that 2,603 of the 3,165 directors he studied sat on only one board, with the remaining 562 directors accounting for 1,404 multiple directorships. Regardless of the focus of interlocking directorate studies, many still contain useful information about the boards themselves.

Dooley (1969) examined interlocking directorships among the 200 largest nonfinancial and the 50 largest financial corporations ranked by assets in 1935 and 1965, taking the list of corporations from the Fortune Directory and the list of officers from Standard and Poor's *Register*. Pfeffer (1972) drew a random sample of eighty corporations from the Dun and Bradstreet *Reference Book of Corporate Managements*, 1969. He excluded holding companies, financial institutions, and companies in which ownership was highly concentrated in the hands of the officers and directors. Industries were the same as those included in Dooley's nonfinancial sector: utilities, transportation, manufacturing, and retail and wholesale trade. Because of the source, all the firms were quite large, with average sales of $531 million. Allen (1974) used the same criterion as Dooley, choosing the 200 largest nonfinancial and the 50 largest financial corporations, ranked by assets, for 1970. Dooley and Allen both included banking and life insurance, whereas Pfeffer excluded them. Ornstein (1976) studied the 200 largest nonfinancial firms, the 30 largest financial institutions, and the 20 largest merchandizing firms in Canada as of 1972.

Organization size.   Large organizations tend to be more diversified and to have a greater impact on their environments. They face high environmental heterogeneity in dealing with a large number of sectors, and gaining legitimacy is very important because of their visibility and environmental impact. For these reasons, theorists argue that large organizations should have large boards of directors, and this hypothesis is confirmed in every study. Pfeffer found a correlation of 0.47 between sales and board size, Allen observed a correlation of 0.34 between size of assets and board size, Ornstein found a multiple correlation of assets and sales size with board size of 0.68, and Dooley found the number of corporate *interlocks* correlated 0.47 with asset size.

Comparison of results across studies is difficult because most investigators relied on zero-order correlation or tabular analysis, and included different variables in their analysis than other investigators. Nonetheless, results from Allen's and Orstein's studies indicate that sales and asset size account for a great deal of the difference between industries in board size. Banks and other financial institutions have much larger boards than other types of organizations, but much of this difference is due to the greater assets of financial institutions.

Capital requirements.   Given that the search for outside funding lies behind much of the externally directed activity of corporate management, we would expect the composition of boards to be affected in several ways—representatives from financial institutions would be placed on boards, and outsiders would be appointed, especially lawyers. Pfeffer found a small positive correlation between the debt/equity ratio of a firm and the proportion of directors from financial institutions, but Allen found a small negative relationship between the debt/equity ratio and number of links to the top fifty financial institutions. However, Allen did not have all the financial interlocks of firms in his sample, but only those to the top fifty financial institutions and so his results are not as complete as Pfeffer's.

Dooley's results in this respect are more rigorous than Allen's or Pfeffer's, as he examined the effect of financial solvency on links to financial institutions, while controlling for industry type and asset size. Including all 200 corporations in a regression analysis, he found that "the incidence of interlocks between the two increases as the nonfinancial corporation becomes less solvent and as the assets of the nonfinancial corporation become larger. Thus many corporations are partially dependent on financial houses for credit and in turn, financial institutions depend on the larger corporations for a substantial portion of their business" (Dooley, 1969, p. 318). His results were even stronger in a more homogeneous sample of fifty utilities, as assets and solvency accounted for almost half of the variation in links to financial institutions.

As for outside directors, Pfeffer found that the higher the debt/equity ratio, the higher the proportion of outsiders on a board. He argued that less solvent corporations need outsiders who may sit on bank boards or have other close ties to members of the financial community, but he did not examine the institutional affiliations of the outsiders. Ornstein found that the proportion of outsiders increased with increasing sales and assets, but that the trend was not very strong. (He presented no information on debt/equity ratios and proportion of outsiders.) Pfeffer argued that firms seeking outside financing require the services of lawyers in drawing up documents and giving advice, and found a modest correlation (0.2) between the proportion of lawyers on a board and a firm's debt/equity ratio.

Interviewing board members and chief executives of 248 very large American corporations, Bacon and Brown (1977, p. 93) found that they were against placing suppliers of services on their boards. This category included commercial bankers, investment bankers, and outside legal counsel. Board members and executives argued that: (1) such board members would be in a conflict of interest situation, being forced to choose between "their" institution and the corporation; and (2) it is difficult to withdraw business from a supplier represented on the board. Instead, respondents said that outsiders are appointed from companies and institutions *not* doing business directly with the corporation. These arguments suggest we should be very cautious in accepting the interpretations advanced by Allen, Dooley, Ornstein, and Pfeffer. All used aggregate data not allowing them to identify whether, in fact, outside directors represented organizations doing business with the corporation on whose board they sat.

External regulation.   Corporations are legally constrained from establishing direct links with governmental regulatory agencies, and thus they must seek influence via indirect routes. One tactic is to appoint outside directors with external political power. Pfeffer argued that this should be observable in the form of an increased proportion of outsiders on the boards of regulated organizations. He found a moderate but significant association between the proportion of outside directors and whether an organization was locally (and nationally) regulated, but unfortunately he was unable to present information on whether, in fact, the outsiders were politically powerful

In a related proposition, Pfeffer argued that government regulation on a national basis requires firms to respond to fairly legalistic and formal rules and regulations. Attorneys are thus useful additions to the board of nationally regulated firms, and he found a very modest correlation between national regulation and the percent of lawyers on a board.

Increased importance of financial interlocks.   The debate regarding whether financial institutions "control" corporations in advanced industrial societies is thus far inconclusive, but there are no doubts regarding the significance of financial institutions in the United States economy. In contrast to Berle's (1954) extreme view that major corporations are almost totally self-financing in their operations, Dooley (1969, p. 322) pointed out that "the total liabilities of nonfinancial business approach one-half trillion dollars, that about one-third of the assets of the 200 largest nonfinancial corporations are financed on credit, and that these 200 corporations interlock 616 times with the 50 largest banks and life insurance companies alone. Stock and bond issues, mergers and acquisitions, and other questions of high finance require expert counsel." In both the United States and Canada, banks and other financial institutions have larger boards of directors and more interlocks than other forms of organization.

Although Allen's data are very restricted in their coverage, being limited to only within-group interlocks, he demonstrated an important pattern of change from 1935 to 1970: The frequency of interlocking between financial and nonfinancial corporations increased over time. The increase was not terribly large, in an absolute sense, and it was greatest for the fifty largest industrial corporations. Mariolis's (1975) cross-sectional but more comprehensive study of the 797 largest United States corporations in all industries found that 10 of the 21 most interlocked corporations were banks and 5 were insurance companies. He also found that banks were much more centrally interlocked than other types of corporations, but he was unable to determine which interlocks indicated "bank control" and which did not. Indeed, as is true of nearly all aggregate data derived from archival sources, the *meaning* of links between financial institutions and corporations is not immediately obvious. Are links established because of capital requirements, need for the economic expertise of banks, or the attempts of bank trust departments (which hold a great deal of corporate stock) to "control" the corporations? Undoubtedly these questions will stand high on the agenda of issues studied by organizational sociology in the next decade.

Limits to existing research on corporate boards. The legal and political environments of corporations changed substantially in the 1970s, and further research is required to determine whether the findings reviewed in this section need to be modified. Corporate boards in the United States are increasingly asserting their independence and authority (Bacon and Brown, 1977). Public confidence in big business and its leadership was shaken by scandals involving corporate contributions to the 1972 Presidential election campaigns, and payoffs and kickbacks to overseas customers and intermediaries. The legal environment moved toward attributing greater potential liability to directors for their actions (and inactions), and politically there was the spectre of increased government intervention. In the business community, criticism of boards increased as outsiders argued that boards were too passive and were manipulated by management.

These changes in boards' environments evoked four specific responses. First, audit subcommittees of boards became more important, monitoring company performance and acquiring information outside of usual channels. Second, executive compensation and nominating subcommittees of boards also gained ground, acquiring more control over who becomes a board member and thus limiting management's ability to handpick members. Third, directors obtained better company information, and fourth, boards began challenging management, forcing more chief executives to leave. Such adaptations were heavily influenced by the courts and regulatory agencies, such as the Securities and Exchange Commission, which demanded higher standards for directors.

A major limitation to the research reviewed in this section is its exclusive focus on United States boards of directors, for the pattern of *who* sits on corporate boards differs substantially across nations. Boards in the United States are single-tiered, whereas many Western European countries have two-tiered boards, with a division of responsibilities and differing membership. Countries differ in their tradition of appointing insiders or outsiders to a board, and in England most boards are made up of company executives. A major difference, of course, is the role played by the national government, and the United States differs substantially from other industrialized nations in this respect. In Western Europe, Japan, and elsewhere, companies are incorporated at the *national* level under uniform rules and regulations, whereas in the United States incorporation is at the *state* level. In Sweden, national law prohibits combining the chief executive and board chairman positions in one person, and in West Germany no members of management may sit on the supervisory board. Until research in the United States takes account of cross-national differences, we must be cautious in generalizing about the impact of societal-level forces on corporate-level behavior.

Boards of directors: Summary. Boards of directors are more than advisors to management or corporate window dressing. They link organizations with essential environmental elements and their composition is a result of compromises between two sets of forces, one based on internal needs and the other on the objectives of other organizations. On the one hand, management uses boards of directors to co-opt or control external sources of uncertainty and influence, such as financial institutions and regulatory agencies. On the other hand, other organizations use their power to coerce changes in board composition and make other changes in corporate activities. Mintz (1977) cited the example of E. T. Barwick Industries, in which Eugene Barwick held 53 percent of the stock and his family an additional 30 percent. Despite owning four-fifths of the shares, Barwick was deposed from control by the banks to which the corporation was indebted. Barwick's authority over operations was taken away and he was allowed to visit his office only with bank permission. Dyadic strategies, in the form of obtaining loans or choosing board members, may enable an organization to manage crucial interdependencies, but the sacrifice in autonomy occasionally brings with it substantial costs.

Mergers and Joint Ventures

Choosing or accepting directors linking an organization to important environmental elements may take care of such problems as stabilizing an action set or removing some uncertainty surrounding how an external agent will behave. More severe problems of dependence and uncertainty, however, because of suppliers', distributors', or competitors' actions, may have to be met through undertaking joint ventures or mergers. A *merger* is the complete absorbtion of one organization by another, or the joining of two or more organizations into a new common identity. Not all mergers involve the obliteration of the acquired organization's identity, as many acquiring organizations retain the staff, facilities, and even the name of the acquired organization. This is especially true of conglomerate mergers undertaken during the past two decades, as some acquisitions involved little more than redirecting the flow of profits to a different set of owners. A *joint venture* is a temporary alliance between two or more organizations carrying out tasks that will benefit all of them. Typically, joint ventures involve organizations in the same or similar industries, and are an adaptive response to constraints on other forms of interorganizational cooperation, such as mergers. Although the number of mergers is small in absolute terms, compared to other forms of interorganizational activities, they have had a major impact on the distribution of assets and market power in the population of business organizations.

Describing the nature of the changes is easier than explaining why they have come about, and in this section I will present only an outline of developments during the past century (see Steiner, 1975). In attempting to summarize the literature on mergers, Scherer (1970, p. 122) remarked that "no simple summary can do justice to the question of mergers' effects and motives. One can, if he looks hard enough, find facts to support almost any hypothesis." He contented himself with a few sweeping generalizations. First, market concentration was substantially increased by an early wave of mergers, but since World War II the major effect of mergers has been to increase the concentration of overall corporate assets, rather than market concentration within any given industry. Second, usually multiple motives guide firms' decisions to undertake mergers and joint ventures. The early wave of mergers was generated by desires for monopoly power, but motives have become more diverse since then. Third, it is not clear whether the public, as consumers and shareholders, have benefited from mergers as much as corporate managers and dominant owners. The Antitrust division of the Justice Department has been struggling to define where the public interest lies in the welter of mergers, acquisitions, and take-overs of the past several decades.

Historical Patterns of Merger Activity

Three great waves of merger activity have swept the United States in the past century: an initial period of massive horizontal mergers between competitors in the period from 1887 to 1904, a transitional period of increasing vertical integration and some mergers for diversification during 1916–1929, and an explosion of conglomerate mergers after World War II (Scherer, 1970). The early wave was sparked by major economic and social structural changes in the United States, and was paralleled to a great extent by a similar pattern of mergers in Great Britain. It ended with the severe recession of 1903–1904 and a federal government crackdown on mergers having anticompetitive effects. The shape of the post-World War II merger wave was also marked by major structural changes in the United States economy and was heavily influenced by the selective government prosecution of vertical and horizontal (but not conglomerate) mergers. Conglomerate mergers created a new organizational form and contributed to the increasing concentration of corporate assets in the hands of the largest firms.

The initial wave: 1887–1904. The last third of the nineteenth century was a period of major transformation in American society. In the decades following the Civil War, the economy completed a transition from an agricultural and commercial base to an industrial-capitalistic one. Industrial cities began to dominate the economy at the expense of commercial cities, as Cleveland, Detroit, and Chicago and other cities grew rapidly. The orientation of financial elites changed from involvement in foreign commerce to American manufacturing and domestic trade. Burgeoning growth in the economy was reflected in several trends: Manufacturing output increased at a rate surpassing population growth; miles of railroad track increased from only 30,000 in 1860 to 206,000 in 1900; pig iron production jumped from 821,000 long tons in 1860 to 13,789,000 long tons in 1900; and the number of employees in the iron and steel industry rose from 36,000 in 1860 to 222,000 in 1900 (Pred, 1966). Total population rose from about 31 million in 1860 to almost 76 million inhabitants in 1900.

As the United States economy recovered from the world-wide depression of

1883, aggressive entrepreneurs and promoters touched off a wave of mergers between competitors that converted over 70 important oligopolistic or near-competitive industries into near-monopolies by 1904 (Scherer, 1970, p. 106). Multi-firm mergers were common, and one study found that three-quarters of independent firm disappearances were due to mergers involving the consolidation of five or more firms. Standard Oil began in Cleveland by consolidating 20 petroleum refineries into one company and then adding about 100 more companies by 1900 through acquiring competitors and related firms, capturing 90 percent of the United States oil refining capacity. Market concentration was significantly increased through mergers in copper, lead, railroad cars, explosives, tin cans, tobacco products, electrical equipment, rubber products, paper, farm machinery, brick-making, chemical, leather, sugar, business machines, photographic equipment, and shoe machinery (Scherer, 1970, p. 105). Many contemporary corporate giants can trace their beginnings to the mergers of this era: General Electric, American Can, American Tobacco, DuPont, Uniroyal, PPG, Eastman Kodak, International Harvester, and U.S. Gypsum.

Opposition to the growing power of giant corporations surfaced in a variety of social movements during this period. The Populists, Knights of Labor, and a variety of socialist and agrarian parties fought the monopolies. However, they were defeated, with the Knights of Labor declining and being replaced by the American Federation of Labor in the 1880s. The Populists dwindled in importance after their electoral defeats in the presidential elections of 1892 and 1896.

Parallel events in England during the period of 1870–1914 provide additional insight into the initial wave of mergers and also highlight differences between the societal context of mergers in the United States and Great Britain (Payne, 1967). As in the United States, most of the large industrial enterprises emerging in Great Britain in the last third of the nineteenth century were formed through incorporation and merger, rather than rapid internal growth of individually owned firms. The limited liability acts of 1855–1856 created the legal basis for the incorporation of private enterprises, but they were not used heavily until the 1880s. English law and courts were very permissive with regard to corporate formation, and tariff charges remained constant. Rail and water transportation were excellent, linking all parts of the country. Perhaps most important were evolutionary changes in methods of financing and promoting limited liability companies—companies that were legal entities in their own right, with shareholders protected from liability for losses exceeding their investment in the company—as described in Chapter 7.

Share holding was opened to the general public, rather than being restricted to the financial elite. A new organizational form appeared: Economic conditions made possible the development of firms specializing in promoting the incorporation of new firms. Initially, these professional intermediaries waited for firms to make the first move, but by the mid 1880s, professional promoters became much more aggressive. Underwriting of shares became widespread in the early 1900s, and thus financial institutions could purchase and subsequently issue to the public shares in newly incorporated firms.

These changes reflected a transformation of English society's economic environment. Growing affluence and the cumulative nature of industrial economic development created a large groups of persons with funds to invest in new enterprises. "The evolutionary changes in Great Britain *created the possibility* of setting up giant companies, by using the limited-liability legislation of the 'fifties, in the very same decade as the liberalization of the corporation laws of New Jersey, Delaware, and New York and the maturing of the market for industrial securities permitted a widespread merger movement in the United States" (Payne, 1967, p. 523). However, the merger movement in Great Britain was on a much smaller scale than in the United States, as indicated in the proportionately smaller number of consolidations, assets of capitalized firms, and market power achieved. Industries in both countries had overexpanded in anticipation of an economic boom, and thus there was surplus productive capacity, resulting in cutthroat competition, falling prices and profits, and attempts to meet competitive interdependence through mergers. Why, then, were mergers in Great Britain proportionately fewer than in the United States?

Arguments developed in Chapter 7 and 8, concerning the creation and persistence of organizational forms, can be drawn upon in analyzing the slower pace of mergers in Great Britain. First, England industrialized much earlier than the United States, with a great deal of development occurring in the early part of the nineteenth century. Most organizations and the industrial support structure were well-developed—albeit on a smaller scale than in the United States—when the economic transformation of the late 1800s occurred. Great Britain's industrial structure was well-adapted to previous conditions, but it was also so firmly established that it created a barrier to further change. The strength of family-owned firms impeded their reorganization, and England's dominant international position made enterpreneurs a bit complacent in the face of new opportunities. Thus, intraorganizational variation was low and constraints on the development of new forms were high.

Second, the small size of the British market and the tendency of firms toward product differentiation and specialization rather than production for a mass market allowed organizations to avoid the pressures of competitive interdependence. British manufacturers used product differentiation as a way of avoiding price competition and relied upon the British public's taste for quality and craftsmanship to keep their small-scale operations alive. Manufacturers looked at markets and saw problems of catering to highly diverse and localized needs, rather than taking opportunities for expanding production. United States manufacturers, by contrast, aimed for the mass market. Specialists are well-adapted to narrow environmental niches, but specialization may be dangerous for their long-term survival because it "tends to become increasingly irreversible, for there takes place a concomitant growth of special mercantile relationships, highly skilled labor forces and the evolution of particular types of managerial talent that makes any return to an earlier, more flexible, position more expensive and difficult" (Payne, 1967, p. 525).

Third, Great Britain's original resource and technological base was quite limited. Dependent upon imports of raw material, such as cotton, England was producing the "wrong things," and also neglecting technical education of its youth. By contrast, the United States was well-endowed with natural resources: iron, coal, oil, and so forth. Fourth, British entrepreneurs may have had too much pride in their own independence and self-sufficiency, as they were reluctant to raise new capital on the open market, which would have weakened family control over their enterprises. Some family firms grew, but the great majority remained relatively small firms "jealous of their heritage" and going nowhere. They became moribund and disappeared. The loss of family control to outside industrialists, professional management, and financiers caused a great deal of intraclass conflict within the elite and also provided an opportunity for "marginal men"—Jews, Quakers, and foreigners—to play important entrepreneurial roles (Francis, 1977).

Fifth, British manufacturers could use methods of managing competitive interdependence that were closed to Americans. A network of trade associations covered the industrial field, and there were numerous "gentlemen's agreements" and understandings in restraint of trade. Because they didn't need to worry about judicial-legislative hostility toward pools and cartels—as did their American counterparts—there was less pressure on British owners to consider amalgamation. These market control arrangements permitted many marginal firms to survive that would have been swallowed up in the American market.

The initial wave of mergers in the United States and Great Britain shaped the structure of the two nations' economies for the twentieth century. The great wave of mergers to combat competitive interdependence occurred in the United States shortly after full-scale industrialization was underway, whereas in Great Britain a substantial industrial structure was already in place. Historical and cultural differences retarded the merger movement's full impact in Great Britain, in contrast to its major impact in the United States.

Explaining Mergers and Joint Ventures

Three sets of overlapping explanations have been proposed to account for the pattern of mergers and joint ventures during the past century. First, mergers and joint ventures are methods of organizational growth that have economic and technical advantages, as well as returning substantial benefits to managers and merger promoters. Second, they allow organizations to cope with symbiotic interdependence by internalizing relations with previously autonomous organizations. Third, competitive interdependence is lessened if mergers or joint ventures with competitors are successful.

Most studies of mergers and organizational expansion stress rationalistic criteria (following the rational selection model), but we must remember that organizations are coalitions of interest groups that occasionally have very different objectives. Mergers may benefit one segment but have only slight relevance to interorganizational dependencies facing another segment. A joint venture, for example, may be a way of heading off the plans of a rival department to expand its operations. This diversity of objectives and interests may be one reason why studies of mergers and joint ventures leave so much variation in outcomes unaccounted for.

Organizational growth and aggrandizement.   Growth allows organizations to realize economies-of-scale on many fronts, and in some instances merger may be an easier way to grow than internal expansion. Merger and expansion allows top management to put its underemployed talent to work, and other economies-of-scale may result: "the acquired firm can gain the acquirer's advertising discounts; sales forces can be consolidated and streamlined; brand names of the new partners can be pooled in such a way as to maximize product differentiation advantages" (Scherer, 1970, p. 118). Technological economies-of-scale are less likely to be realized, if only because most such economies are obtained at the plant rather than the firm level and it is rare that plants are close enough to each other to allow their physical merger. (A notable exception was the British Leyland Cowley Motor Works; the two plants that merged to form this new firm were just across the road from one another.)

Merger is simply a faster way of growing than internal expansion, and a management impatient to achieve "bigness" may choose to grow via acquiring other companies rather than expanding from within. "Under the 1970 amendments to the Holding Company Act of 1956, banks may establish offices for their nonbanking operations throughout the nation, regardless of state laws prohibiting the interstate expansion of banking itself" (Nadler, 1974, p. 89). Banks have acquired or established finance companies, mortgage-banking operations, and other financial service companies to generate loan business. First National City Corporation, parent of Citibank, established the Acceptance Finance Corporation, with eighty-five offices in fourteen states; the Advance Mortgage Company, with twenty-four offices in eleven states; and other operations in the United States and abroad. In 1974, the BankAmerica Corporation, based in San Francisco, acquired the 445 offices of General Acceptance Corporation, located in forty-one states and Canada. Although it was required to divest itself of offices in western states, it was allowed to keep 317 offices in the rest of the country.

Growth objectives are most easily realized when surplus funds are available and the economy as a whole is growing. Accordingly, the rate of mergers increases during periods of economic expansion—as in the 1960s—and decreases with contraction in the economy. Corporations that experience temporarily higher than normal profits or that suddenly find funds cheaper to borrow are more likely than others to make acquisitions. Summarizing a large body of research findings, Mueller (1977, p. 25) suggested that "cheap" internal and external capital leads to mergers, with "cheap" referring to capital that management does not feel compelled to use in maximizing stockholder welfare.

Growth confers major benefits on managers and promoters of mergers, as "managerial salaries, bonuses, stock options, and promotions all tend to be more closely related to the size or changes in size of the firm than to its profits" (Mueller, 1969, p. 644). After reviewing the potential economic justifications for conglomerate-type mergers (mergers by acquiring companies with firms in unrelated areas of business), Mueller concluded that many benefits claimed for mergers could be achieved equally well through other activities, such as buying the stock or bonds of another firm. However, only mergers offer top managers the direct opportunity for large economic gain. Noting the increasing proportion of conglomerate mergers, Mueller (1969, p. 698) remarked that "these trends seem to be consistent with the growth maximization hypothesis"; that is, top management maximizes managerial as opposed to stockholder welfare.

In the early waves of mergers, unscrupulous promoters made their fortunes by putting together questionable mergers and selling shares in such ventures to an unsuspecting public. Shares were sold at many multiples of a firm's intrinsic value, a practice labelled "stock watering" at the time. The Securities Act of 1933 and the Securities Exchange Act of 1934 did away with the more flagrant abuses, but was not able to do so entirely. Scherer (1970) noted that the "go-go" conglomerate mergers of the 1960s made many company executives and speculators rich, while the ultimate collapse of the boom left many investors poorer but not necessarily wiser.

Managing symbiotic interdependence.   Relations with suppliers, distributors, and other noncompetitor organizations may pose problems of uncertainty and dependence for a focal organization. As long as supplying organizations are independent, supply reliability cannot be assumed and disruptions are inevitable, such as when a resource becomes scarce and suppliers ration it to their "preferred" customers. Other organizations can use their control over strategic resources to maneuver themselves into a dominant position vis-à-vis the focal organization, extracting onerous concessions from it. Merger is a central strategy for coping with problematic interdependencies, assuming the focal organization retains control over the outcome of the merger.

Firms may merge backwards to incorporate sources of supplies or raw materials, thus attaining greater control over them and avoiding their being acquired by other firms. Paper companies buy lumber companies, food processing companies acquire farms and plantations, and steel companies merge with producers of iron ore. Organizations may merge forward to gain control over wholesale or retail distribution of products and services. Many tire and auto accessory manufacturers have established their own retail outlets, and some airlines have gone into the hotel business so they can sell travel packages for the tourist market.

Many benefits follow from internalizing transactions within one organization that were previously conducted as interorganizational transactions in the open market (Williamson, 1975). In dealing with an autonomous organization, authorities must rely on information furnished by persons who have a vested interest in concealing things that would put their organization in a disadvantageous bargaining position. By acquiring the organization, authorities gain access to its records and have the power to conduct audits as the need arises. In dealing from a distance with another organization, managers lack refined and selective ways of gaining compliance with their directives, as they have no sanctioning power over the other's employees and behaving in a heavy-handed way could abort the relationship. Internalization of the relationship gives managers more degrees of freedom in resolving problems and allows conflict resolution to take place in a unified context. Rather than the structured-in conflict of interest confronting administrators of two organizations, a single authority structure brings a semblance of shared purposes to relationships.

Joint ventures carry some of these same benefits, and have the added advantage of a temporary life. Parent organizations can disband or sell joint ventures after they have served their purposes. Nine schools of theology in Chicago formed a joint venture in the late 1960s known as "the Cluster." It "binds the seminaries in a web of curriculum agreements, faculty-sharing and joint use of library resources in an attempt to cut costs and implement the ecumenical mandate adopted by the denominations that support them" (Briggs, 1977). Each seminary retains its own identity, with the Cluster supplementing its course offerings and library facilities and allowing activities that would not be possible without the joint venture. Denominational boundaries are not threatened because commitments to the cluster are ultimately revocable.

Research findings on mergers' manageability of symbiotic interdependence. A number of studies of mergers and joint ventures have been carried out from an interorganizational relations perspective, but there are severe limitations on our ability to generalize from them. First, they tend to focus on manufacturing and the extractive industries because of data availability, thus excluding the bulk of the organizational population. Second, analyses are conducted at an industry rather than organizational level of analysis, again because of data availability, and there is thus a problem of aggregation bias in the results.

Pfeffer (1972b) studied patterns of merger at the industry level, being mainly concerned with symbiotic interdependence. The question he addressed was how can we account for industry j's percent of the total number of mergers of industry i? This is different from asking, Why did organization i merge with organization j? Pfeffer examined 854 mergers of manufacturing companies and mergers of petroleum refiners with producers of natural gas and crude oil. The data were aggregated at the level of twenty two-digit Standard Industrial Classification codes so that the effect of resource interdependence could be examined, given that this was the only level for which such information was available.

Two dependent variables were included: (1) the percent of the total number of mergers of industry i that were with industry j, and (2) the percent of the total assets acquired in mergers of firms in industry i that were from firms in industry j. To measure resource flows, Pfeffer had to use interindustry transactions, as no data was available on firm-to-firm transactions. Three independent variables were defined: (1) the percent of industry i's *sales* made to industry j; (2) the percent of industry i's *purchases* made from industry j; and (3) the percent of industry i's *total transactions* (across all industries) that were with industry j, created by aggregating sales and purchases. Three control variables were included. First, to control for the fact that industries with a large number of firms have a greater opportunity of being chosen than industries with a few firms, the number of firms in the acquired firm's industry was added. Second, to control for the possibility that profitable industries are more likely to attract firms interested in mergers than nonprofitable industries, the average rate of return on equity for firms in an industry was added. Third, the concentration ratio of the acquired firm's industry was also included because it is a standard indicator of market structure.

Pfeffer found that the three resource flow variables were highly correlated with the percent of mergers and assets acquired in another industry. Profitability and concentration ratios were not significant predictors, and the number of firms in an industry was only slightly correlated with the three dependent variables. Because of the way the three resource flow variables were defined, they were highly correlated with one another. Thus the three of them together explained only slightly more of the variance in the two dependent variables than any one taken by itself. The three together explained about half of the variation in the percent of mergers between two industries, and about two-fifths of the variance in percent of assets acquired.

Although in a footnote Pfeffer (1972b, p. 390) described the Federal Trade Commission's classification of mergers into three categories as "both arbitrary and not relevant to the analysis undertaken here," he also showed that the FTC's classifications were strongly related to the profitability of acquired firms. Mergers to absorb competitors, suppliers, or customers are basically limited to a firm's organization set, and thus opportunities to search for a highly profitable acquisition are strictly limited. The FTC labels such mergers *vertical* and *horizontal*, and Pfeffer called them *mergers for absorption*. Mergers to diversify leave open a wide range of acquisition possibilities, and so an acquiring firm can search for a highly profitable acquisition. The FTC labels these mergers *conglomerate*, and Pfeffer called them *mergers for diversification*. His expectation that mergers for diversification would result in the acquisition of more profitable firms than mergers for absorption was upheld, as a higher percent of conglomerate mergers than of other mergers involved the acquisition of firms with a rate of return on equity of 15 percent or more in the year prior to acquisition. Most research on mergers has found that firms acquired via conglomerate mergers are more profitable than the acquiring firm (Mueller, 1977).

Pfeffer asserted that his results illustrated the impact of symbiotic interdependence in pushing organizations into mergers to absorb such interdependencies. Interindustry transactions were significantly related to patterns of merger activity, but two limitations to the analysis should make us cautious in accepting the results without qualification. First, regardless of the motives of top management in seeking a merger, it would seem that they would attempt to acquire firms in industries with which they were familiar. This means acquiring firms in industries with which they had done business. Pfeffer's measure of "transactional interdependence" might simply be a surrogate for top management's knowledge of merger opportunities.

Indeed, even people in top management seeking mergers for diversification would look for firms in industries that they had some familiarity with so they could evaluate performance data (Cable, 1977). Given the aggregate nature of Pfeffer's analysis, there is no way to refute this alternative (and more parsimonious) explanation. We don't know whether, in fact, an acquired firm had *any* resource transactions with an acquiring firm. Second, the above qualification is deepened by Pfeffer's own finding that the FTC's classification of mergers into three categories has predictive value. The FTC reported that about 71 percent of the mergers during this period were of the conglomerate variety, undertaken for diversification. By this definition, less than 30 percent of the mergers Pfeffer investigated involved symbiotic or competitive interdependence between firms.

Pfeffer conducted a pioneering study of merger activity patterns, but many questions remain unanswered. Future research should be carried out at the organizational rather than industry level, with actual transactions between firms examined. Unfortunately, data availability problems are nearly overwhelming, as firms treat such information as highly confidential.

Managing competitive interdependence.   Organizations are often able to cope with competitors through some of the proprietary strategies discussed previously, such as hiring competitors' employees or attempting greater product differentiation. Merger is another adaptive response, although it is much more common in the public than the private sector. Merger between large businesses in the same industry is extremely difficult, due to a strengthening of antitrust laws in 1950 and increasing government surveillance. Nevertheless, such mergers still occur; between 1948 and 1969 about 16 percent of the mergers reported by the FTC were of the horizontal variety—taking place within the same industry.

During the first great wave of mergers in England and the United States, the great majority of mergers were undertaken to reduce competitive interdependence, but the United States federal government policy today discourages such mergers. Mergers between competitors are still possible in highly competitive industries, such as book publishing. In 1977 there were about 6,000 hard-cover trade book publishers in the United States, and more than 300 mergers had taken place in the previous two decades. However, even this once fiercely competitive industry has come under Justice Department and FTC scrutiny, as sales concentration has increased. "Seven paperback publishers now control the bulk of the mass paperback industry, and all of them are part of larger corporations. Ten companies account for 89 percent of all book-club sales in 1976" (Crittenden, 1977, p. 1).

In contrast to government policies discouraging mergers between business competitors, mergers in the public sector are often encouraged by governmental bodies in the name of "efficiency" and "avoiding duplication of effort" (Aldrich, 1978). Duplication and overlapping services in the private sector are treated as a stimulus to innovation and as meeting consumer demands for freedom of choice, whereas in the public sector duplication is merely "wasteful." Hospitals, police departments, universities, and school systems are urged to merge in the interests of economy and efficiency.

Joint ventures are a method for competitive, larger business firms to avoid the legal problems posed by outright mergers. In studying fifty-three joint ventures between firms in the iron and steel industry, Fusfeld (1958) found that all involved backward integration to the production of a raw material required by the companies. Pfeffer and Nowak (1976, p. 409), examining 166 joint ventures in the manufacturing, oil, and gas extraction industries between 1960 and 1971, found that 92 were between parent firms in the same industry: "There is little evidence that there are many conglomerate joint ventures, or joint activities undertaken by firms operating in very different industries." As in Pfeffer's (1972b) analysis of mergers, Pfeffer and Nowak found that interindustry measures of resource transactions were highly correlated with joint venture activity in most industries examined.

In the 1970s, the General Electric Corporation found itself losing out in competition with foreign-owned companies selling televisions and electronic products. The impact of this losing battle was especially severe in New York State, where General Electric was the largest manufacturing company; in Syracuse, employment dropped from over 17,000 employees to just over 5,000 from 1967 to 1977. General Electric responded by forming a joint venture with Hitachi Ltd. of Japan to manufacture television sets at several locations in the United States. Other Japanese manufacturers were also seeking American partners for joint ventures as a way of avoiding restrictions on imports produced by Japanese-United States "orderly marketing agreements," voluntarily limiting Japanese imports to the United States.

Joint ventures are also used among public sector and human service organizations. Urban universities often create joint degree programs, and multi-community mass transit systems are encouraged in the United States by federal subsidies. Vanderbilt University has a joint university library with George Peabody Teachers' College and Scarritts Methodist College, and the Bay Area Rapid Transit System links San Francisco, Alameda, San Mateo, and Contra Costa counties. National governments cooperated in the 1970s on joint space exploration efforts, and national professional associations have created many overarching international organizations.

Diversification—expanding into other product or service markets—can be a result of desires for growth, or managing symbiotic or competitive interdependence. Mergers with organizations in unrelated fields can be classified as mergers for diversification on the basis of their results, but they defy simple classification by authorities' motives. Diversification, as an active strategy, most often is an attempt to reduce organizational dependence on one segment of the environment. American tobacco companies have diversified into the production of soft drinks and other products as a way of hedging bets against the long-term future of smoking in the United States. Auto dealers selling United States manufactured cars often also sell foreign made compact cars so as to spread their coverage of customer income classes. General Electric, besides producing consumer applicances and light bulbs, also sells railroad locomotives and Australian coking coal.

Conglomerate mergers after World War II.   In the years immediately following World War II, most mergers were still of the horizontal or vertical type, with conglomerates not accounting for half of the large mergers (acquisitions with $10 million or more in assets) until the early 1950s. Counting all mergers recorded by the FTC, there were 16,601 from 1945 through 1968. Over one-quarter of the manufacturing firms, ranking from the five hundred and first to the one thousandth largest in size, were acquired by mergers between 1950 and 1962. Very large firms accounted for most of the assets acquired during this period. "Firms with assets of $100 or more accounted for 59 percent of the number of manufacturing and mining firms with assets exceeding $10 million acquired between 1948 and 1967, and 72 percent of the value of assets acquired" (Scherer, 1970, p. 108). Almost all of the firms on *Fortune* magazine's list of the top 500 industrial corporations participated in the merger movement. Large organizations' dominance of merger activity continued into the 1970s, as 961 of the 1,919 acquiring firms in 1973 had assets of $50 million or more, while 1,580 of the acquired companies had assets of less than $1 million. Merger activity by large firms was partially responsible for the increase in aggregate concentration of industrial assets within the 200 largest firms, but it had less of an impact on industry-specific concentration ratios (Weiss, 1965).

Conglomerate mergers totalled 83 percent of all large manufacturing and mining firm acquisitions recorded by the FTC in 1967–1968. Thus, by the 1970s conglomerate mergers had become the dominant form of acquisition involving assets of $10 million or more. Given the importance of such mergers, the FTC distinguished between three subtypes: (1) product extension, when both firms are functionally linked in production and/or distribution but sell in different product markets; (2) market extension, when both firms manufacture the same products but sell in different geographic markets; and (3) "other" types, which include firms with neither a buyer-seller nor a division-of-labor direct relationship. Product extension mergers are the most numerous of conglomerate mergers.

The shift to conglomerate as opposed to horizontal or vertical mergers was heavily influenced by governmental constraints. The Celler-Kefauver amendment in 1950 to the Clayton Anti-Trust Act gave the FTC and the Justice Department strong weapons against traditional forms of merger, but left a large grey area through which conglomerate mergers could slip (Alexander, 1971). The Celler-Kefauver amendment extended the Clayton Act to prohibit the acquisition of assets rather than just stock and also liberalized the definition of competition to include "any line of commerce in any section of the country." With a stronger base to work from, the FTC and the Justice Department challenged a high proportion of mergers in the two decades after 1950. However, these were mainly challenges to traditional forms of merger.

While challenging 36 percent of horizontal, 29 percent of vertical, and 20 percent of market extension mergers, these agencies challenged only 3 percent of the product extension and one of the "other" conglomerate mergers. One obvious strategic choice for organizations seeking to escape or mitigate the impact of competitive interdependence (although not symbiotic interdependence) was to diversify. Blocking one alternative, the Celler-Kefauver amendment led to the choice of another.

One reason conglomerate mergers were seldom fought is that their status in both economics and law is ambiguous. Their impact on competition is not well understood or agreed upon, even by economists, and no case law was built up to cover them. Antitrust cases take from seven to ten years to complete, and regulatory agencies want to put their resources into reasonably rewarding ventures. The FTC and the Justice Department pursued cases where a favorable outcome was more certain, or at least the ground rules were well understood.

Negative consequences of conglomerate mergers.   Conglomerate firms, as a new organizational form, have the potential for changing the selection cirteria facing other firms. Many of their alleged consequences concern negative effects on competitors (Alexander, 1971). If merger results in significant cost reductions for the acquired firm, it may drive out competitors. Competition in the industry of the acquired firm may lessen because existing firms fear the power of the conglomerate and new firms don't want to enter a situation stacked against them. Rivals do have something to fear, for the enormous size of conglomerates gives them the ability to outlast rivals in long, drawn-out competition. They can make up losses in one area with profits in another, and can thus use such tactics as predatory pricing. The FTC has been pushing conglomerates to break down their annual financial reports by lines of trade so that such practices can come under public scrutiny.

If the acquiring firm uses merger as an alternative to setting up its own operation in the same product market, to avoid expensive start-up costs and first-year losses, then a potentially competitive effect on the market is lost. Conglomerates can cope with symbiotic interdependence by establishing reciprocity agreements with firms that they deal with, such as by trading buyer-seller roles in different product markets, shutting out other potential suppliers or customers in these markets. In spite of all these potential negative consequences, available evidence indicates that the aggregate effect of mergers on industrial concentration has been slight (Weiss, 1965; Scherer, 1970, p. 109). This is partially due to FTC and Justice Department vigilance and partially to the fact that most industries in the United States already possess a sizeable degree of oligopoly. Economists and other investigators have also become more aware of the possible political as well as economic effects of industry concentration, as in Pittman's (1976) study of the effects of concentration and regulation on political campaign contributions.

Mergers and joint ventures: Summary.   Managers' motives for undertaking mergers and joint ventures are as diverse as the outcomes themselves, and some forms of organization find their choice of strategies sharply constrained by external factors. Many of the "growth" benefits claimed by business managers for mergers are more easily realized through other strategies, and the continued enthusiasm of managers and promoters for conglomerate mergers suggests that other forces are at work. After reviewing the empirical literature on mergers through 1976, Mueller (1977, p. 29) asserted that the only clear winners in mergers were corporate managers and that mergers result in no net gains to acquiring firms' stockholders: "this evidence is broadly consistent with the hypothesis that managers pursue corporate growth or other objectives that are not directly related to stockholder welfare and economic efficiency."

The advantages of internalizing previously external transactions, through mergers to reduce symbiotic interdependence, are substantial, although as with all dyadic strategies, it means taking on new problems of administering new departmental and role relationships. Coping with competitive interdependence is easiest for public sector organizations and most difficult for private sector businesses, given the prevailing societal norms concerning "competition" and "eliminating duplication of effort." Businesses often turn to joint ventures, less subject to federal scrutiny, and some studies indicate most joint ventures are between firms standing in a competitive or buyer-seller relation to one another (Pate, 1969). The most significant wave of industrial mergers took place at the turn of the century in the United States and England, and the economic phenomenon most akin to it in the 1970s is undoubtedly the increasing importance of multinational corporations in the world economic system.

ACTION SET FORMATION

Many sources of dependence and uncertainty can't be managed through proprietary or dyadic strategies, requiring instead cooperative action among many organizations. Action sets—groups of organizations coming together for a specific purpose within a limited time frame—can arise whenever environmental conditions dangle incentives before organizations that are attractive enough to over-come the "collective rationality" problem. Simply put, the collective rationality problem arises in situations where a collective response would be effective, but because participation in the collective action is voluntary, individual organiza-tions hang back in the expectation that others will do the work (Olson, 1968). Allowing others to do the work is a rational strategy for individual organizations to pursue, for their marginal contribution to the collective effort's success is likely to be small, whereas their costs in time and resources are large. Therefore, a collective strategy is likely to occur only under special conditions: extremely attractive incentives are offered, organizations are coerced into participation, or authorities subscribe to an overarching set of values stressing collective cooperation.

Simple oligopolies—environments in which a small number of organizations possess enough power to collectively influence outcomes—develop tacit agree-ments among member organizations to collectively manage problematic inter-dependencies. Business firms may agree to restrain price competition so as to maximize collective profits. Action set agreements within oligopolies may be formalized, as in the heavy electrical equipment scandal of the 1950s, in which firms fixed a price for all sellers to use and split up the market between them-selves. Wall Street stockbrokers enjoyed an open price-fixing agreement prior to 1975, when the Securities and Exchange Commission ordered brokerage firms to set rates competitively. A similar phenomenon exists in the public sector among social service organizations, according to Warren et al. (1974). Social service organizations carve up territories among themselves and subscribe to values limiting competition between agencies.

Consortia form when a large number of organizations pool their resources for providing a collective service to members that no single organization could man-age, such as metropolitan fire, police, and water districts. The Interuniversity Consortium for Political and Social Research furnishes social science data sets and other services to members at a substantial savings over the cost of collecting the primary data anew. Joint lobbying groups are created when organizations with similar interests combine to exert pressure on government agencies, such as coalitions of antiwar groups in the 1960s or coalitions of environmental protec-tion groups in the 1970s. The Sierra Club and the Environmental Defense Fund won many battles through cooperative lobbying.

The Development of Action Sets

Economists label implicitly coordinated interorganizational actions in the private sector as "interfirm organizations." In some instances the interfirm organization is quite similar to a large organization, with a procedure for making and enforc-ing collective decisions. However, most action sets fall short of this degree of bureaucratization, as members retain partial autonomy. Conditions under which action sets arise are most clearly illustrated by examples from the private sector, and the following discussion depends heavily on discussions of business organizations by Caves (1972) and Phillips (1960).

Under conditions of pure competition, with large numbers of buyers and sellers and with no organization having more power than any other, building an action set to restrict competition is next to impossible. Many environments, however, depart from this ideal, especially taking into account the local or regional character of many markets. Situations of oligopoly are especially prevalent in the manufacturing sector, in which there are many product markets with only a few sellers. As I pointed out when discussing barriers to entry limiting organizations' choices of environments, industries vary widely in their degree of seller concentration.

In a situation where a small number of organizations share a market, interorganizational arrangements restraining competition can be largely informal. "Mutual restraint" or "gentlemen's agreements" suffice to resolve conflicts to the advantage of all firms. By avoiding price wars, sudden changes in product policy, raids on a competitor's territory, and so forth, uncertainty is reduced and collective profits maximized. The situation in the auto manufacturing industry, with three large producers and one small one, resembles "simple monopoly" quite closely.

A simple monopoly occasionally acts as if it were a corporate group, with its own goals and interorganizational division of labor. The general objective of the collective arrangement is reducing the indeterminancy characterizing oligopolistic markets, where the number of organizations is small enough so that the aggressive actions of one can have a detrimental effect on the rest. If an interorganizational arrangement is to be successful, individual organizations have to forego some actions unique to themselves or in their own individual interest because they conflict with the tacit group objective. The central problem of an oligopoly is thus inducing cooperation and policing deviance, such as secret price cutting. The more unique the needs held by members of the action set, the more complex it has to be to meet them.

Creation and integration of an action set is much more problematic in situations of complex as opposed to simple oligopoly. The concept of complex or linked oligopoly (Phillips, 1960) is isomorphic with the definition of a loosely coupled system presented in Chapter 4. Given a large, heterogeneous environment, with resources concentrated in widespread segments, local subsystems of similar organizations form. Each organization has its own small group of rivals in its segment of the environment. In large metropolitan areas, this description applies to neighborhood grocery stores, metal fabricating firms making the same product, limited price general merchandise stores, and motion picture theaters.

The whole population of organizations, of all types, can be conceptualized as a series of linked oligopolies, or a loosely coupled system. Most potential competition lies within a highly circumscribed segment of the environment, and organizations have the opportunity to observe the behavior of competitors. The informal collusion that was possible under simple monopoly conditions is difficult to achieve under these more complex conditions, because of the larger number of organizations involved. Phillips (1960) identified four conditions affecting the degree to which an action set will be able to achieve coordinated actions that restrain interorganizational competitive interdependence.

Number of organizations in the action set.   The larger the number of organizations whose actions must be coordinated, the more formalized the action set must become. Large action sets require more planning and coordination than small ones, and they lead to increasing bureaucratization—increasing formalization, standardization, the development of written documents, and all the other components of a bureaucratic apparatus. Beyond some point, of course, an action set simply cannot be formed, as problems of coordination and conflicting interests become overwhelming. With a small action set, by contrast, coordination can be very informal.

The larger the action set, the greater the need for executive or authoritative action by an organization acting as leader. Individual organizations are likely to attempt secret price-cutting or other antiset action, cloaked in the anonymity of being only one organization among many. Successful action sets need either an organization acting as a policing agent or an effective mechanism for information sharing among members, making surveillance of members' actions easier.

Movement of top executives between organizations within an industry is one method of increasing interorganizational information sharing and thus stabilizing an action set. In a study of the movement of top executives between firms in twenty selected industries, Pfeffer and Leblebici (1973b, p. 456) found that "when there are more organizations [in an industry] and hence the development of a collective structure of behavior among the organizations is less likely, there is less movement within the industry and more stability in executive positions." They found that the greater the number of organizations in an industry, the lower the percent of executives whose last job was in the same industry, the lower the average number of job changes per executive, and the higher the average number of years spent in the same company. Although not an explicit variable in their analysis, the intervening link between the number of firms in an industry and executive movement could be a perception on the part of top management that an action set is necessary and an awareness that such action is feasible when the number of firms is fairly small. The population ecology model predicts that interfirm movement of executives would persist as long as it was successful in dampening competitive interdependence, and thus such movement would eventually cease in large industries with poor prospects for true action set formation.

Leadership within action sets.   Leadership within sets will be assumed by the most powerful or influential organization, and the greater the concentration of power in the hands of one organization's authorities, the easier action set coordination will be. The presence of a powerful organization may be a substitute for elaborate plans and detailed lines of authority within an action set. There are many possible bases for power within an action set, some of which were specified in the discussion of dependence relations.

One firm may have a large volume of sales, relative to others, and thus be better insulated against a price-cutting war, if a less powerful firm should start one. A firm may have a reputation for making "correct" decisions, and thus be copied by others. In many oligopolistic industries, certain firms take the lead in announcing their price and other firms then follow in it setting their own prices. This is the most likely pattern in industries selling undifferentiated products to knowledgeable buyers, such as in the steel or copper industries. Without price coordination among firms, knowledgeable buyers would desert their former supplier and go for the lowest price, thus making sellers' market shares extremely volatile (Caves, 1972).

Community-wide associations play a similar role in the social services sector (Turk, 1973). Voluntary associations with uncontested community-wide significance are seen as neutral and thus in a good position to mediate community conflicts. They are usually dominated by elites and help promote high consensus among community leaders on controversial issues. The wider their scope, the more they constitute a means of dampening heated interorganizational conflict, given that most elites have overlapping memberships in many community organizations. Turk found that community-wide associations played a leadership role in the formation of hospital councils—associations of local hospitals—and in the integration of anitpoverty networks.

Similarity of values and attitudes.   The more alike members are in their values and perceptions, the less the need for formalized procedures and a strong authority structure for coordinating an action set. At the extreme, an action set with perfectly homogeneous, shared values—perfect domain consensus—would be as efficient as a simple monopoly. Organizations could anticipate how others would react to situations and no formal decision-making arrangements would be necessary. Homogeneous values make collusion easier to perpetrate, and lay the groundwork for authorities' perceiving that collective action will benefit like-minded organizations.

Communication channels between organizations are an important means by which interorganizational actions are coordinated. Pfeffer and Leblebici (1973b, p. 451) argued that "personnel flows are one mechanism of information transfer and communication" between firms in an industry, especially when top executives are involved. In discussing limits to strategic choice, I pointed out that common socialization routes, reliance on similar information sources, and other mechanisms increase the probability that choices will be made on the basis of highly similar views of the environment. These factors also smooth the way for the formation of action sets, if the number of organizations linked through competitive interdependence is small enough.

Other procedures have a similar effect in producing a uniformity of outlook among set members. Product standardization, often achieved with the assistance of government agencies, removes a possible source of competitive pressures. Uniform costing methods, such as a basing-point system, enable competitors to predict rivals' prices accurately. Trade publications and fairs allow the pooling of information, and joint lobbying for Fair Trade Laws is an ideal form for ensuring similar behavior across organizations—manufacturers can fix prices from which retailers cannot deviate. In mature industries, executives use their knowledge of past practices and industry "rules of thumb" to obtain fairly accurate market forecasts.

Impact of other action sets.   The evolutionary model posits that complex environments eventually generate complex structures. The more organized and effective the action sets dealt with by a focal action set, the more it must change its structure to match. This is, of course, Galbraith's (1952) concept of "countervailing power"—when "seller concentration is high the buyers will coalesce to oppose it" (Caves, 1972, p. 32). In many Western European countries, associations of employers within an industry have called forth matching associations of unions to bargain collectively over industry-level wages and working conditions.

In professional sports in the United States, players' associations have formed in response to action sets of employers that have attempted to minimize interteam competition for new players. Many of the earlier practices used by the associations of team owners have been ruled illegal restraints on competition, but the associations persist.

Action sets: Summary.   Action sets are fragile structures, as they bind organizations that usually have an inherent conflict of interest. Thus, stable and effective action sets only emerge under a fairly limiting set of conditions: The number of organizations in a potential set is fairly small; one organization takes on a recognized leadership role; values and attitudes of authorities are similar enough to induce perceptions of shared collective interests; and other action sets are not so powerful as to inhibit their creation. Once begun, however, stable action sets have a cumulative effect on their environments, as they call forth other action sets. The number of multi-organization associations in the United States is growing inexorably, although most are still fairly limited in their effectiveness.

SUMMARY

Interorganizational relations are not simply a consequence of the interorganizational division of labor, and more than just "exchange" is at stake in many transactions. The principle of maintaining autonomy and avoiding unnecessary dependence guides leaders and administrators in choosing strategies for managing relations with their environments. A hierarchy of preferred strategies exists, treating "strategy" from the viewpoint of organizational authorities; proprietary, dyadic, and action set strategies make up the preference ordering. Whether authorities are able to exercise their preferences is always problematic: Some projects are not feasible under the proprietary strategy, no partners are found for a cooperative venture, and external pressures force action sets into existence when a battle places survival at issue.

Adherence to a consistent strategy is often impossible, with changes in environmental selection parameters and the nature of intraorganizational variation ruling out preferred actions. Opportunities for managing competitive interdependence by wiping out or absorbing one's competitors, for example, vanished with rigorous governmental enforcement of the Sherman and Clayton Acts and subsequent legislative additions. Thus, organizational change is partially shaped by authorities' strategies and partially by what opportunities are available. Whether opportunities are seized depends upon whether they are recognized, the skills and resources of authorities, the nature of external constraints, and the whims of fortune. When authorities are constrained by existing opportunities, they contribute to maintaining established selection parameters, but the evolving economic and political context creates new opportunities fairly often. Organizations able or willing to vary adaptive strategies can take advantage of their changing environments to improve their chances of retention in the population.

13 Organizational Networks and Economic Power

The population ecology model is best applied at the population level of analysis, but most investigators of organizational change have focused on individual organizations. This level of analysis has been encouraged by the attention paid to leadership, decision making, and case studies of successful organizations. Proprietary and dyadic strategies, reviewed in the previous chapter, are preferred administrative methods for dealing with environmental contingencies and constraints, and it is possible to examine them at the organizational level without being led too far astray. Action set analyses and many other interorganizational transactions, however, require an explicit analytic recognition that the major environmental elements are other organizations. The concepts of organization set, action set, and network were created in response to the complexity introduced into organization theory by multiorganization fields of action. When change occurs among a large number of linked organizations, traditional conceptions of isolated organizations are no longer applicable.

The concept of organizational networks takes full account of environments as multiorganization aggregates, and also links the study of organizations to the study of economic power and social change. Organizations control the flow of capital, goods and services, labor, information, and almost all other essential resources in industrial societies. A corollary to the argument that new organizations are constrained by the terms on which resources are available in a society is that societal change is controlled through and reflected in organizational change. Organizations, as major centers of resource concentrations, are at the core of any theory of social change. In Marxist theory, large industrial firms stand at the focal point of class antagonisms, as capitalists and laborers struggle for control of the surplus of production. In functionalist theory, employing organizations allocate prestige and economic reward to members of society on the basis of their contribution to societal effectiveness. In the population ecology model, organizations are arranged in a hierarchy of resource control, with dominant organizations setting the conditions of existence for subordinate organizations and thus structuring the environment within which selection occurs.

Regardless of which theory of social change is adopted, investigators face a nearly overwhelming task of comprehending the structure of society in all its organizational complexity. Network concepts have been the salvation of many theorists, although more often than not the notion of networks has been used in a purely metaphorical sense. Rather than pushing on from the network metaphor to inquiring what a full-blown network analysis would consist of, theorists have stopped short with analogies and allusions to "social networks." Organizational sociology is favorably equipped to go beyond this stage, as theorists have developed a vocabulary for describing relations between organizations in networks (dependence, formalization, standardization, and so forth) and terms for describing network subcomponents (organization sets and action sets). Moreover, the population ecology model directs our attention to the conditions under which networks arise and are stabilized, and the resource dependence perspective suggests explanations for the role dominant organizations play in such networks.

In this concluding chapter a model of interorganizational network evolution is presented that is based on the concepts of loosely coupled systems and organizational adaptation in heterogeneous and changing environments. Conditions that favor the selection and retention of network structures are illustrated with several examples, with the role of dominant organizations given special attention. A general model of organizational change ought to shed some light on an issue addressed by social theorists for the past century, and thus a final section uses network concepts in an analysis of economic power and domination in industrial societies.

EVOLUTION OF NETWORKS

Interorganizational networks are identified by tracking down all of the ties binding organizations in a population defined and explicitly bounded by an investigator. Any population could be defined for a network analysis, but investigators generally limit themselves to populations in which the concept of network is theoretically meaningful. Examples of contexts permitting meaningful network analysis include: (1) relations between all the organizations in a community concerned with social services, including provider and funding agencies (Aldrich, 1978); (2) relations between the National Collegiate Athletic Association, athletic conferences, the Amateur Athletic Union, television and radio broadcasting networks, and non-member as well as member institutions (Stern, 1977); (3) relations between banks and large corporations, identified through interlocking directorships (Beardon *et al.*, 1975); and (4) relations between the National Science Foundation, the Physical Science Study Committee, book publishers, manufacturers of scientific apparatus, educational film distributors, teacher training colleges, and local educational authorities (Clark, 1965). The networks identified in these examples were not corporate bodies and were not capable of "action" in the organizational sense, but they did constrain or facilitate the activities of organizations and action sets in a systematic way.

Environmental selection pressures affect populations of organizations through new organizational forms eliminating old ones, the modification of established forms, or the creation of new niches that call forth new forms. Two classes of forms were introduced in the previous two chapters: forms resulting from dyadic interorganizational strategies (mergers, joint ventures) and multiorganization action sets (cartels, consortia, and so forth). These classes are important for the analysis of organizational change because they represent significant new accumulations of organizational power that may change the distribution of resources and the terms on which they are available in a society. Action sets may raise barriers to entry in an industry, collaborate to exploit unorganized consumers through price-fixing, lobby to change government domestic policy, and perhaps even prolong—or end—a war. Interorganizational arrangements and action sets may cohere into larger networks of organizational ties, and, if stable, networks may affect the path of societal change. They may create the necessary preconditions for the formation of new action sets, facilitate the spread of innovations disrupting the fabric of the established order, or make it easier for economic elites to exercise dominance.

Networks and Loose Coupling

The concept of loosely coupled systems was used in describing within-organization variation, and the same ideas are applicable in comprehending the structure of interorganizational networks. The connection between networks being loosely joined and an investigator's ability to understand network structure has been recognized by theorists from many disciplines (Granovetter, 1973). In his analysis of the social anthropology of politics, Bailey (1969, p. 10) noted "if a particular political structure were intimately connected with every other structure of social action, so that everything which went on in economics or religion or on the domestic scene vitally affected it, the task of analysis could never be finished." Fortunately for political scientists, only some parts of the larger environment are linked to political events and organizations, and most aspects of the environment may be safely ignored. In his studies of corporate mergers, Pfeffer (1972b) used input-output tables for interindustry transactions (Leontif, 1966), indicating that industries are tightly coupled to a few and only loosely coupled to many other industries. Loose coupling in the political sector is mainly a function of constitutional provisions and other devices limiting the range of demands on the political system, whereas loose coupling between industries is a function of organizational resource and technology requirements.

Members of complex evolving populations adapt to their environments and the inherent limits on organization by assuming the form of hierarchical loosely coupled systems (Simon, 1962). Adaptation of members' components occurs at the lowest level necessary for effective functioning. Complex systems thus evolve that are composed of many subsystems, with each responsible for the performance of a limited range of functions. Links between subsystems are only as loose or tight as is necessary to ensure the system's survival. The overall configuration of members changes very slowly over time, but subsystems within their structures change more rapidly.

Subsystems of complex systems are not only loosely joined but also are arranged in hierarchies reflecting the evolutionary importance of stable intermediate forms of organization. Recall that in a system of n elements, the number of potential links of all elements are directly connected is $n(n-1)/2$, assuming symmetry in relations. In a richly coupled system—with each element connected directly in an influence relation with every other element—any disturbing influences spread rapidly. Richly coupled nonhierarchical systems would have difficulty reaching stable states, as each environmental disruption would tear apart whatever stable form had been reached up to that point.

By contrast, a hierarchical loosely coupled system is composed of many intermediate level systems with only scattered links between elements of different levels. Each subsystem is richly joined within itself and thus is sensitive to external influence in a way that affects the entire subcomponent, but relations between subsystems are fairly weak. Influence between subsystems flows through only a limited number of directly connected elements, rather than through them all. In the short-run, subsystems of loosely coupled systems are highly independent, and in the long-run they exhibit interdependence only in an aggregate way. The overall system is fairly stable, due to the absence of strong ties between elements and subsystems, but individual subsystems are free to adapt quickly to local conditions.

In complex, heterogeneous, and changing environments, we would expect most organizational forms that appeared to resemble loosely coupled systems. Loosely coupled systems enjoy the benefits of size and specialization of function, while remaining flexible enough to cope with a wide range of contingencies—they are true "generalists," in Hannan and Freeman's (1977) terms. From the perspective of administrators and organizations interested in rapid response from an organization or set of organizations, however, there are disadvantages to loosely coupled systems. There is a inevitable increase in communication delays and ineffectiveness, and if a crisis occurs that demands an immediate system-wide response, a loosely coupled system may not respond in time to prevent catastrophe. In large-scale systems where crises are common, administrators often plan for a richly coupled system in spite of the increased cost of maintaining it, as in the armed services, emergency warning systems, and disaster relief organizations.

We must be cautious in theorizing about the evolution of networks as if they are bounded and purposeful entities, always keeping in mind that networks are constructs created by investigators to guide analysis, and may not have an independent existence. Dominant organizations, government elites, and special interest groups often seek the creation or modification of networks as a primary objective and therefore play an active role in assembling network components. Likewise, readily identifiable networks often emerge as an unintended by-product of organizational activities, especially under conditions where action sets are easily formed. Thus, even though networks themselves are not corporate actors, enough organizational action is centered around them to give life to the concept. Investigators will not err flagrantly if they begin with the assumption that networks of organizations are loosely joined, hierarchically differentiated, and integrated—if at all—by their ties to centrally-located organizations.

Selection Pressures and the Role of Linking-pin Organizations

A defining characteristic of networks is a pattern of interorganizational relations joining otherwise highly dispersed organizations into a loosely joined system. Three population-level processes affect the creation of the key links joining network subcomponents: (1) the adaptation of new organizations to their local environments, including establishing interorganizational relations for division of labor and dominance reasons; (2) the formation of action sets around joint interorganizational objectives; and (3) the role played by linking-pin organizations centrally located in networks.

The *adaptation of new organizations* to their local environments is the starting point for network analyses. New organizations in a population adapt to local environments consisting of clients and members, action sets, other organizations, and nonorganized elements. Other organizations and action sets are presumptively the most important sources of external constraints, as they control more resources than isolated individuals or unorganized elements. New organizations adapt their goals, technologies, and boundaries to take account of pre-existing organizations. Usually this process creates so little disruption at the population level that it passes unnoticed, although dislocations for individual organizations can be troublesome. In the social services sector, Warren *et al.* (1974) found little evidence of overt conflict between new and older organizations, as most new agencies adopted the definition of the situation held by existing organizations. In the business sector, new businesses adapt to prevailing wage rates, imitate others' technologies and operations, utilize existing channels of supply and distribution, and come to terms with unions and local laws and regulations (Hawley, 1971).

Stable action sets are the typical subnetwork units in interorganizational networks, with the specific type of subcomponents depending on the scope of the network studied. In analyzing national economic networks, industries can be treated as subsystems aggregated into a loosely joined system through resource interdependence. At the industry level, oligopolistic coalitions and cartels form somewhat unstable actions sets, and mergers and joint ventures solidify some linkages.

Studies of local community structures often treat a "power elite" and other grouping of vested interests as the building blocks of community power structures (Perucci and Pilisuk, 1970). In his community power study of forty-nine highly active organizations in Syracuse, Freeman (1968) found they formed eight clusters, ranging from two to eight organizations. The eight clusters were heterogeneous, containing different types of organizations, with clusters integrated on the basis of their similar interests in particular community issues. Sutton (1969) studied 100 organizations in a Kentucky county and was able to identify five main coalitions, with the various coalitions playing different roles in community innovation. Stentz (1972), however, was not able to identify any meaningful subgroups in her study of ninety-three health organizations in Suffolk County, perhaps because most organizations were highly involved with other health organizations and nonhealth organizations were not included in the sample. This example illustrates the importance of investigators choosing meaningful boundaries for their analysis when tracing out network patterns in an organizational population.

Subnetwork components, such as action sets and interorganizational dyads, are only relatively rather than completely isolated, making their precise identification difficult. Identifying coalitions, clusters, and action sets in networks by the use of matrices and graphs is somewhat arbitrary, and a variety of techniques are used to decrease the degree of arbitrariness involved (Phillips and Conviser, 1972; Bernard and Killworth, 1973; Harary *et al.*, 1965; Alba, 1973; White *et al.*, 1976). A common technique is to identify a subcomponent by the intensity of interaction among its members compared to lack of interaction with outsiders, or similarity in interaction patterns among members and dissimilarity between members and non-members.

Linking-pin organizations having extensive and overlapping ties to different parts of networks play a central role in integrating organizational networks. Having ties to more than one action set or subcomponent, linking-pin organizations are the nodes through which networks are loosely coupled. Three functions are particularly important: (1) they serve as communication channels between or-

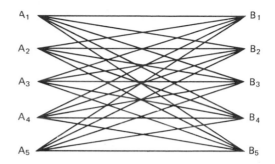

(a) Richly Joined Set of Organizations: 25 Links

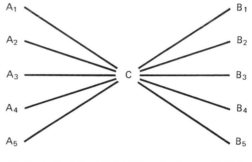

Figure 13.1 The importance of linking-pin organizations: communication links between 10 organizations

(b) Centrally Joined Set of Organizations: 10 Links

ganizations, typically through contact between boundary-spanning personnel; (2) they provide general services linking other organizations to one another by transferring information, staff, clients, or other resources from one part of a network to another; and (3) they serve as models to be imitated by others, or use the dependence of others on themselves to direct the activities of action sets and organizations. Clearly linking-pin organizations play a central role, but are there any reasons for expecting such organizations to arise?

The population ecology model posits that new organizational forms will be positively selected if they adopt forms giving them a relative advantage over existing forms, or if they happen onto a niche not yet occupied. The three-stage model does quite well in accounting for the survival and growth of linking-pin organizations, given the relative superiority of this form and the power and influence dominant organizations have in such niches.

Consider the example of a population divided into two major types of organizations, A and B (such as buyers and sellers), where some method of interorganizational communication is needed between the two types. Communication is possible if all organizations of one type are directly joined to all organizations of the other type, thus creating a richly joined system. The total number of relations in the population would equal A times B, assuming a link is established in each direction. If there were five organizations of each type, the total number of links would be twenty-five (see Figure 13.1a).

Each new organization added to either subpopulation—A or B—increases the number of required links linearly. If another buyer is added, five more links are created, and if yet another is added, another five links are created. If an organization is added to *each* subpopulation, the increase in links is exponential. If one pair is added, the number of links jumps from twenty-five to thirty-six and adding another pair increases the number of links to forty-nine. In large populations, individual organizations would find the maintenance of a large set of links quite costly, especially if the number of organizations in both subpopulations is increasing.

The population ecology model would predict that any innovation or random variation that happened to create a less costly solution to the linkage problem would be selected quickly. Any cost-saving variation would give the organization that adopted it a relative advantage, and thus a selective survival prospect over others in environments where resources are limited and more efficient users of resources have a selective advantage. Similarly, any new organizational form that enabled organizations to communicate with one another more quickly would be in a niche with an initially overwhelming advantage, as there would be a strong demand for its services.

If an intermediary organization were created linking the As and Bs, the number of links in the network would be reduced to A plus B, rather than A times B (see Figure 13.1b). Each A would have one link to the intermediary, C, and so would each B. The process of sorting out the various messages and information channeled between the As and Bs would be internalized by C. This is a complex task for C, but C specializes in the role of intermediary and only a fraction of the links would be active at a time. The selective advantages of an intermediary are greatest when the population of As and Bs is sufficiently heterogeneous to rule out either using stereotypes of the other in its operations. If all As were alike, then any given B would need only a single link to an A to provide all the information it needs.

More than one intermediary or linking-pin organization would surely arise, as the selective advantages in this niche are substantial. An intermediary is not positively selected on the basis of its contribution to joint A-B survival, but rather because of its obvious appeal to As and Bs as a method for cutting their own costs. The intermediary, C, survives in its new niche because those As or Bs using C have a selective advantage over others that do not, and their survival, in turn, allows C to survive. Examples of intermediary roles include money lending or credit institutions in the financial sector and wholesaling and distributing organizations in the industrial sector.

Dominant or high status organizations can be expected to occupy the role of linking-pin organization, as they achieve their position in organizational hierarchies partly by strategic maneuvering into central positions and partly by retaining power through manipulating interorganizational relations. Research on community power emphasizes the coordinating role of organizations that represent local vested interests: Chambers of Commerce, country clubs, and local economic development associations (Turk, 1977). Freeman's (1968, p. 62) study of local community leadership in Syracuse found that the Metropolitan Development Association seemed to "provide a basis for coordination of the policies of many private organizations in Syracuse. This represents an attempt both to mediate between potentially competing interests through the formation of an association for mutual self-help and to promote community projects of which members approve."

The manipulation of authority to gain a dominant position or to avoid dependence on others is a common strategy followed by dominant organizations (Buckley and Burns, 1974). Vertical integration through mergers, horizontal expansion, interlocking directorates, discriminatory pricing, and other tactics are used by business firms to achieve dominant positions in hierarchies. In the public sector, agencies attempt to control coordinating councils, acquire exclusive rights to domains, and in other ways achieve authoritative control over the allocation of resources to other organizations. Nations differ greatly in the freedom allowed business organizations to manipulate networks with the American system generally prohibiting practices restricting competition, whereas "European legislation in principle accepts cartels, trusts, and other combinations, even if they involve restraints of trade and commerce, and will interfere only in cases where it appears that their consequences are to the detriment of the public interest" (Boserup and Schlichtkrull, 1962, p. 61).

National and local governments both facilitate and constrain the freedom of organizations to manipulate networks, with their actions occasionally increasing network complexity. Hierarchy in networks is often a consequence of constraints imposed by governments, particularly in the social services sector. Under these circumstances, hierarchy is not a result of organizational adaptation to local environments, but rather a consequence of "constraint from above" (Glassman, 1973). Some hierarchical networks spring full-blown from the results of legislative action. The federal Comprehensive Employment and Training Act of 1973 specified that federal, regional, state, and local components were to be arranged in a hierarchy of authority, leaving horizontal relations to the discretion of authorities at each level. Within program or issue areas subject to governmental supervision, levels of hierarchy are often inserted without strong pressures for such developments from the lower levels, such as the "review and comment" authority given to regional bodies by United States federal legislation in the transportation, pollution control, and other fields.

Under certain conditions, the hierarchical structure of government agencies and private sector organizations may impede the growth of action sets and other network components. Van de Ven (1975, p. 12) pointed out that "the vertical patterns [of government programs] are usually highly structured by clearly defined contracts, charters, laws, administrative policies and procedures. They are usually bureaucratically organized with rational planning, specified goals, prescribed means, and clear authority and sanctioning patterns. As a result, horizontal integration, particularly at the local level, is difficult to achieve." Local branches of national private sector organizations may not be allowed to participate in community programs, charters of federated organizations may forbid such participation, and the fulfillment of mandated objectives may leave no freedom for local initiative. In several New York State communities with local labor-management committees, subsidiaries of nationally owned corporations have been prevented from participating on the committees, despite the widespread community support for the programs.

Network Stability: The Retention Problem

Investigators using network concepts in studying social service delivery systems, interlocking economic interests, or the diffusion of innovations need some assurance that a "network" is more than an ephemeral will-o'-the-wisp. Unlike organizations and action sets, networks are largely investigator-derived constructs, with only the *potential* for more than a transitory existence. A network identified for a particular analysis is only a partial network from a larger or different schema that might have been constructed. Nevertheless, an examination of tendencies toward hierarchy and loose coupling in organizational populations, and consideration of the objectives of dominant organizations, suggests that some networks may be stable enough to be studied in their own right.

Environmental selection is usually treated as selecting individuals, not specific configurations or populations of individual elements. In biological ecology models, interrelationships between species and subpopulations in any given environment are simply the accidental by-product of the selection of the most fit individuals (Margalef, 1968). Environmental pressures, however, while not directly selecting a pattern of species or subpopulation interrelations, account indirectly for the maintenance of patterns whenever environmental stability preserves the selection criteria to which individual elements have adapted. From this viewpoint, an interorganizational network is a consequence of the adaptation of organizations and action sets to their environments, rather than the result of selection of the network itself. As long as environments are stable, the network may be stable, but organizational maneuvering for relative advantage may disrupt the network even under these conditions. To understand why a network has emerged or is stable, we must search for the conditions supporting its component links or for environmental selection criteria operating specifically at the level of networks, such as governmental regulations.

Instability.   Network stability can be defined as a condition in which interorganizational relations in a bounded population remain the same over some specified time interval. Disregarding the effect of external interventions, internal network stability depends on four factors: (1) duplication and (2) multiplexity in relations between any two organizations or action sets; (3) the probability of failure of a link; and (4) the impact that the failure of one link has on the probability of other links failing.

Consider a population of five organizations joined by ten two-way relations, with a probability of 0.8 that a single one-way relation remains stable over one year. Assuming that the probability of one relation's failing does not depend upon what happens to any other relation, the probability of the network of ties between these ten organizations being exactly the same at the end of the year as at the beginning is 0.8^{10} or 0.11. If the probability of a single one-way link remaining stable rises to 0.9, then the probability of network stability rises to 0.35, and if single one-way link stability increases to 0.95, the probability of complete network stability increases to 0.60. All calculations are based on the assumption that relations are independent of one another in the impact of their failing. If, as seems probable, this assumption is unwarranted, the prospects for network stability are sharply reduced.

Multiplexity in relations—multiple relations joining two organizations—greatly improves the probability of network stability, even if individual relations fail. If each organization is joined by five *different* types of links in each direction, and the probability of any single link failing is 0.2 (or the probability of stability is 0.8), then the probability of a dyadic interorganizational relationship failing is only 0.0003 and the network itself is extremely stable. This example again assumes that failure of any one of the five links has little, if any, impact on the other links. The assumption of independence of links is more reasonable in this instance, as multiple ties between two organizations could well involve different boundary-spanners at different levels of the organizations. A network composed of organizations joined by multiplex ties would therefore be quite stable. Indeed, it is doubtful that single-stranded relations could form the basis for truly stable networks. If there is only a single-purpose relation joining two organizations, and even if its probability of failure is fairly low, a network based on the aggregation of such relations would be quite unstable and actually misleading in its cross-sectional complexity.

An interorganizational network is thus most stable when relations between organizations are multiplex rather than single-purpose, each dyadic relation is highly stable, and unstable relations have little, if any, effect on other relations. Research on boundary-spanning roles shows that multiplex relations are common and that boundary-spanners have an interest in pursuing multiplex ties because of benefits to their own positions (Aldrich and Herker, 1977). Unfortunately, there is almost no longitudinal research on the stability of dyadic relations, and some findings suggest that instability may be the norm (Aldrich, 1976a, 1976b). A network where interorganizational relations are relatively independent across pairs of organizations is, by definition, a loosely coupled system, and there are strong theoretical reasons for expecting most networks to fall into this category.

Stabilizing forces. Environmental factors, such as (1) a noncompetitive market structure, (2) bureaucratizing pressures, and (3) the manipulation of dependence relations are forces that might stabilize a network and thus facilitate its retention. The natural selection model of change implies that structures are only as complex as the environments supporting them, and without consistent external pressure, complex systems drift back toward simplicity. Network stability is thus enhanced by any conditions that allow organizational forms to persist unchanged or that maintain consistent environmental selection parameters, as discussed in previous chapters. Competitive market conditions, for example, make network stability unlikely: If barriers to entry are low and if economies-of-scale are not present, many small organizations can enter easily and will continuously divide the market among themselves. If each is similar to the others and if none can make strategic moves to dominate the field, a network involving organizations in this market will be highly unstable. If barriers to entry are high, turnover may be lower and agreements worked out among would-be competitors to mitigate the impact of competition. An action set or network containing organizations in this field would very likely be a stable one.

Occasionally selection criteria operate specifically at the level of networks, coaxing new networks into existence. Government bureaucracies often prescribe a certain pattern of interorganizational relations in implementing new programs, or mandate a formalized relation between organizations wishing to take advantage of government grants. United States manpower training legislation in the 1960s not only mandated a formalized relation between local Employment Service offices and manpower training programs, but also between Employment Services offices and Social Service Departments. The result was not an action set, as these organizations did not form a coalition, but rather a network that indirectly linked Employment Service offices to large numbers of previously ignored social service agencies.

Dependence relations as a stabilizing force.   Except for situations where environmental selection criteria operate specifically at the level of network functioning, it is likely that most stable networks owe their existence to individual organizations and action sets adapting to their environments. Conditions that increase the dependence of one organization on another heighten the probability of stability in a relationship, and we would expect dominant organizations to take an active role in promoting such stability. In addition to conditions affecting dependence already discussed in this and previous chapters, three other factors are important: (1) kinship ties between members of different organizations; (2) resource control, including control over the nature of interorganizational coupling and over new network resources; and (3) increases in the multiplexity of relations.

Kinship ties have been neglected by most theorists, apparently because of an uncritical acceptance of the thesis of managerial ascendance in the control of large corporations (Berle and Means, 1932). To counter proponents of the managerial control thesis, Lundberg (1937) reported research findings supporting his position that "America's sixty families" controlled much of the corporate wealth in the United States, and Zeitlin *et al.* (1974), Knowles (1973), and Domhoff (1967) supplied evidence that key families still wield a great deal of economic power in industrial societies. Many of the largest corporations in Chile, for example, are controlled by a small group of families through an intricate system of interlocking directorates (Zeitlin *et al.*, 1974).

Kinship ties are certainly an extremely stable basis for interorganizational relations, as long as family members retain control of their organizations. They last the lifetime of the persons involved and obligate members to respond to a wide range of requests, in all circumstances, making them the ultimate in multiplex ties. A network of family ties, ranging across a number of corporations, serves as a framework within which action sets are quickly mobilized. Wealthy families, such as the Rockefellers and Mellons, have extended and consolidated their financial power through strategic intermarriage (Knowles, 1973).

Minority ethnic groups have used kinship and ethnic ties in the creation of self-help networks to achieve economic success (Light, 1972; Bonacich, 1973; Aldrich, 1977). Japanese and Chinese migrants to the United States were able to draw upon their kin and earlier immigrants, first for employment and later for assistance in capitalizing their businesses. Indian and Pakistani immigrants to Great Britain created communal institutions to assist persons from their families and villages, and when General Amin ordered Asians expelled from Uganda in 1971, over 30,000 migrated to Great Britain. By drawing upon kinship and ethnic networks, many were able to start their own businesses within a few years of their arrival. The relative decline of small business ownership in the United States and the low volume of foreign immigration (from any one nation) indicate that kinship is less important in this sector than previously, but it is still significant among subgroups such as among Cuban immigrants to Florida and New York, and Korean immigrants to California.

Resource control by dominant organizations can take a variety of forms, including attempts to control the nature of coupling and to capture the flow of new resources in networks. In some situations, dominant organizations gain advantages by shifting networks from loosely to more tightly coupled structures. Relations between suppliers and distributors of petroleum products provide an example of dominant organizations (the suppliers, in this case) attempting to stabilize relations for their own benefit (Howard, 1956). When the supply of oil products falls below the demand for them, some suppliers ration the short supply to all their customers, whereas many major company refiners increase distribution through their own wholesale stations, at the expense of independent wholesalers. Marketers without fixed sources of supply are unable to obtain supplies and thus operate at unprofitable levels or go out of business. Periodic instances of this situation discourage petroleum jobbers from acquiring their supplies on the spot market or shifting between suppliers for short-term price advantages. The dependence of independent jobbers on large oil refineries thus partially stabilizes an otherwise competitive and unstable network.

Loose coupling protects dominant organizations from the impact of potentially threatening innovations, and thus they have a vested interest in maintaining positions at the center of interorganizational networks. If proposed innovations are compatible with the interests of linking-pin organizations, then change may occur rapidly, even in loosely coupled systems. Linking-pin organizations spread information about innovations, and loose coupling allows each organization to adapt innovations to suit its circumstances. Conversely, loose coupling makes it easier for linking-pin organizations to block innovations incompatible with their interests, as information spreads slowly in such networks when dominant organizations refuse to play an information-transmittal role.

In discussing constraints on distributing new medical resources in communities, Rushing (1971) noted that medical intervention assistance programs are often imported into communities without taking into account patterns of power relations between organizations. New programs create activity patterns that are never integrated into existing power and influence networks. "Consequently, when the external assistance is removed, the new patterns that have been established may disappear" (Rushing, 1971, p. 33). Lack of support from dominant organizations makes it difficult, if not impossible, to implement new programs, such as building new hospitals or mental health clinics.

Dominant organizations can stabilize networks by controlling the flow of resources into them. Powerful organizations often subscribe to a shared paradigm that defines the nature of community problems and the form of acceptable solutions (Warren et al., 1974). Such paradigm control is especially important in the public sector, as powerful interest groups shape the legislative directives defining which organizations are eligible for government grants and assistance. "Model Cities" agencies made little progress in changing patterns of interaction between urban social service agencies in the 1960s because the shared interorganizational paradigm diagnosed social problems as due to individual deficiencies rather than failures of the social system.

Clark (1965) argued that social and political change in the United States resulted in the centralization of educational policy-making in the hands of state and federal agencies in the 1950s and early 1960s. These centralized bodies, in turn, exerted influence on other public agencies and private groups through a network of formal and voluntary relations. Educational policy concerning the teaching of the physical sciences was changed very rapidly because these linking-pin organizations were able to redirect the flow of educational resources into new uses.

Multiplexity or redundancy of relations between organizations increases the stability of their relationship. To the extent that authorities recognize the advantages of multiplex relations, we would expect them to seek network stability through establishing multiple channels of access to interacting organizations. Dominant organizations would be especially likely to adopt this strategy, as it increases the dependence of subordinate organizations and enhances the probability of their acquiescence in future demands. Conglomerate firms often use this strategy in gradually asserting control over the corporations they acquire, as more and more local functions are assumed by headquarters staff during a transitional period (Aldrich and Sproule, 1977). Eventually, the new acquisition is totally dependent on corporate headquarters for vital functions such as budgeting, capital investment, and product innovation.

An Example of Network Evolution: The NCAA

Many of the principles of interorganizational network evolution are illustrated by Stern's (1977) analysis of the growth of the National Collegiate Athletic Association (NCAA), an organization regulating college athletic competition from 1906 to 1952. This example also illustrates the relevance of other concepts and environmental trends discussed in previous chapters, especially increasing environmental capacity and national social and economic interdependence. The NCAA arose as a linking-pin organization in a field characterized by a high degree of competitive and symbiotic interdependence, and through various adaptations and strategies eventually assumed a dominant position in the intercollegiate athletic network. From an initially weak position as an information disseminator, the NCAA gained enough strength through manipulating the network that by 1952 it could sanction member schools not abiding by NCAA rules on recruitment and competition.

The NCAA grew in an environment marked by increasing public interest in college athletics, increases in the amount of resources flowing into collegiate competition, and a broadening of the scope of athletic recruitment and competition from a purely local to a national level. The NCAA was formed in 1906 by thirty-eight colleges and universities and benefited from several developments in the next half century. Just as major changes were occurring in the industrial sector at the turn of the century, increasing affluence and the rebirth of the Olympic games in 1896 were kindling public interest in college athletics. The federal government took an active interest in physical conditioning during World War I and encouraged intercollegiate competition as a stimulus to developing the physical and leadership abilities of future soldiers. After the war, interest remained high as the affluence of the 1920s permitted the building of college stadiums, gate receipts increased, and full-time coaches were hired. The media began to devote extensive coverage to college athletics.

The depression of the 1930s only partially impeded the growth of athletic programs, as improved communication technology spread information about players and games widely, and radio broadcasts of football games gained wide audiences. Improvements in transportation networks made long-distance travel easier and cheaper, thus promoting interregional rivalries and national competition. The Rose Bowl game was begun in 1919 as an East-West competition, and recruiting also spread to become a nationwide talent search. The advent of television broadcasting of games in the late 1940s and early 1950s added new stakes to the already lucrative business of selling college athletics to the public.

Heightened public interest and nationwide competition changed the nature of the environment facing college athletic programs, increasing competitive interdependence between colleges and increasing symbiotic interdependence between colleges and merchandisers of sport, such as radio and television. In addition, the growth of a rival organization—the Amateur Athletic Union—posed problems for the NCAA with regard to the sanctioning of competition and, perhaps most important, affected relations with the international Olympic games. Regional conferences of colleges and universities, such as the Big Ten, the Pacific Conference, the Big Eight, and the Southwestern Conference, mitigated somewhat the impact of competitive interdependence, but national environmental changes laid the groundwork for a national organization. When the NCAA emerged and began its cautious growth in the early decades of this century, it was filling a national niche in which it had no direct competitors.

The NCAA, as an organization at the center of a network of links to athletic conferences and individual colleges and universities, benefited from all the mechanisms discussed in the previous section in gradually asserting dominance in the network: (1) increasing formalization and hierarchy within the network; (2) growing dependence, through the NCAA's controlling the nature of linkages and new resources; and (3) the success of the NCAA in increasing the multiplexity of ties between the central office and members. Many of the events and activities promoting the NCAA's rising dominance were not of its own making, as they were simply responses to constraints and contingencies that forced members to turn to the NCAA for assistance.

Formalization of the NCAA's relations with members began with two activities: publication of standard rules of play for intercollegiate games, and the division of the country into districts, each with an official NCAA representative to look after its interests. The NCAA did not try to supersede regional athletic conferences, such as the Big 10 or the Southern Conference, but rather used them as a node through which NCAA rules and regulations on recruiting and competition were promoted. The conferences were thus the key action sets within the loosely coupled network, linked through their common membership in the NCAA.

Internal formalization of the NCAA's administrative structure was marked by increasing bureaucratization and growth of the office staff, and the establishment of specialized committees. Major increases in bureaucratization took place in response to periods of increased environmental complexity, such as the expansion of competition in the 1920s, the creation of national championship tournaments in the 1920s and 1930s, and the enactment and enforcement of tighter rules in the late 1940s and early 1950s. As the administrative component grew, its strength allowed staff to pursue policies strengthening the association at the expense of the membership, a process similar to that described by Michels (1962) in his "iron law of oligarchy."

Originally the NCAA's network was quite loosely coupled, as legislation was not binding on members if they filed written objections to it. Attempts during the early stages to enforce tighter coupling would have undoubtedly meant the end of the NCAA. Instead, a great deal of local autonomy was permitted, and the NCAA worked to establish strong conferences that would use NCAA rules in regulating their members. Loose coupling meant that administrative expenses were kept low and resources could be devoted to the battle with the AAU over international competition. Loose coupling also minimized internal conflict and allowed the NCAA to present a united face to the nation, thus furthering the impression that the NCAA represented most colleges and universities.

Movement toward tighter coupling came with the NCAA's increasing control over new network resources and an increase in the multiplexity of ties to members. The NCAA's external prestige and internal credibility were reinforced by the recognition given it by the government and mass media. The mass media treated the NCAA as representing college athletics, and the federal government legitimated the NCAA's position by placing it on numerous committees. New network resources were then easier to control, as external organizations channeled their inquiries and activities into the network through the NCAA. The NCAA became the administrative agent for dealing with the television and radio networks, gaining control over a critical source of funding. It also gained a major voice in appointing coaches for Olympic teams and conducting tryouts, thus standing as an intermediary between members and the international Olympic games.

Ties between the NCAA and member organizations became increasingly multiplex as it increased services and resources provided to colleges and universities. Every sport added to intercollegiate competition required a new NCAA rules committee, and every national championship competition required an NCAA tournament committee. Because the NCAA was first and thus preempted the field, there was no other route to determining a national champion in a sport except by going through the NCAA's tournament. The tournaments generated income, which the NCAA then distributed to competing institutions.

The culmination of the NCAA's movement toward dominance in the network occurred in 1952, when the NCAA council met in response to extreme external pressure and internal conflict over a series of scandals involving recruiting, gambling, and general commercial penetration of college athletics. The council voted to allow the NCAA to enact legislation that would be mandatory for all member institutions and enforced through control over access to television and radio revenues, championship competitions, and other resources. The NCAA thus acquired ultimate power over collegiate athletics—the power to exclude members from NCAA controlled activities and resources—and total control over entry and exit was achieved.

Interorganizational network evolution is amply illustrated by the NCAA's rise to power within the network of intercollegiate athletics. Through the joint effects of external pressures and internal adaptations, the NCAA's growing administrative bureaucracy spun a web of linkages that ultimately gave it control over new network resources and the terms on which members could remain in the network. Action sets within the network—the various regional conferences—are still important subcomponents today, and thus the network is not as tightly coupled as possible. Nevertheless, the multiplexity of ties to members and the NCAA's dominant position make it the key actor in the network. Court challenges to the NCAA's sanctioning power in the late 1970s may redress the balance somewhat back toward individual members.

Evolution of Networks: Summary

Interorganizational networks are generally loosely coupled, hierarchically differentiated, integrated by the actions of linking-pin organizations, and probably rather unstable. The concept of network is similar to that of organization set in that the boundaries of both depend on the sensitivity of observers in locating meaningful limits to an organizational aggregate. Just as authorities strive for control over organizations in their organization set without necessarily having a clear conception that such an entity exists, so linking-pin and dominant organizations act in ways that give structure to the networks in which they are implicated without necessarily intending to do so. Occasionally, of course, networks are deliberately designed structures, such as those created by government legislation or shrewd authorities in dominant organizations.

Human service delivery systems, systemic patterns of interlocking corporate directorates, and the diffusion of educational innovations are difficult to comprehend unless all the organizations involved are portrayed as an interorganizational network. This does not mean that all organizations are assumed to be directly connected. On the contrary, the benefit of the loosely coupled system concept is that it alerts us to the incomplete and shifting relations characterizing most networks. Instability can not be total, for then there is no point in using the network concept, and several factors were discussed that could lend some stability to networks: government intervention, dependence relations in the form of kinship ties, resource control via controls over the degree of coupling and the flow of new resources, and increasing multiplexity of ties.

NETWORKS AND ECONOMIC POWER

Although supposedly put to rest by the maturation of "post-industrial" society, the issue of corporate ownership and control has come alive again in the past decade. Proponents of the "managerial revolution" position asserted that the separation of ownership and control in modern corporations, and the disappearance of a visible "dominant class," meant that a marxist class analysis of modern society was not longer appropriate. Skeptics, however, pointed to the weak and inconsistent evidence marshalled in support of the managerialist position and called for continued research into whether ownership and control really have been separated, and whether a capitalist class exists in modern industrial societies. A vast program of research on these questions is underway, and it is clearly impossible to do justice to the issues or summarize the research in this concluding section. Instead, I want to explore the extent to which the concept of interorganizational networks might prove useful in guiding research on such issues.

The concept of a dominant capitalist class is central to the investigation of where economic power lies in industrial societies: "Classes are constituted of freely intermarrying families variously located in the social process of production and system of property relations" (Zeitlin, 1974, p. 1109). Persons in the same class position associate more frequently with one another than with outsiders and thus intermarry frequently. Upper-class cohesion is strengthened by social clubs, resorts, private schools, elite colleges, and other integrative mechanisms (Domhoff, 1967; Mills, 1957). Research on the social conditions facilitating upper-class cohesion is relevant here only insofar as it shows that it appears there is something worth investigating. I will leave open the larger question of the size and composition of the dominant capitalist class, and treat only the question of whether network analysis of relations between corporations and financial institutions indicates that networks of economic power *could* facilitate a dominant class's control of the economy.

Four distinct positions exist with respect to the issue of ownership and control (Mintz, 1977). First, some theorists follow Berle and Means (1932) in arguing that the proportion of a corporation's stock held by any one person or interest is generally so small that there is no external locus of control. In the absence of external control, the corporation's managers assume control, appointing persons to the board of directors and making major policy decisions that stockholders are powerless to overturn. Second, some marxists accept the argument that managers have assumed effective control of most corporations, but assert that managers belong to the same class as the powerless stockholders and have a similarly strong financial stake in the corporation through high salaries, stock options, and other benefits. These two positions imply that the relevant unit of analysis in studying economic power is the corporation itself, as corporations are in competition with one another for resources, favorable government action, and other advantages.

Third, some theorists, marxist and non-marxist, reject the notion that effective control of corporations has passed into the hands of their managers. Recent research, discussed in Chapter 12, has found that a substantial number of corporations classified as "under management control" in earlier studies were misclassified, and that through diligent and time-consuming research it is possible to track down an effective center of control for many of them. Marxist theorists argue that many corporations are, in fact, controlled by a single, family-centered interest group. Fourth, the finance capital position asserts that an effective external source of control exists, and that such control is in the hands of banks and financial institutions, which supply credit to and own or control stock in large corporations. These two positions imply that the relevant unit of analysis in studying economic power is not an individual corporation but the network of relations in which it is implicated; the third position identifies this network as kinship- and class-based, whereas the fourth position asserts that networks are dominated by financial institutions that may not be family-controlled. In the following discussion, I focus on linkages between corporations, and not on the ownership dispute itself.

Kinship Ties Between Corporations

Combining class analysis with network analysis, the hypothesis could be advanced that financially powerful action sets form around kinship-based interorganizational networks, with network stability enhanced because of the overlap of kinship and economic interests. Knowles (1973, p. 3) argued that the old capitalist families "have transferred their ownership and active participation out of largely non-financial corporations . . . to financial institutions, primarily banks, through which they continue to dominate the affairs not only of their traditional non-financial family companies but of a host of others which their augmented financial powers permits them to control." Bank directorships facilitate the retention of financial power, as they assure a powerful family of a line of credit, give them indirect access to the vast stockholdings of a bank's trust department, and allow the use of the bank as a focal point for forging alliances with other powerful organizations.

The network of ties formed by kinship relations between branches of the same powerful family was found to be quite stable in Knowles' (1973) case study of the Rockefeller family and its associates. Two branches of the Rockefeller family have their base of power in four large banks and three large mutual life insurance companies: the Chase Manhattan Bank; First National City Bank; Chemical Bank; the First National Bank of Chicago; and the Metropolitan, Equitable, and New York Life insurance companies. In 1969, these seven organizations had assets of over $113 billion. In his case study, Knowles mapped the network of interorganizational relations maintained through ties between Rockefeller family members, persons with long-term allegiances to the family, and other wealthy families traditionally allied with the Rockefellers, such as the Milbank and Grace families.

The weakest part of Knowles' analysis, unfortunately, is his attempt to show the economic implications of interlocking kinship ties. Lacking direct access to information on how corporate decisions were made, he fell back on comparing the outcome of an event with what an ideal outcome would have been from the Rockefeller group's viewpoint. He reported, for example, that there was a greater amount of product duplication among petrochemical firms in the Rockefeller interest group than between this group and other firms, suggesting that the Rockefeller-connected firms had found some joint method of dealing with competitive interdependence. With respect to the wielding of political power, he examined the Rockefeller group's reputed influence on the formation of foreign policy and its attempt to protect its foreign oil investments. Although mainly circumstantial, Knowles' analysis of the consequences of kinship ties suggests that comparative research on other wealthy families would be a fruitful application of network analysis.

Investigating the usefulness of the concept of a kinship-based economic group, Zeitlin *et al.* (1974) examined the network of relations between large corporations in Chile. They concluded that kinship-based economic groups own and control the large corporations in Chile through a complex intertwining of economic interests and kinship bonds. An examination of single corporations, rather than networks, would have led to serious errors in their analysis of economic power, and they emphasized the significance of taking networks as units of analysis. To determine the size of a single family's control of a firm, it was necessary to examine the "many legally distinct holdings, together with those held through personal and family holding companies, trusts, and estates (and/or such intermediaries as nominees and brokers)" (Zeitlin *et al.*, 1974, p. 102).

Whitley (1973) discovered an astonishingly high degree of family-based ties between the twenty-seven major English financial institutions he studied. Eight families accounted for ties between sixteen financial institutions through members of the immediate family, usually brothers. Taking kinship ties beyond the nuclear family into account, twenty-six of the twenty-seven institutions were connected, many by more than one kinship tie. The existence of extensive ties does not prove that a small group of families controls these large financial institutions, but kinship ties do form a more stable basis for possible joint action than ones based purely on acquaintanceship.

In the United States, the Mellon family has controlling interests in at least four of the largest 500 nonfinancial corporations—Gulf Oil, Alcoa, Koppers Company, and Carborundum Company—and three large financial corporations—the First Boston Corporation, the General Reinsurance Corporation, and the Mellon National Bank and Trust Company (Zeitlin, 1974). Mellon National Bank, in turn, owns almost 7 percent of the common stock in another of the top 500 corporations—Jones and Laughlin Steel. The Mellons control these corporations through membership on boards of directors, family and charitable trusts and foundations, and various other connections.

Interlocking Directorates

In discussing boards of directors, I noted that corporations in the United States are extensively interlocked via shared directors. Whether this pattern of interlocking directorates represents a power and influence structure is a matter of some controversy, as there is little evidence on the behavioral consequences of interlocks at the aggregate level (Mace, 1971). Some economists have argued that interlocking directorates are simply irrelevant for competition, although their evidence is not strong (Stigler, 1968, p. 261). Following arguments developed earlier, it could be argued that the potential influence represented by a loosely coupled network can be converted into actual influence when action sets form around central points in the network.

Studies of interlocking directorates have been made for the United States by the House of Representatives Committee on Banking (1968), Dooley (1969), Allen (1974), Mariolis (1975), Beardon et al. (1975), and Levine (1977); for Great Britain by Whitley (1973), and Stanworth and Giddens (1975); for Canada by Ornstein (1976); for Belgium by Daems (1978); and for Chile by Zeitlin et al. (1974). In the United States, federal action has been quite permissive with respect to director interlocks between corporations. "In operation, the body of Federal legislation has not effectively prevented interlocks in corporate managements in the fields it covers. Enforcement of the Clayton Act's prohibitions against interlocking directorates was neither prompt nor vigorous" (U.S. House of Representatives, 1965, p. 226). Only thirteen complaints were filed by the Federal Trade Commission between 1914 and 1965 under section eight of the Clayton Act, and the Department of Justice delayed systematic application of the law against interlocking directorates until 1946. The first case actually tried before a court was not brought to trial until 1952.

Extensive interlocks between corporations in the United States have been found in all studies. Only 17 of the 250 largest corporations in 1965 had no interlocking director positions with another corporation that was also among the 250 largest, and the average number of interlocks was 9.9 (Dooley, 1969). The Clayton Act's prohibition against interlocks between competitors has not eliminated the practice, and 297 interlocks were found between corporations that appeared to be in direct competition with each other. Mariolis (1975) examined *Fortune* magazine's 1970 list of the top 500 industrials, the top 50 banks, the top 50 insurance companies, the top 50 retailers, the top 50 utilities, the top 50 transportation companies, and 47 miscellaneous large corporations, all ranked by either sales or assets. Of the 797 corporations studied, 92 percent were interlocked at least once with another large corporation, 85 percent had at least two interlocks, and 10.5 percent had twenty-five or more interlocks. The median number of interlocks was eight. Banks ranked highest in interlocks, with an average of 27.8, and the miscellaneous firms ranked lowest, with an average of 6.4.

Two problems prevent us from generalizing Mariolis's results to the total corporate population of the United States. First, his data set excludes all corporations too small to make the *Fortune* magazine lists, and the smaller corporations omitted might well be linked to many of the larger corporations. This omission could lead an investigator to overlook the importance of smaller corporations within the 797 because, and while they aren't central to the largest corporations, they *do* play a significant role for the smaller corporations not on the list. Second, the population of directors—and thus interlocks—was derived from the sample of corporations, thus excluding all United States board memberships falling outside the limits of the *Fortune* lists. Results might have been different had a sample of directors been drawn and then their board memberships—and corporations—recorded (Levine, 1977).

Beardon *et al.* (1975), in a study under Michael Schwartz's direction, studied the 1,131 largest corporations in the United States during the period 1962–1973, using a data set with the same limitations as Mariolis's. As of 1962, these companies had 13,574 directors and a total of 11,252 interlocks, or an average of 10 interlocks per corporation. When all interlocks were weighted equally, a network created by the ties was found to be almost totally inclusive of the corporations in the sample—only about 12 percent of the firms had no interlocks within the system. The network included 5 pairs of corporations interlocked only with each other, in addition to the 132 corporations with no interlocks within the system. The remaining 989 corporations were linked together into a single continuous network. To search for clusters or subcomponents in the network, the investigators examined only interlocks involving directors who were officers in one of each pair of linked corporations. This analysis revealed five "peaks" in the network, centered on five banks: Continental Illinois, Mellon Bank, J. P. Morgan, Bankers Trust of New York, and United California Bank.

Levine (1977), using Mariolis and Schartz's data, followed up Beardon *et al.*'s attempt to find the structure underlying the pattern of interlocking among the 797 largest corporations. He replicated their findings: Beyond 62 isolates and 5 small subsets of organizations, all the 724 remaining corporations were linked in one giant network, constituting one connected set. Using network matrices as described in Chapter 11, Levine found that paths between corporations were fairly short. Paths could vary from 1 to 723 in length: A path of 1 indicates two corporations directly linked; a path of 2 indicates two corporations indirectly linked by an intermediary; and at the extreme, a path of 723 would be a single chain, end to end, of organizations. The median shortest path was three: 61 percent of all shortest path connections were completed in three steps or less, and 91 percent of all shortest paths were completed in four steps or less. "The network of corporations and directors appears to be as intricately and tightly tied together as is a small community with its multiplicity of cross-cutting ties" (Levine, 1977, p. 16).

In an attempt to find dominant organizations that played linking-pin roles, Levine removed all the banks, but 83 percent of the network was still connected. In a second, more crude attempt, he systematically removed corporations, beginning with the most-linked. Going as far as removing the top twenty-one corporations still left 88 percent of the network connected, and other attempts to break up the network by massive destruction of its components also failed. Levine argued that his results gave no comfort to marxist or pluralist scholars:

There is no evidence that a subset of elite organizations or many subsets of separate competing organizations exist. Resistance of the network to deterioration under the wholesale destruction of its parts was taken as evidence for its nondifferentiability.

These conclusions are highly speculative, as Levine recognized, given the data limitations described above. Moreover, Levine's results are quite compatible with the argument that a strong commonality of interest unites almost all major United States corporations and that upper-class cohesion, as described by Zeitlin, Domhoff, and others, obviates the need for any dominant linking-pin organizations among the largest corporations. A critical test of this proposition is not possible until samples of corporations are expanded to include the thousands of smaller corporations in the United States. None of these studies examined decision-making or patterns of influence between corporations, and so it is premature to draw conclusions about intercorporate competition—or the lack of it—solely from interlock data.

The existence of extensive interlocks between financially powerful corporations indicates that there is a potential for action sets to form along network lines, but direct evidence of action set formation is not presented in these studies. An indirect indicator of possible action set formation is the fact that the most common interlocks are between corporations with their head offices in the same city or region. Dooley (1969) found that almost half of the 250 largest corporations belonged to one of fifteen clearly identifiable local interest groups, identified by the number of times members were interlocked among themselves. Seven local groups contained members interlocked four or more times, and eight groups had members interlocked two or three times. Banks and life insurance corporations formed the core of local groups, acting as linking-pins through which others were joined. Levine's (1972) more limited study of fourteen banks interlocked with the boards of seventy large industrial corporations showed a similar pattern of bank centrality.

One of the most thorough attempts to relate patterns of director interlocks to action set creation and maintenance was a study of thirty-seven large corporations in Chile by Zeitlin et al. (1974). They found that complex patterns of interlocking directorates, reciprocal stockholdings, and other arrangements united groups of corporations under the control of wealthy family-based interest groups. These groups responded with political action when they perceived their economic interests threatened by the Allende government, supporting its overthrow.

Two studies of businesspeople's community development committees found that some committees had a major impact on city politics through their members' interlocking directorships. Of thirty directors of the Greater Philadelphia Movement, ten also served on more than one board of a nonprofit corporation, three directors served on five other civic or quasi-public bodies, and nine served on two or three boards (Petshek, 1973). In St. Louis, members of Civic Progress held eighty-two board positions and filled half of the officer positions in eight pivotal community agencies influencing social welfare policy (Edgar, 1970). Interlocking directorates between community organizations is a subtle, nonobtrusive way for elites to influence civic policies in the name of organizational rationality, claiming to speak for their organizations rather than for an interest group.

Bank Centrality

Results from studies by Dooley (1969), Zeitlin (1974), Beardon *et al*. (1975), Mariolis (1975), Levine (1972), and others summarized previously show that banks and other financial institutions occupy central positions in interorganizational networks of business corporations. Theorists holding a finance capital perspective argue that banks are therefore able to manipulate and control network and action set activities, directing them toward their own profitability. The twin pillars supporting the central network position of banks are their control of capital and their control of corporate stocks and debt obligations through their trust departments, with board membership on nonfinancial corporations following from the exercise of this power. Legislative changes in the 1970s that permitted banks to own nonbanking subsidiaries anywhere in the United States gave major banks an additional avenue through which to generate traffic in loans. Nadler (1974, p. 87) asserted that "their techniques for raising monies to fund loans of virtually any size at any time are helping them to lever themselves into the economies of all our geographical regions. . . ."

Congressman Wright Patman's staff (U.S. House of Representatives, 1968) assembled data on relations between banks, and between the largest corporations and selected banks in ten Standard Metropolitan Statistical Areas (SMSAs). They found a pattern of banks holding, in their trust departments, their own stock as well as the stock of competing banks. Among the 210 largest commercial banks, about 57 percent held more than 5 percent of their own stock, and 29 percent held more than 10 percent. Patman's staff also found a high number of director interlocks between banks and large corporations, with the extent of interlocking positively related to the volume of stock the bank held in the corporation. The forty-nine banks studied held 5 percent or more of the common stock in 147 of the 500 largest industrial corporations.

Between four and six banks were studied in each of the ten SMSAs. Interlocks between these forty-nine banks and corporations listed in *Fortune* magazine's directory were examined, with a total of 768 director interlocks found with 286 of the 500 largest industrials. There were 64 director interlocks with 26 of the 50 largest merchandising firms, 73 interlocks with 27 of the 50 largest transportation firms, 146 interlocks with 29 of the 50 largest insurance companies, and 86 interlocks with 22 of the 50 largest utilities. Dooley's (1969, p. 322) results were similar, as the 200 largest corporations interlocked 616 times with the fifty largest banks and life insurance companies. In studies by Dooley (1969), Mariolis (1975), and Beardon *et al*. (1975), banks and life insurance companies had the highest average number of corporate interlocks of all industries studied. Banks in West Germany obtain seats on the supervisory boards of corporations because of power gained through directly purchasing shares in the corporation and through soliciting the proxy votes of customers whose shares are in the bank's custody (Bacon and Brown, 1977).

The central position of banks is demonstrated not only through their being represented on corporate boards, but also through the composition of their own boards. Bank boards of directors can serve as meeting places for supposed competitors in other industries. In 1973, the First National City Bank of New York board of directors brought together the following executives from major firms in the chemical industry: Charles McCoy, President of DuPont; Charles Sommer, Chairman of the Board of Monsanto; Gordon Grand, President of Olin; and J. Peter Grace, President of W. R. Grace.

Kinship ties and interest groups surrounding wealthy families are implicated in bank as well as industrial corporation control. Burch's (1972) investigation of the fifty largest banks provided a minimum estimate of the proportion of banks controlled by family interests. He concluded that "30 percent were probably under family control, another 22 percent possibly under family control, and 48 percent probably under management control" (Zeitlin, 1974, p. 1105). The Rockefeller family group holds over 5 percent of the stock in the Chase Manhattan Bank and has a substantial interest in the First National City Bank (Citibank); the Fisher and Mott families, whose wealth comes from their interests in General Motors, hold over 5 percent of the stock in the National Bank of Detroit; Henry Ford's family holds 4 percent of the stock in Manufacturer's National Bank; and the Hanna family, controlling the National Steel and Consolidation Coal Corporations, have at least a 3 percent interest in the National City Bank of Cleveland. Zeitlin noted that these are not isolated examples and that it may not be possible to argue that banks "control" industry in cases where financial and industrial interests are so obviously intertwined.

A pattern of frequent interlocks between organizations controlling a high proportion of a society's assets may be an indication that the organizations involved have a vested interest in stable interorganizational relations. The Patman report, Zeitlin's papers, and other studies raise questions about the extent of collusive behavior between financially powerful organizations. Such activities would have a major impact on the allocation of societal resources, affecting the terms on which resources are available to less powerful organizations and ultimately having an impact on the economic well-being of all citizens.

Networks and Economic Power: Summary

Acceptance of the thesis of a separation of ownership and control in modern corporations appears premature, as studies showing that no identifiable interest grouping owns more than a given proportion of a corporation's stock tell us little about where effective control resides. Research underway in the United States (Zeitlin, 1974), England (Nyman and Silberston, 1977), and other industrial countries should shed light on this issue. Studies reviewed in this section suggest that individual corporations are not the appropriate units of analysis for examining the persistence of a capitalist class and its economic power. Greater attention must be paid to the role of interorganizational networks affecting the activities of corporations in capitalist societies.

SUMMARY

Interorganizational networks are derived constructs that may have an existence independent of observer perceptions if selection criteria favor the retention of their components. Network evolution can be conceptualized as the formation of a hierarchical, loosely coupled system, with dominant organizations, government elites, and special interest groups playing an important entrepreneurial role. Network-like patterns of interorganizational relations may also arise as by-products of organizations and action sets pursuing their own specific objectives. Whether an interorganizational network is retained depends on the role played by linking-pin organizations and selection criteria rewarding linkage stability. Stability is enhanced when multiple ties exist between boundary-spanners at different hierarchical levels or in different organizational subunits, and loose coupling makes the links relatively independent of one another. Dependence relations may fill these criteria, especially kinship and ethnic ties or relations based on resource control.

Extensive links exist between large corporations in the financial and nonfinancial sectors of the economy, with a central role played by banks and other financial institutions. Only partial information is available on the extent of kinship-based interorganizational links, and so the role of family ties in stabilizing economic networks is unclear at present. Investigators often speculate about the behavioral consequences of interorganizational networks of economic interest, but the task remains of documenting such behavior, beyond simply showing it is a plausible outcome. Zeitlin (1974, pp. 1107–8) did not use the term "network analysis," but his prescriptive statement for would-be investigators of the corporate ownership and control issue is surely relevant here: "Research must focus at the outset on the complex relationships in which the single corporation is itself involved; . . . the relationships between it and other corporations; the forms of personal union or interlocking between corporate directorates and between the officers and directors and principal shareholding families . . ." and connections between the financial and governmental units that affect the selection criteria to which corporations must adapt.

Approaching the study of social change and stability through interorganizational networks links the population ecology model of organizational change with central issues in the sociological tradition. Organizations—producing goods, delivering services, maintaining order, challenging the established order—are the fundamental building blocks of modern societies, and must stand at the center of the analysis of social change. Focusing on populations rather than isolated organizations forces us to come to terms with the complexity of industrial societies, directing our attention to what goes on outside as well as within organizations. Proper application of the variation-selection-retention model presents a challenge to traditional conceptions of organizational analysis, for it requires a great deal of collaboration with other social science disciplines (especially history, economics, and political science). Fortunately, there are signs of a growing interest in such cross-disciplinary cooperation, and students of organizational change in the coming decade will benefit from the halting steps made in that direction in the 1970s.

References

ADAIR, ROSS. 1960. "The Indian Health Worker," *Human Organization*, 19 (Summer): 59–63.

ADAMS, J. STACY. 1976. "The Structure and Dynamics of Behavior in Organizational Boundary Roles," in *Handbook of Organizational and Industrial Psychology*, ed. Marvin Dunnette. Chicago: Rand McNally, pp. 1175–99.

ADLER, LEE. 1964. "A New Orientation for Plotting Marketing Strategy," *Business Horizons*, 4 (Winter): 37–50.

AGUILER, FRANCIS. 1967. *Scanning the Business Environment*. New York: MacMillan Publishing Co., Inc.

AIKEN, MICHAEL, and JERALD HAGE. 1968. "Organizational Interdependence and Intraorganizational Structure," *American Sociological Review*, 33 (December): 912–30.

ALBA, RICHARD. 1973. "A Graph-Theoretic Definition of a Sociometric Clique," *Journal of Mathematical Sociology*, 3: 113–26.

ALCHIAN, A. 1950. "Uncertainty, Evolution, and Economic Theory," *Journal of Political Economy*, 58 (June): 211–21.

ALDRICH, HOWARD E. 1971a. "The Sociable Organization: A Case Study of MENSA and Some Propositions," *Sociology and Social Research*, 55 (July): 429–41.

351

————. 1971b. "Organizational Boundaries and Interorganizational Conflict," *Human Relations*, 24 (August): 279–87.

————. 1972a. "Technology and Organizational Structure: A Re-examination of the Findings of the Aston Group," *Administrative Science Quarterly*, 17 (March): 26–43.

————. 1972b. "An Organization-Environment Perspective on Co-operation and Conflict in the Manpower Training System," in *Conflict and Power in Complex Organizations*, ed. A. Negandhi. Kent, Ohio: Center for Business and Economic Research, pp. 11–37.

————. 1976a. "Resource Dependence and Interorganizational Relations Between Local Employment Service Offices and Social Services Sector Organizations," *Administration and Society*, 7 (February): 419–54.

————. 1976b. "An Interorganizational Dependency Perspective on Relations Between the Employment Service and its Organization Set" in *The Management of Organization Design*, Vol. II, eds. Ralph H. Kilman, Louis R. Pondy, and Dennis P. Slevin. New York: Elsevier North-Holland, Inc., pp. 231–66.

————. 1977. "Asian Shopkeepers as a Middleman Minority: A Study of Small Businesses in Wandsworth." Paper presented at the annual meeting of the American Sociological Association, Chicago.

————. 1978. "Centralization Versus Decentralization in the Design of Human Service Delivery Systems: A Response to Gouldner's Lament," in *Issues in Service Delivery in Human Service Organizations*, eds. Rosemary Sarri and Yeheskel Hasenfeld. New York: Columbia University Press.

ALDRICH, HOWARD E., and DIANE HERKER.   1977. "Boundary Spanning Roles and Organization Structure," *Academy of Management Review* (April): 217–30.

ALDRICH, HOWARD E., and SERGIO MINDLIN.   1978. "Uncertainty and Dependence: Two Perspectives on Environment," in *Organization and Environment*, ed. Lucien Karpik. Beverly Hills, Calif: Sage Publications, Inc., pp. 149–70.

ALDRICH, HOWARD E., and JEFFREY PFEFFER.   ©1976. "Environments of Organizations," in *Annual Review of Sociology*, Vol. II, ed. A. Inkeles. Palo Alto: Annual Review, Inc., pp. 79–105. All rights reserved.

ALDRICH, HOWARD E., and A. J. REISS, JR.   1971. "Police Officers as Boundary Personnel," in *The Police in Urban Society*, ed. H. Hahn. Beverly Hills, Calif: Sage Publications, Inc., pp. 193–208. By permission of the publisher.

————. 1976. "Continuities in the Study of Ecological Succession: Changes in the Race Composition of Neighborhoods and Their Businesses," *American Journal of Sociology*, 81 (January): 846–66.

ALDRICH, HOWARD E., and CLAIRE SPROULE.   1977. "Mergers and the Industrial Relations Process." Unpublished paper, NYSSILR, Cornell University.

ALEXANDER, KENNETH.   1971. "Conglomerate Mergers and Collective Bargaining," *Industrial and Labor Relations Review*, 24 (April): 354–74.

ALKER, HAYWARD JR., WALTER BUCKLEY, and TOM R. BURNS. 1976. "Introduction and Overview," in *Power and Control*, eds. Tom R. Burns and Walter Buckley. Beverly Hills and London: Sage Publications, Inc., pp. 1–23.

ALLEN, MICHAEL PATRICK. 1974. "The Structure of Interorganizational Elite Cooptation: Interlocking Corporate Directorates," *American Sociological Review*, 39 (June): 393–496.

ALLEN, THOMAS. 1967. "Information Needs and Uses," *Annual Review of Information Science and Technology*, Vol. 4, ed. Carlos Cuadra. Chicago, Ill.: Encyclopedia Britannica.

ALLEN, THOMAS, and STEPHEN COHEN. 1969. "Information Flow in Research and Development Laboratories," *Administrative Science Quarterly*, 14 (March): 12–19.

ALLISON, GRAHAM T. 1971. *Essence of Decision: Explaining the Cuban Missile Crisis*. Boston, Mass.: Little, Brown & Company.

ANDERSON, PERRY. 1974a. *Lineages of the Absolutist State*. New York: Humanities Press.

———. 1974b *Passages from Antiquity to Feudalism*. London: New Left Books.

ARGYRIS, CHRIS. 1972. *The Applicability of Organizational Sociology*. London: Cambridge University Press.

AVERITT, ROBERT. 1968. *The Dual Economy*. New York: W. W. Norton & Co., Inc.

BACHARACH, SAMUEL. 1977. "Environmental Heterogeneity and the Open Organization." Presented at the 1977 Academy of Management Meetings, Orlando, Florida.

———. 1978. (Forthcoming) "Morphologie et Processus: Une Critique de la Recherche Intra-Organisationelle Contemporaire," *Revue de Sociologie du Travail*.

BACHARACH, SAMUEL, and MICHAEL AIKEN. 1976. "Structural and Process Constraints of Influence in Organizations: A Level Specific Analysis," *Administrative Science Quarterly*, 21 (December): 623–42.

BACHARACH, SAMUEL, and EDWARD J. LAWLER. 1976. "The Perception of Power," *Social Forces*, 55 (September): 123–34.

BACON, JEREMY, and JAMES BROWN. 1975. *Corporate Directorship Practice: Role, Sanction, and Legal Status of the Board*. New York: The Conference Board.

———. 1977. *The Board of Directors: Perspectives and Practices in Nine Countries*. New York: The Conference Board.

BAILEY, F. G. 1969. *Strategems and Spoils: A Social Anthropology of Politics*. Oxford: Basil Blackwell.

BAIN, JOE. 1956. *Barriers to New Competition: Their Character and Consequences in Manufacturing Industries*. Cambridge, Mass.: Harvard University Press.

BANFIELD, EDWARD. 1961. *Political Influence*. New York: The Free Press.

BARKER, LUCIUS, and DONALD JANSIEWICZ. 1970. "Coalitions in the Civil Rights Movement," in *The Study of Coalition Behavior*, eds. S. Groennings, E. W. Kelley, and M. Leiserson. New York: Holt, Rinehart and Winston, pp. 192–208.

BARNARD, CHESTER I. 1938. *The Functions of the Executive*. Cambridge, Mass.: Harvard University Press.

BARRY, BRIAN. 1974. "Review Article: 'Exit, Voice, and Loyalty,' " *British Journal of Political Science*, 4 (January): 79–107.

BARTON, ALLAN. 1969. *Communities in Disaster*. Garden City, N.Y.: Doubleday & Co., Inc.

BATY, GORDON, WILLIAM EVAN, and TERRY ROTHERMEL. 1971. "Personnel Flows as Interorganizational Relations," *Administrative Science Quarterly*, 16 (December): 430–43.

BEARDON, JAMES, WILLIAM ATWOOD, PETER FREITAG, CAROL HENDRICKS, BETH MINTZ, and MICHAEL SCHWARTZ. 1975. "The Nature and Extent of Bank Centrality in Corporate Networks." Paper presented at the Annual Meeting of the American Sociological Association, San Francisco, Calif.

BECKER, MARSHALL. 1970. "Sociometric Location and Innovativeness: Reformulation and Extension of the Diffusion Model," *American Sociological Review*, 35 (April): 267–82.

BENDIX, REINHARD. 1956. *Work and Authority in Industry*. New York: John Wiley & Sons, Inc.

BENSON, J. KENNETH. 1971. "Models of Structure Selection in Organizations: On the Limitations of Rational Perspectives." Paper presented at the Annual Meeting of the American Sociological Association, Denver, Colorado.

———. 1975. "The Interorganizational Network as a Political Economy," *Administrative Science Quarterly*, 20 (June): 229–49.

———. 1977. "Organizations: A Dialectical View," *Administrative Science Quarterly*, 22 (March): 1–21.

BENSON, J. KENNETH, and ROBERT DAY. 1976. "On the Limits of Negotiation: A Critique of the Theory of Negotiated Order," Paper presented at the Annual Meeting of the American Sociological Association, New York.

BERG, IVAR. 1969. *Education and Jobs: The Great Training Robbery*. New York: Praeger Publishers, Inc.

BERGER, PETER. 1963. *Invitation to Sociology*. Garden City, N.Y.: Doubleday, Anchor Books.

BERGER, PETER L., and THOMAS LUCKMANN. 1967. *The Social Construction of Reality*. Garden City, N.Y.: Doubleday, Anchor Books.

BERLE, ADOLPH. 1954. *The 20th Century Capitalist Revolution*. New York: Harcourt Brace Jovanovich, Inc.

BERLE, ADOLPH, and GARDINER MEANS. 1932. *The Modern Corporation and Private Property*. New York: MacMillan Publishing Co., Inc.

BERNARD, H. RUSSELL, and PETER KILLWORTH. 1973. "On the Social Structure of an Ocean-Going Research Vessel and Other Important Things," *Social
Science Research*, 2: 145–84.

BERRY, BRIAN J. L., and JOHN D. KASARDA. 1977. *Contemporary Urban
Ecology*. New York: Macmillan Publishing Co., Inc.

BIRCH, A. H. 1975. "Economic Models in Political Science: The Case of
'Exit, Voice, and Loyalty,' " *British Journal of Political Science*, 5
(January): 65–82.

BLAU, PETER M. 1951. *The Dynamics of Bureaucracy*. Chicago: University of
Chicago Press.

———. 1962. "Studies on Formal Organizations," *American Journal of
Sociology*, 68 (November): 289–90.

———. 1964. *Exchange and Power in Social Life*. New York: John Wiley &
Sons, Inc.

———. 1972. "Interdependence and Hierarchy in Organizations," *Social Science Research*, 1 (April): 1–24.

BLAU, PETER M., and RICHARD A. SCHOENHERR. 1971. *The Structure of Organizations*. New York: Basic Books, Inc.

BLAU, PETER M., and W. RICHARD SCOTT. 1962. *Formal Organizations*. San
Francisco, Calif.: Chandler Publishing Co.

BLAUNER, ROBERT. 1964. *Alienation and Freedom*. Chicago: University of
Chicago Press.

BLUMER, HERBERT. 1966. "Sociological Implications of the Thought of
George Herbert Mead," *American Journal of Sociology*, 71 (March): 535–
44.

BOISSEVAIN, JEREMY. 1974. *Friends of Friends: Networks, Manipulators, and
Coalitions*. Oxford: Basil Blackwell.

BOLTON COMMITTEE. 1971. *Report of the Committee of Inquiry on Small
Firms*. London: HMSO.

BONACICH, EDNA. 1973. "A Theory of Middleman Minorities," *American
Sociological Review*, 38: 583–94.

BOSERUP, WILLIAM, and UFFE SCHLICHTKRULL. 1962. "Alternative Approaches to the Control of Competition," in *Competition, Cartels, and Their
Regulation*, ed. John Miller. Amsterdam: North-Holland, pp. 59–113.

BOSWELL, JONATHAN. 1973. *The Rise and Decline of Small Firms*. London:
Allen and Urwin.

BOWLES, SAMUEL, HERBERT GINTIS, and PETER MEYER. 1975. "Education,
I.Q. and the Legitimation of the Social Division of Labor," *Berkeley Journal
of Sociology*, 20: 233–64.

———. 1975. *Schooling in Capitalist America: Educational Reform and the
Contradictions of Economic Life*. New York: Basic Books, Inc.

BRAVERMAN, HARRY. 1974. *Labor and Monopoly Capital*. New York:
Monthly Review Press.

BRENNER, ROBERT.   1977. "The Origins of Capitalist Development: A Critique of Neo-Smithian Marxism," *New Left Review*, No. 104 (July–August): 25–90.

BRIGGS, KENNETH.   1977. "Chicago Seminaries Share Students, Faculty and Ecumenical Ideas," *New York Times*, May 1, p. 28. ©1977 by the New York Times Company. Reprinted by permission.

BUCKLEY, WALTER.   1967. *Sociology and Modern Systems Theory*. Englewood Cliffs, N.J.: Prentice-Hall, Inc.

BUCKLEY, WALTER, and TOM BURNS.   1974. "Power and Meta-Power: Relational Control of the Development of Hierarchical Control Systems." Working paper, Department of Sociology, University of New Hampshire.

BUKSTI, JACOB.   1976. "The Adaptability of Organizations to Environmental Changes: The Case of the Danish Agriculture and Fisheries." Institute of Political Science, University of Aarhus, Denmark. Paper presented at a colloquium of the European Group on Organizational Sociology.

BURCH, PHILIP H. J. 1972. *The Managerial Revolution Reassessed*. Lexington, Mass.: D. C. Heath & Company.

BURNS, LAWTON R.   1977. "Ecological Processes and Organizational Sociology: The Chicago School." Unpublished paper presented at the 1977 Meeting of the American Sociological Association, Chicago.

BURNS, TOM, and G. M. STALKER.   1961. *The Management of Innovation*. London: Tavistock.

BURT, RONALD S.   1977. "Power in a Social Typology," *Social Science Research*, 6 (Winter): 1–83.

CABLE, JOHN.   1977. "Searching By Merger." International Institute of Management, Berlin.

CAMPBELL, DONALD.   1969. "Variation and Selective Retention in Socio-Cultural Evolution," *General Systems*, 16: 69–85.

CAPLOW, THEODORE, and KURT FINSTERBUSH.   1968. "France and Other Countries: A Study of International Interaction," *Journal of Conflict Resolution*, 12 (March): 1–15.

CARLSON, R.   1964. "Environmental Constraints and Organizational Consequences," *Behavioral Science and Educational Administration*. Chicago, Ill.: National Society for the Study of Education.

CAVES, RICHARD.   1972. *American Industry: Structure, Conduct, and Performance*. Englewood Cliffs, N.J.: Prentice-Hall, Inc.

CERRA, FRANCES.   1977. "Eight-Year Skirmish Continues on Consumer Protection." *New York Times*, September 26, p. 24. ©1977 by The New York Times Company. Reprinted by permission.

CHANDLER, ALFRED.   1962. *Strategy and Structure*. Cambridge, Mass.: The M.I.T. Press.

———.   1977. *The Visible Hand*. Cambridge, Mass.: Harvard University Press.

CHEVALIER, J. M.   1970. *La Structure Financiere de L'Industrie Americaine*. Paris: Editions Cujas.

CHILD, JOHN.   1969. *The Business Enterprise in Modern Industrial Society*. London: Collier-MacMillan Limited.

————.   1972. "Organization Structure, Environment, and Performance—The Role of Strategic Choice," *Sociology*, 6 (January): 1–22.

————.   1973. "Strategies of Control and Organizational Behavior," *Administrative Science Quarterly*, 18 (March): 1–17.

————.   1976. "Participation, Organization, and Social Cohesion," *Human Relations*, 29 (May): 429–51.

————.   1977. *Organization: A Guide to Problems and Practice*. London: Harper and Row Publishers, Inc.

CLARK, BURTON.   1956. "Organizational Adaptation and Precarious Values," *American Sociological Review*, 21 (June): 327–36.

————.   1965. "Interorganizational Patterns in Education," *Administrative Science Quarterly*, 10 (September): 224–37.

————.   1972. "The Organizational Saga in Higher Education," *Administrative Science Quarterly*, 17 (June): 178–84.

CLARK, PETER B., and JAMES Q. WILSON.   1961. "Incentive Systems: A Theory of Organizations," *Administrative Science Quarterly*, 6 (September): 129–66.

CLARK, TERRY N.   1968. *Community Structure and Decision-Making: Comparative Analyses*. San Francisco: Chandler.

COHEN, MICHAEL D., JAMES G. MARCH, and JOHAN P. OLSEN.   1972. "A Garbage Can Model of Organizational Choice," *Administrative Science Quarterly*, 17 (March): 1–25.

COLEMAN, JAMES S.   1970. "Social Inventions," *Social Forces*, 49 (December): 163–73.

————.   1974. *Power and the Structure of Society*. New York: W. W. Norton & Co., Inc.

COLEMAN, JAMES S., ELIHU KATZ, and HERBERT MENZEL.   1957. "The Diffusion of Innovation Among Physicians," *Sociometry*, 20 (December): 253–70.

COLLINS, N. R. and L. E. PRESTON.   1961. "The Size Structure of the Largest Industrial Firms, 1909–1958," *American Economic Review*, 51 (December): 986–1011.

COLLVER, ANDREW.   1970. "Interaction Between Organizations." Unpublished paper, State University of New York, Stony Brook.

COOK, KAREN S.   1976. "Exchange and Power in Networks of Interorganizational Networks," *Sociological Quarterly*, 18 (Winter): 62–82.

CRITTENDEN, ANN.   1977. "Merger Fever in Publishing," *New York Times*, Financial Section, October 23, pp. F1, 9. ©1977 by The New York Times Company. Reprinted by permission.

CROSS, THEODORE.   1969. *Black Capitalism*. New York: Atheneum Publishers.

CROZIER, MICHAEL. 1964. *The Bureaucratic Phenomenon*. Chicago, Ill.: University of Chicago Press.

CYERT, RICHARD M., and JAMES G. MARCH. 1963. *A Behavioral Theory of the Firm*. Englewood Cliffs, N.J.: Prentice-Hall, Inc.

CZEPIEL, JOHN A. 1974. "Patterns of Interorganizational Communications and the Diffusion of a Major Technological Innovation in a Competitive Industrial Community," *Academy of Management Journal*, 18, no. 1 (March): 6–24.

———. 1977. "Communications Networks and Innovation in Industrial Communities." Unpublished paper, New York University, Graduate School of Business Administration.

DAEMS, HERMAN. 1978. *The Holding Company and Corporate Control*. The Hague: Martinus Nyhoff, Social Sciences Division.

DAHRENDORF, RALF. 1959. *Class and Class Conflict in Industrial Society*. Stanford, Calif.: Stanford University Press.

DALTON, MELVILLE. 1959. *Men Who Manage*. New York: John Wiley & Sons, Inc.

DAVIS, RALPH. 1966. "The Rise of Protection in England, 1669–1786," *Economic History Review*, 19 (August): 306–17.

DELACROIX, JACQUES. 1977. "The Export of Raw Materials and Economic Growth: A Cross-National Study," *American Sociological Review*, 42 (October): 795–808.

DEMERATH, NICHOLAS J., and VICTOR THIESSEN. 1966. "On Spitting Against the Wind: Organizational Precariousness and American Irreligion," *American Journal of Sociology*, 71: 674–87.

DEUTSCH, KARL. 1953. *Nationalism and Social Communication*. New York: John Wiley & Sons, Inc.

DEUTSCH, MORTON, and H. G. GERARD. 1955. "A Study of Normative and Informational Social Influences Upon Individual Judgement," *Journal of Abnormal and Social Psychology*, 51 (November): 629–36.

DILL, WILLIAM R. 1958. "Environment as an Influence on Managerial Autonomy," *Administrative Science Quarterly*, 2 (March): 409–43.

———. 1962. "The Impact of Environment on Organizational Development," in *Concepts and Issues in Administrative Behavior*, eds. S. Mailick and E. H. VanNess. Englewood Cliffs, N.J.: Prentice-Hall, Inc., pp. 29–48.

DOERINGER, PETER, and MICHAEL PIORE. 1971. *Internal Labor Markets and Manpower Analysis*. Boston, Mass.: D. C. Heath and Company.

DOMHOFF, WILLIAM. 1967. *Who Rules America*. Englewood Cliffs, N.J.: Prentice-Hall, Inc.

DOOLEY, PETER. 1969. "The Interlocking Directorate," *American Economic Review*, 59 (June): 314–23.

DOWNEY, H. KIRK, D. HELLRIEGEL, and J. SLOCUM. 1975. "Environmental Uncertainty: The Construct and Its Application," *Administrative Science Quarterly*, 20 (December): 613–29.

DUNCAN, OTIS, and BEVERLY DUNCAN.   1957. *The Negro Population of Chicago: A Study of Residential Succession*. Chicago: University of Chicago Press.

DUNCAN, ROBERT.   1972. "Characteristics of Organizational Environments and Perceived Environmental Uncertainty," *Administrative Science Quarterly*, 17 (September): 313–27.

DURKHEIM, EMILE.   1933. *The Division of Labor in Society*. New York: Macmillan Publishing Company.

DUTTON, JOHN, and RICHARD WALTON.   1966. "Interdepartmental Conflict and Cooperation: Two Contrasting Studies," *Human Organization*, 25 (Fall): 207–20.

EDGAR, R. E.   1970. *Urban Power and Social Welfare: Corporate Influence in an American City*. Beverly Hills, Calif.: Sage Publications, Inc.

EMERSON, RICHARD M.   1962. "Power-Dependence Relations" *American Sociological Review*, 27 (February): 31–40.

———.   1972. "Exchange Theory, Part I: A Psychological Basis for Social Exchange," and "Exchange Theory, Part II: Exchange Relations, Exchange Networks, and Groups as Exchange Systems," in *Sociological Theories in Progress*, Vol. II, eds. Joseph Berger, *et al*. Boston, Mass.: Houghton Mifflin Company.

EMERY, F. E., and E. L. TRIST.   1965. "The Causal Texture of Organizational Environments," *Human Relations*, 18 (February): 21–32.

ENOS, J. L.   1962. "Invention and Innovation in the Petroleum Industry," in *The Rate and Direction of Inventive Activity*, ed. R. R. Nelson. Princeton: Princeton University Press.

ETZIONI, AMITAI.   1961. *A Comparative Analysis of Complex Organizations*. New York: The Free Press.

EVAN, WILLIAM.   1966. "The Organization-Set: Toward a Theory of Inter-Organizational Relations," in *Approaches to Organizational Design*, ed. James Thompson. Pittsburgh, Pa.: University of Pittsburgh Press, pp. 175–90.

———.   1972. "An Organization-Set Model of Interorganizational Relations," in *Interorganizational Decision-Making*, eds. M. Tuite, M. Radnor, and R. Chisholm. Chicago, Ill.: Aldine, pp. 181–200.

———.   1976. *Organization Theory*. New York: John Wiley & Sons, Inc.

FELLMETH, ROBERT C.   1970. *The Interstate Commerce Commission*. New York: Grossman Publishers.

FESTINGER, LEON.   1954. "A Theory of Social Comparison Processes," *Human Relations*, 7 (No. 2): 117–40.

FISCHER, CLAUDE S.   1975. "Toward a Subcultural Theory of Urbanism," *American Journal of Sociology*, 80 (May): 1319–41.

FORM, WILLIAM H.   1954. "The Place of Social Structure in the Determination of Land Use: Some Implications for a Theory of Urban Ecology," *Social Forces*, 32 (May): 317–23.

FRANCIS, ARTHUR.   1977. "Families, Firms, and Finance Capital." Unpublished paper, Nuffield College, Oxford.

FRANK, ANDRE.   1966. "Sociology of Development and Underdevelopment of Sociology," *Catalyst*, 2 (Summer): 20–73.

FREEMAN, JOHN.   1978. "Effects of the Choice of the Unit of Analysis on Organizational Research," in *Studies on Environment and Organizations*, ed. Marshall Meyer, *et al.* San Francisco, Calif.: Jossey-Bass, Inc., Publishers.

FREEMAN, JOHN, and MICHAEL T. HANNAN.   1975. "Growth and Decline Processes in Organizations," *American Sociological Review*, 40 (April): 215–28.

FREEMAN, JOHN, and JERROLD KRONENFELD.   1973. "Problems of Definitional Dependency: The Case of Administrative Intensity," *Social Forces*, 52 (September): 108–21.

FREEMAN, LINTON.   1968. *Patterns of Local Community Leadership*. Indianapolis, Ind.: Bobbs-Merrill Co., Inc.

FREIDSON, ELIOT.   1970. *Profession of Medicine*. New York: Harper & Row, Publishers, Inc.

FUSFELD, DANIEL.   1958. "Joint Subsidiaries in the Iron and Steel Industry," *American Economic Review*, 48 (May): 578–87.

GAILBRATH, JAY.   1973. *Designing Complex Organizations*. Reading, Mass.: Addison-Wesley Publishing Co., Inc.

GALBRAITH, JOHN K.   1952. *American Capitalism: The Concept of Countervailing Power*. Cambridge, Mass.: Houghton Mifflin Company.

———.   1967. *The New Industrial State*. Cambridge, Mass.: Houghton Mifflin Company.

GALTUNG, JOHAN.   1971. "A Structural Theory of Imperialism," *Journal of Peace Research*, 8: 81–117.

GAMSON, WILLIAM.   1967. *Power and Discontent*. Homewood, Ill.: Dorsey Press.

———.   1975. *The Strategy of Social Protest*. Homewood, Ill.: Dorsey Press.

GAMSON, WILLIAM, and NORMAN SCOTCH.   1964. "Scapegoating in Baseball," *American Journal of Sociology*, 70 (July): 6–29.

GEORGE, KENNETH D., and AUBREY SILBERSTON.   1974. "The Causes and Effects of Mergers." Paper presented at the First International Institute of Management Conference on Economics of Industrial Structure, Deidescheim, West Germany.

GERTH, HANS, and C. WRIGHT MILLS.   1958. *Essays in Sociology: Max Weber*. New York: Oxford University Press.

GIDDENS, ANTHONY.   1973. *The Class Structure of Advanced Societies*. London: Hutchinson.

GLASSMAN, ROBERT.   1973. "Persistence and Loose Coupling," *Behavioral Science*, 18 (March): 83–98.

GOFFMAN, ERVING.   1961. "On the Characteristics of Total Institutions," in *The Prison*, ed. Donald R. Cressey. New York: Holt, Rinehart and Winston.

GORDON, LAURA KRAMER. 1975. "Bureaucratic Competence and Success in Dealing with Public Bureaucracies," *Social Problems*, 23 (December): 197–208.

GOULDNER, ALVIN W. 1954. *Patterns of Industrial Bureaucracy*. New York: The Free Press.

————. 1955. "Metaphysical Pathos and the Theory of Bureaucracy," *American Political Science Review*, 49 (June): 496–507.

GRAFTON, CARL. 1975. "The Creation of Federal Agencies," *Administration and Society*, 7 (November): 328–65.

GRANOVETTER, MARK. 1973. "The Strength of Weak Ties," *American Journal of Sociology*, 78 (May): 1360–80.

————. 1974. *Getting a Job: A Study of Contacts and Careers*. Cambridge, Mass.: Harvard University Press.

GREER, SCOTT 1965. *Urban Renewal and American Cities*. Indianapolis, Ind.: Bobbs-Merrill Co., Inc.

GRUSKY, OSCAR. 1961. "Corporate Size, Bureaucratization, and Managerial Succession," *American Journal of Sociology*, 67 (November): 261–69.

————. 1969. "Succession with an Ally," *Administrative Science Quarterly*, 14 (June): 155–70.

GUEST, ROBERT H. 1962. "Managerial Succession in Complex Organizations," American Journal of Sociology, 68 (July): 47–56.

GUSFIELD, JOSEPH R. 1955. "Social Structure and Moral Reform: A Study of Women's Christian Temperance Union," *American Journal of Sociology*, 61 (November): 221–32.

————. 1963. *Symbolic Crusade: Status Politics and the American Temperance Movement*. Urbana, Ill.: University of Illinois Press.

HAAS, J. EUGENE, and THOMAS E. DRABEK. 1973. *Complex Organizations: A Sociological Perspective*. New York: Macmillan Publishing Co., Inc.

HAGE, JERALD, and MICHAEL AIKEN. 1967. "Program Change and Organizational Properties," *American Journal of Sociology*, 72 (March): 503–19.

————. 1970. *Social Change in Complex Organizations*. New York: Random House, Inc.

HAGE, JERALD, and ROBERT DEWAR. 1973. "Elite Values, Social Structure, and Organizational Performance," *Administrative Science Quarterly*, 18 (September): 279–90.

HALL, RICHARD. 1963. "The Concept of Bureaucracy: An Empirical Assessment," *American Journal of Sociology*, 69 (July): 32–40.

————. 1968. "Professionalization and Bureaucratization," *American Sociological Review*, 33 (February): 92–104.

————. 1977. *Organizations: Structure and Process* (2nd Ed.). Englewood Cliffs, N.J.: Prentice-Hall, Inc.

HALL, RICHARD, JOHN CLARK, PEGGY GIORDANO, PAUL JOHNSON, and MARTHA VAN ROCKELL. 1977. "Patterns of Interorganizational Relationships," *Administrative Science Quarterly*, 22 (September): 457–74.

HALL, RICHARD, J. EUGENE HAAS, and NORMAN J. JOHNSON.   1967. "Examination of the Blau-Scott and Etzioni Typologies," *Administrative Science Quarterly*, 12 (June): 118–39.

HAMBERG, DANIEL.   1963. "Invention in the Industrial Research Laboratory," *Journal of Political Economy*, 71 (April): 95–115.

HANNAN, MICHAEL, and JOHN FREEMAN.   1977. "The Population Ecology of Organizations," *American Journal of Sociology*, 82 (March): 929–64.

HARDIN, RUSSELL.   1976. "Stability of Statist Regimes: Industrialization and Institutionalization," in *Power and Control*, eds. T. Burns and W. Buckley. London and Beverly Hills, Calif.: Sage Publications, pp. 147–168.

HARARY, FRANK, ROBERT NORMAN, and DORWIN CARTWRIGHT.   1965. *Structural Models: An Introduction to the Theory of Directed Graphs*. New York: John Wiley & Sons, Inc.

HARRISS, C. LOWELL.   1961. "Subsidies in the United States," *Public Finance*, 16: 3–4.

HASENFELD, YEHESKEL.   1972. "People-Processing Organizations: An Exchange Approach," *American Sociological Review*, 37 (June): 256–63.

HAUG, MARIE, and MARVIN SUSSMAN.   1969. "Professional Autonomy and the Revolt of the Client," *Social Problems*, 17 (Fall): 256–63.

HAUSKNECHT, MURRAY.   1962. *The Joiners*. New York: Bedminster.

HAWLEY, AMOS.   1950. *Human Ecology*. New York: The Ronald Press Company.

———.   1971. *Urban Society*. New York: The Ronald Press Company.

HELFGOT, JOSEPH.   1974. "Professional Reform Organizations and the Symbolic Representation of the Poor," *American Sociological Review*, 39 (August): 475–591.

HELMICH, DONALD, and WARREN BROWN.   1972. "Successor Type and Organizational Change in the Corporate Enterprise," *Administrative Science Quarterly*, 17 (September): 371–81.

HERMANN, CHARLES F.   1963. "Some Consequences of Crisis Which Limit the Viability of Organizations," *Administrative Science Quarterly*, 8 (June): 61–82.

HERNES, GUDMUND.   1976. "Structural Change in Social Processes," *American Journal of Sociology*, 82 (November): 513–47.

HICKSON, DAVID J.   1966. "A Convergence in Organizational Theory," *Administrative Science Quarterly*, 11 (September): 224–37.

HICKSON, DAVID J., C. R. HININGS, C. A. LEE, R. E. SCHNECK, and J. M. PENNINGS.   1971. "A Strategic Contingencies' Theory of Intraorganizational Power," *Administrative Science Quarterly*, 16 (June): 216–29.

HINDLEY, BARBARA.   1970. "Separation of Ownership and Control in the Modern Corporation," *Journal of Law and Economics*, 13: 185–222.

HIRSCH, PAUL.   1972. "Processing Fads and Fashions: An Organization-Set Analysis of Cultural Industry Systems," *American Journal of Sociology*, 77 (January): 639–59.

————. 1975a. "Organizational Analysis and Industrial Sociology: An Instance of Cultural Lag," *American Sociologist*, 10 (February): 3–12.

————. 1975b. "Organizational Effectiveness and the Institutional Environment," *Administrative Science Quarterly*, 20 (September): 327–44.

HIRSCHMAN, ALBERT O.   1972. *Exit, Voice, and Loyalty*. Cambridge, Mass.: Harvard University Press.

————. 1973. "Exit, Voice, and Loyalty: Further Reflections and a Survey of Recent Contributions," *Social Science Information*, 13, No. 1: 7–26.

————. 1976. "Discussion," *American Economic Review*, 66 (May): 386–9.

HOFSTADTER, RICHARD.   1945. *Social Darwinism in American Thought, 1860–1915*. Philadelphia, Pa: University of Pennsylvania Press.

HORVATH, DEZSO, DAVID HICKSON, and CHARLES MCMILLAN.   1974. "Organizational Control Structures: International Comparison." Paper presented at the Annual Meetings of the American Sociological Association, Montreal.

HOWARD, MARSHALL.   1956. "Interfirm Relations in Oil Products Markets," *Journal of Marketing*, 20: 356–66.

HUBER, JOAN, and WILLIAM FORM.   1973. *Income and Ideology: An Analysis of the American Political Formula*. New York: The Free Press.

HUGHES, EVERETT C.   1928. *A Study of a Secular Institution: The Chicago Real Estate Board*. Ph.D. Dissertation, University of Chicago.

————. 1964. "Good People and Dirty Work," *Social Problems*, 10 (Summer): 3–11.

INKELES, ALEX, and D. H. SMITH.   1974. *Becoming Modern*. Cambridge, Mass.: Harvard University Press.

JACOBS, DAVID.   1974. "Dependency and Vulnerability: An Exchange Approach to the Control of Organizations," *Administrative Science Quarterly*, 19 (March): 45–59.

JANOWITZ, MORRIS.   1959. "Changing Patterns of Organizational Authority: The Military Establishment," *Administrative Science Quarterly*, 3 (March): 45–59.

JENCKS, CHRISTOPHER, *et al*.   1972. *Inequality: A Reassessment of the Effect of Family and Schooling in America*. New York: Basic Books, Inc.

JEWKES, JOHN, DAVID SAWERS, and RICHARD STILLERMAN.   1958. *The Sources of Invention*. London: MacMillan.

KAHN, ROBERT P., J. DIEDRICK SNOEK, and ROBERT A. ROSENTHAL.   1964. *Organizational Stress: Studies in Role Conflict and Ambiguity*. New York: John Wiley & Sons, Inc.

KAMENS, DAVID.   1977. "Legitimating Myths and Educational Organization: The Relationship Between Organizational Ideology and Formal Structure," *American Sociological Review*, 42 (April): 208–19.

KANTER, ROSABETH.   1977. *Men and Women of the Corporation*. New York: Basic Books, Inc.,

KAPLAN, J. B.   1967. "Implementation of Program Change in Community Agencies," *Milbank Memorial Fund Quarterly*, 45: 321–31.

KARPIK, LUCIEN. 1972. "Le Capitalisme Technologique," *Sociologie du Travail*, 13 (January–March): 2–34.

KELLER, ROBERT, and WINFORD HOLLAND. 1975. "Boundary-Spanning Roles in a Research and Development Organization," *Academy of Management Journal*, 18 (June): 388–93.

KELLER, ROBERT, ANDREW SZILAGYI, and WINFORD HOLLAND. 1976. "Boundary-Spanning Activity and Employee Reactions," *Human Relations*, 29 (July): 699–710.

KIMBERLY, JOHN. 1976a. "Issues in the Design of Longitudinal Organizational Research," *Sociological Methods and Research*, 4 (February): 321–48.

———. 1976b. "Organizational Size and the Structuralist Perspective: A Review, Critique, and Proposal," *Administrative Science Quarterly*, 21 (December): 571–97.

———. 1978. "The Diffusion, Adoption, and Effectiveness of Managerial Innovation." Unpublished paper, Yale University.

KLINGSBORN, M. J. 1973. "The Significance of Variability," *Behavioral Science*, 18 (November): 441–47.

KNOWLES, JAMES. 1973. "The Rockefeller Financial Group," Andover, Massachusetts: *Warner Modular*, Module 343: 1–59.

KOCHAN, THOMAS. 1975. "Determinants of the Power of Boundary Units in an Interorganizational Bargaining Relation," *Administrative Science Quarterly*, 20 (September): 434–52.

KOLARSKA, LENA. 1977. "The Functioning of 'Voice' in the Polish Economy." Paper presented at a seminar on Organizations in their Societal Context, Dansk Management Center, Copenhagen, December 5–7.

KOLARSKA, LENA, and HOWARD ALDRICH. 1978. "Critical Notes on Exit, Voice, and Loyalty." Unpublished paper, NYSSILR, Cornell University.

KORNHAUSER, ARTHUR, ROBERT DUBIN, and ARTHUR ROSS. 1954. *Industrial Conflict*. New York: McGraw-Hill Book Company.

KUNZ, PHILLIP. 1969. "Sponsorship and Organizational Stability: Boy Scout Troops," *American Journal of Sociology*, 74 (May): 666–75.

KUZNETS, SIMON. 1959. *Six Lectures on Economic Growth*. Glencoe, Ill.: The Free Press.

LAMMERS, CORNELIUS. 1969. "Strikes and Mutinies: A Comparative Study of Organizational Conflicts Between Rulers and Ruled." *Administrative Science Quarterly*, 14 (December): 558–72.

LANDAU, MARTIN. 1969. "Redundancy, Rationality, and the Problem of Duplication and Overlap," *Public Administration Review*, 29 (July/August): 346–58.

LARNER, ROBERT J. 1970. *Management Control and the Large Corporations*. New York: Dunellen Publishing Company.

LAVER, MICHAEL. 1976. " 'Exit, Voice, and Loyalty' Revisited," *British Journal of Political Science*, 6 (October): 463–82.

LAWLER, EDWARD J., and SAMUEL BACHARACH. 1976. "Outcome Alternatives and Value as Criteria for Multi-Strategy Evaluations," *Journal of Personality and Social Psychology*, 34 (November): 885–94.

LAWRENCE, PAUL R., and JAY W. LORSCH. 1967. *Organization and Environment*. Cambridge, Mass.: Harvard University Press.

———. 1973. "Reply to Tosi *et al.*," *Administrative Science Quarterly*, 18 (September): 397–98.

LEFTON, MARK, and WILLIAM ROSENGREN. 1966. "Organizations and Clients: Lateral and Longitudinal Dimensions." *American Sociological Review*, 31 (December): 802–10.

LENSKI, GERHARD E. 1966. *Power and Privilege: A Theory of Social Stratification*. New York: McGraw-Hill Book Company.

———. 1975. "Social Structure in Evolutionary Perspective," in *Approaches to the Study of Social Structure*, ed. Peter Blau. New York: The Free Press, pp. 135–53.

———. 1976. "History and Social Change," *American Journal of Sociology*, 82 (November): 548–64.

LENSKI, GERHARD E., and JEAN LENSKI. 1974. *Human Societies: A Macro Level Introduction to Sociology*. New York: McGraw-Hill Book Company.

LEONTIF, WASSILY. 1966. *Input-Output Economics*. New York: Oxford University Press.

LEVINE, JOEL H. 1972. "The Sphere of Influence," *American Sociological Review*, 37 (February): 14–27.

———. 1977. "The Network of Corporate Interlocks in the United States: An Overview." Unpublished paper, Department of Sociology, Dartmouth College.

LEVINE, S. and P. E. WHITE. 1961. "Exchange as a Conceptual Framework for the Study of Interorganizational Relationships," *Administrative Science Quarterly*, 5 (March): 583–610.

LIEBERSON, STANLEY, and JAMES F. O'CONNOR. 1972. "Leadership and Organizational Performance: A Study of Large Corporations." *American Sociological Review*, 37 (April): 117–30.

LIGHT, IVAN. 1972. *Ethnic Enterprise in America*. Berkeley, Calif.: University of California Press.

LINTON, RALPH. 1936. *The Study of Man*. New York: Appleton-Century.

LIPSET, SEYMOUR M., MARTIN A. TROW, and JAMES S. COLEMAN. 1956. *Union Democracy*. Glencoe, Ill.: The Free Press.

LITWAK, EUGENE, and LYDIA HYLTON. 1962. "Interorganizational Analysis: A Hypothesis on Coordination." *Administrative Science Quarterly*, 6 (March): 395–420.

LUNDBERG, FERDINAND. 1937. *America's Sixty Families*. New York: Vanguard Press, Inc.

MAANEN, JOHN VAN. 1975. "Police Socialization: A Longitudinal Examination of Job Attitudes in an Urban Police Department," *Administrative Science Quarterly*, 20 (June): 207–28.

MACAULAY, S.   1963. "Non-contractual Relations in Business: A Preliminary Study," *American Sociological Review*, 28 (February): 55–67.

MCCARTHY, JOHN, and MAYER ZALD.   1977. "Resource Mobilization and Social Movements: A Partial Theory," *American Journal of Sociology*, 82 (May): 1212–41.

MCCULLOUGH, ARTHUR, and MICHAEL SHANNON.   1977. "Organization and Protection," in *Critical Issues in Organizations*, eds. Stewart Clegg and David Dunkerley. Boston, Mass.: Routledge and Kegan Paul.

MACE, M.   1971. *Directors: Myth and Reality*. Boston: Graduate School of Business Administration, Harvard University.

MCKELVEY, BILL.   1975. "Guidelines for the Empirical Classification of Organizations," *Administrative Science Quarterly*, 20 (December): 509–25.

MADISON, J. H.   1974. "The Evolution of Commercial Credit Reporting Agencies in Nineteenth Century America," *Business History Review*, 48 (Summer): 164–86.

MANIHA, JOHN K.   1974a. "The Persistence of Organizational Forms: A Case Study of a Police Control Board," *Social Science Quarterly*, 54 (March): 800–14.

———.   1974b. "The Standardization of Elite Careers in Bureaucratizing Organizations," *Social Forces*, 53 (December): 282–88.

MANIHA, JOHN K., and CHARLES PERROW.   1965. "The Reluctant Organization and the Aggressive Environment," *Administrative Science Quarterly*, 10 (September): 238–57.

MANNHEIM, KARL.   1936. *Ideology and Utopia*. London: Routledge and Kegan Paul.

MARCH, JAMES G., and HERBERT A. SIMON.   1958. *Organizations*. New York: John Wiley & Sons, Inc.

MARGALEF, RAMON.   1968. *Perspectives in Ecological Theory*. Chicago: University of Chicago Press.

MARIOLIS, PETER.   1975. "Interlocking Directorates and Control of Corporations: The Theory of Bank Control," *Social Science Quarterly*, 56 (December): 425–39.

MARRETT, CORA.   1971. "On the Specification of Interorganizational Dimensions," *Sociology and Social Research*, 56 (October): 83–99.

MARX, KARL.   1967. *Capital, Vol. II*. Moscow: Progress.

———.   1973. *Grundrisse: Foundations of the Critique of Political Economy*, trans. Martin Nicolaus. London: New Left Review and Penguin Books.

MATHIESEN, THOMAS.   1972. *Across the Boundaries of Organizations*. Berkeley, Calif.: Glendessary Press.

MAYER, KURT, and SIDNEY GOLDSTEIN.   1961. *The First Two Years: Problems of Small Firm Growth and Survival*, Small Business Research Series No. 2, Washington, D. C.: U.S. Government Printing Office.

MERTON, ROBERT K. 1957. *Social Theory and Social Structure*. Glencoe, Ill.: The Free Press.

MESSINGER, SHELDON L. 1955. "Organizational Transformation: A Case Study of Declining Social Movement," *American Sociological Review*, 20 (February): 3–10.

MEULLER, WILLARD. 1964. "The Measurement of Industrial Concentration," in *Hearings before the Subcommittee on Antitrust and Monopoly of the Committee on the Judiciary*, U. S. Senate, 88th Congress.

MEYER, JOHN, JOHN BOLI-BENNETT, and CHRIS CHASE-DUNN. ©1975. "Convergence and Divergence in Development," in *Annual Review of Sociology*, Vol. I, ed. A. Inkeles. Palo Alto, Calif.: Annual Review, Inc., pp. 223–460. All rights reserved.

MEYER, MARSHALL. 1972. "Size and the Structure of Organizations: A Causal Analysis," *American Sociological Review*, 37 (August): 434–40.

MEYER, MARSHALL, and M. CRAIG BROWN. 1977. "The Process of Bureaucratization," *American Journal of Sociology*, 83 (September): 364–85.

MICHELS, ROBERT. 1962. *Political Parties*. Glencoe, Ill.: The Free Press.

MILES, ROBERT. 1976. "Role Requirements as Sources of Organizational Stress," *Journal of Applied Psychology*, 61 (April): 172–79.

———. 1977. "Boundary Relevance." Paper presented at the Annual Meeting of the Academy of Management, Kissimmee, Florida, August 15.

MILLS, C. WRIGHT. 1957. *The Power Elite*. New York: Oxford University Press.

MINDLIN, SERGIO. 1974. *Organizational Dependence on Environment and Organizational Structure: A Reexamination of the Findings of the Aston Group*. M.S. Thesis, ILR, Cornell University.

MINDLIN, SERGIO, and HOWARD ALDRICH. 1975. "Interorganizational Dependence: A Review of the Concept and a Reexamination of the Findings of the Aston Group," *Administrative Science Quarterly*, 20 (September): 382–92

MINTZ, BETH. 1977. "Managerialism, Stockholding and the Role of Finance Capital." Unpublished paper, State University of New York, Stony Brook.

MINTZBERG, HENRY. 1973. *The Nature of Managerial Work*. New York: Harper & Row Publishers, Inc.

MITCHELL, J. CLYDE. 1969. *Social Networks in Urban Situations*. Manchester, England: University of Manchester Press.

———. 1973 "Networks, Norms, and Institutions," *Network Analysis: Studies in Human Interaction*, eds. Jeremy Boissevain and J. Clyde Mitchell. The Hague: Mouton.

MOCH, MICHAEL. 1976. "Structure and Organizational Resource Allocation," *Administrative Science Quarterly*, 21 (December): 661–74.

MOCH, MICHAEL, and EDWARD MORSE. 1977. "Size, Centralization and Organizational Adoption of Innovations," *American Sociological Review*, 92 (October): 716–25.

MOORE, BARRINGTON, JR.   1966. *Social Origins of Dictatorship and Democracy*. Boston: Beacon Press.

MUELLER, DENNIS C.   1972. "A Life Cycle Theory of the Firm," *Journal of Industrial Economies*, 20 (July): 199–219.

———.   1977. "The Effects of Conglomerate Mergers: A Survey of the Empirical Evidence." Unpublished paper, Department of Economics, University of Maryland.

MUELLER, HANS.   1969. "The Policy of the European Coal and Steel Community Toward Mergers and Agreements by Steel Companies," *Antitrust Bulletin*, (Summer).

MYERS, SUMNOR, and DONALD MARQUIS.   1969. *Successful Industrial Innovations*. Washington, D.C.: National Science Foundation.

MYTINGER, ROBERT.   1968. "Innovation in Local Health Services." Washington, D.C.: USGPO, Public Health Service Publication No. 1664-2.

NADEL, MARK.   1971. *The Politics of Consumer Protection*. Indianapolis, Ind.: Bobbs-Merrill Co., Inc.

NADLER, PAUL.   1974. "The Territorial Hunger of Our Major Banks," *Harvard Business Review*, 52: 87–98.

NEWTON, KENNETH.   1975. "Voluntary Associations in a British City," *Journal of Voluntary Action Research*, 4 (January–April): 43–62.

NISBET, ROBERT.   1969. *Social Change and History*. New York: Oxford Galaxy.

NUNNALLY, JUM C.   1967. *Psychometric Theory*. New York: McGraw-Hill Book Company.

NYMAN, STEVE, and AUBREY SILBERSTON.   1977. "The Ownership and Control of Industry," in *Welfare Aspects of Industrial Markets*, eds. A. P. Jacquemin and H. W. deJong. Leiden, the Netherlands: Martinus Nijhoff.

O'CONNOR, JAMES.   1973. *The Fiscal Crisis of the State*. New York: St. Martin's Press.

OGBURN, WILLIAM F.   1937. *Technological Trends and National Policy,* Report of the Subcommittee on Technology to the National Resource Committee. Washington, D.C.: U.S. Government Printing Office.

OLSON, MANCUR, JR.   1968. *The Logic of Collective Action*. New York: Schocken Books, Inc.

ORNSTEIN, MICHAEL.   1976. "The Boards and Executives of the Largest Canadian Corporations: Size, Composition, and Interlocks," *Canadian Journal of Sociology*, 1 (Winter): 411–37.

OUCHI, WILLIAM, and MARY ANN MACGUIRE.   1975. "Organizational Control: Two Functions," *Administrative Science Quarterly*, 20 (December): 559–69.

PARSONS, TALCOTT.   1956. "Suggestions for a Sociological Approach to the Theory of Organizations," *Administrative Science Quarterly,* 1 (June and September): 63–85, 225–39, respectively.

————. 1966. *Societies: Evolutionary and Comparative Perspectives*. Englewood Cliffs, N.J.: Prentice-Hall, Inc.

PATE, J. L.   1969. "Joint Venture Activity, 1960–1978," *Economic Review of the Federal Reserve Bank of Cleveland* (July): 16–23.

PAYNE, P. L.   1967. "The Emergence of the Large-Scale Company in Great Britain, 1870–1914," *Economic History Review*, 20 (1967): 519–42.

PENNINGS, JOHANNES.   1973. "Measures of Organizational Structure: A Methodological Note." *American Journal of Sociology*, 79 (November): 686–704.

————. 1975. "The Relevance of the Structural-Contingency Model for Organizational Effectiveness," *Administrative Science Quarterly*, 20 (September): 393–410.

————. 1978. "Coordination Between Strategically Interdependent Organizations," Unpublished paper, Graduate School of Industrial Administration, Carnegie Mellon University.

PERROW, CHARLES.   1961. "Goals in Complex Organizations," *American Sociological Review*, 26 (December): 854–65.

————. 1965. "Hospitals, Technology, Goals and Structure," in *Handbook of Organizations*, ed. James March. Chicago, Ill.: Rand McNally College Publishing Company.

————. 1967. "A Framework for Comparative Organizational Analysis," *American Sociological Review*, 32, No. 2 (April): 194–208.

————. 1970. *Organizational Analysis: A Sociological View*. Belmont, Calif.: Wadsworth Publishing Co., Inc.

————. 1972. *Complex Organizations: A Critical Essay*. Glenview, Ill.: Scott, Foresman & Company.

PERRUCCI, ROBERT, and MARC PILISUK.   1970. "Leaders and Ruling Elites: The Interorganizational Bases of Community Power," *American Sociological Review*, 35 (December): 1040–56.

PETSHEK, K. R.   1973. *The Challenge of Urban Reform: Policies and Programs in Philadelphia*. Philadelphia, Pa.: Temple University Press.

PETTIGREW, ANDREW.   1972. "Information Control as a Power Resource," *Sociology*, 6 (May): 187–204.

————. 1975. "Towards a Political Theory of Organizational Intervention," *Human Relations*, 28 (April): 191–208.

PFEFFER, JEFFREY.   1972a. "Size and Composition of Corporate Boards of Directors," *Administrative Science Quarterly*, 17 (June): 218–28.

————. 1972b. "Merger as a Response to Organizational Interdependence," *Administrative Science Quarterly*, 17 (September): 382–94.

————. 1974. "Administrative Regulation and Licensing: Social Problem or Solution?" *Social Problems*, 21 (April): 468–79.

————. 1977. "Power and Resource Allocation in Organizations," in *New*

Directions in Organizational Behavior, eds. Barry Staw and Gerald Salancik. Chicago, Ill.: St. Clair Press, pp. 235–65.

PFEFFER, JEFFREY, and HUSEIN LEBLEBICI.   1973a. "The Effect of Competition on Some Dimensions of Organizational Structure," *Social Forces*, 52 (December): 268–79.

————.   1973b. "Executive Recruitment and the Development of Interfirm Organizations," *Administrative Science Quarterly*, 18 (December): 4457–61.

PFEFFER, JEFFREY, and PHILLIP NOWAK.   1976. "Joint Ventures and Interorganizational Dependence," *Administrative Science Quarterly*, 21 (September): 398–418.

PFEFFER, JEFFREY, and GERALD SALANCIK.   1974. "Organizational Decision Making as a Political Process: The Case of a University Budget," *Administrative Science Quarterly*, 19 (June): 135–51.

PHILLIPS, ALMARIN.   1960. "A Theory of Interfirm Organization," *Quarterly Journal of Economics*, 74 (November): 602–13.

PHILLIPS, DAVID, and RICHARD CONVISER.   1972. "Measuring the Structure and Boundary Properties of Groups: Some Uses of Information Theory," *Sociometry*, 35: 235–54.

PITTMAN, RUSSELL.   1976. "The Effects of Industry Concentration and Regulation on Contributions in Three 1972 U.S. Senate Campaigns," *Public Choice*, 27 (Fall): 71–80.

PRED, ALLAN.   1966. *The Spatial Dynamics of U. S. Urban-Industrial Growth, 1800–1914*. Cambridge, Mass.: The M.I.T. Press.

PRICE, JAMES.   1963. "The Impact of Governing Boards on Organizational Effectiveness and Morale," *Administrative Science Quarterly*, 8 (December): 361–68.

PUGH, DEREK, DAVID HICKSON, and ROBERT HININGS.   1969. "The Context of Organizational Structures," *Administrative Science Quarterly*, 14 (March): 91–114.

PUGH, DEREK, DAVID HICKSON, ROBERT HININGS, and CHRIS TURNER.   1968. "Dimensions of Organizational Structure," *Administrative Science Quarterly*, 13 (June): 65–104.

ROSENBERG, NATHAN.   1963. "Technological Change in the Machine Tool Industry," *Journal of Economic History*, 23 (December): 414–43.

ROTHSCHILD-WHITT JOYCE.   1976. "Conditions Facilitating Participatory-Democratic Organizations," *Sociological Inquiry*, 46, no. 2: 75–86.

RUESCHEMEYER, DIETRICH.   1977. "Structural Differentiation, Efficiency, and Power," *American Journal of Sociology*, 83 (July): 1–25.

RUMMELT, RICHARD.   1974. *Strategy, Structure, and Economic Performance*. Harvard Business School, Harvard University.

RUSHING, WILLIAM.   1971. "Public Policy, Community Constraints, and the Distribution of Medical Resources," *Social Problems*, 19: 21–36.

SADLER, PHILIP and BERNARD BARRY. 1970. *Organizational Development*. London, England: Longmans, Green, and Co.

SALAMAN, GRAEME. 1974. "The Sociology of Assessment: The Regular Commissions Board Assessment Procedure," in *People and Organizations: Media Booklet II*. Milton Keynes, England: The Open University Press.

SALISBURY, ROBERT. 1969. "An Exchange Theory of Interest Groups," *Midwest Journal of Political Science*, 13 (February): 1–32.

SCHERER, FREDERICK. 1970. *Industrial Market Structure and Economic Performance*. Chicago, Ill.: Rand McNally.

SCHMOOKLER, JACOB. 1966. *Invention and Economic Growth*. Cambridge, Mass.: Harvard University Press.

SCHUMPETER, JOSEPH A. 1934. *The Theory of Economic Development*. Cambridge, Mass.: Harvard University Press.

SCRIVEN, MICHAEL. 1959. "Explanation and Prediction in Evolutionary Theory," *Science*, Vol. 130: 477–82, 2 August 1959.

SELZNICK, PHILIP. 1943. "An Approach to a Theory of Bureaucracy," *American Sociological Review*, 8 (February): 47–54.

————. 1949. *TVA and the Grass Roots*. Berkeley, Calif.: University of California Press.

————. 1957. *Leadership in Administration*. Evanston, Ill.: Row, Peterson.

————. 1960. *The Organizational Weapon*. Glencoe, Ill.: The Free Press.

SHARP, MARGARET. 1973. *The State, the Enterprise, the Individual*. New York: John Wiley & Sons.

SHORTER, EDWARD, and CHARLES TILLY. 1974. *Strikes in France, 1830–1968*. Cambridge, Mass.: Cambridge University Press.

SIEBER, SAMUEL. 1974. "Toward a Theory of Role Accumulation," *American Sociological Review*, 39 (August): 567–78.

SILLS, DAVID. 1957. *The Volunteers*. Glencoe, Ill.: The Free Press.

SILVER, ALLAN. 1967. "The Demand for Order in Civil Society: A Review of Some Themes in the History of Urban Crime, Police, and Riot," in *The Police*, ed. D. Bordua. New York: John Wiley & Sons, Inc., pp. 1–24.

SILVERMAN, DAVID. 1970. *The Theory of Organizations: A Sociological Framework*. New York: Basic Books, Inc., Publishers.

SIMMEL, GEORG. 1950. *The Sociology of Georg Simmel*. New York: The Free Press.

————. 1955. *Conflict*. New York: The Free Press.

SIMON, HERBERT A. 1961. *Administrative Behavior* (2nd ed.). New York: Macmillan Publishing Co., Inc.

————. 1962. "The Architecture of Complexity," *Proceedings of the American Philosophical Society*, 106 (December): 467–82.

SKOCPOL, THEDA. 1976. "Old Regime Legacies and Communist Revolutions in Russia and China," *Social Forces*, 55 (December): 284-315. Copyright © The University of North Carolina Press.

————. 1977. "Wallerstein's World Capitalist System: A Theoretical and Historical Critique," *American Journal of Sociology,* 82 (March): 1075–90.

SMIGEL, ERWIN O. 1964. *The Wall Street Lawyer.* New York: The Free Press.

SMITH, CONSTANCE, and ANNE FREEDMAN. 1972. *Voluntary Associations, Perspective on the Literature.* Cambridge, Mass.: Harvard University Press.

SNOEK, J. DIEDRICK. 1966. "Role Strain in Diversified Role Sets," *American Journal of Sociology,* 71 (January): 363–72.

STANWORTH, PHILIP, and ANTHONY GIDDENS. 1975. "The Modern Corporate Economy: Interlocking Directorships in Britain, 1906–1970," *The Sociological Review,* 23: 5–28.

STARBUCK, WILLIAM. 1976. "Organizations and Their Environments," in *Handbook of Organizational and Industrial Psychology,* ed. Marvin Dunnette. Chicago, Ill.: Rand McNally, pp. 1069-1123.

STAW, BARRY, and E. SZWAJKOWSKI. 1975. "The Scarcity-Munificence Component of Organizational Environments and the Commission of Illegal Acts," *Administrative Science Quarterly,* 20 (September): 345–54.

STEINER, PETER. 1975. *Mergers.* Ann Arbor, Mich.: University of Michigan Press.

STENTZ, BARBARA. 1972. *Interaction Patterns of Health Organizations.* MA Thesis, Department of Sociology, State University of New York, Stony Brook.

STERN, ROBERT. 1977. "The Evolution of an Interorganizational Control Network." Unpublished paper, New York State School of Industrial and Labor Relations, Cornell University.

STIGLER, GEORGE C. 1968. *The Organization of Industry.* Homewood, Ill.: Richard D. Irwin, Inc.

STINCHCOMBE, ARTHUR L. 1959. "Bureaucratic and Craft Administration of Production: A Comparative Study," *Administrative Science Quarterly,* 4 (September): 168–87.

————. 1965. "Social Structure and Organizations," in *Handbook of Organizations,* ed. J. G. March. Chicago, Ill.: Rand McNally, pp. 142–93.

STRAUSS, GEORGE. 1962. "Tactics of Lateral Relationship: The Purchasing Agent," *Administrative Science Quarterly,* 7 (September): 161–86.

STURMTHAL, ADOLF. 1977. "Unions and Industrial Democracy," *The Annals,* 431 (May): 12–21.

SUTTON, WILLIS, JR. 1969. "The Sociography of a Community's Interorganizational Relations: The Network of Perceived Group Contact in a Kentucky County." Unpublished Paper, Department of Sociology, University of Kentucky.

SYKES, GRESHAM. 1956. "The Corruption of Authority and Rehabilitation," *Social Forces,* 34 (March): 257–62.

TAIJFEL, HENRI. 1969. "Social and Cultural Factors in Perception," in *Hand-*

book of Social Psychology, Vol. 3, eds. G. Lindzey and E. Aronson. Reading, Mass.: Addison Wesley Publishing Co., Inc.

TAUSKY, CURT.   1970. *Work Organizations: Major Theoretical Perspectives*. Itasca, Ill.: F. E. Peacock Publishers, Inc.

TERREBERRY, SHIRLEY.   1968. "The Evolution of Organizational Environments," *Administrative Science Quarterly*, 12 (March): 590–613.

THOMAS, W. I.   1928. *The Child in America*. New York: Alfred A. Knopf, Inc.

THOMPSON, JAMES.   1960. "Organizational Management of Conflict," *Administrative Science Quarterly*, 4 (March): 389–409.

————.   1962. "Organizations and Output Transactions," *American Journal of Sociology*, 68 (November): 309–24.

————.   1967. *Organizations in Action*. New York: McGraw-Hill Book Company.

THOMPSON, JAMES, and WILLIAM MCEWEN.   1958. "Organizational Goals and Environment: Goalsetting as an Interaction Process," *American Sociological Review*, 23 (February): 23–31.

THOMPSON, WILBUR.   1965. *A Preface to Urban Economics*. Baltimore, Maryland: Johns Hopkins Press.

TILLY, CHARLES.   1973. "Do Communities Act?" *Sociological Inquiry*, 43 (3, 4): 209–40.

TOSI, HENRY, RAMON ALDAG, and RONALD STOREY.   1973. "On the Measurement of the Environment: An Assessment of the Lawrence and Lorsch Environmental Subscale," *Administrative Science Quarterly*, 18 (March): 27–36.

TUMIN, MELVIN.   1953. "Some Principles of Stratification: A Critical Analysis," *American Sociological Review*, 18 (August): 387–93.

TURK, HERMAN.   1973. "Comparative Urban Structure from an Interorganizational Perspective," *Administrative Science Quarterly*, 18 (March): 37-55.

————.   1977. *Organizations in Modern Life*. San Francisco, Calif.: Jossey-Bass, Inc., Publishers.

TURNER, BARRY.   1976. "The Organizational and Interorganizational Development of Disasters." *Administrative Science Quarterly*, 21 (September): 378–97.

ULLMAN, EDWARD.   1941. "A Theory of Location for Cities," *American Journal of Sociology*, 46 (May): 835–64.

U. S. HOUSE OF REPRESENTATIVES.   1965. *Interlocks in Corporate Management*. Report from the Committee on the Judiciary, Antitrust Subcommittee. Washington, D.C.: U. S. Government Printing Office.

————.   1968. *Commercial Banks and Their Trust Activities: Emerging Influence on the American Economy*. Report from the Banking and Currency Committee, Subcommittee on Domestic Finance. Washington, D.C.: U. S. Government Printing Office.

374   References

UTTERBACK, JAMES.   1971. "The Process of Technological Innovation Within the Firm," *Academy of Management Journal*, 14 (March): 75–88.

VAN DE VEN, ANDREW.   1975. "Design for Evaluating Inter-Agency Networks Among Texas Early Childhood Organizations." Unpublished paper, Department of Administrative Sciences, College of Business, Kent State University.

WALLERSTEIN, IMMANUEL.   1974. *The Modern World System: Capitalist Agriculture and the Origins of the European World-Economy in the Sixteenth Century*. New York: Academic Press, Inc.

————.   1976. "From Feudalism to Capitalism: Transition or Transitions?" *Social Forces*, 55 (December): 273–82.

WALTON, RICHARD E., and JOHN N. DUTTON.   1969. "The Management of Interdepartment Conflict: A Model and Review," *Administrative Science Quarterly*, 14 (December): 73–90.

WARNER, W. LLOYD.   1953. *American Life: Dream and Reality*. Chicago: University of Chicago Press.

WARNER, W. LLOYD, *et al*.   1949. *Democracy in Jonesville*. New York: Harper & Row Publishers, Inc.

WARREN, ROLAND.   1967. "The Interorganizational Field as a Focus for Investigation," *Administrative Science Quarterly*, 12 (December): 396–419.

————.   1973. "Comprehensive Planning and Coordination—Some Functional Aspects," *Social Problems*, 20 (Winter): 355–64.

WARREN, ROLAND, STEPHEN ROSE, and ANN BERGUNDER.   1974. *The Structure of Urban Reform*. Lexington, Mass.: D. C. Heath & Company.

WEBER, MAX.   1947. *The Theory of Social and Economic Organization*. Translated and edited by A. M. Henderson and Talcott Parsons. New York: Oxford University Press.

WEICK, KARL.   1969. *The Social Psychology of Organizing*. Reading, Mass.: Addison-Wesley Publishing Co., Inc.

————.   1976. "Educational Organizations as Loosely Coupled Systems," *Administrative Science Quarterly*, 21 (March): 1–19.

WEISS, LEONARD.   1965. "An Evaluation of Mergers in Six Industries," *Review of Economics and Statistics*, 47 (May): 172–81.

WHETTEN, DAVID.   1974. *Predicting Organization Set Size*. Doctoral Dissertation, NYSSILR, Cornell University.

WHETTEN, DAVID, and HOWARD ALDRICH.   1978. "Organization Set Size and Diversity: Links Between People Processing Organizations and Their Environments," Unpublished paper, University of Illinois, Champaign-Urbana.

WHITE, HARRISON, SCOTT BOORMAN, and RONALD BREIGER.   1976. "Social Structure From Multiple Networks. I. Blockmodels of Roles and Positions," *American Journal of Sociology*, 81 (January): 730–80.

WHITE, LESLIE.   1949. *The Science of Culture: A Study of Man and Civilization*. New York: Farrar, Straus & Giroux, Inc.

WHITE, PAUL E. 1974. "Resources as Determinants of Organizational Behavior," *Administrative Science Quarterly*, 19 (September): 366–79.

WHITLEY, RICHARD. 1973. "Commonalities and Connections Among Directors of Large Financial Institutions," *The Sociological Review*, 31: 613–32.

WHITTINGTON, G. 1972. "Changes in the Top 100 Quoted Manufacturing Companies in the U.K., 1948 to 1968," *Journal of Industrial Economy*, 21, 1 (November): 17–34.

WHYTE, WILLIAM F. 1955. *Street Corner Society* (2nd Ed.). Chicago, Ill.: University of Chicago Press.

WIENER, M. 1958. "Certainty of Judgment as a Variable in Conformity Behavior," *Journal of Social Psychology*, 48 (November): 257–63.

WILENSKY, HAROLD L. 1967. *Organizational Intelligence*. New York: Basic Books, Inc., Publishers.

WILEY, MARY, and MAYER ZALD. 1968. "The Growth and Transformation of Education Accrediting Agencies: An Exploratory Study in Social Control of Institutions," *Sociology of Education*, 41 (Winter): 36–56.

WILLIAMSON, OLIVER. 1963. "Managerial Discretion and Business Behavior," *American Economic Review*, 53 (December): 1032–57.

————. 1975. *Markets and Hierarchies: Analysis and Antitrust Implications*. New York: The Free Press.

————. 1976. "The Economics of Internal Organization: Exit and Voice in Relation to Markets and Hierarchies," *American Economic Review*, 66 (May): 369–77.

WILSON, JAMES Q. 1971. "The Dead Hand of Regulation," *The Public Interest*, 25 (Fall): 39–58.

————. 1973. *Political Organizations*. New York: Basic Books, Inc.

WILSON, THOMAS. 1970. "Conceptions of Interaction and Forms of Sociological Explanation," *American Sociological Review*, 35 (August): 697–710.

WOOD, JAMES R. 1972. "Unanticipated Consequences of Organizational Coalitions: Ecumenical Cooperation and Civil Rights Policy," *Social Forces*, 50 (June): 512–21.

WOODWARD, JOAN. 1965. *Industrial Organization: Theory and Practice*. London: Oxford University Press.

YUCHTMAN, EPHRAIM and STANLEY SEASHORE. 1967. "A System Resource Approach to Organizational Effectiveness," *American Sociological Review*, 32 (December): 891–903.

ZACHARIAH, MATHEW. 1971. "The Impact of Darwin's Theory of Evolution on Theories of Society," *Social Studies*, 62: 69–76.

ZALD, MAYER N. 1969. *Power in Organizations*. Nashville, Tenn.: Vanderbilt.

————. 1970. *Organizational Change: The Political Economy of the YMCA*. Chicago: University of Chicago Press.

ZALD, MAYER N., and ROBERT ASH.   1966. "Social Movement Organizations: Growth, Decay, and Change," *Social Forces*, 44 (March): 327–41.

ZALD, MAYER N., and MICHAEL BERGER.   1978. "Social Movements in Organizations: Comp d'Etat, Insurgency, and Mass Movements." *American Journal of Sociology*, 83 (January): 823–861.

ZALD, MAYER N., and PATRICIA DENTON.   1963. "From Evangelism to General Service: The Transformation of the YMCA," *Administrative Science Quarterly*, 8 (September): 214–234.

ZEITLIN, MAURICE.   1974. "Corporate Ownership and Control: The Large Corporation and the Capitalist Class," *American Journal of Sociology*, 79 (March): 1073–1119.

ZEITLIN, MAURICE, LYNDA EWEN, and RICHARD RATCLIFF. 1974. "New Princes for Old? The Large Corporation and the Capitalist Class in Chile," *American Journal of Sociology*, 80 (July): 87—123.

ZUCKER, LYNN.   1977. "The Role of Institutionalization in Cultural Persistence," *American Sociological Review*, 42 (October): 726–42.

Index

377